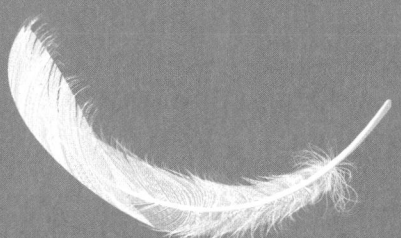

On the Set of

Forrest Gump

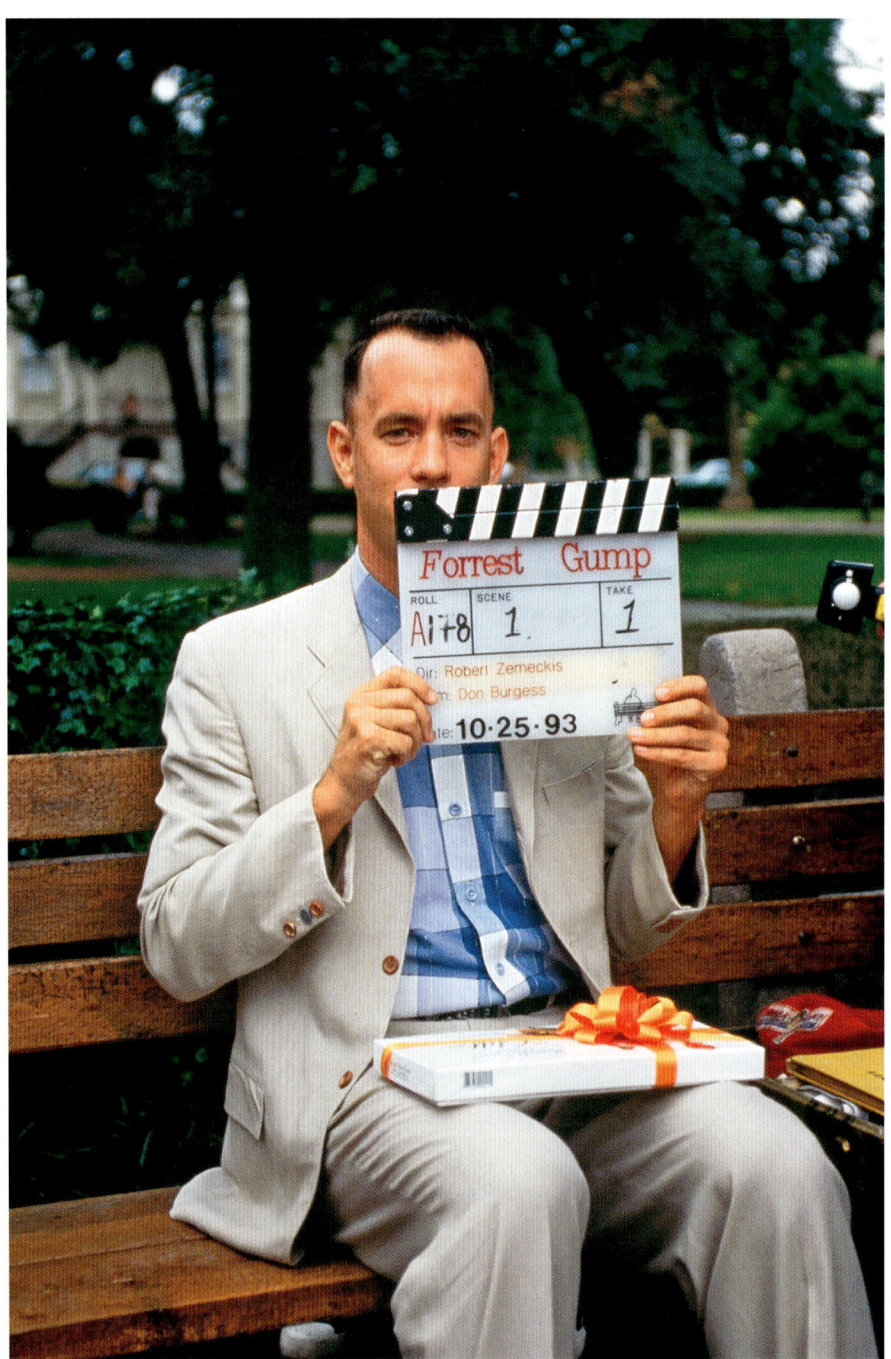

On the Set of
Forrest Gump

Steve Starkey

Foreword by

Tom Hanks

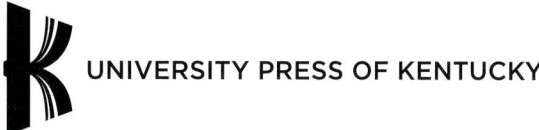

UNIVERSITY PRESS OF KENTUCKY

Scholarly publisher for the Commonwealth, serving Bellarmine University, Berea College, Centre College of Kentucky, Eastern Kentucky University, The Filson Historical Society, Georgetown College, Kentucky Historical Society, Kentucky State University, Morehead State University, Murray State University, Northern Kentucky University, Simmons College, Spalding University, Transylvania University, University of Kentucky, University of Louisville, University of Pikeville, and Western Kentucky University.

Editorial and Sales Offices: The University Press of Kentucky
663 South Limestone, Lexington, Kentucky 40508-4008
www.kentuckypress.com

Grateful acknowledgment is made to Paramount Pictures for the use of all the photographs as well as any excerpts from the original screenplay for *Forrest Gump* that appear in the body of the book. All photographs and any excerpts from the original screenplay are © Paramount Pictures.

Special thanks to Rick Carter for the use of his Gump House watercolor.

Cataloging-in-Publication data available from the Library of Congress

ISBN 978-1-9859-0367-8 (hardcover)
ISBN 978-1-9859-0368-5 (pdf)
ISBN 978-1-9859-0369-2 (epub)

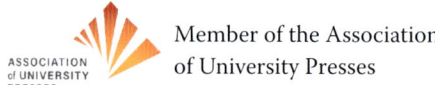

ASSOCIATION of UNIVERSITY PRESSES

Member of the Association of University Presses

To Arthur (Artie) Schmidt. He made his last cut on August 5, 2023.

Contents

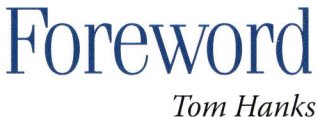

Foreword

Tom Hanks

WHEN I THINK BACK on the making of *Forrest Gump,* my mind swirls in disbelief at what I and the film company went through to get that movie done. In order to get the cross-country run on film, we worked twenty-seven days in a row, with travels up and down the Eastern Seaboard—to New Hampshire, Vermont, and Maine. We'd shoot all week in South Carolina, then take a helicopter from Fripp Island to a plane out of Savannah to fly to, like, North Carolina and beyond. We'd shoot upon arrival and do that all weekend. Come Monday, we would be back on the set for the week and do the same thing again and again. That turned into twenty-six days of shooting with one for travel—a full month of straight shooting—with hair and makeup and beards and wigs and extras and locations and never stopping. Adventures!

After I finally got my day off, we were constantly grabbing the cross-country shots—in Santa Monica, in the Navajo Nation in Monument Valley. In addition to that, there was the traveling unit with my brother, Jim, as Forrest in places like Wisconsin. He and I still argue about who was running in what shot.

Since there were so many scenes to shoot, there were twin units filming at the same time. I shot with Bob on the A unit, then had a police escort to take Bob and me to the location Starkey's B unit had set up for a huge shot that needed to be done with the daylight still available.

The Vietnam battle scenes were pure chaos—and scary. Very physical and intense, all under the command of Dale Dye, USMC, Ret. From then on I worked with Dale on *Saving Private Ryan* and *Band of Brothers,* among others. The Vietnam set on *Gump* was a quarter mile from where we were living. I walked home.

The Washington, DC, scenes were crazy as we were smack in the middle of the nation's capital, outside the White House and at the Reflecting Pool, shooting where Schwarzenegger had just shot some of *True Lies* on a horse.

Back in LA, I had a terrible flu when we shot the football sequences at East LA College. I caught the bug in the crowded bar for the New Year's Eve scene with Gary as Lieutenant Dan, and knew it. I could feel my throat constricting and my body going feverish. I was comatose all weekend, then showed up at the football stadium, telling Bob I was sick as a dog with a terrible flu. He said, "That's too bad 'cause you have a shitload of running to do!" Some of the football players dislocated their shoulders throwing blocks while shooting the kickoff scene.

The show was relentless, but we got through it and maybe got a little bruised in the process, but, at the end of the day, we made the film we set out to make.

On the Set of
Forrest Gump

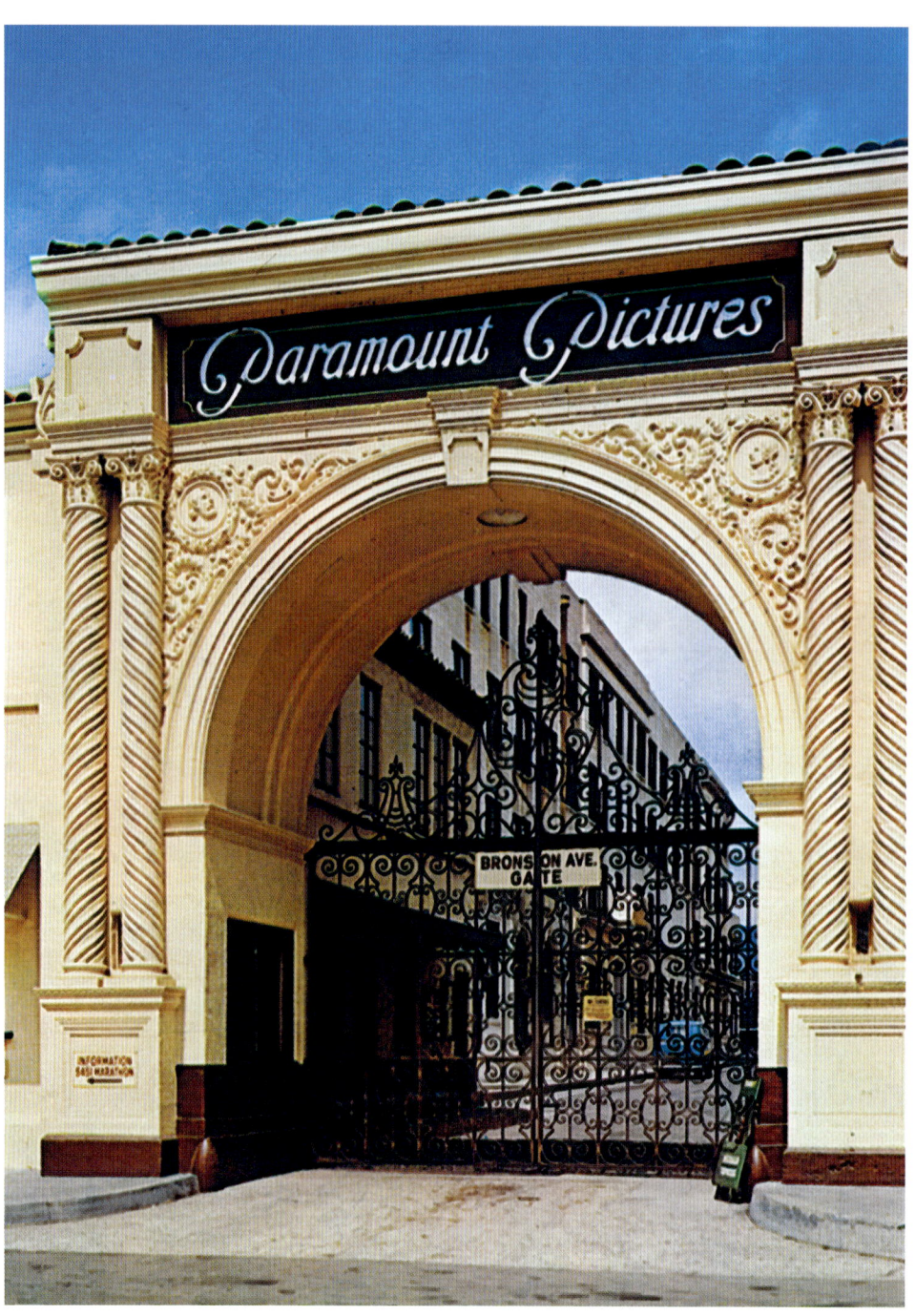

Prologue

WHEN I DROVE ONTO the lot at Paramount Studios in the spring of 1994, I was both excited and anxious. I was always excited to walk on the lot of any studio. I felt privileged. But on that day, anxiety clouded my excitement. We were about to do the first preview screening of *Forrest Gump.* In addition to the filmmakers, the studio executives would be present, which only increased my anxiety. They wielded power, and we had a rather acrimonious relationship.

I had watched the film for the first time a few weeks before, and I looked forward to sharing that emotional experience with others. At the same time, I was worried that the audience wouldn't feel what I had felt. Even though I had been moved by the screenplay and had similar feelings during shooting, I never expected the movie to be as powerful as it was. The director, Bob Zemeckis, had put together a film that was much bigger than what I had imagined. After watching the movie assembled for the first time, I called Bob to tell him how proud I was to be a part of it. No matter what happened, nothing would take away the feeling I had that day in that screening. In that sense, I felt good as I walked toward the theater.

The preview was set up in the Paramount Theatre. We had agreed to the screening but requested that we forgo the usual preview cards filled out by the audience. We thought the film was playing well and we had little to gain from what the audience might say on a questionnaire. Those comments might give the studio a reason to "fix" the film when it wasn't broken in the first place. By sitting in the audience during the screening, we would learn what, if anything, we needed to change. The studio had agreed.

We all secured seats toward the back of the theater, filmmakers on one side, studio executives and their marketing team on the other. The theater was small, so we would be able to sense the audience reactions from where we were sitting. Tom Hanks, who had not seen the film since an early rough cut, came along for the ride. I met him in the lobby shortly after the film started and guided him to his seat in the back, where he could come and go unnoticed.

The film played beautifully. The audience laughed when we expected them to, but for the most part, you could hear a pin drop. No one got up to go to the bathroom during the screening. As the final scene was winding down, I moved to where Tom was sitting and told him it was time to go if he wished to avoid being recognized by the audience. He got up, and I escorted him to the lobby to say good-bye. To my surprise, standing there were several employees from the National Research Group, a company that presents and evaluates preview screenings. They were armed with questionnaires and pencils to hand out to the audience at the conclusion of the film. I told them there had been a mistake. We had decided not to use preview cards at the screening, so they could take off.

"Who asked you to come?" I challenged them.

"Sherry Lansing," they answered. More beholden to Sherry, the chair of Paramount Pictures' Motion Picture Group, than to me, they proceeded to enter the theater.

I followed them in, and as I passed Bob's seat, I told him that Sherry had ordered cards. He looked up in dismay. I quickly marched down the aisle and yelled out to the audience, "There has been a mistake. You do not need to fill out the cards. Please pass your pencils and questionnaires back to the aisle."

From the opposite aisle in the back of the theater I heard Sherry shout, "Please keep your seats and fill out the questionnaire before you leave the theater." The back-and-forth continued for a few minutes until a guy almost dead center in the audience stood up and said, "I don't know what you two are arguing about, because this is the best movie I have ever seen!"

I glanced back and saw that Jack Rapke, Bob's agent, was escorting him out of the theater. They wanted no part of this. As the cards were distributed, I made my way back to the lobby and met Sherry and said, "I thought we agreed not to have cards."

"I decided I wanted them," she countered.

Giving in to the standoff, I offered a compromise: "What if we have the audience complete the cards and then I take them back to the editing room. We will read them first, then send them back to the studio." She nodded in agreement.

A short time later, as I was heading out of the theater, Sherry and her team confronted me. This included Jonathan Dolgen, who was attending his first preview as the new chairman of Viacom Entertainment. Sherry stopped me in my tracks, put her face close to mine, and said, "One day you will learn that you do not work for Robert Zemeckis. You work for me and Paramount Pictures!" With that, I left and placed the cards safely in the trunk of my car.

I met up with Bob and told him the outcome. I suggested that we go back to our offices and regroup. We knew the cards wouldn't lie. We had a wonderful film on our hands.

I got into my car and sat there in shock. What had I done? I had yelled at the head of the studio, and she had yelled right back at me. This was crazy! The guy in the audience was right. We had a wonderful film on our hands, so what were we screaming about?

After everything I had been through on the film, I should not have been surprised it had come to this.

Throughout the making of the movie, I had come to represent all the studio's fears and all the budget overages. I was held responsible for all the problems. How did that happen? Stupid is as stupid does, I guess. As with all good tales, it is best to start at the beginning.

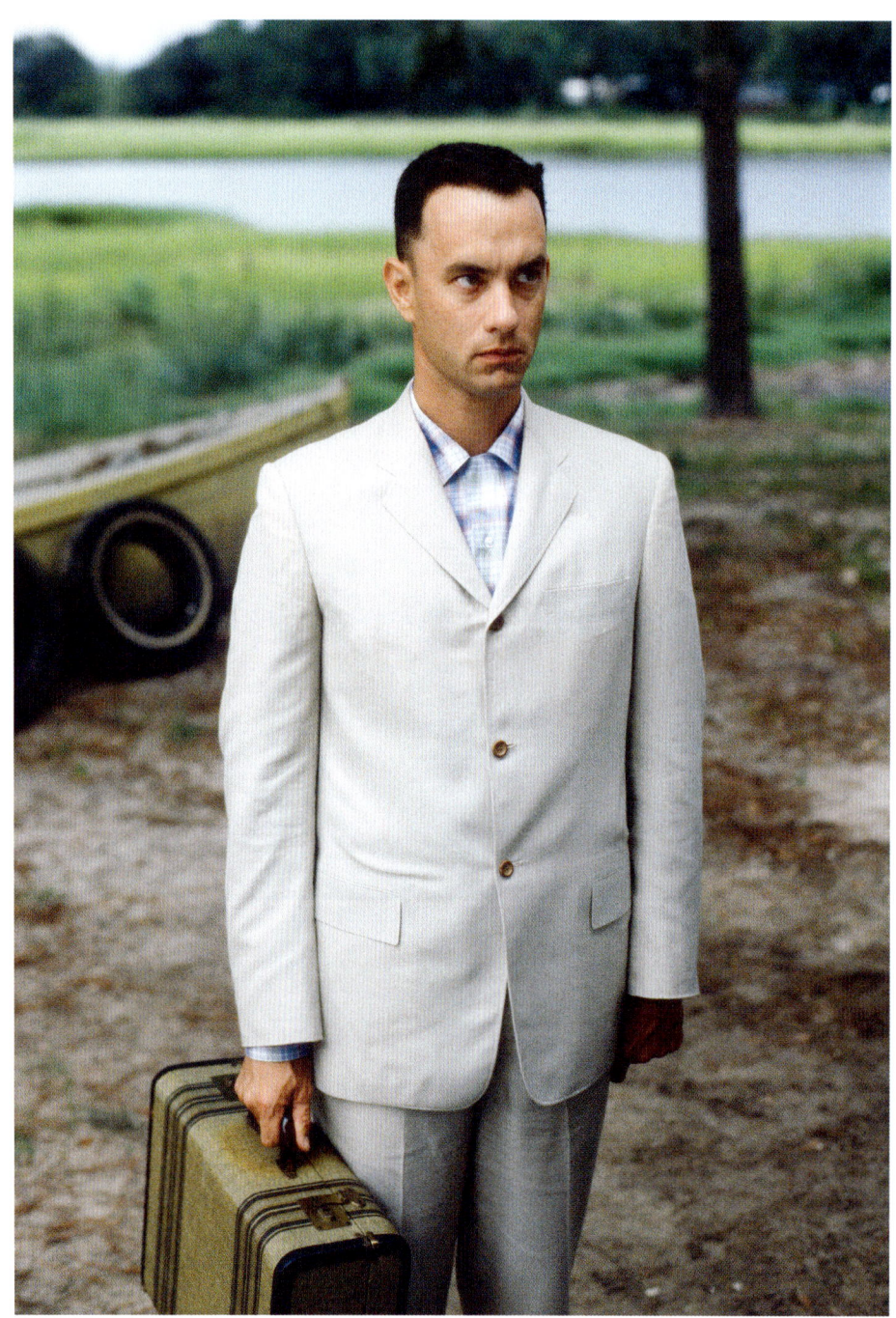

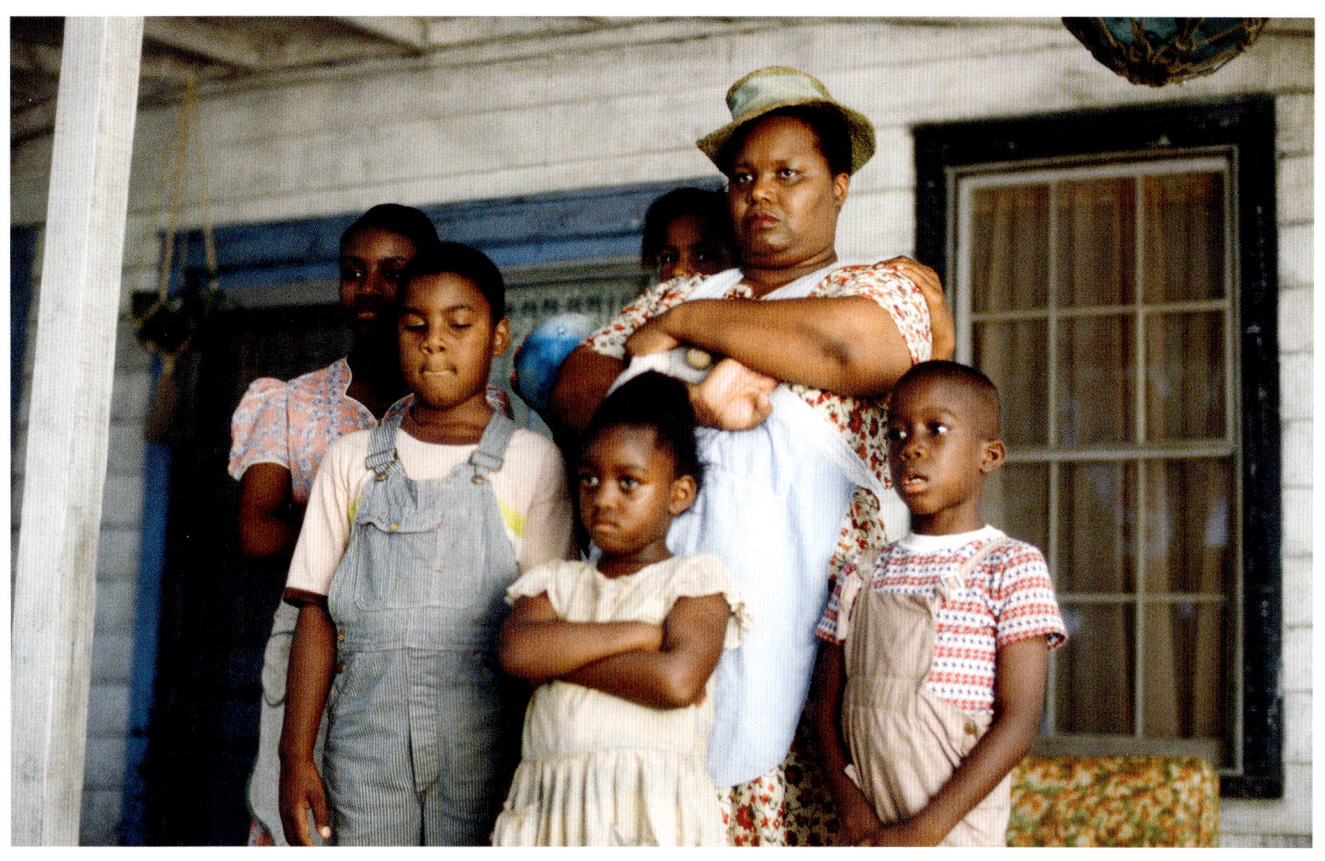

EXT. A SHACK, BAYOU LA BATRE—DAY (1974)
And we see Bubba's mother, her arms folded across her chest, standing with
Bubba's brothers and sisters on the porch of a small shack, looking at Forrest.

                    BUBBA'S MOTHER
          Are you crazy or just stupid?

                       FORREST
                       (shrugs)
          Stupid is as stupid does, Mrs. Blue...

                    BUBBA'S MOTHER
                        (nods)
          I guess...

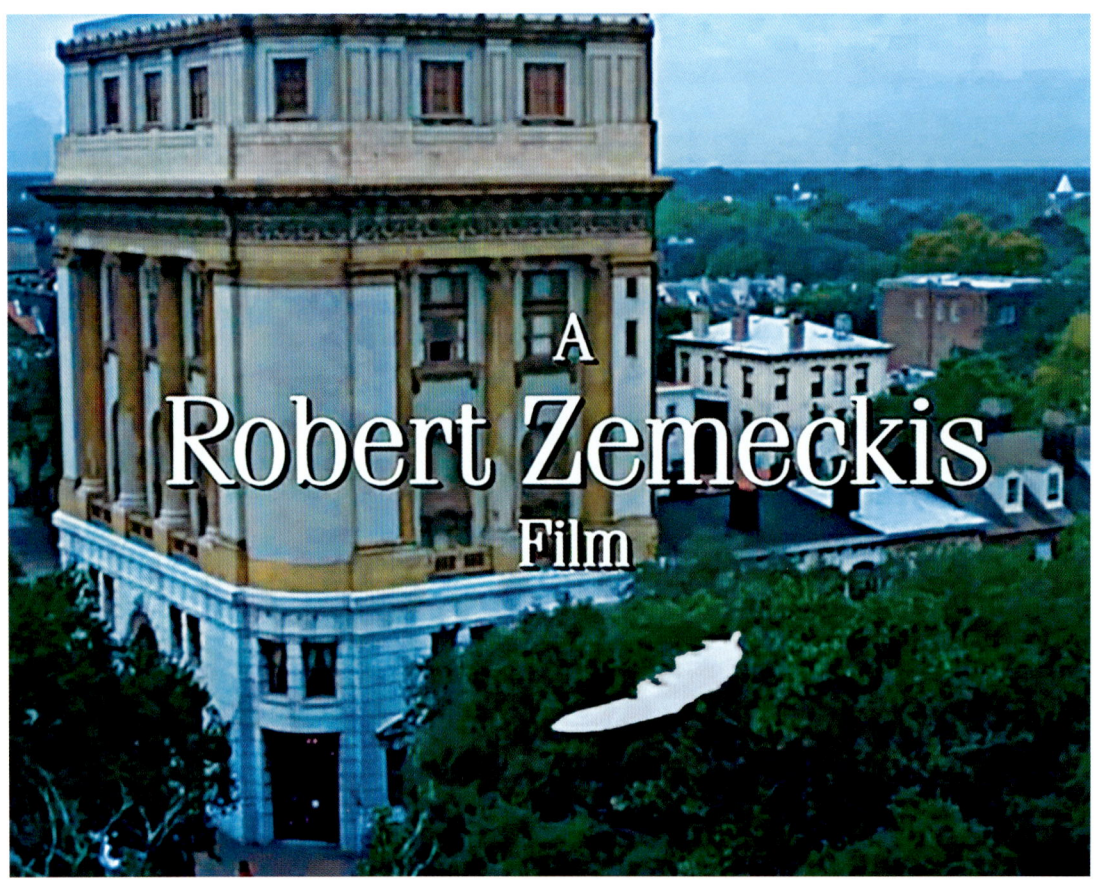

FADE IN:

There's nothing but blue sky. And we see a feather, lighter than air, floating, like time passing, slowly floating by. And we see it's over a city. A breeze catches it, moving it here and there above the city. It slowly floats down past the buildings. It seems to hover for a moment over a busy sidewalk among the people hurrying by. It starts to land on a man's head, but as if it had a mind of its own, it changes direction. It starts to land on a woman's shoulder, but it changes its "mind" again. And taken by a small breeze it lightly falls, and silently lands, by "chance" at this time, at this place, on this street, at a MAN's feet, wearing dilapidated running shoes, sitting on a bench, in Savannah, Georgia.

From the screenplay for Forrest Gump, *by Eric Roth.*

1 | Life Is Like a Box of Chocolates

JUST AS THE FEATHER lands by "chance" at the feet of Forrest Gump in the movie, by similar "chance" the script for *Forrest Gump* came to rest on my desk. It was placed there by Robert Zemeckis, my producing partner and the director of the film. That's how it all started for me. Bob said, "Let me know what you think." Bob already knew what he thought. He was not looking for confirmation or validation. He wanted to know my thoughts, but he was past the stage of ambivalence. This would be his next movie. From that point forward, he would do anything and everything in his power to get it made. What he really wanted to know, beyond my thoughts about the screenplay, was how the hell we were going to make the movie. Before he left the room he turned and said, "Tom Hanks is attached to do the film."

I opened the script and started reading: "Hello, I'm Forrest. Forrest Gump." From that line on, I couldn't stop reading. Page after page. As each scene unfolded, I wanted to read the next. I laughed and I cried. And then I smiled. A smile of satisfaction for a story well told. The story of a simple man who lived an extraordinary life, and it all happened by chance. Or was it destiny? I was taken aback by the serendipity of the fact that Forrest and I had lived through the same era, which made the story resonate even more deeply. This was the story of my life—and the movie of a lifetime.

When I walked into Bob's office, I was full of questions, but first and foremost I asked where the story had come from. I learned that Eric Roth had adapted the screenplay from a book of the same name by Winston Groom. The project originated at Warner Brothers, where producers Steve Tisch and Wendy Finerman acquired the rights to the book. Finerman and Tisch brought the project to Paramount after it had been put into turnaround, or shelved, at Columbia Pictures. Finerman remained determined to get the movie made. She got Tom Hanks on board and offered the film to Bob Zemeckis to direct.

But that's where things got muddy. Sherry Lansing, John Goldwyn, and Michelle Manning, the executives at Paramount, didn't know what to make of it. It was clearly a large production with an unconventional script. It did not fit into any box of chocolates they had ever seen. It was not a sure bet at the box office by any means, even with Zemeckis

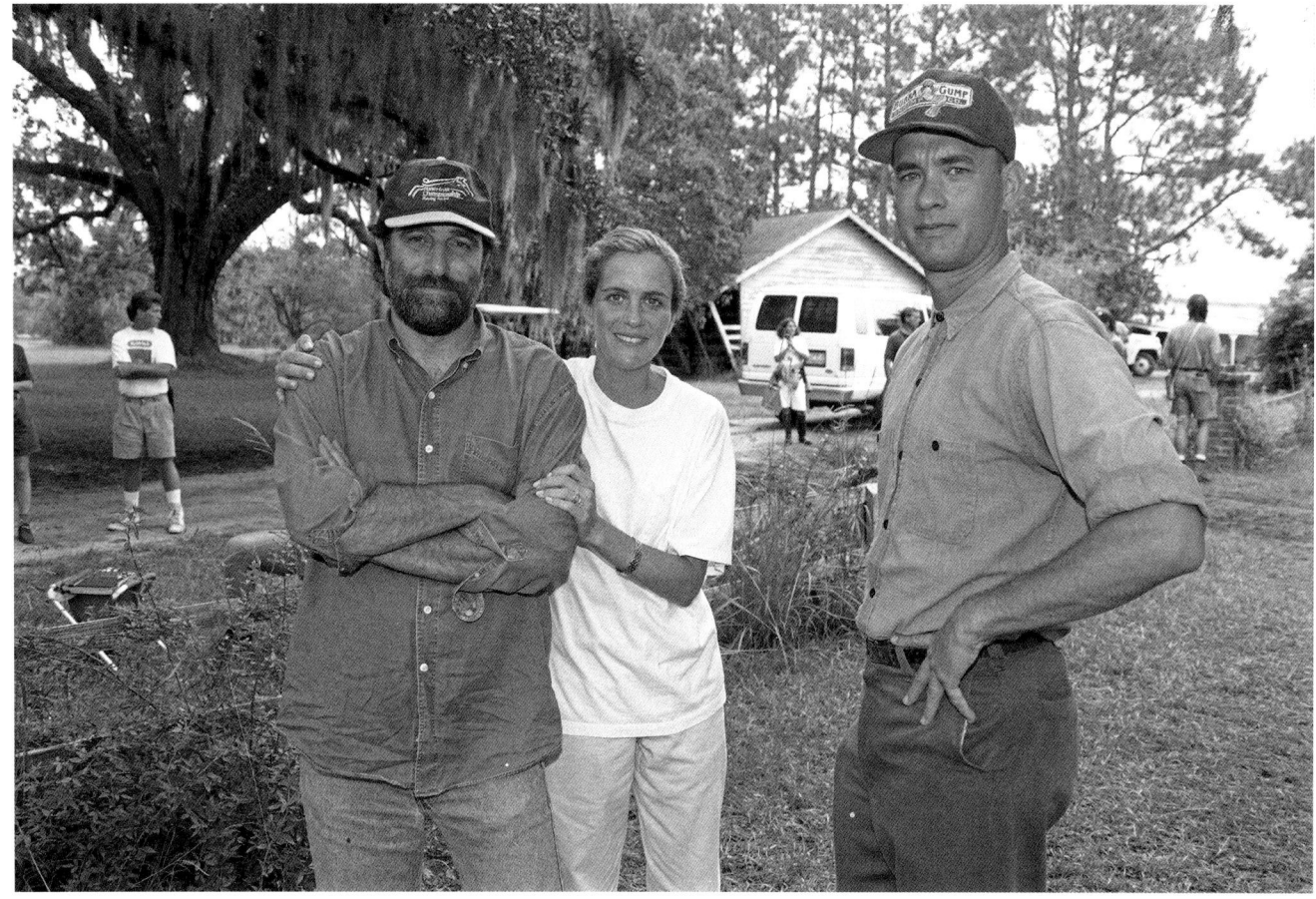

Eric Roth, Wendy Finerman, and Tom Hanks

and Hanks attached. The studio heads found it difficult to say no but were hesitant to say yes. They needed to know more, which really meant they needed to know how much it would cost. Once Finerman handed the reins of the project over to Zemeckis, the burden of answering the studio's budget question and managing the production fell onto Bob's and my shoulders.

To try to answer that question, I decided to travel down two roads. First, I would read the book by Winston Groom to see how that informed the screenplay. Then I would put together a scouting trip to the South to get a feel for the shooting possibilities. For this, I needed seed money, which meant preparing a cash-flow estimate for the studio. I needed a few collaborators on board

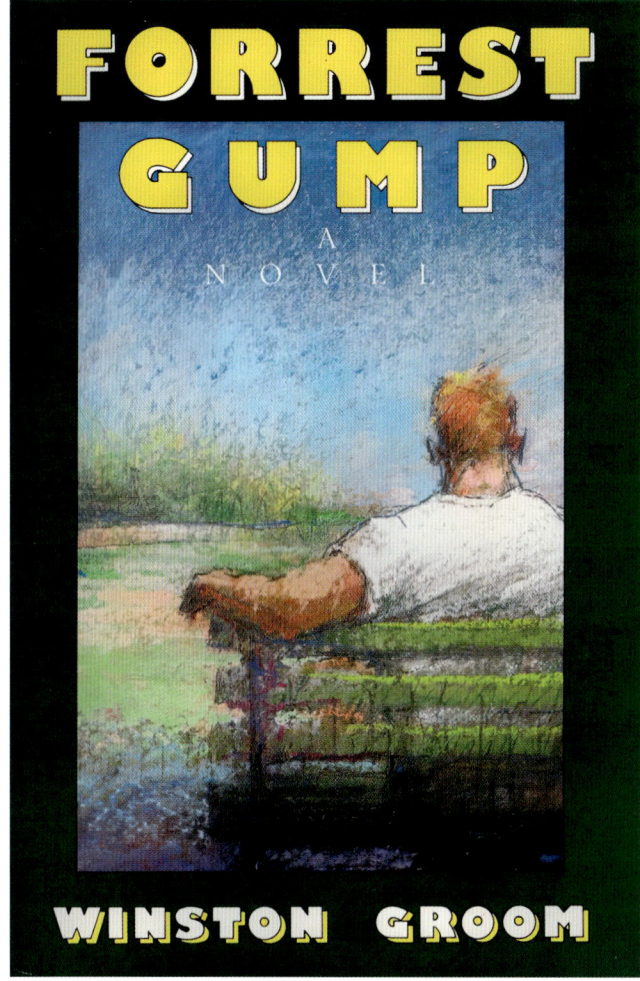

Cover of *Forrest Gump* by Winston Groom

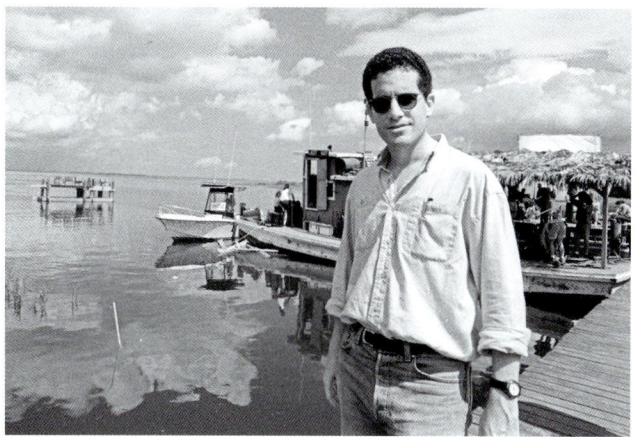

Charles Newirth

to help me figure things out. I wanted to hire a production designer, location manager, and line producer and also get an allowance for location scouting. Paramount quickly agreed to fund my exploration, hoping this exercise would lead to a fair budget.

I started by trying to nail down a line producer/production manager to put together a shooting schedule and work with me on a budget. This person would also be instrumental in suggesting which crew members to hire and helping to negotiate their deals. I approached Joan Bradshaw, whom Bob and I had worked with on previous movies, but she was already committed. Instead I signed Charles Newirth, a seasoned production manager who came highly recommended. Most recently he had worked on two of Barry Levinson's films, *Bugsy* and *Avalon*.

As I had done as associate producer on *Roger Rabbit* and *Back to the Future II* and *III* and as producer on *Death Becomes Her,* I consulted Bob on most of the talent we hired, beginning with Rick Carter. Rick had been our production designer on *Death Becomes Her* and on a number of other Zemeckis projects. He and I had also pieced

11

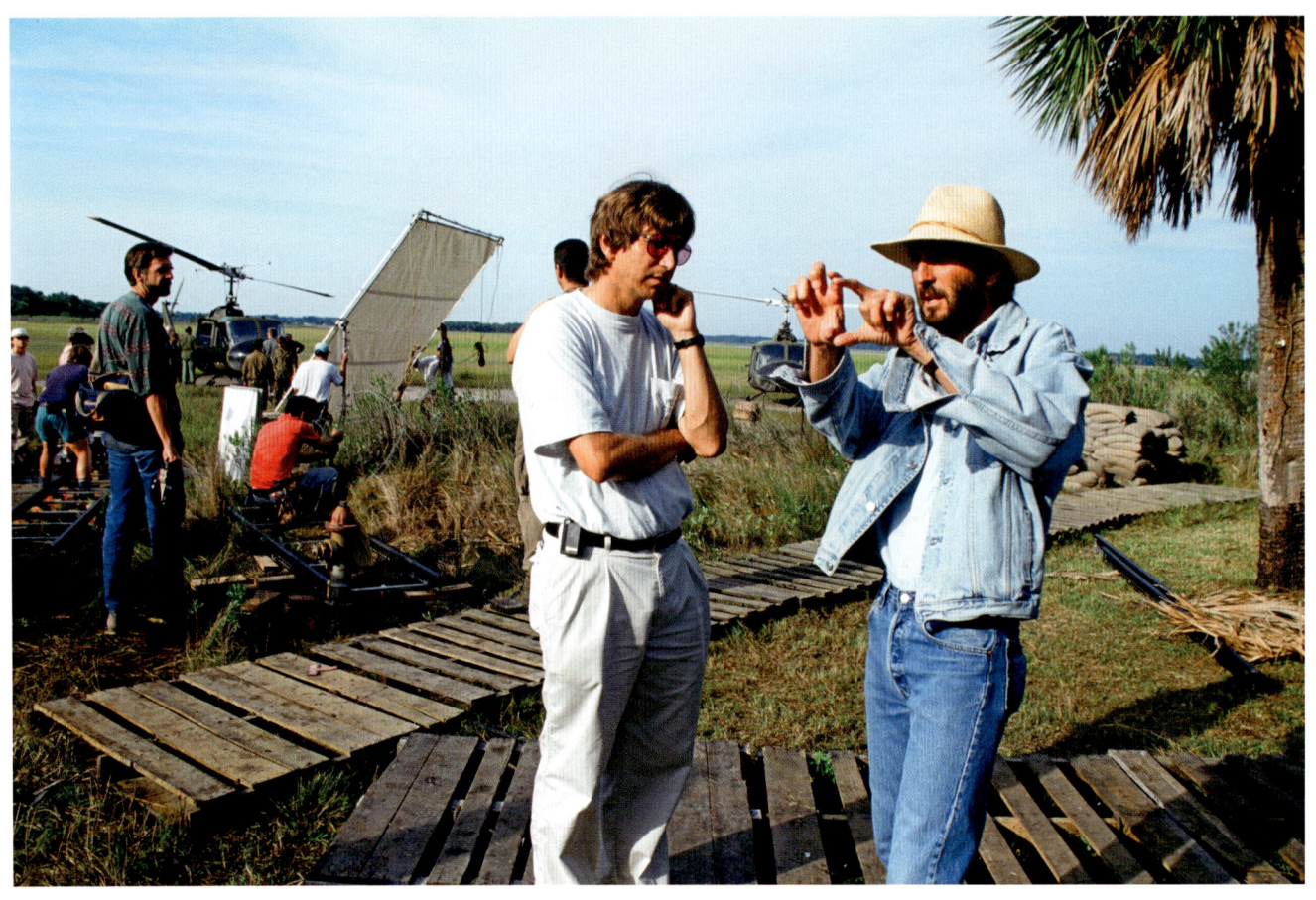

Rick Carter and me on location

together the plan to make *Jurassic Park,* although I moved on before that film was shot. Rick was my age and, like me, had gone to college at Berkeley in the 1970s. Much of the film would be like reliving our past.

While the war in Vietnam was raging, Rick and I had attended antiwar rallies, much like the one Forrest stumbles into in Washington, DC, after he returns from the war. Forrest meets with the presidents of our lifetime—Kennedy, Johnson, and Nixon. And, with a wink, he is responsible for bringing to light the Watergate break-in, which was instrumental in Nixon's downfall. So many incidents in the film—from the US Table Tennis team going to China to the moon landing—formed the tapestry of our lives. But most of all, we were

Beatles fans, so when Forrest appears on *The Dick Cavett Show* and inspires the lyrics to John Lennon's song "Imagine," we were hooked.

What also excited us, which is true of all films, was immersing ourselves in a place we were unfamiliar with. On this adventure we would travel into the Deep South and discover the world of Forrest Gump. After working with Rick time and again, I knew he was up to the challenge. Bob agreed that he was ideal for the project.

We invited Rick to come on board, and he immediately suggested Mary Morgan as the location manager. We trusted his choice. Mary hit the road right away. She started in Winston Groom's actual hometown of Mobile, Alabama, and fanned out from there. She was trying to find a town that might stand in for the fictional Greenbow, Alabama, where we hoped to discover the Gump house. Mary would also scout for a Louisiana bayou for the scenes where Forrest fulfills a promise to Bubba Blue, his Vietnam buddy, to start a shrimping business. Along the way, she was also hoping to find a stand-in for Vietnam. Many locations were needed for the film, some in Washington, DC, and some in Los Angeles. But we had to start in the South, painting with large strokes at first and fine-tuning as we went along. With this fact-finding, we would have an honest approach to our location work and could solidify our budget.

But other questions remained: How does a feather fall from the sky and land at Forrest's feet? How do we shoot the scenes with Lieutenant

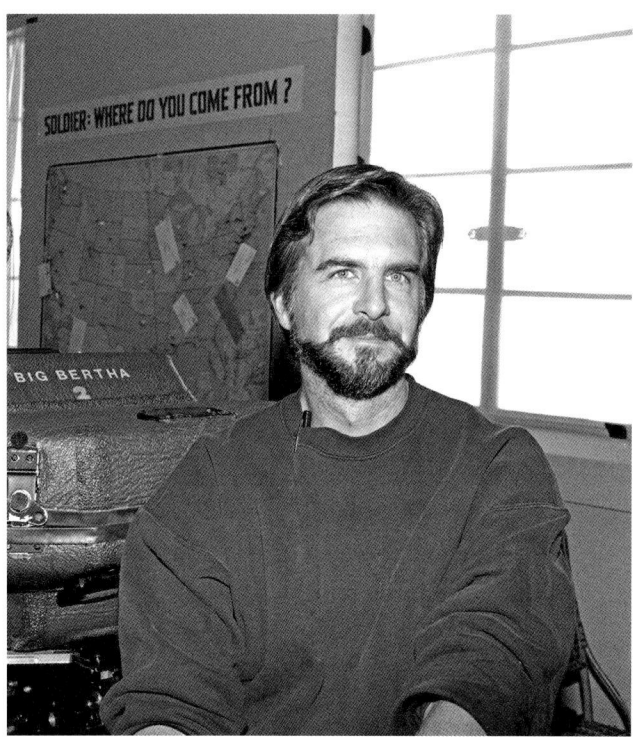

Ken Ralston

Dan—Forrest's commander in Vietnam—after he loses his legs? How does Forrest interact with all those past presidents? To answer these questions, I called on Ken Ralston, the visual-effects wizard who had worked with Bob on every one of his films since the original *Back to the Future.* He would have the answers. At least he would have a way to approach all my special-effects queries, and then I could get a number from Industrial Light & Magic, the visual-effects house, to plug into the budget.

At the same time, we got the approval to begin casting, starting with the most important role:

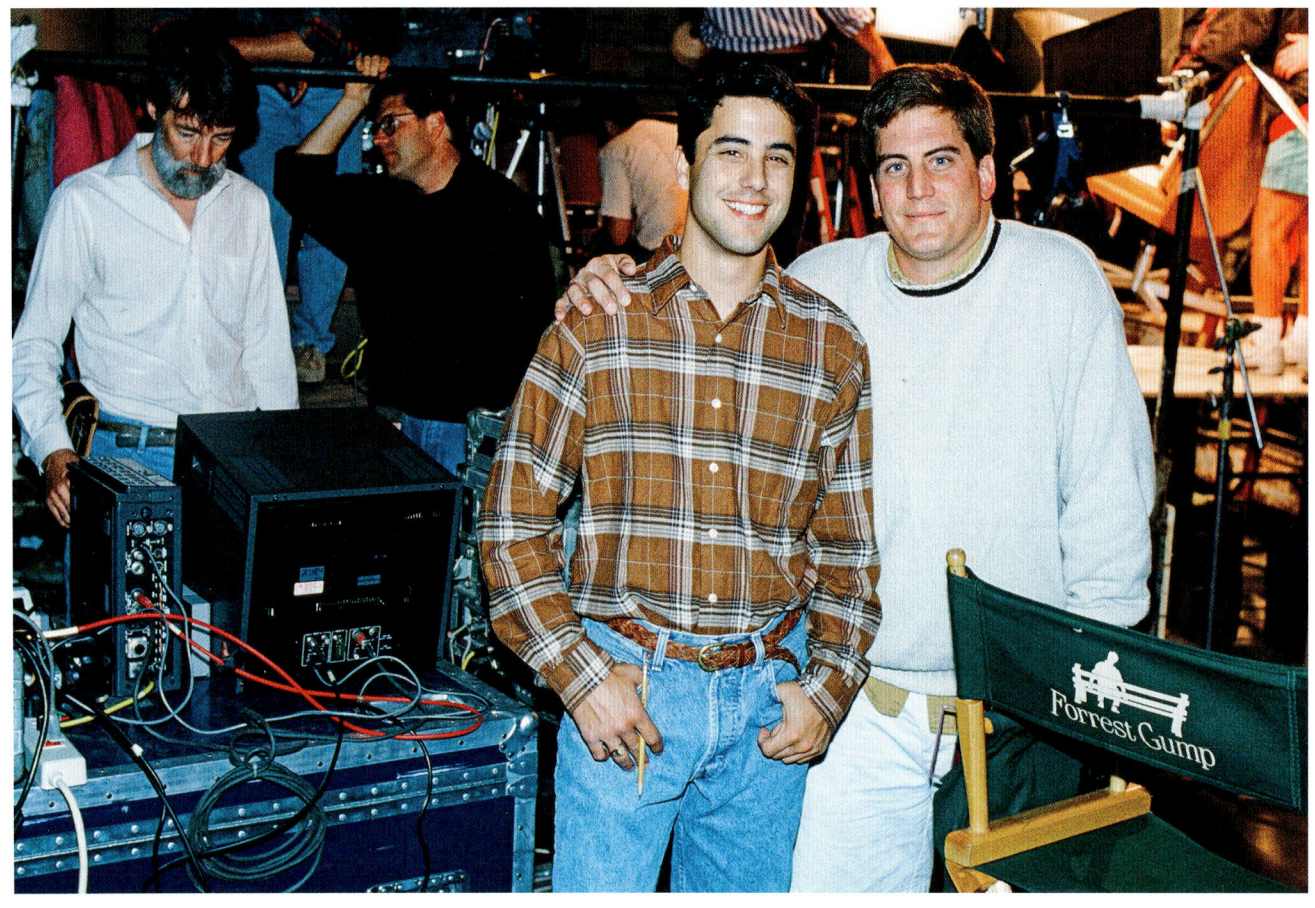

Rick Porras and Steve Boyd

Jenny Curran, Forrest's boyhood best friend and eventually the love of his life. We knew it would be difficult to find the young Forrest and young Jenny. Even though we didn't have a start date, we were eager to start looking. Wendy Finerman suggested we hire New York casting guru Ellen Lewis, and we were fortunate to get her. Ellen wasted no time putting calls out.

While all this was going on, Bob and Eric were tinkering with the script. They were desperate to find stock film footage for some scenes they had roughed out in the screenplay: Forrest meeting the presidents in the White House, happening upon the George Wallace standoff at the University of Alabama, and being a guest with John Lennon on *The Dick Cavett Show.* Bob and Eric needed the historical footage in order to design and finish writing those scenes. The final script, along with the accompanying videos, would help all the relevant departments re-create the sets, the props, and the look of the background characters. It was a colossal undertaking. Rick Porras and Steve Boyd, with whom I'd worked on *Death Becomes Her,* were assigned to comb through hours of footage hidden in dark vaults nationwide to find the gems we needed.

Meanwhile, I opened Groom's book, hoping to get additional inspiration for the location search and the tone of the film. From the opening line, I could tell that the book and the screenplay were decidedly not like peas and carrots. The central characters were very different. Groom's Forrest wants readers to know that being stupid is not easy: "Let me say this: bein an idiot is no box of chocolates." Groom's Forrest continues by comparing himself to other idiots, from those in Shakespeare and Dostoevsky to others in modern literature's *To Kill a Mockingbird* and *Of Mice and Men.* He concludes with a story that illustrates Forrest is not as stupid as he seems. In fact, Groom's Forrest is a savant, and his mathematical abilities often drive the book's plot.

The Forrest in the film has a different perspective: "Life was like a box of chocolates . . . you never know what you're going to get." His mama taught him that the world is full of possibilities, and you never know what surprises may come your way. He never ponders the characters in classical literature. He is a humble man with endearing qualities.

He is driven in life to do what is right and what is good and by his love for his mama and Jenny. He acknowledges that he may not be smart, but he knows what love is.

The more I read, the more I realized how brilliant Eric's screenplay was. He had included highlights of the remarkable places Forrest travels to in the Groom novel (the University of Alabama, Vietnam, China) but excluded the most outrageous, like going to space with an ape and winding up on a desert island. He changed what happens to Forrest's mama—in the novel, she ends up in the poorhouse—and altered Forrest's relationship with Lieutenant Dan. And while Jenny was an important character in the book, in the film, Forrest and Jenny's love story is a crucial continuous thread. In the end, Eric and Bob took some of Groom's ideas but then shaped the movie's characters and added many gems of their own.

A few things were true in both the book and the film: Forrest has to pee at the most inopportune times and, as the Groom character says, "I got no complains, cause I reckon I done live a pretty interestin life."

After I finished the book, Bob asked me if he should read it. I told him it would probably only confuse him, and he should stick to the script. I don't know if he ever read it or not.

Now with the script in hand and the book back on the shelf, it was time to roll up my sleeves, head to the South, and get to work on a shooting plan and a budget.

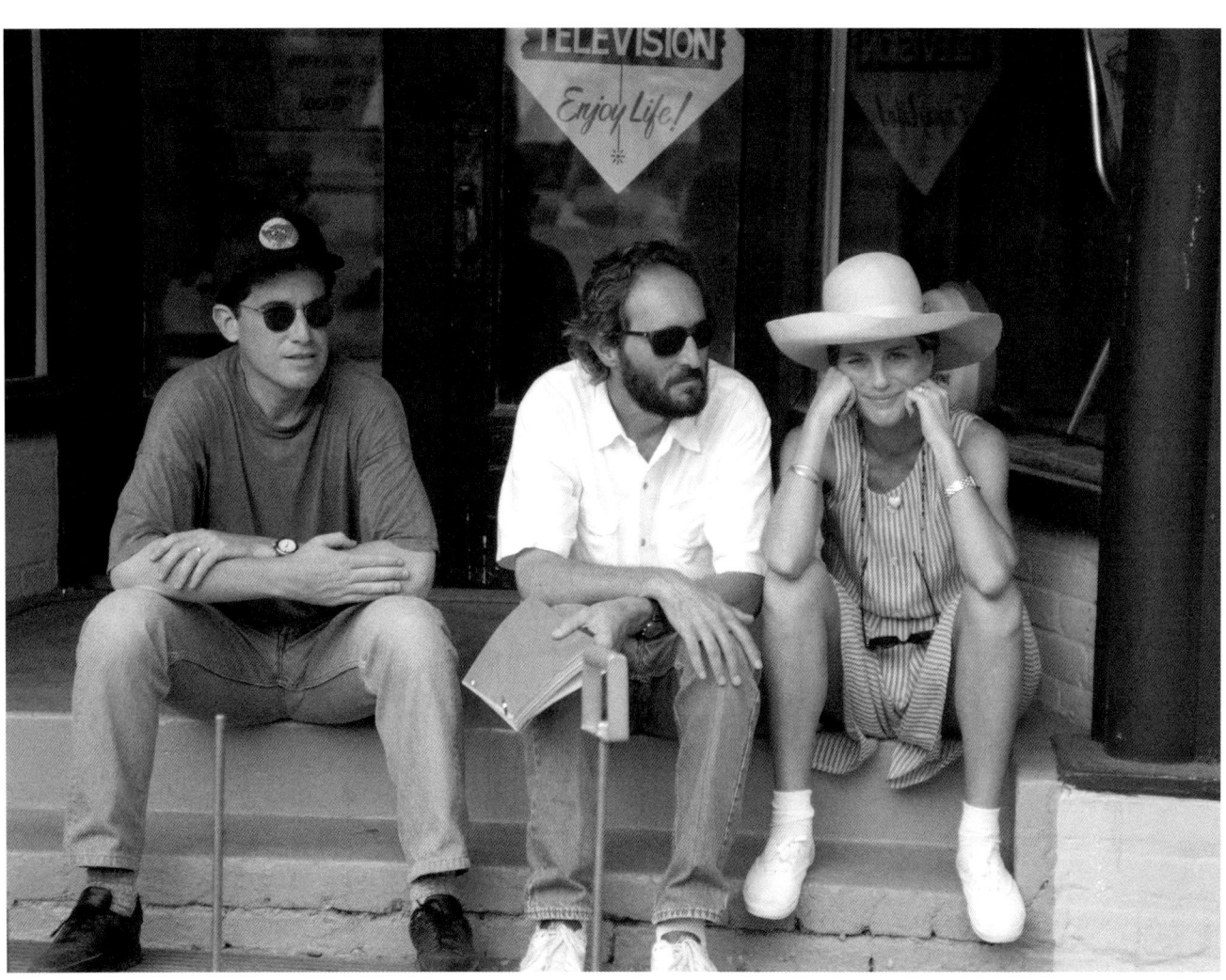

2 | Searching for Greenbow, Alabama

I AM ON A VOYAGE of discovery in a time capsule transporting me to the world of Forrest Gump. Instead of traveling in Doc Brown's DeLorean as we did in *Back to the Future,* the screenplay for *Forrest Gump* has fixed our time and place, and Bob Zemeckis is at the helm. The era we are heading to extends from the 1950s through the early 1980s, and our destination is the Deep South.

We started by scouting in Louisiana, looking for Forrest Gump's hometown along with possible locations to shoot the wartime scenes in Vietnam and shrimping in the bayou. The filmmaking team was crammed together in a van, sharing stories of recent film experiences and talking excitedly about scenes in the new screenplay. Everyone was looking out the windows, hoping to discover the perfect town around the next bend in the road.

As I listened to the murmur of voices around me, I gazed at the wide-open spaces along the highway and let my thoughts wander to images of Vietnam. I imagined the fields of the Mekong Delta and Forrest on patrol with his platoon. Later, as we passed through bayou country closer to the coast, I could see a few fishermen heading

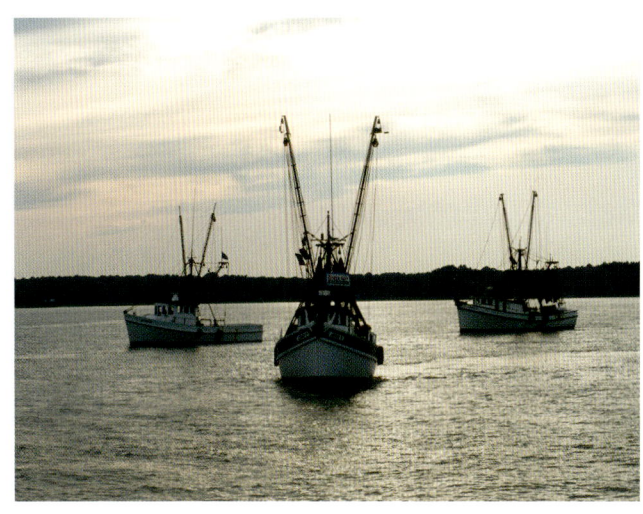

out to sea. Were they shrimp boats? That could be Forrest, trying his luck in the shrimping business. Louisiana was beginning to look promising. Hopefully we would find Forrest's hometown in the surrounding area.

Location scouting always gives me the feeling that the film is getting real. Up until now, we had been on pins and needles while the budgeting and art department prep were done on a shoestring. The studio had kept the cash flow tight, but now money was trickling in. Although the light was not yet green, it was blinking yellow. We might get to make this film, but it would be a fight.

That's the way it always is: The studio exerts pressure on the filmmakers by holding back funds. First, the studio says it won't allow scouting until the budget number comes down or some above-the-line deal is made with the director or the star. Knowing that the filmmakers are chomping at the bit to get started, the studio heads often use this as leverage when making a deal. They never let you forget who holds the purse strings. *Gump* felt like a risky venture to the studio, so the purse strings were being held very, very tightly.

As we drove for miles on the open highway, every signpost at the edge of a new town seemed to promise what we were looking for. Our excitement was palpable. Could this be it? But as each new town failed to meet our expectations, I started to wonder where we might go next.

Go where the script tells you to go, they say, which in this case was where the book sent the screenwriter: Alabama. Eric Roth had taken Winston Groom's place of origin to heart when he wrote the screenplay and called Forrest's hometown Greenbow, Alabama. So we followed in his footsteps and went to Mobile, Groom's hometown, to see if any place nearby might work. We quickly found that the area had little to offer. We would have to cast a wider net.

On to Georgia. We knew *Fried Green Tomatoes* had been shot in Juliette, and that movie had a good southern look. We decided to check the place

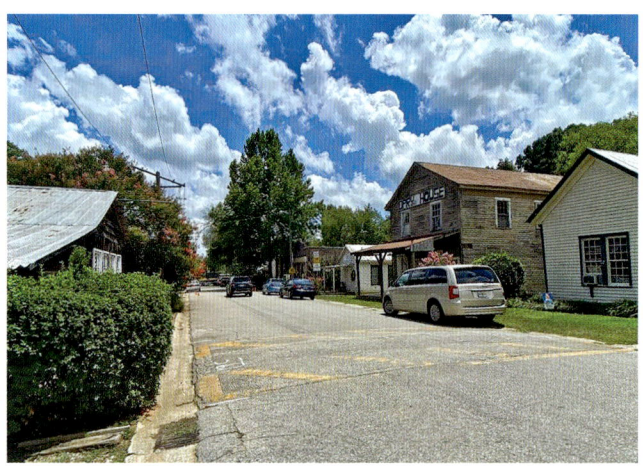

McCrackin Street in Juliette, Georgia

out. The funny thing was, as we wandered the small streets of the town, we realized that Juliette did not definitively evoke the South. It could just as easily have been somewhere in the Midwest. We began to wonder, what defines the South? Would we know it when we saw it?

As we drove, Bob, who was sitting shotgun, started to contemplate the scope of the movie and all the locations beyond Forrest's hometown. He turned and said, "You know how we should make this movie? Just like Coppola's film *The Rain People.* Francis drove around from town to town, shooting as he went. Small crew. Just the actors, camera, sound. You know, just what he needed."

I knew what Bob was talking about. I had watched *Filmmaker*, George Lucas's behind-the-scenes documentary on *The Rain People*, and it was just as Bob described it. The crew would arrive

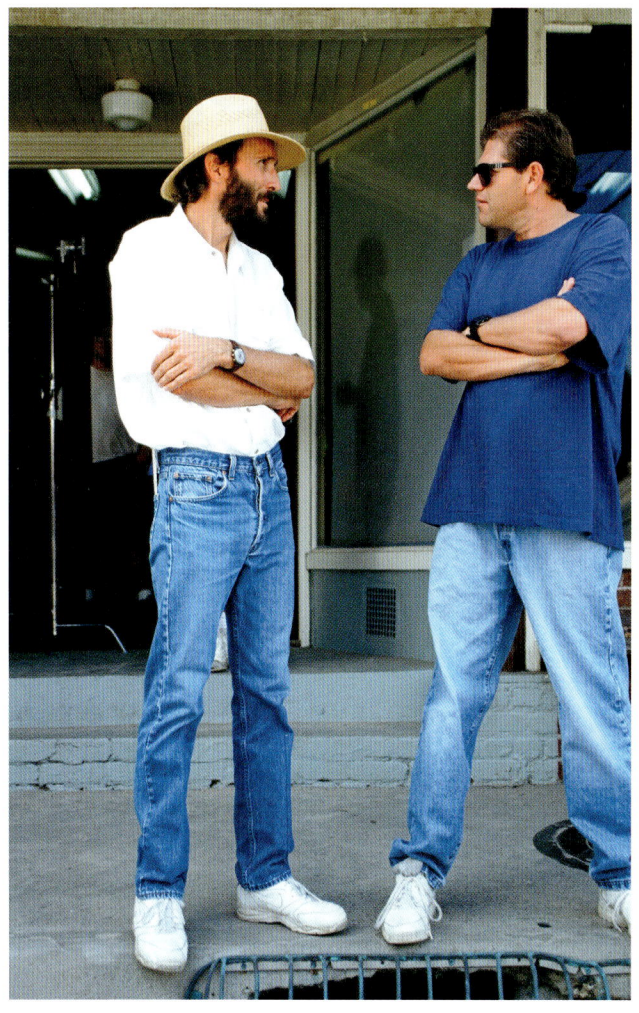

Bob and me, scouting the towns of the South

idea of being lean and mean. He loved the idea of shooting a movie with a skeleton crew. Although he needed big crews for his movies, he wished the process could be scaled back to only those absolutely necessary to get each shot. In our case, that was unrealistic, but the truth was that big crews slow things down.

In my mind, the next best thing was to find a hub where the production could be based, with all the other film locations fanning out like the spokes of a wheel. The less we had to move the company or the crew, the better. Contrary to Bob's run-and-gun thinking, I was looking to stay in one place and keep the production as tight as possible.

Still, our first priority as we traveled those miles of highway was to find Forrest's hometown. We were about to discover, however, that we were looking down the wrong road. We would soon learn that it was not the town we needed to find. It was something else.

in a town. Francis would bless the location. Production would scramble to secure permission to shoot and scour the area to accommodate everyone overnight.

But *Forrest Gump* was not *The Rain People.* We had a bigger beast on our hands. Bob liked the

We made our discovery in South Carolina's Low Country. There, freshwater and seawater collided and mixed to form beautiful, brilliantly colored salt marshes that stretched to the horizon. The shorebirds were plentiful, the sea life abundant. But the towns were not impressive. In fact, they looked poor or derelict. Mary Morgan, our location manager, took us on a detour down a country highway. Far from any town, we pulled off the

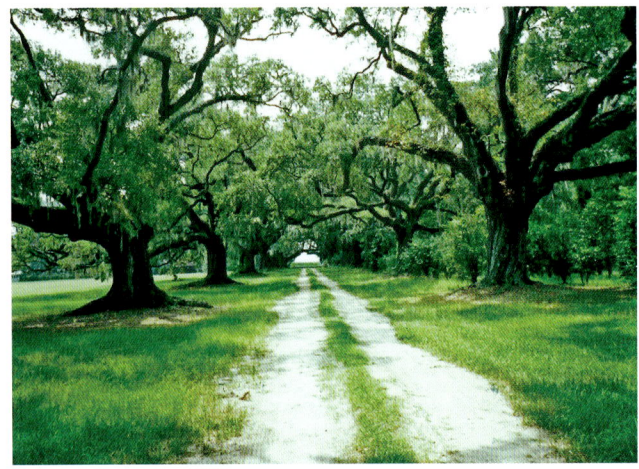

Oak Alley in South Carolina's Low Country

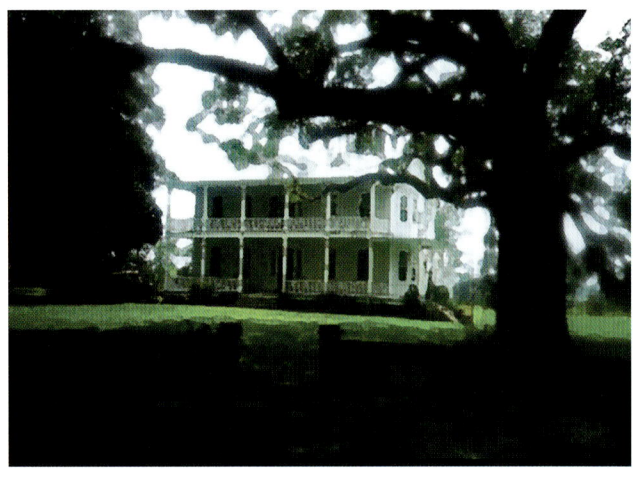

Watercolor of the Gump house by Rick Carter

road and stopped the van, stepped out, and looked down a small dirt track lined with majestic oak trees dripping with Spanish moss.

Like Dorothy in *The Wizard of Oz* when she says, "We're not in Kansas anymore," we realized the oak alley in front of us could only be in the South. It caused us all to rethink what we were calling Forrest's home.

We walked up the road under the canopy of trees, avoiding mounds of fire ants and swatting away mosquitoes, to an open field overgrown with grass and weeds. Rick Carter, our production designer, told us a house had once stood there on the original Bluff Plantation. He thought one could stand there again.

It was not hard to imagine a stately house there, next to the Combahee River. We had finally found Forrest's home. It would ground the film, just as

it would Forrest. This is where he would grow up and where he would return after his world travels and life's adventures.

It's funny how things like this happen. Finding where to plant your flag is a process. You know it when you feel it. If you get fixated on the town, you can end up on a wild goose chase. The real discovery was not the town at all; it was Forrest's home. There wasn't any second-guessing. The oak alley became as iconic as the house it led to. Mama led Forrest up the alley to their home. He took his first ride to school there. He was liberated from his leg braces and found freedom from his tormentors there. Everything was falling into place.

Once we found our setting for the Gump house, we turned our sights back to the town, whose distinctive nature became relatively less important. A quick tour of the area took us to Varnville, which

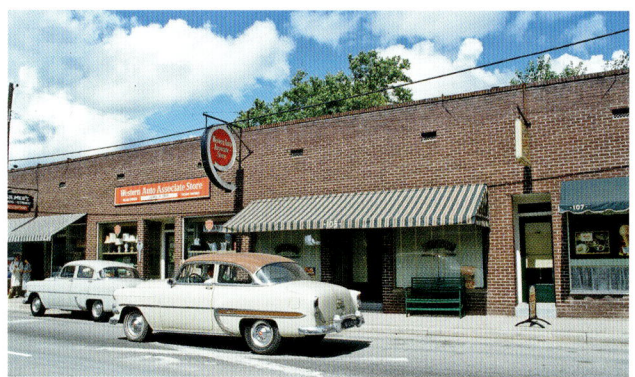

Downtown Varnville, South Carolina

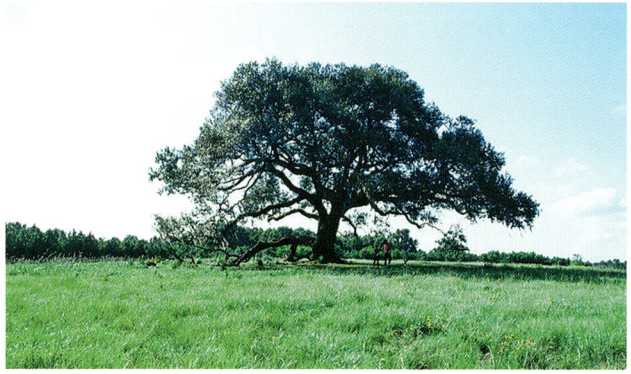

Forrest and Jenny's tree on the Bluff Plantation property

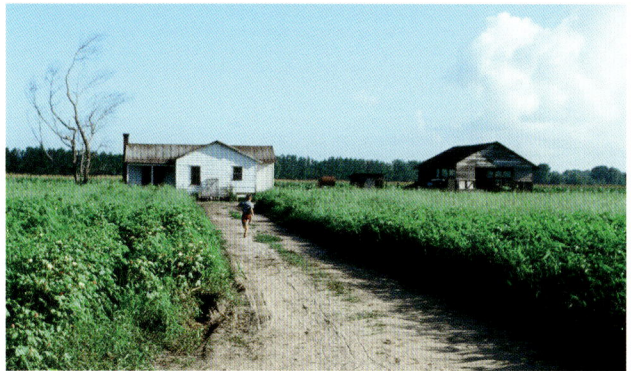

Jenny's farmhouse

fit our needs quite nicely, with a simple main street and a classic barbershop.

When we returned to the Bluff Plantation property, the film started to open before our eyes. We found an iconic oak tree, where Forrest and Jenny would play as children and where Forrest would eventually lay Jenny to rest. We located a spot for Jenny's farm nearby, where we could plant crops with time to grow before filming.

We also discovered open marshlands that could stand in for Vietnam and waterways that would serve for the shrimping scenes. What initially appeared to be a daunting number of locations all seemed to be present in and around the Bluff Plantation.

The nearby town of Beaufort, South Carolina, proved to be the production center I was looking for. The town had been used for *The Big Chill.* And although we had no call to shoot on the old streets of Beaufort, we soon discovered that it had plenty of the infrastructure we needed, including housing for the crew and a multistory building with space for our production offices. It all looked good.

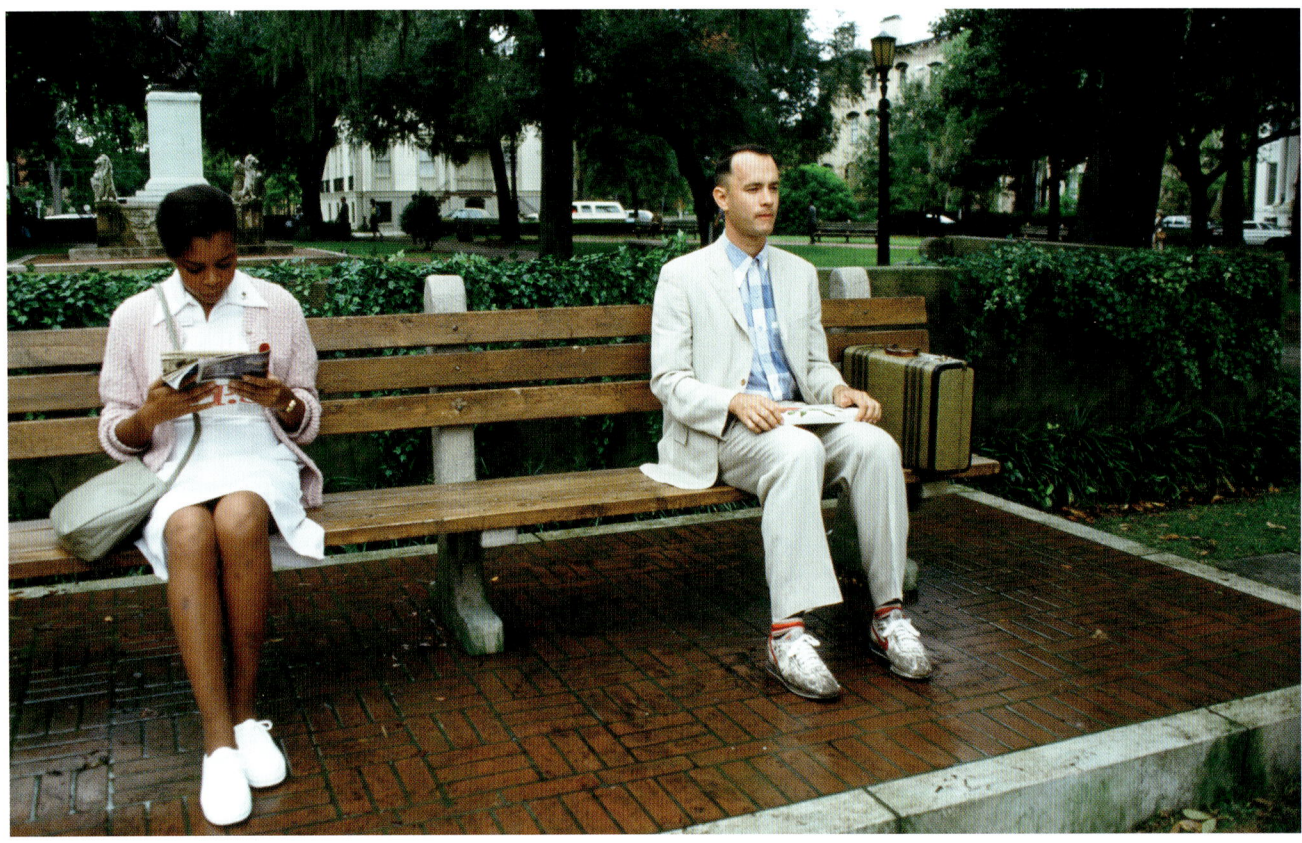

Forrest on the bench in Chippewa Square in Savannah

Before we left the South, Rick Carter and Mary Morgan took us to Chippewa Square in the historic section of Savannah, Georgia. The timeless resonance of the setting captured our hearts. We would place Forrest on a bench here. This is where he would tell his story.

After our revealing and productive scouting trip, we continued to Washington, DC, and reviewed the film's iconic locations there: the Jefferson Memorial, the Reflecting Pool in front of the Lincoln Memorial, the Capitol, the White House, and more. We even scouted the interior of the White House in order to design the set we planned to build.

With all this in our hip pocket, we were ready to head back to Los Angeles, figure out our local locations and stage work, and put together a plan and a budget. We were also eager to see what casting surprises Ellen Lewis might have for us.

22

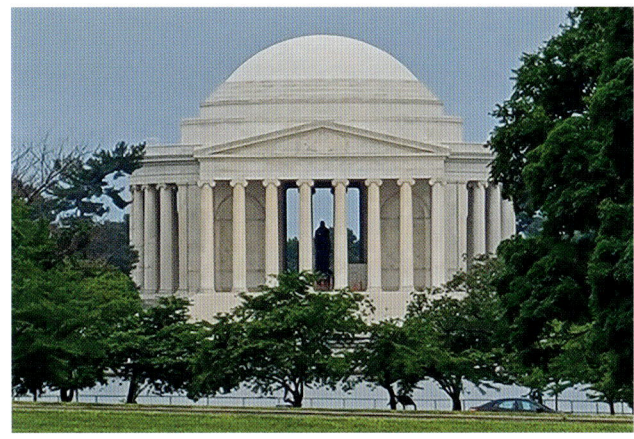

Jefferson Memorial

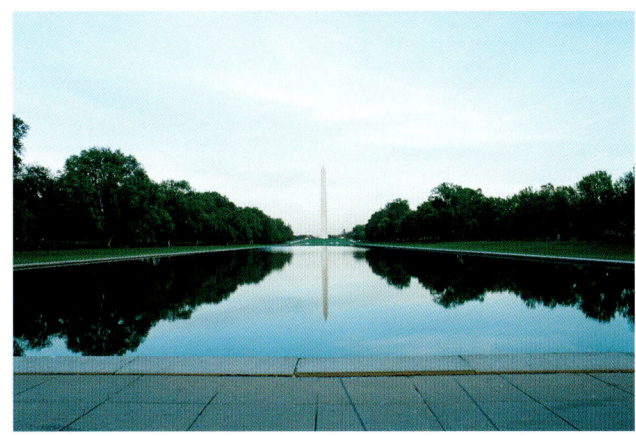

Reflecting Pool

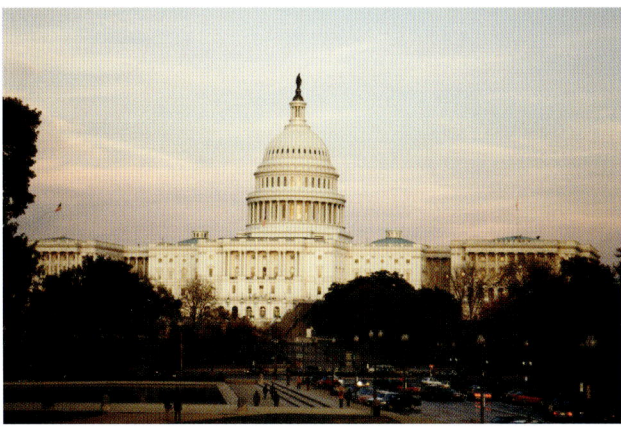

US Capitol

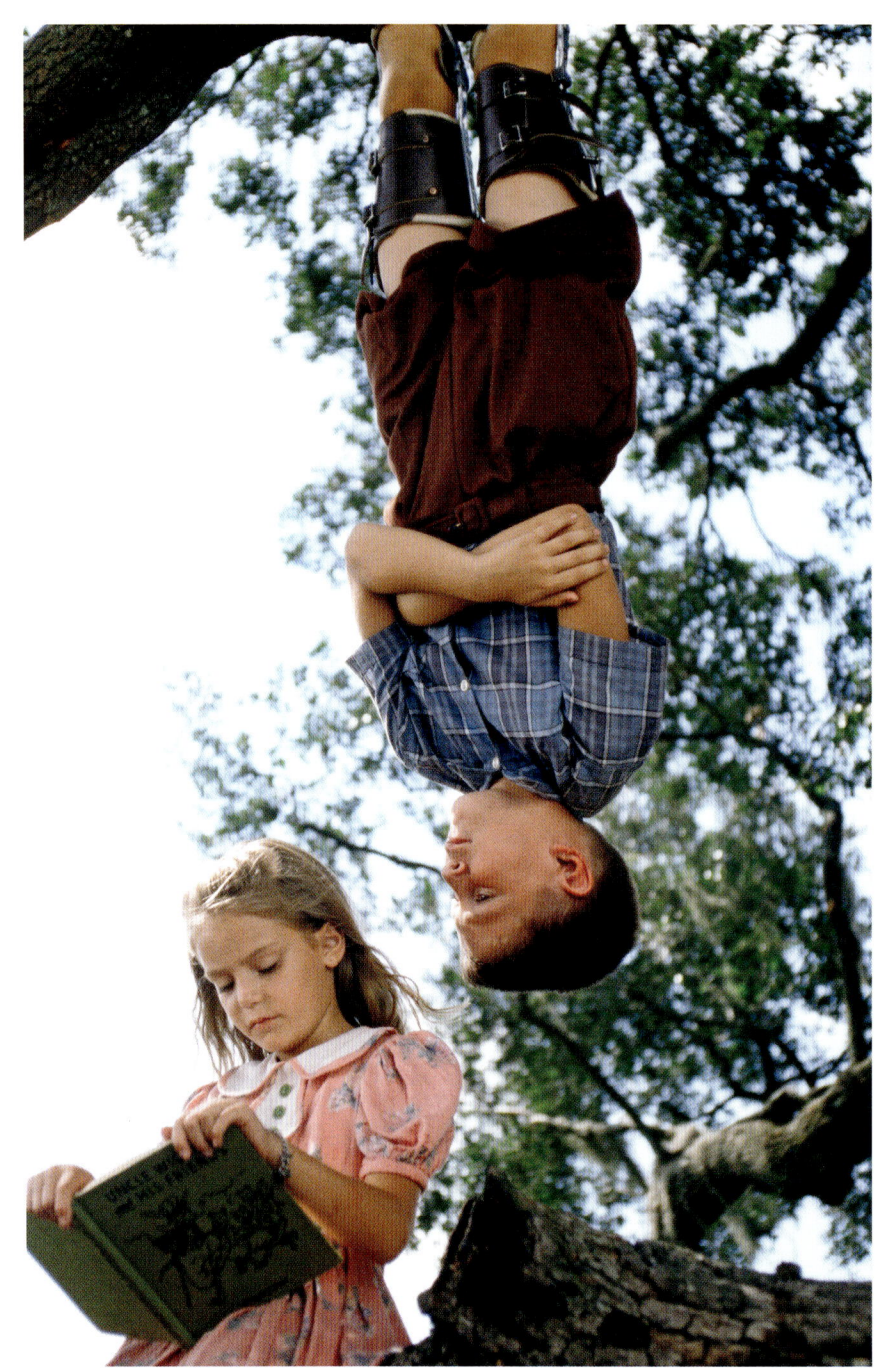

3 | Do You Have Any Peanut Butter?

LOOKING OVER THE CRAFT-SERVICE table, Michael Conner Humphreys asked me if we had any peanut butter. The usual assortment of raw vegetables, fruit, and energy bars was not appealing to him. I understood. I love peanut butter. His mom was embarrassed. I ran off the soundstage to the craft-service truck to try to rectify the situation. I was charmed by this young boy from Mississippi. None of us—Bob Zemeckis, Tom Hanks, Wendy Finerman, or casting director Ellen Lewis—had seen any boys who could play the young Forrest Gump until Michael captured our imagination. His thick southern accent—a little goofy sounding, in fact—was unlike anything we had heard during our casting search, or ever, for that matter. His body language was also unlike any other's. But would he freeze in front of the camera? What would he do when acting opposite the young Jenny? All this would reveal itself during the screen test, which would take place after he got his peanut butter sandwich.

On a whim, Michael had attended an open casting call in Memphis, Tennessee. His mom had driven him up from their small town of Independence, Mississippi, after she saw an ad in the local paper, and we flew them out to Los Angeles for a screen test. This was surely their first trip to Hollywood.

For months we had watched hours of tape of young Forrest wannabees. We even tested a few. Ellen had begun her readings in Los Angeles and New York, then cast her net to other large cities in the hopes of finding the right boy, actor or not. When that didn't work, she asked if she could do regional calls to try to uncover a hidden gem. In Memphis, she found her boy.

Our young Jenny proved to be equally difficult to find, especially as she was described by Forrest in voice-over (V.O.) from his bench in Savannah:

```
             FORREST (V.O.)
I  had  never  seen  anything  so
beautiful  in  my  life.  She  was  like
an  angel.
```

Hanna Hall, the young actress we finally cast in the role, did not come from the South. She too had attended an open call, but in her home state of Colorado. For her, the accent would have to be

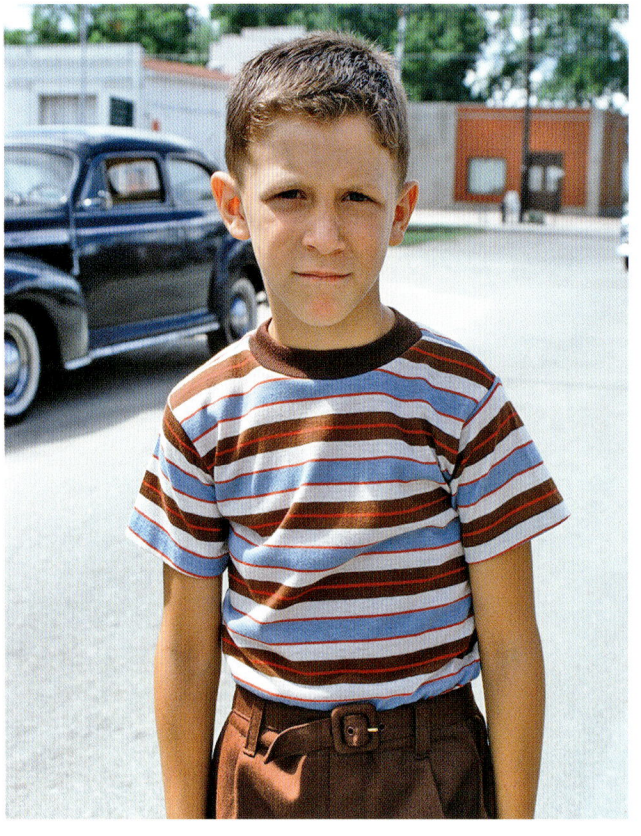

Michael Conner Humphreys as young Forrest

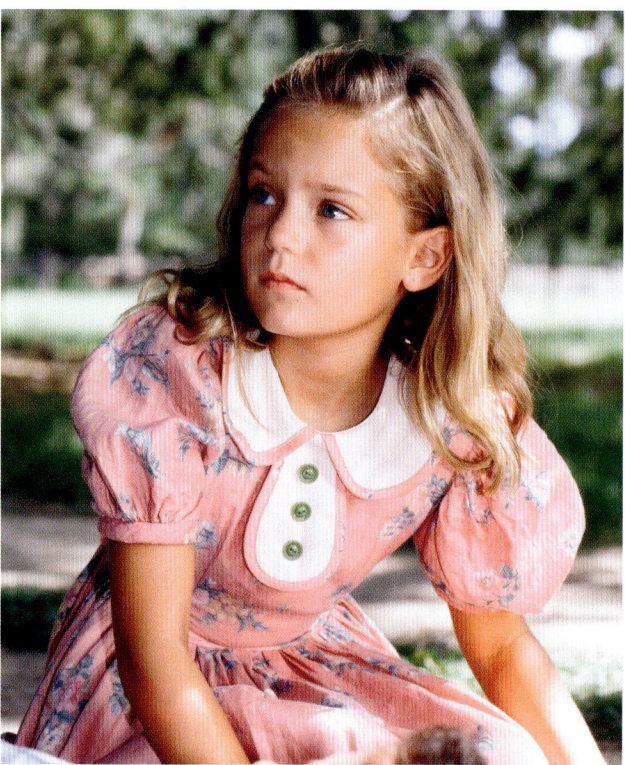

Hanna Hall as young Jenny

learned under the guidance of a dialect coach. But Hanna's magical qualities outweighed the fact that she was not from the South. She was a beautiful girl and was somehow able to convey Jenny Curran's troubled childhood through her eyes. These dual qualities had been difficult to find until Hanna read for the part.

When Michael and Hanna performed opposite each other, we knew we had our young Forrest and Jenny.

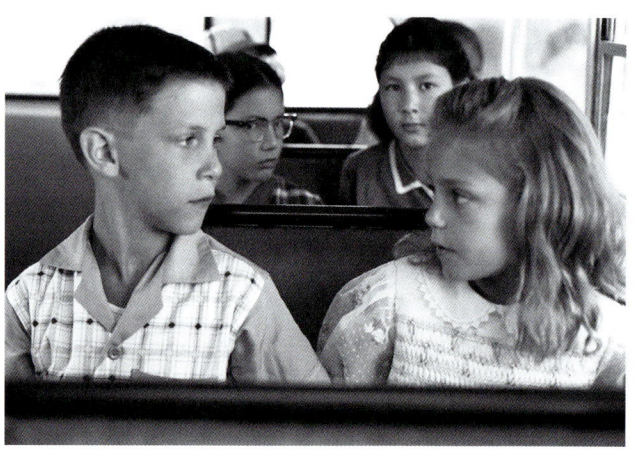

Forrest and Jenny on the school bus

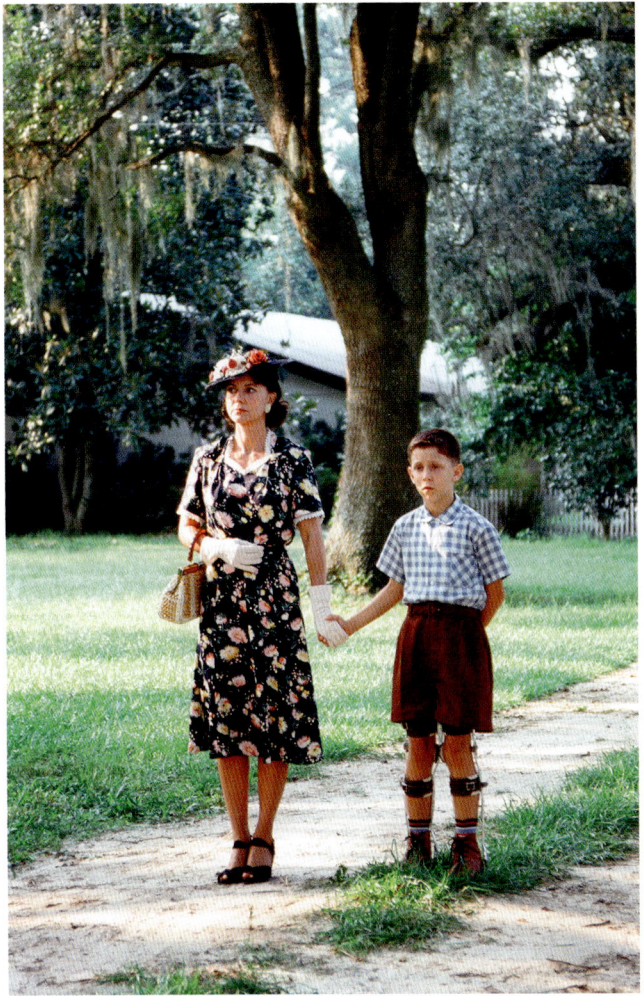

Sally Field as Mama Gump

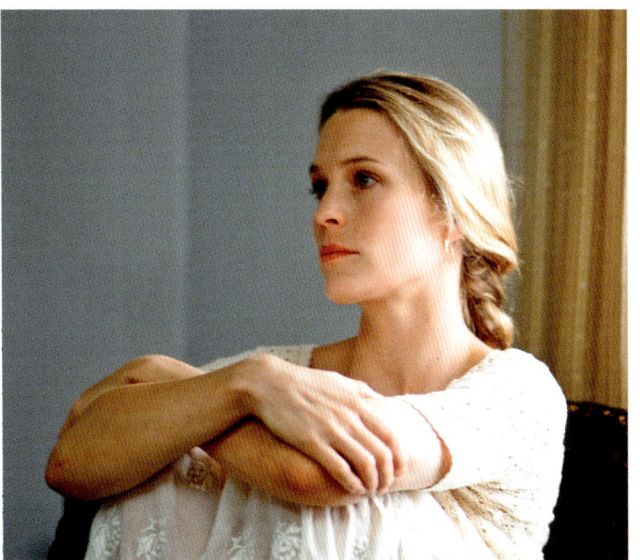

Robin Wright as adult Jenny

While we were obsessed with finding our young Forrest and Jenny, we also focused our attention on the role of the adult Jenny. After reviewing many, many actresses for the part—Demi Moore even came to the office dressed as a hippie—we invited Robin Wright and Laura Dern to come in for screen tests with Tom. Robin performed a beautiful audition. She was like the angel young Forrest described. She walked off the set with the role. A short time later we found out she was pregnant, but that didn't sway our decision. Production would have to make it work and shoot around her.

One morning I came into Bob's office and said, "I think I found Lieutenant Dan! I was at Dominic's last night [our go-to restaurant/bar at the time]

Bob, still fearful of having these two young actors carry the film for the first twenty minutes, wanted a seasoned pro to play Mama Gump. He turned to Sally Field. There was no question in his mind. Sally could hold young Forrest's hand, both as his mama and as an actress.

27

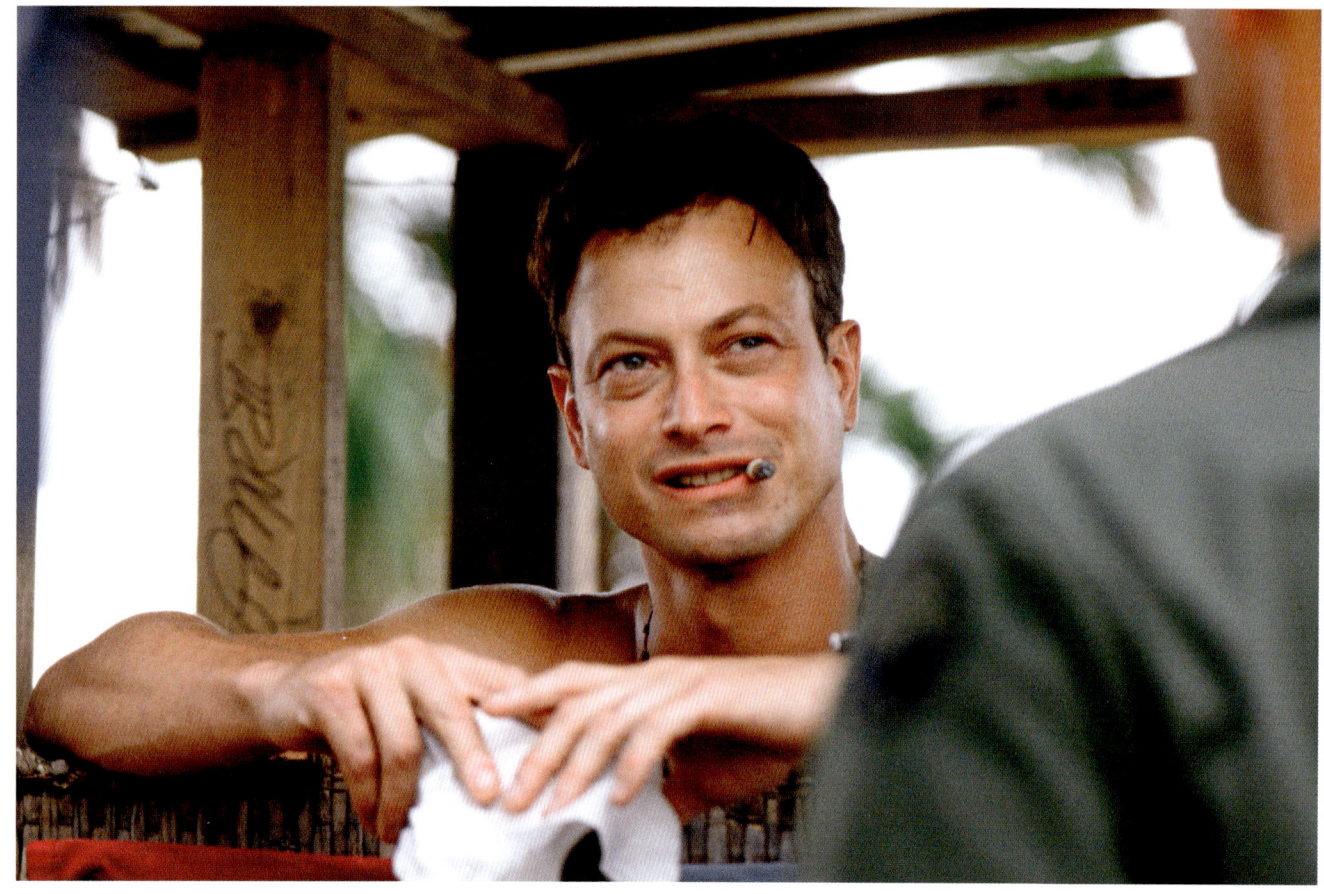

Gary Sinise as Lieutenant Dan

having a drink and shooting some pool with Gary Oldman. He may be our man."

"He is a great actor," Bob agreed, "but I want to keep looking. Put him on the list."

When Bob isn't convinced an actor is right for a part, he says to put him on the list.

Then we auditioned Gary Sinise for the role. Before the actor walked in the door, we reviewed his work in *Of Mice and Men.* That film showed the great range of his acting ability. We felt he could bring the same sensibilities to the entire character arc of Lieutenant Dan, beginning as an army lieutenant, then an embittered "cripple" and angry drunk, and finally a renewed man.

After the audition the list evaporated. Gary became Lieutenant Dan.

28

The search for the actor to play the part of Bubba Blue, Forrest's best friend, started in the pursuit of stunt casting. We considered a wide array of well-known actors and comedians, from Dave Chapelle to Ice Cube, looking for someone with name recognition. That proved to be a fool's errand. When Ellen Lewis brought in Mykelti Williamson and he auditioned for the group, we stopped in our tracks. His performance, done with a lip plumper, captured the character's endearing down-home qualities. He warmed our hearts and was awarded the role.

While all this casting was going on, we brought Tom Hanks into a recording studio to read all the dialogue he would later perform on the bench in Savannah, Georgia. We needed the timing of his lines long before we shot the dialogue for real. Later, while filming, we would watch a video play-back of the recorded line against the shot to see if the timing was correct. If necessary, we could make alterations to the camera movement or the actor's performance by either slowing things down or speeding them up. In addition, when a shot came into the editing room, the editor would be able to lay the dialogue up against a shot or a cut and feel the rhythm of what he was cutting.

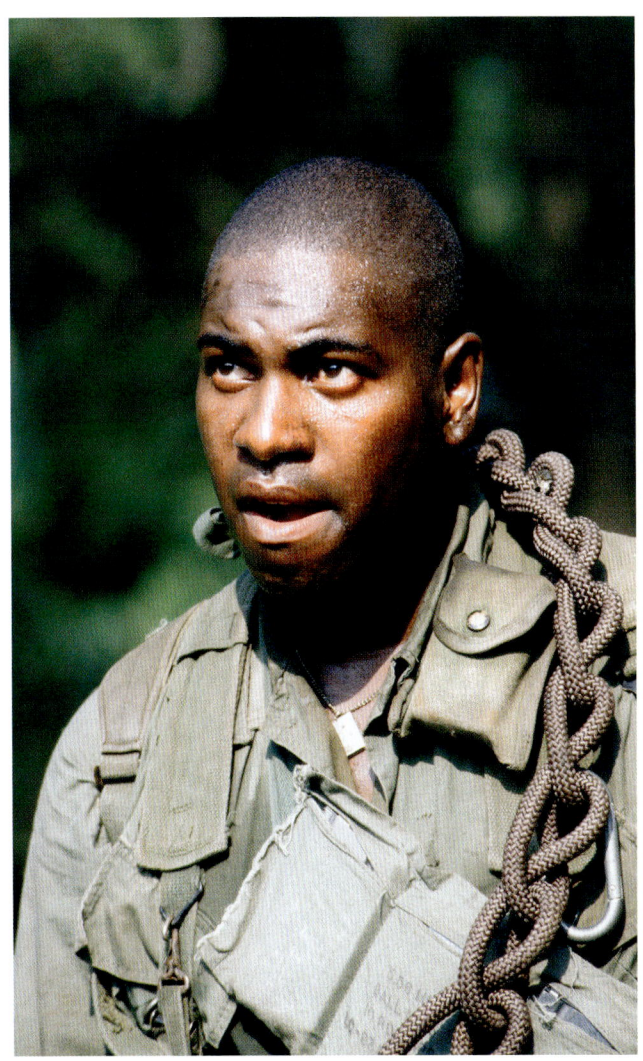

Mykelti Williamson as Bubba Blue

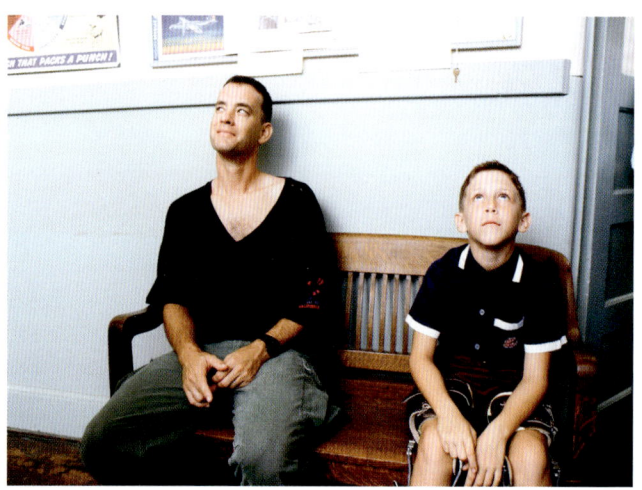

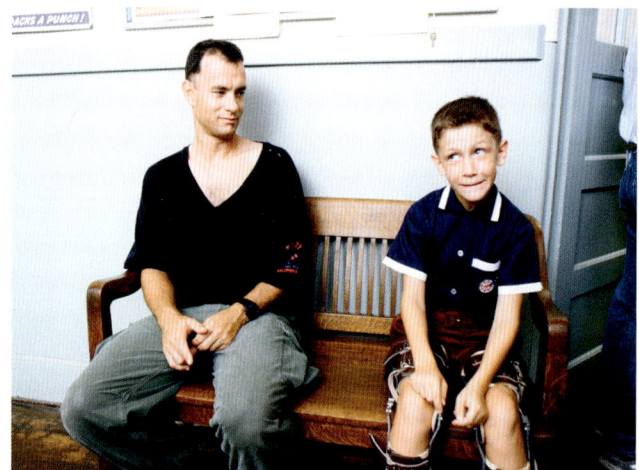

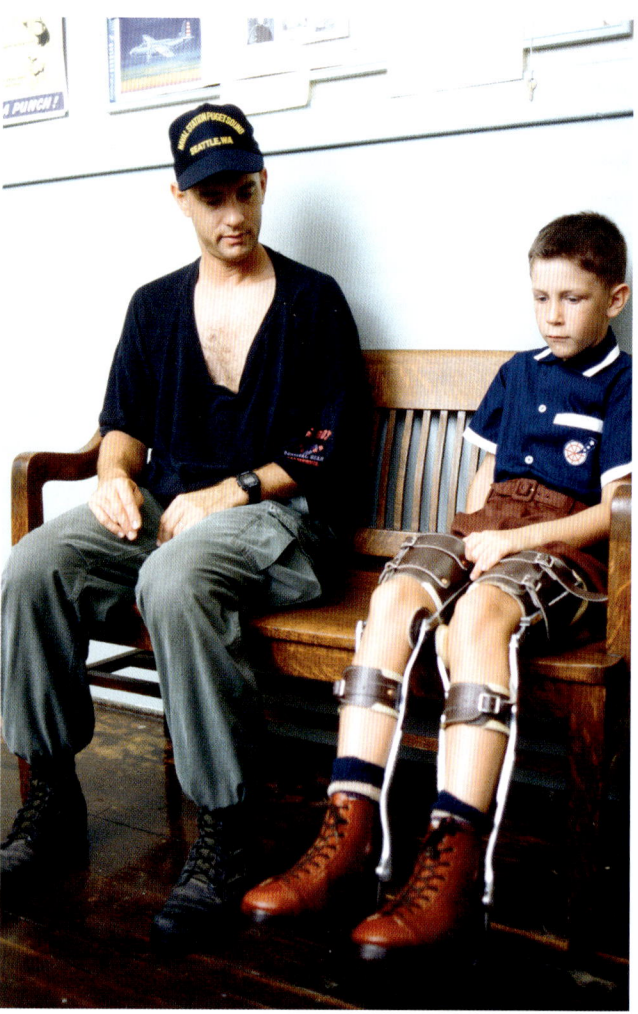

Tom Hanks and Michael Humphreys

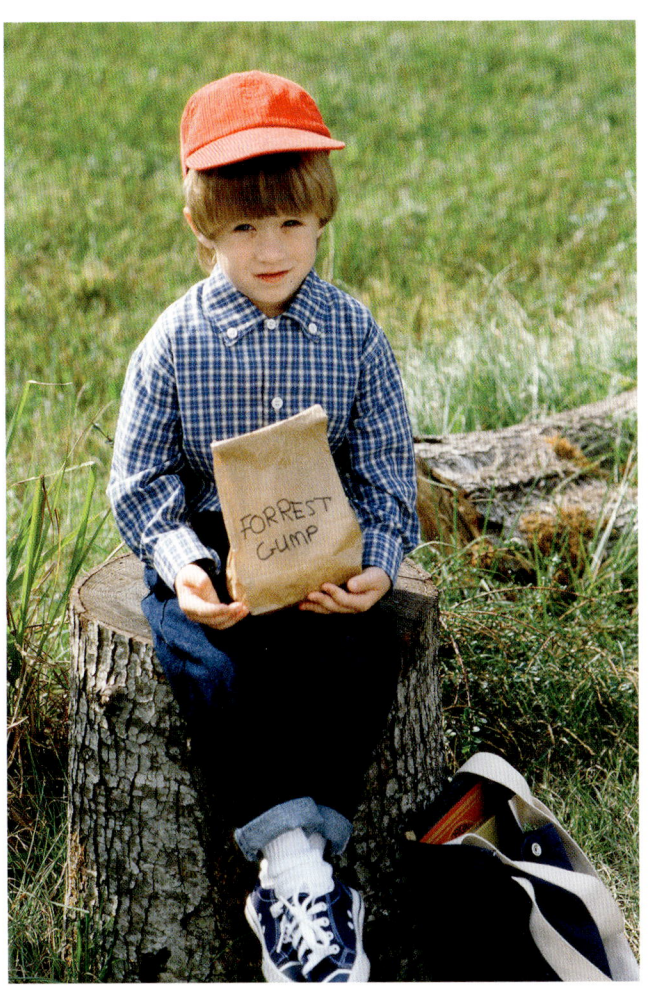

Haley Joel Osment as Forrest Jr.

While performing these temporary lines, Tom took a wild stab at a southern accent. But hearing Michael Humphreys' appealingly thick accent turned Tom's head around, and his Forrest started to take shape. Tom shadowed Michael, learned his accent and his body language, and modeled his character on the young boy from Mississippi.

Bob and Tom eventually had to fight with the studio to keep Tom's distinctive voice. I think Michael's quirky voice was so different from what anyone had ever heard that it was just another reason for the studio to be anxious.

Casting is a process, and like all aspects of filmmaking, it's always full of surprises. None of the casting was more surprising than when Ellen showed us a tape of a little boy, Haley Joel Osment, whom she had seen in a pizza commercial. "Guys," she told us, "I've found our Forrest Jr." And just like that, he was cast. Haley would play the young son of Jenny and Forrest, near the end of the film.

The surprises didn't end in casting, as I'd find out during my first budget meeting with Paramount.

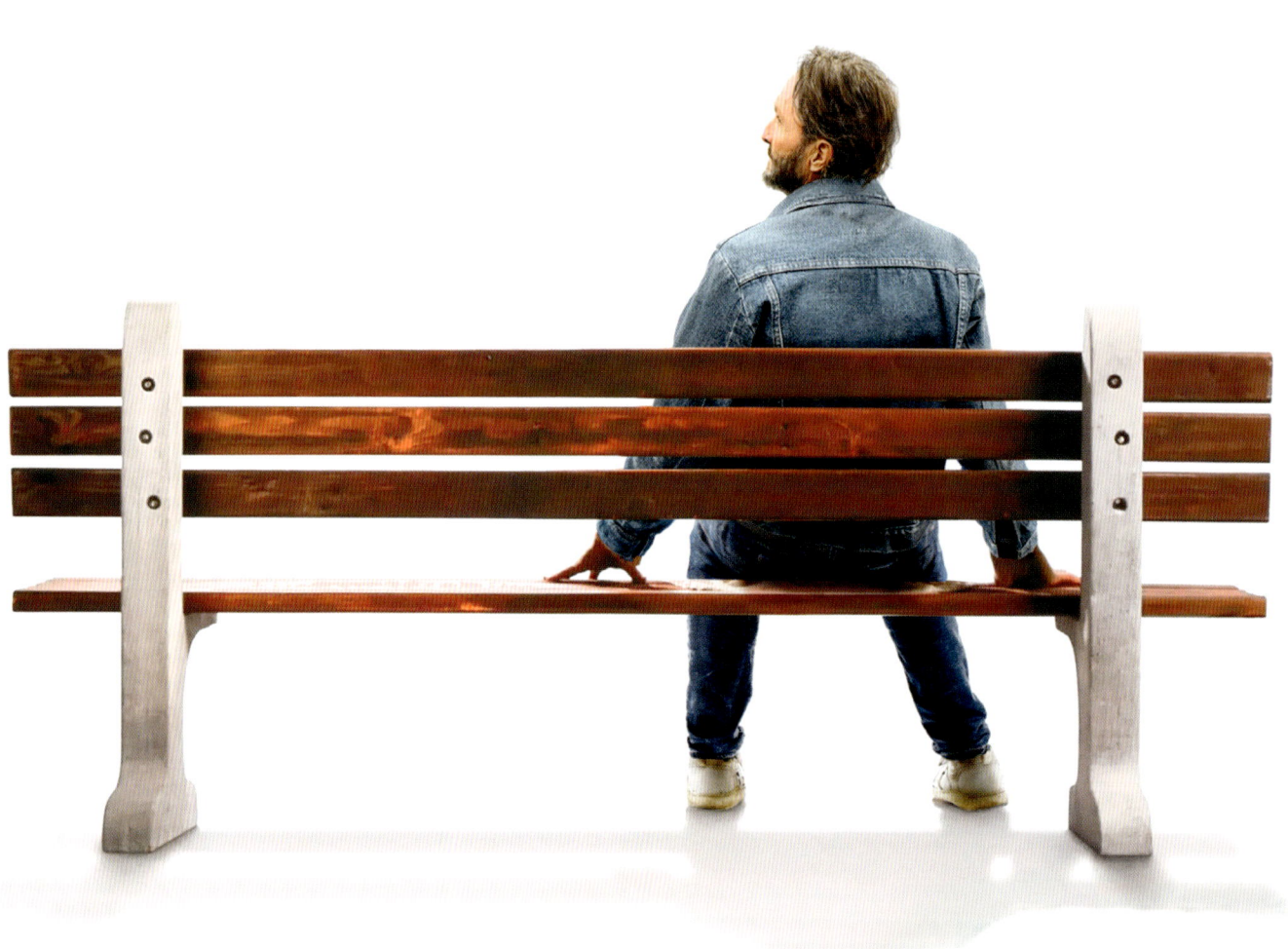

4 | Dreaming of a Greenlight

I WALKED UP THE stairs of the two-story production building on the Paramount lot and looked for the office of the head of physical production, Bill Tadross. He invited me in, took my budget, and handed it to his accountant, who was seated on a couch. I took a seat in a chair by the window. I wasn't sure why Bill wanted to meet only with me and not include Charles Newirth, my production manager, or our accountant, but I felt comfortable defending our budget. I knew it inside and out. Still, I thought it was strange.

While taking a few practice golf swings, Bill asked me if I golfed. I told him I hadn't taken up the sport yet, but I thought I might someday. Then he asked how I felt about the budget. I said it was tight, but we had a good plan, and I thought we could make the film for the number. I opened my copy of the budget, thinking there might be a few questions. There weren't any. Bill kept the meeting short. He said I was good to go. If I was happy, he was happy. That was it. I may have been happy, but I was dumbfounded.

As I walked back to my car, I didn't know what to think. I felt like I had just shot a hole in one. I

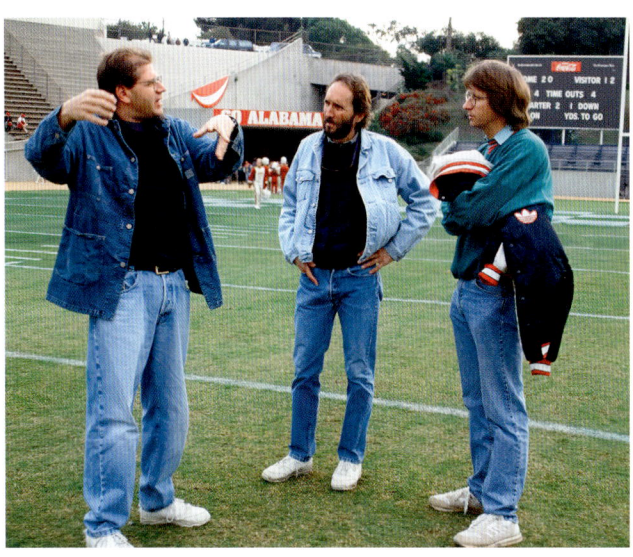

Zemeckis, me, and Rick Carter scouting the football stadium

had taken my best shot, and it had gone in. How lucky was I? Was the whole production going to go this smoothly? Would the studio simply give us the greenlight to make the movie?

I went back and reported the news to Bob and Charles, who both had more experience with meetings of this sort than I did. Charles thought I might be holding back some of the details of what went on. Did Bill go through the budget line by

33

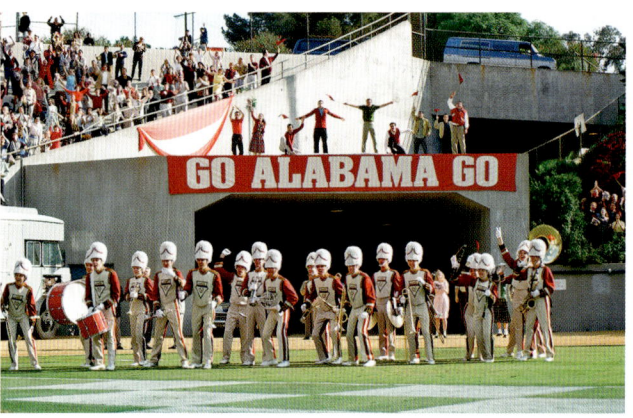

Set of the University of Alabama football field at
East Los Angeles College

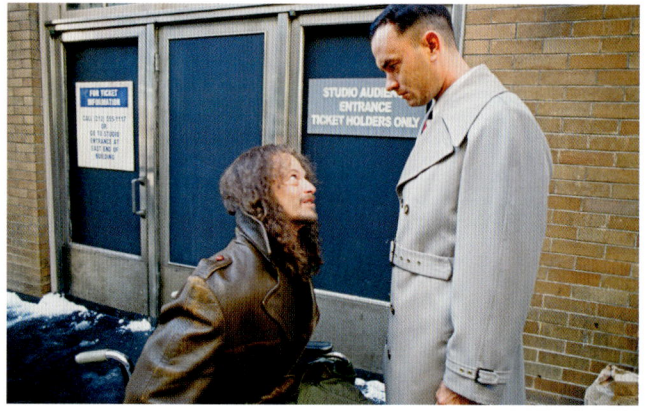

Lieutenant Dan and Forrest reunite after
The Dick Cavett Show

line, department by department? No, he didn't even look at it. He simply blessed it.

With smiles on our faces, we accepted our surprising bit of luck and went to work. We had a lot to button down before leaving town and setting up camp on location. We turned our focus to the work in and around Los Angeles. We secured our many local locations, starting with East Los Angeles College, which would double for the University of Alabama, where Forrest played football.

We continued to downtown LA, where we planned to do all the exterior New York work, beginning with the daytime scene outside the stage door where Lieutenant Dan reunites with Forrest following his appearance on *The Dick Cavett Show.*

The night work would take place first in a bar where Lieutenant Dan celebrates the New Year with Forrest and then outside, where he crosses a busy New York street. The upstairs of the First

Congregational Church had a great room we could dress as an infirmary where Forrest and Lieutenant Dan recover from their war wounds.

We also had Jenny's dark period to shoot. We scouted the Ambassador Hotel for a scene where she takes cocaine in a nightclub and checked out the rooftop of an apartment building for the place where Jenny considers suicide.

We planned to shoot all the blue-screen shots—those involving visual effects—onstage. These included Forrest meeting presidents in the Oval Office and appearing as a guest with John Lennon on *Dick Cavett.* Along with a few other sets, Lieutenant Dan's apartment would also be built and shot onstage. It seemed like the LA shoot would be a movie unto itself. Then, with the budget approved and a plan in place for our return to town, we packed up for Beaufort, South Carolina.

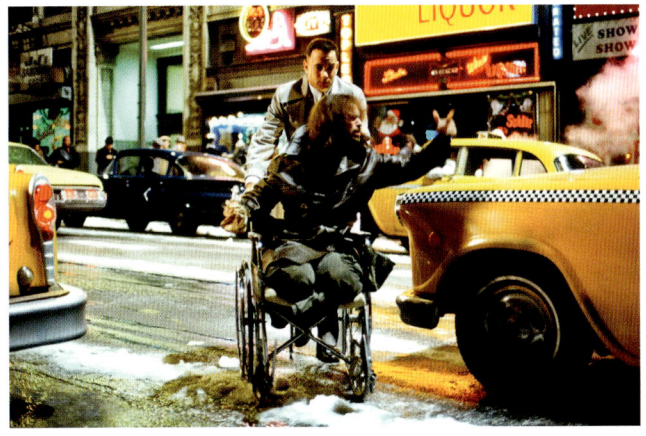

Lieutenant Dan yells at the cabbie, "I'm walkin' here, I'm walkin' here!"

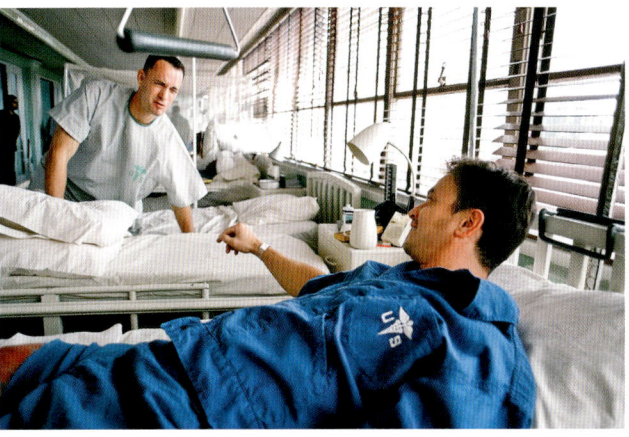

Infirmary set on the second floor of the First Congregational Church

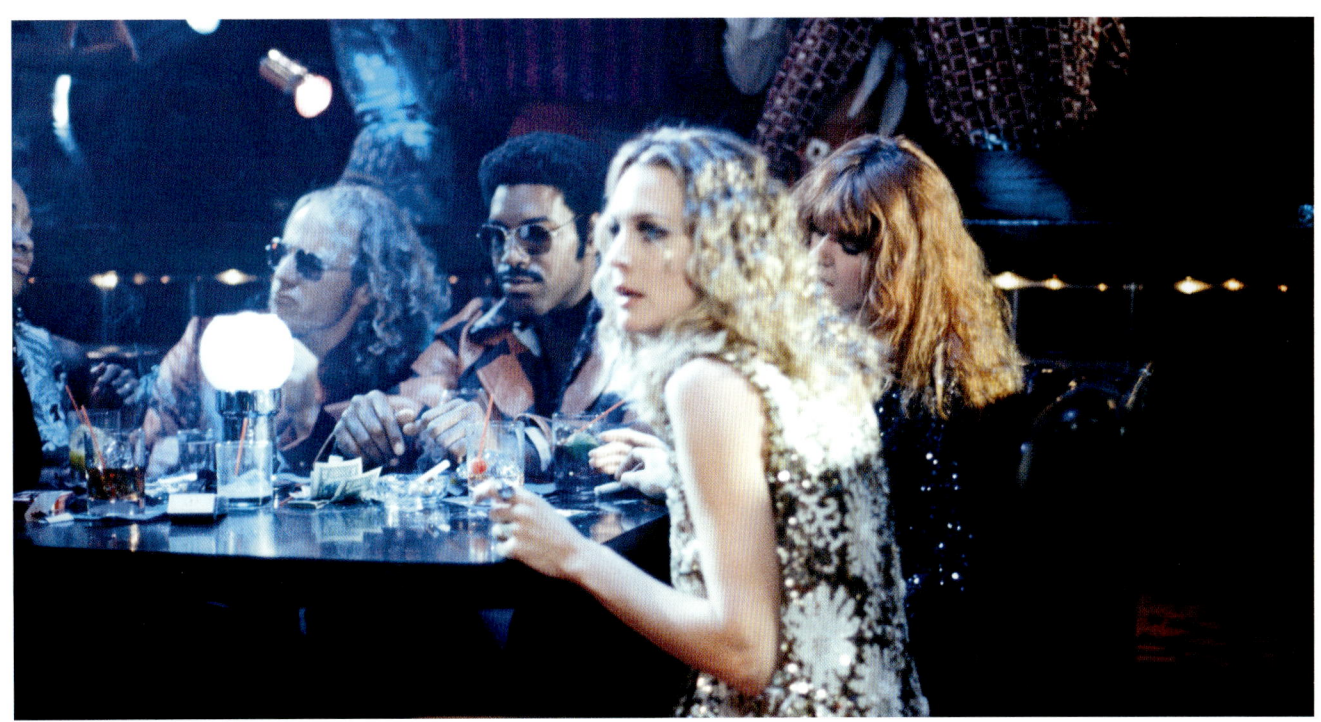

The Ambassador Hotel in Los Angeles, dressed as a nightclub

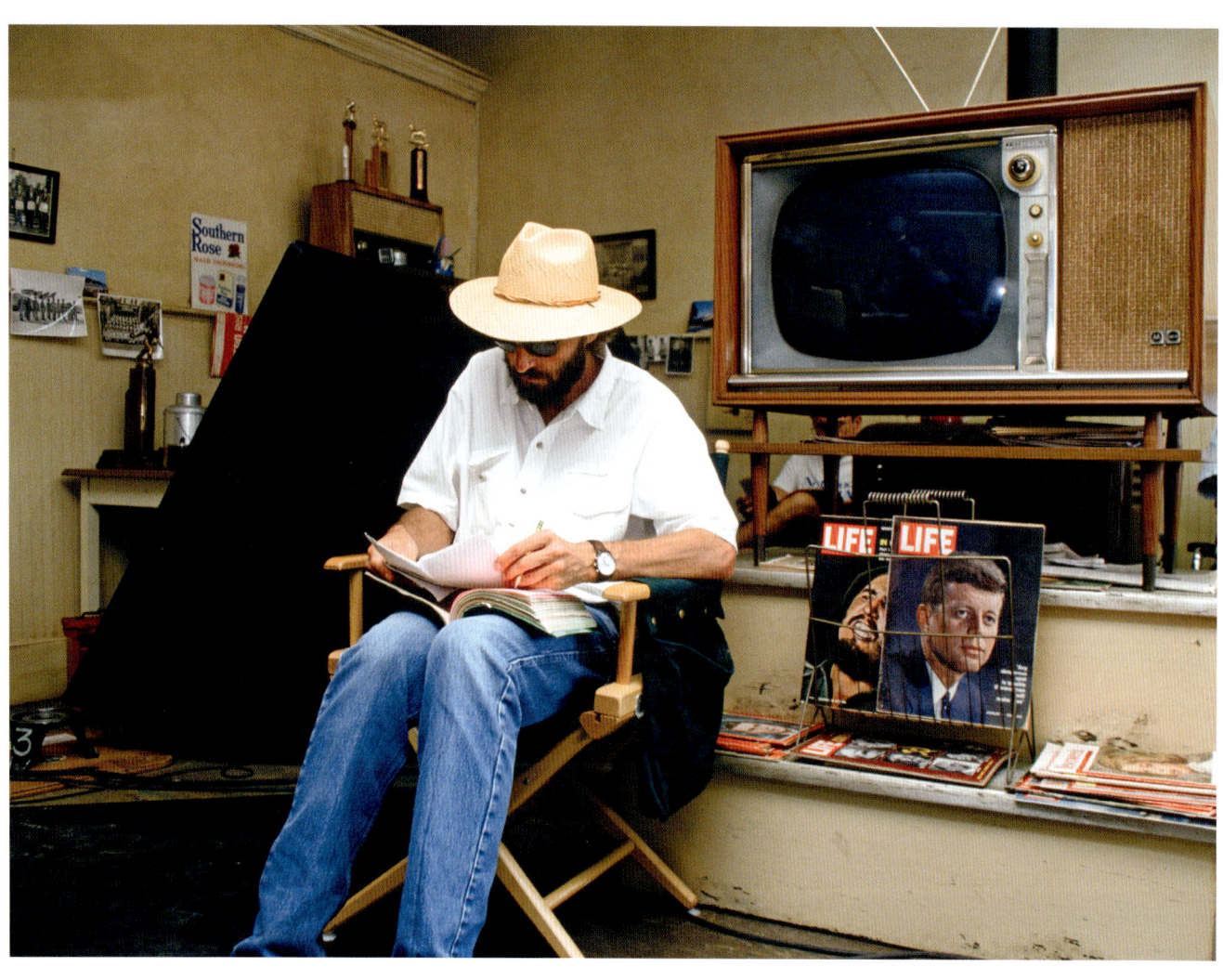

5 | Diving for Dollars

SUDDENLY, AS THE START date closed in on us, it felt like we had no time to lose. On our distant locations, we had a lot of movies within the movie to prep. Not just the scenes in and around the Gump house and the town of Greenbow, Alabama, but also shrimping (including Forrest and Lieutenant Dan getting caught in a hurricane), Vietnam, the bench in Savannah, the sites in Washington, and Forrest's run across the country. But the filming in the South took precedence. We had to get ready for the first few weeks of shooting there and then continue prepping as we went. This meant we'd have to kick a few parts of the movie down the road a bit. We would be shooting by day and prepping by night. What a way to live!

Then I got a call from Paramount, revealing their trepidation about the film. They wanted to cut around $10 million from our $55 million budget. Now? In the final weeks before the start of principal photography? I thought that since the scale of the film was so large, our budget was a bargain. We planned to film all around the country: South and North Carolina, Georgia, DC, Los Angeles, Maine, Montana, and Arizona. The film spanned several decades, requiring period wardrobe, set dressing, and cars throughout. Comparing the budget and scale to other films I had worked on, from *Roger Rabbit* to *Death Becomes Her,* $55 million wasn't out of line. It didn't matter. The studio just wanted cuts.

Bob was unwilling to cut scenes. He wanted to protect the film that he and Tom had set out to make. I argued that without lifting scenes from the script, a number like $10 million was not attainable. When preparing the budget for *Jurassic Park,* I had learned that lesson. Little savings here and there would not do the trick. I had only produced one movie at this point, but I knew enough not to negotiate against myself. I did not want to offer up cuts until I knew the endgame. How deep did we really need to go? We might cut, cut again, and then be asked for more cuts, arbitrarily making unnecessary cuts to placate the studio. But I had to make it appear that I was a team player. I said I would give it a shot.

I started diving for dollars. Above-the-line expenses were set: the deals for the producers, the director, and the principal actors had been made. We were attempting to find the remainder of the cast locally and hire them at scale, so no cuts could be made there either. Extras could always be trimmed, though. This would also reduce the need for other department personnel to accommodate the extras' wardrobe, hair, makeup, and so on.

Then we attacked the below-the-line costs—all the production departments on the film. Once again, many of the crew had already been hired, and their deals were set. Could we make a few less pieces of wardrobe and shop locally? Could we cut out a day with rain? Could we use the camera crane for fewer days? We went through each department with a fine-tooth comb, taking bites wherever we could. But all these things added up to little or nothing in savings. Our contingency funds, spread throughout the budget as a pad for any problems that might arise during production, were now down to the bare bones. I told Bob that we were not even getting close to where we needed to be to make the studio happy. I was stumped, worried we would not hit whatever arbitrary number the studio was looking for.

But the studio executives were adamant. They became irrational. Michelle Manning, the executive assigned to our show, had been reasonable up to this point, but her demeanor suddenly changed. She reported back to us that the studio didn't care what we cut. "Get rid of shrimping," she suggested. "It's expensive to shoot on water anyway. Or Vietnam. Cut it. How about the hurricane? You can live without it. And Forrest's cross-country run? It's

too long. Get rid of it." All the studio cared about was getting the number down.

"You figure out what to cut," they told us. "If you don't cut the budget, we'll shut the show down." That threat, idle or not, caused us to dig in our heels even further. Our attitude became, "Fuck the studio!" I didn't know what to do. I just wanted to make everyone happy and get on with it.

In a moment of desperation, I made a bold suggestion to Bob. What if we did cut the hurricane sequence? It was a stand-alone scene and very expensive, and quite possibly the movie could live without it. We would simply have to rework the transition from what came before the hurricane to what followed it. I knew it was a crazy idea, but it was all I could come up with. Bob digested the proposal with a blank stare. Other than that, I didn't have any scene-cutting suggestions.

The only other thing I could think of was to falsify our savings. I could cut the number of shooting days—and save money—by scheduling more material than was possible to complete each day. The studio would applaud our gamesmanship and accept our run-and-gun approach. I could do the same in each department, making cuts that weren't really practical. For example, I could show fewer extras in the budget for each location, claiming that some of the scenes had been reduced in scope to justify the new budget number. Then we would simply hire as many as needed on the day of shooting.

Each day, when we reported our "hot costs" (actual daily expenditures against budgeted costs),

I would show a small amount of bleeding, so it wouldn't be apparent that we had underestimated what we needed to complete the shoot. We could do the same with shooting days, showing us a day over when we didn't meet the shortened schedule. Eventually, we would wind up where we thought we'd be in the first place. It was common to go over schedule a bit, but not as much as we would.

This was crazy, but I believed it was our only way out of this pickle. I knew at some point the bomb would explode. The studio would realize that the number was climbing back to the original budget, and there would be hell to pay.

Bob asked how long I could pull the rug over their eyes. "Can you get us back to LA?" I couldn't be sure, but I thought I could. So that's what we did.

It turned out the cuts I made were still not enough. The damn studio executives wanted to take a bite out of Bob and Tom. They wanted the two of them to have some skin in the game. Bob and Tom would have to step up to the plate and give up part of their fees, but they would earn it back—and more—if the film was a success. This was a huge risk, not just to them financially but also to our reputations and to the film itself. Despite the high stakes, Bob and Tom agreed. They really had no choice. And while the studio may have hoped for deeper cuts, what I had slashed appeared to be enough. They had squeezed as much as they could out of us. We were given the green light. The time bomb started ticking.

My problem then became how to deal with all the departments. They needed to know which budget number they were dealing with. Should they make any cuts? I told them all to stick with the original plan.

Bruce Moriarty, the first assistant director, who was in charge of the schedule and running the set, had the same question: "Which schedule are we using? The original schedule or the reduced schedule?" I said to stick with the original plan. That meant he would have to prepare two shooting schedules—the original schedule to keep the production on track, and the shortened one to prepare our production reports and cost reports for the studio. But what we were shooting today and what we would be shooting tomorrow would all be based on the original plan.

Bob started to worry about cutting the hurricane scene. "Can you please just give me one day?" he asked. "One day with all the bells and whistles? Then you can shoot a stand-up with a news anchor reporting on the aftermath of the storm, and with that, we can make it work."

I could see where this was going. We had a good plan at the outset, and we had been given the blessing to make that movie. Clearly, Bob was not in the mood to compromise his film, and I was behind him 100 percent. We were going to stick to our guns. I was more than happy to do whatever it took to get our movie made, regardless of what the studio might do to try to stop us. This was going to be one hell of a wild ride!

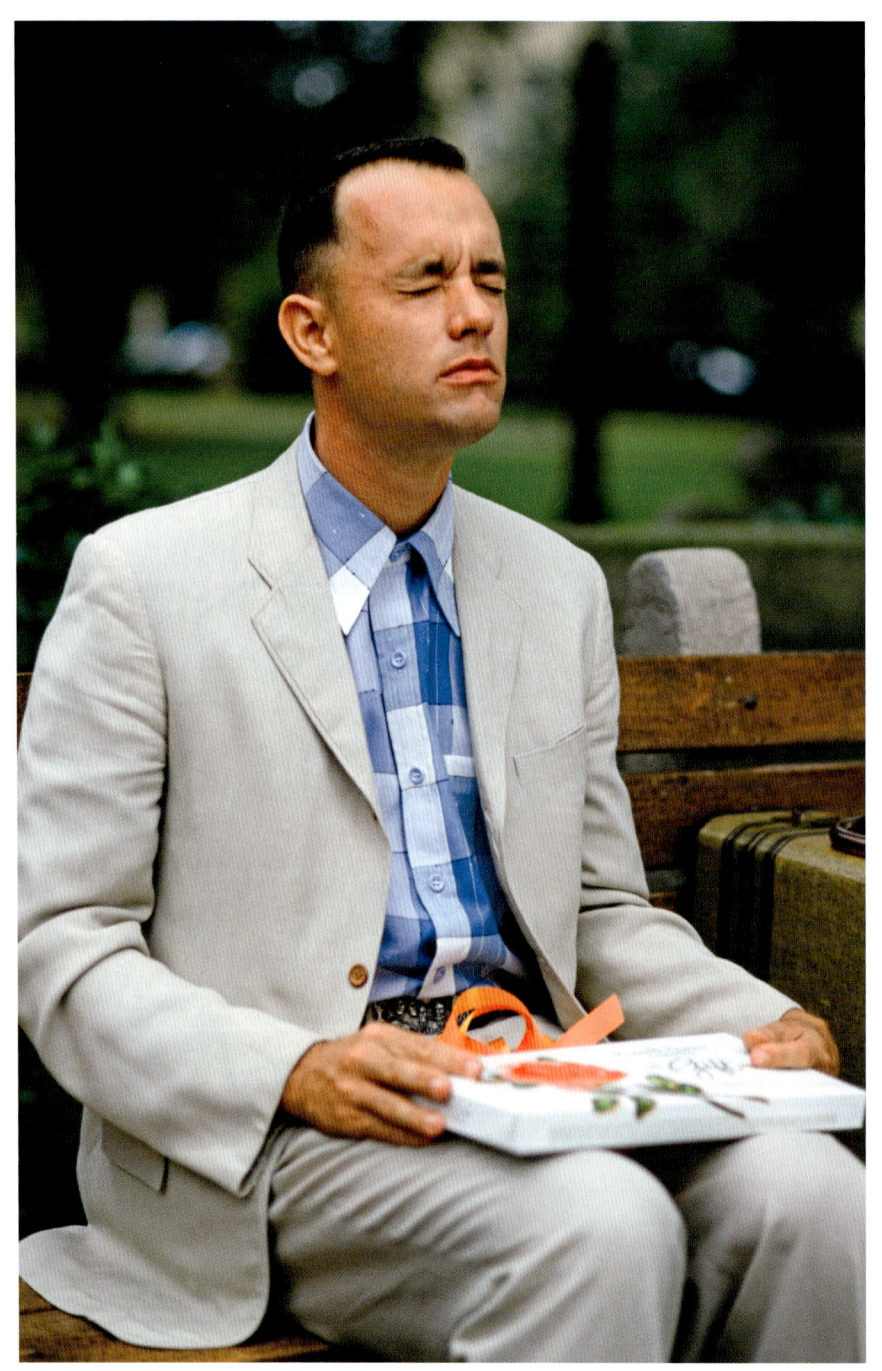

6 | My Magic Shoes

                    FORREST
    I bet if I think about it real
    hard I could remember my first
    pair of shoes.

    (He closes his eyes, thinking real
    hard.)

                    FORREST
                  (continuing)
    Mama said they'd take me
    anywhere.
    She said they was my magic shoes.

JUST LIKE FORREST, I thought back real hard to August 1993, the first day of shooting. We were in Varnville, South Carolina, thirty-five miles northwest of Beaufort, shooting at nearby Hampton Street Elementary School. Magic was in the air. This felt like a real adventure. On that first day everyone was on pins and needles. Just like the first day of school. We were getting settled in, meeting new coworkers. By the end, it would feel like we had gone through the war together and become the best of friends, but for now, we were all wishing one another a pleasant good morning as we bustled forward, attending to the business at hand.

When I drove up to the location, my thoughts were filled with worry. So many things could go wrong. I could only wish and hope that none of my fears would come to pass. I arrived a little earlier than usual, giving myself time to check in with everyone. Everything seemed to be buttoned down when I entered base camp. I would soon learn that with Mary Morgan overseeing locations and Joel Marrow at the head of our transportation department, I had little to fear.

I started my rounds by looking in on the cast. Sally Field was in makeup and seemed happy and excited. The other cast members would be arriving shortly, so I took off for the set. That first day of shooting was one of the most contained, involving sets for the principal's office in Forrest's school and his doctor's office. Both sets were at the elementary school in the town of Walterboro. There were no location moves. That would be rare on this show. It would be good to "make" the day—get the work done—and feel that we were off to a good start—good for the cast, the crew, the director, and, most importantly, in the eyes of the studio.

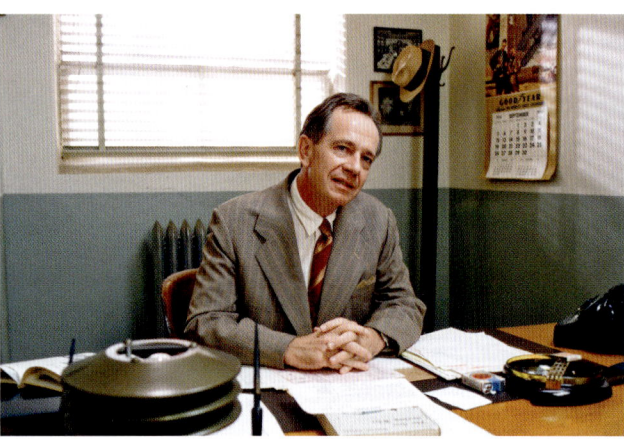

Interior set, principal's office, with actor Sam Anderson

I entered the principal's office and found Nancy Haigh, the set decorator, putting the final touches on it. The set looked perfect. I was stunned. I felt like I had traveled back to my youth, the same period as the film's. The color of the walls, the tall window with Venetian blinds, and the solid desk took me back to my own elementary school days. Rick Carter, working alongside Nancy, seemed pleased. He wanted it to be just right.

Then I approached Bruce Moriarty. As first assistant director, he had his finger on the pulse of all the production departments, and with his staff chiming in with updates on his walkie-talkie, it was hard to get his attention. I felt confident about Bruce. We had connected on the second unit on *Back to the Future II* and *III,* where he, along with the second-unit director, did a great job supervising the filmmaking team responsible for the action sequences and hair-raising stunts on

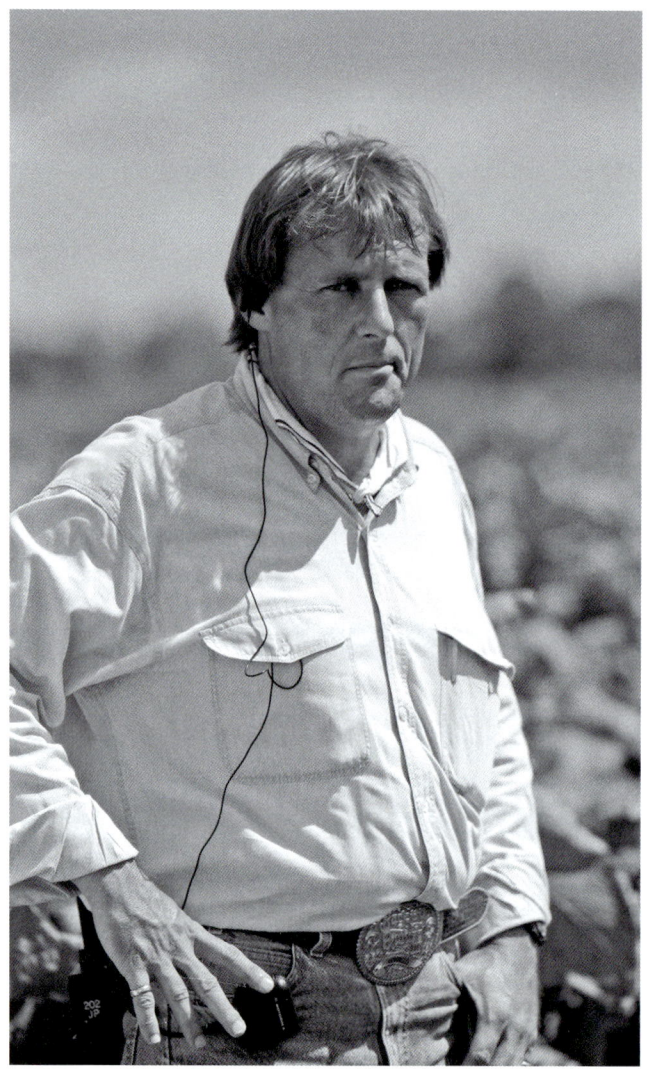

Bruce Moriarty

the show. Bob had worked with him briefly, too, and was happy to have him with us.

In addition, we had brought along Don Burgess from the second unit on *Back to the Future II* and

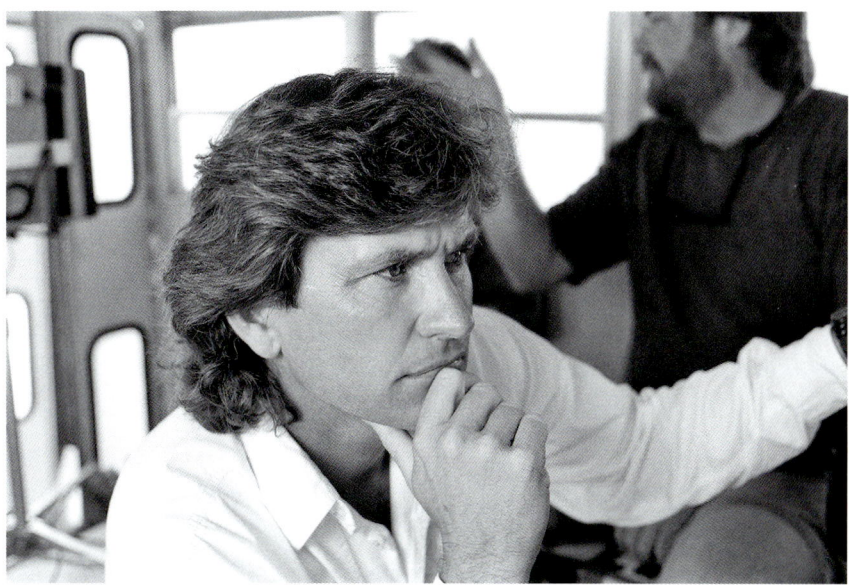

Don Burgess

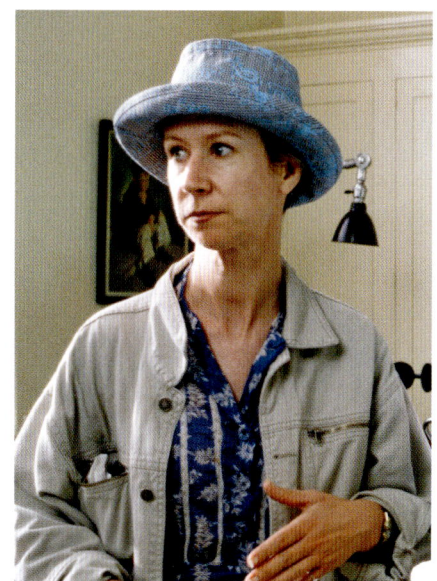

Joanna Johnston

III as director of photography. This would be a big break for Don, one he had been waiting for and deserved.

Bruce told me that Bob had just pulled into base camp. A few minutes later he opened the door to the set. The tension rose. Not only because he was the director but also because he had a discerning eye. He might notice something about the set dressing that no one else had caught. Bob wanted everything to be ready for a rehearsal when the cast arrived. No waiting.

Bob checked in with Don, who was looking at the lighting for the scene. Would the key light coming through the window remain consistent as the sun moved across the sky while we were

shooting? Don reassured him that the lighting was under control. Bob asked Bruce when the cast would be ready. Bruce said they were moments away. To fill that short time Bob offered to go over the shot list for the scene. He always came prepared with a list of his planned camera setups. He huddled around the script supervisor with Don and Bruce and previewed the day's work. Since we had scouted the location with all the department heads, everyone had a good idea of what was in store. But the full list of shots often came as a surprise.

After listening in on the game plan, I left the set to check on the remaining cast, starting with young Forrest. I found Michael Humphreys with

43

his mom and asked her how they were doing. Was Michael nervous? He seemed nonplussed about the whole situation. She reassured me that everything was okay.

I rapped on the doors of Harold Herthum, playing the doctor, and Sam Anderson, playing the principal. They were both seasoned actors, in fine fettle and ready to go. Just as Ellen, our casting director, had hoped, she was able to find experienced actors who did not necessarily come from New York or Los Angeles. Our goal was to hire professionals who lived locally or in nearby states, and we uncovered some great talent—often from small or regional theaters—while saving money on their travel and living expenses.

When I saw the actors in wardrobe, their characters seemed a step closer to coming alive on film. Joanna Johnston, our costume designer, had magically transformed them, carefully dressing each one to reflect their roles: the smarmy school principal, the country doctor, impeccable Mama Gump, and young Forrest, proper in his Sunday best. It was remarkable how she individualized the many characters in the film; you could tell at a glance who they were, even if they were only in one brief scene.

Returning to the set, I found Don putting the finishing touches on the lighting. This was familiar territory to me from my first job as a lighting technician. Then in walked the cast. Most of the crew left the set as Bob rehearsed with Sally Field, young Forrest, and the principal. I sat in my chair hoping that Sam Anderson would live up to his audition. Shooting always raises the stakes, so you never know. I certainly could not predict how Michael Humphreys was going to do, since this was his first scene in front of a camera.

Finally, after all the drama, the budget craziness, and the prep, we were ready to roll the cameras. There is nothing as exciting as watching the cast bring a scene to life. The actors take the scripted words to a new level. From her first scene questioning the principal about Forrest's test scores, Sally surprised me with the nuance and depth of her acting. I had always been impressed by her acting chops, but watching her on our first day of shooting brought a smile of appreciation to my face.

INT. AN ELEMENTARY SCHOOL, ALABAMA—THE PRINCIPAL'S OFFICE—DAY

                       MRS. GUMP
                     (Indignant)
What's "normal" mean anyway? He might be a little on the slow side, but my boy Forrest is going to have the same opportunities as everybody else. He isn't going to a "special school" to learn how to retread tires...We're talking about five little points here...There must be something can be done...

The principal studies her, attracted to her.

                      PRINCIPAL
We're a progressive school system, we don't want to see anybody left behind...
(smiling)...is there a Mr. Gump, Mrs. Gump?

                       MRS. GUMP
                (fingering her hat)
He's on vacation.

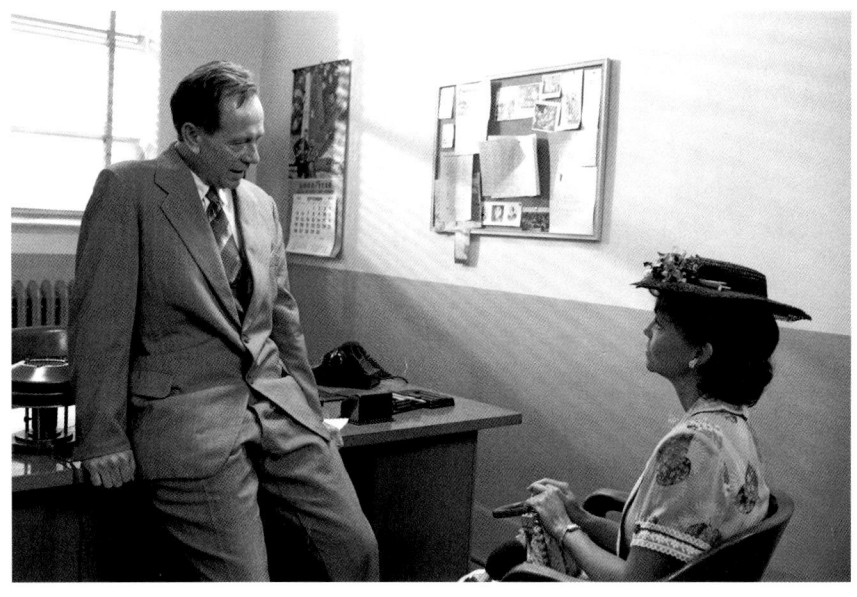
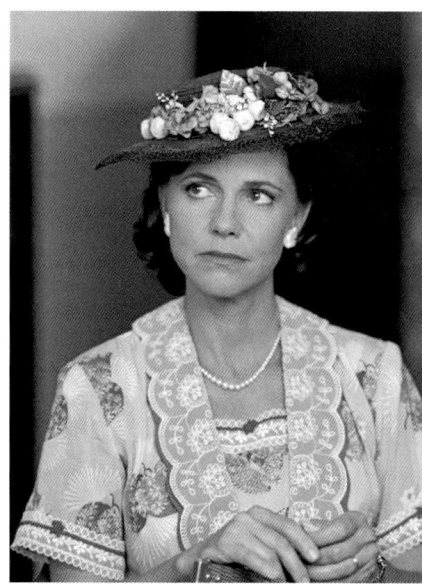

I watched her shift gears as she spoke to the principal. At first she was protective of Forrest, forceful as she fought on behalf of her son. When she saw that her pleas were falling on deaf ears, she took a different approach, seducing the principal with her suggestive tone and smile. It was beautiful to watch. Sam certainly held his own.

```
INT. AN ELEMENTARY SCHOOL, ALABAMA—HALLWAY OUTSIDE PRINCIPAL'S OFFICE—DAY

We see Forrest, now about eight, still in his leg braces, sitting,
like a Norman Rockwell painting, waiting in an empty hallway
outside the Principal's office.
```

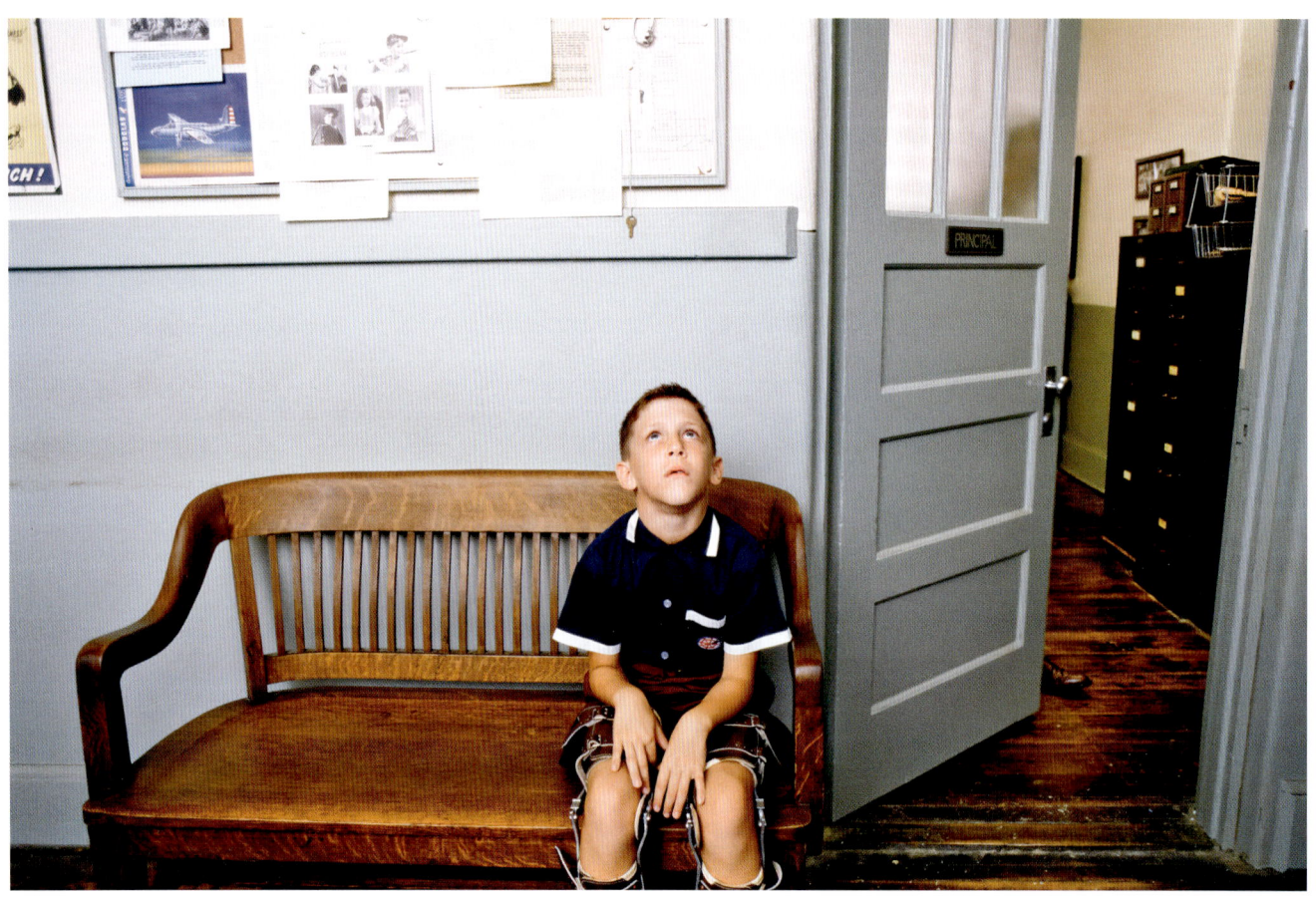

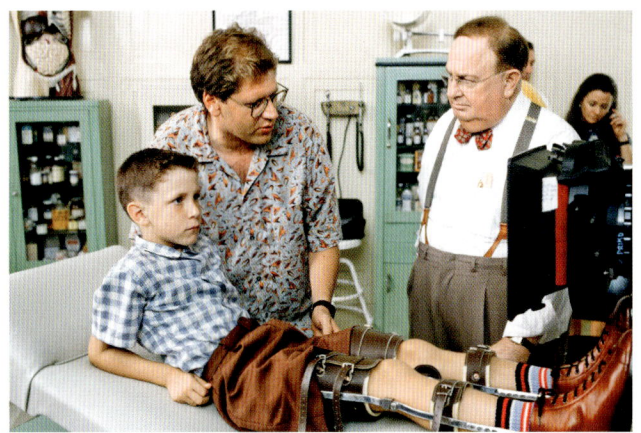

Forrest gets fitted for his "magic shoes"

This was a perfect first scene for Michael Humphreys. All he had to do was be himself and not look into the camera.

The second scene of the day, where Forrest is fitted for his "magic shoes," pushed our young actor further. His goofy smile while looking at his orthopedic shoes and his expressions while clanking around the doctor's office were priceless. I couldn't help thinking that Michael was not only going to be okay; he would actually give us more character than we had hoped for.

The day ran much longer than anticipated, but we got it. It was a success on all fronts.

Meanwhile, once I felt comfortable that all the elements for filming at the school were in place, I took off for Varnville, where we would be shooting the following day. This became my routine. As soon as I felt secure that the day would go as planned, that the director and cast were happy, the location and set dressing were in place, and the props and wardrobe were handled, I would look ahead at what was in store for the next day's work.

In Varnville the final crunch was on, and the crew was getting ready for tomorrow. When I pulled into the base camp, Mary Morgan greeted me and said there were no surprises—no problems with shooting permits and no store owners up in arms. In fact, the shopkeepers were looking forward to getting paid for the use of their stores. This was a poor town, and it looked just right for the film.

Creating the barbershop with its old-timers was the perfect way to add color to an otherwise plain thoroughfare. It was here on Main Street that Mama Gump, in the face of unfriendly townsfolk, imparted the first of many words of encouragement to her son:

Forrest and his mother walking through a small town. As they move along the dusty
street, little Forrest clanking in his braces, people stop what they're doing,
watching them pass. Mrs. Gump slows, looking at their faces.

                              MRS. GUMP
                              (sharp)
   What are you all looking at? Haven't you ever seen a boy with braces on his
   legs before?

And as the team of Gump and Gump move off along the street...

                              MRS. GUMP
                       (Continuing to her boy)
   Don't ever let anybody tell you they're better than you, Forrest...If God
   intended everybody to be the same, he'd have given us all braces on our legs.

                           FORREST (V.O.)
   Mama always had a way of explaining things so I could understand them...

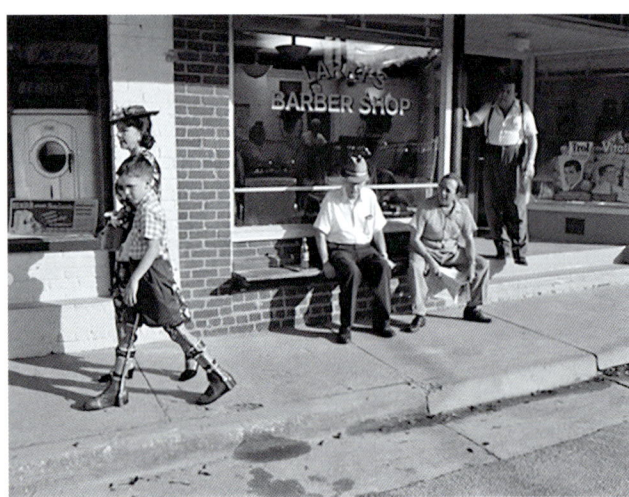 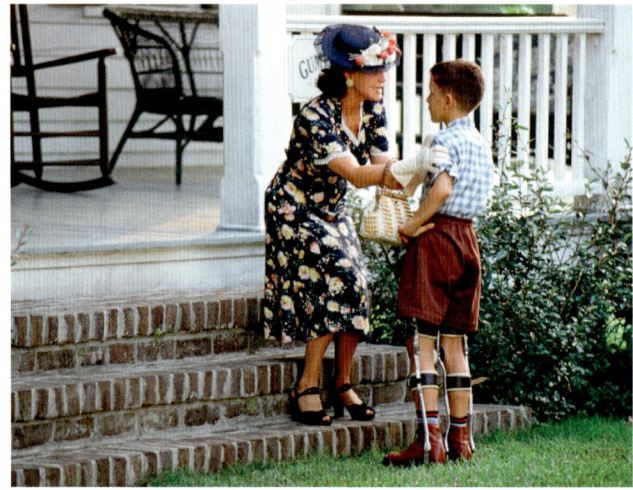

Heading into the weekend after a short first week, I was optimistic. Everything was working well: the locations, the actors. It seemed perfect.

But then summer in the South reared its ugly head. Hurricane Emily was barreling across the Atlantic and had the Carolina coast in its crosshairs. What should we do? Charles Newirth and I went back and forth about it. Although the storm appeared to be heading a bit north of us, there was no way to tell until it made landfall. We had to get prepared. We booked rooms inland in Charlotte, North Carolina, so if the crew had to evacuate, they would have a place to go. We would wait until the first thing Monday morning to decide whether the entire crew would report to work or to the production office, where buses would be ready to transport them out of town.

To protect our prize set from the unpredictable storm, the Gump house was boarded up with plywood. It would have been a disaster if the house were damaged. Charles and I agreed to speak on Sunday and again early Monday morning to make the call. We equipped ourselves with weather radios, so we could get the latest predictions. With frayed nerves, we parted ways. Early Monday morning it appeared we were out of harm's way. Hurricane Emily was moving north. It came ashore on the Outer Banks of North Carolina and damaged 553 homes, but we were spared.

Sleep-deprived but relieved, I headed to the location early Monday morning. I hadn't slept much, so again I got to the set before most of the crew. We were shooting at Oak Alley, the same spot where we had piled out of the van on our scouting trip and decided we had finally found our home in the South. The first scene was at the foot of the driveway by the two-lane highway.

```
We see Forrest and his mother walk-
ing along a two-lane country road.

At some rural mailboxes, they turn
onto a small country road. And ahead
of them, nestled in the shade of some
old oak trees, an old two-story wood
frame HOUSE. The "Gump House"...
```

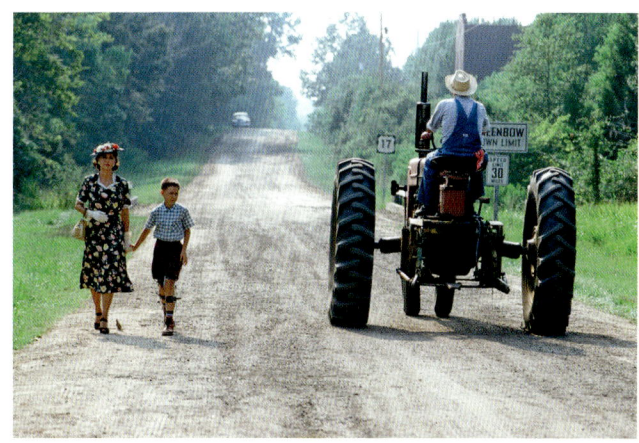

When Sally Field stepped out of her golf cart on the first day of shooting in front of the Gump house, she marveled at our luck in finding it, and she was curious how old the building was. I paused before breaking the news to her: we had built the house, completing it just a few days before.

"You can't be serious," she said.

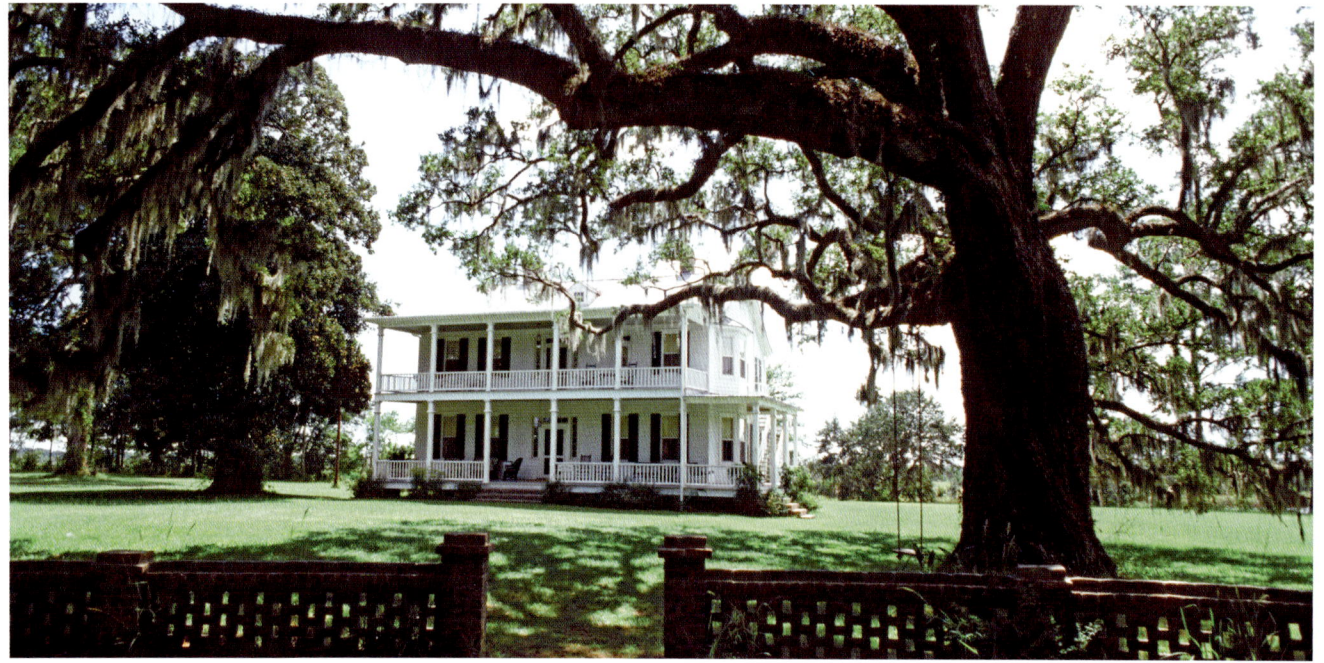

The Gump house exterior

"It's true. They are running around putting the final touches on the set dressing as we speak." By Sally's reaction, I knew that Rick and his construction team had built the perfect set.

We had debated how much of the house to actually construct. The exterior was a straightforward decision. Bob said we would never see the left side of the house (as we faced the front) or the back. That saved us a lot of time and money. How much of the interior we planned to build evolved. We knew we had to build the entryway, the living area, and the dining room, all in the front part of the house. Those rooms were in multiple scenes throughout the film, and we would see them both

from the outside and when we entered the foyer. The downstairs rooms at the back of the house, though, would never be seen on camera.

Also, while we planned to build the stairs leading to the second floor, what would be built upstairs was up for discussion. Conceivably, those rooms could be constructed onstage. But Bob lobbied hard to finish off the upstairs rooms, and the house was getting closer to becoming a real residence, not just a film set.

The first few scenes on the second floor take place in Forrest's bedroom and a guest room, where we hear a famous voice and the sound of a guitar.

We're just able to make out the familiar figure of a young man holding a guitar, sitting on the bed. The young ELVIS PRESLEY, playing an early version of "HOUND DOG":

> *You ain't nothin' but a hound dog*
> *Crying all the time*
> *You ain't nothin' but a hound dog*
> *Crying all the time*
> *You ain't never caught a rabbit*
> *And you ain't no friend of mine*

FORREST (V.O.)
I liked that guitar. It sounded good, and I just started to move along with the music, swinging my hips.

Since his braces restrict his leg movement, he furiously swings his little hips.

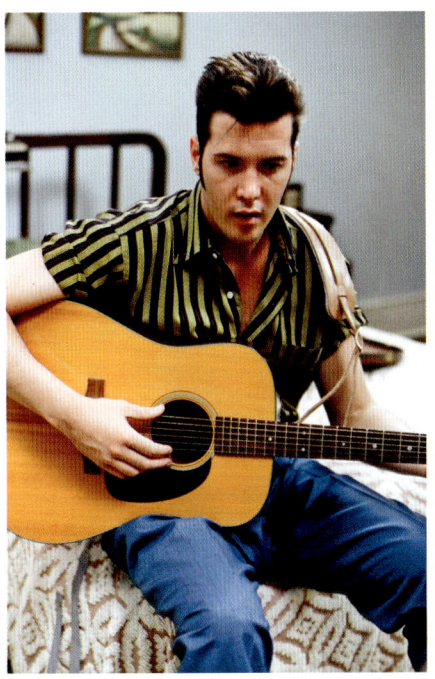
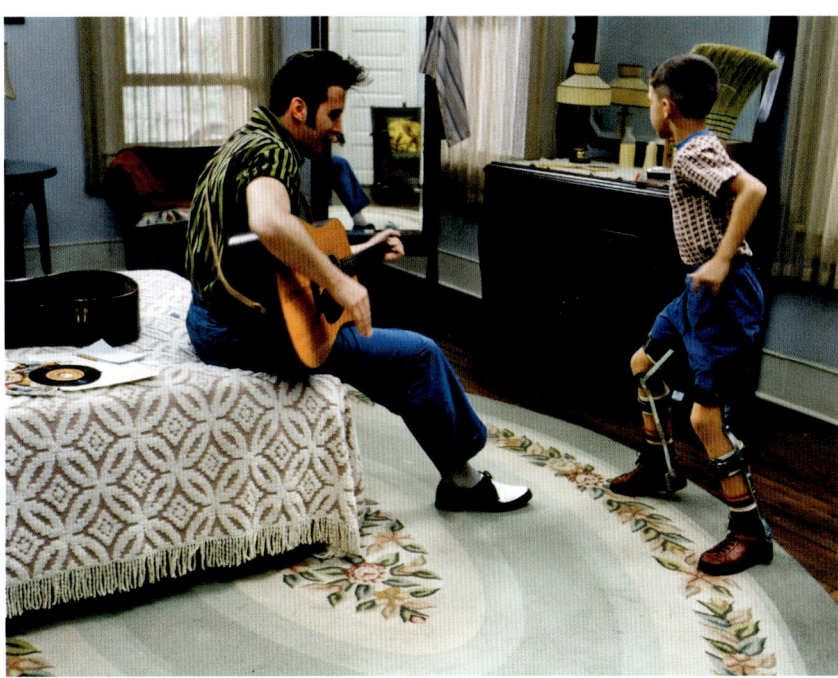

An actor named Peter Dobson had heard about the scene with Elvis and immediately came in to audition for the part. We knew Peter; he was the star of a TV series we'd made a year earlier called *Johnny Bago.* Peter was an Elvis nut. He even offered to get himself to South Carolina on his own dime, just to be in the film. We cast him as Elvis. His performance was fine, but his voice needed some help.

Bob recalled that his friend Kurt Russell had played Elvis in a film and was quite good. Kurt later came to a recording studio and recorded all of Elvis's dialogue, replacing what Peter had done. It proved to be a perfect combination of talent.

On young Forrest's first day of school, he catches the bus at Mailbox Corner, at the bottom of the road leading to the Gump house. This landmark location marked the beginning and end of many of Forrest's life adventures.

Inside the school bus, he encounters a nasty group of country kids who are unwilling to give him a seat. That scene would be shot on a separate day, on a more controlled country road, but I felt confident it would never be cut, and not just because it's where Forrest meets Jenny. Many of the "country bumpkins" on the bus were related to the filmmakers.

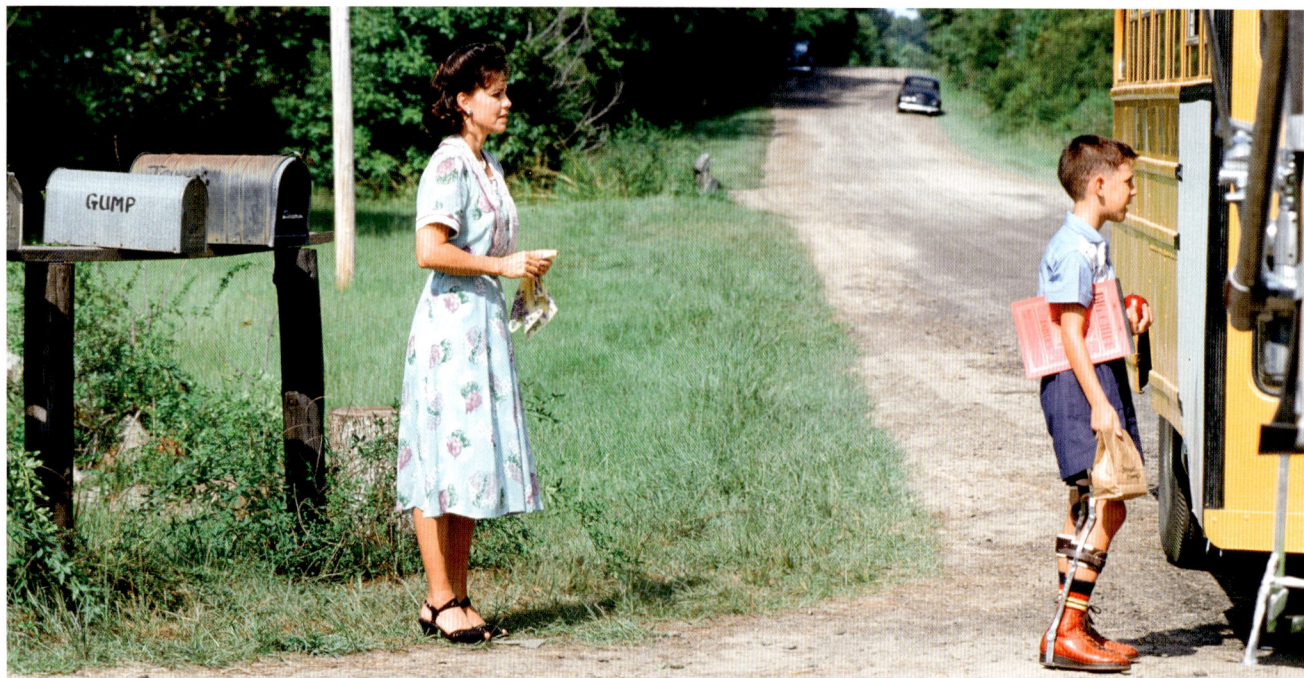

Forrest catches the bus at Mailbox Corner

The bus pulls off. Forrest CLANKS along the aisle, looking for a seat. The children all stare at him, afraid of him. Forrest only smiles. He starts to sit by a BOY.

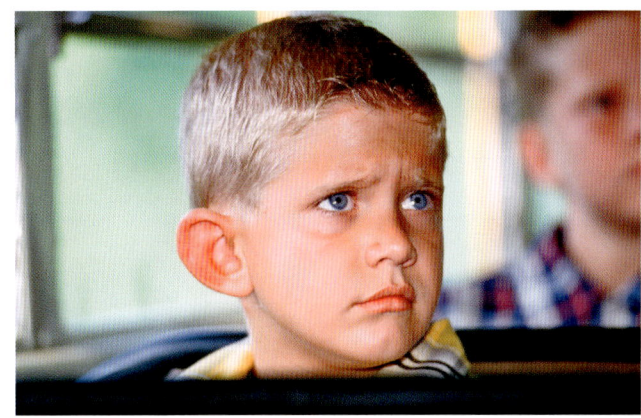

                    BOY
     (Alex Zemeckis, Bob's son)
     Seat's taken.

He looks for another seat.

                    BOY #2
     It's taken.

Forrest takes another step. Looks again.

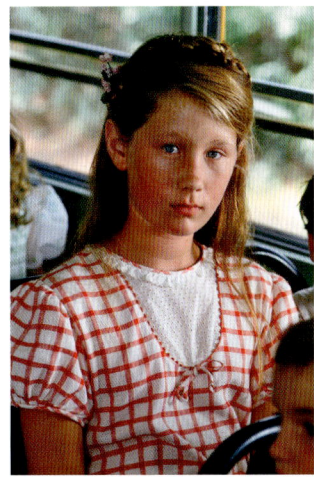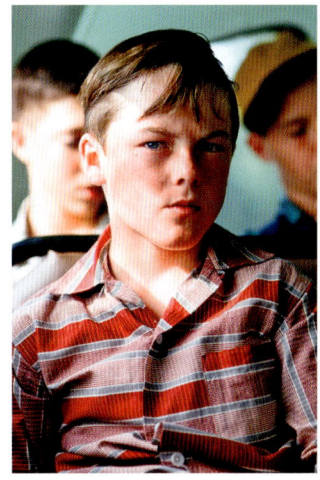

                    GIRL
     (Elizabeth Hanks, Tom's daughter)
     Shakes her head, NO.

Forrest looks further. Stops in front of a bigger BOY.

                    BOY #3
     (Ben Waddell, Steve Starkey's nephew)
     Can't sit here.

Forrest turns and heads toward the front of the bus. A BOY (Don Burgess's son, Michael) looks up and follows Forrest. FORREST stares, looking ahead, wondering what to do.

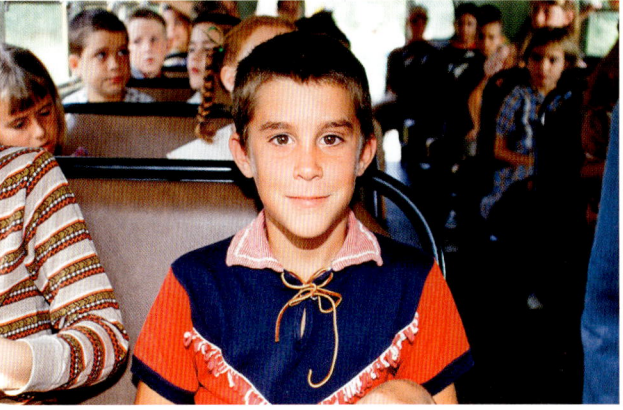

Top: Alex Zemeckis; *Middle left:* Elizabeth Hanks; *Middle right:* Ben Waddel; *Bottom:* Michael Burgess

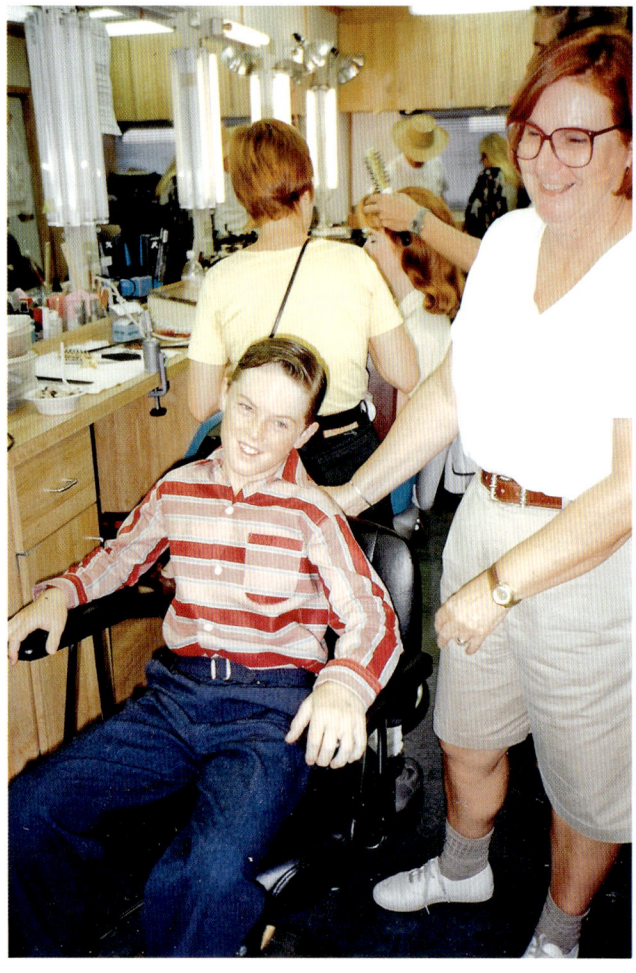

Ben, after his haircut by Judy Cory

For most of these kids, this was their first time on camera. It was their three seconds of fame. My nephew Ben required a little convincing to accept his moment of fame. He was on summer vacation and had traveled by himself from southern Colorado. He arrived with long blond hair almost touching his shoulders. Mostly he was interested in sneaking up on the alligators that lay in the sun by the pond on the golf course near the house I was renting. When it came time for his wardrobe fitting and makeup-and-hair meeting, an assistant director knocked on the door of my motor home to inform me that my nephew refused to cut his hair.

A man after my own heart, I thought, except he wasn't playing a hippie. So my wife, Liv, and I, acting as Ben's chaperones, explained a few rules of movie life and reminded him of the big paycheck hanging in the balance. The cash came with a haircut. It was up to him: he could keep the long hair, but he'd be off the picture and would get no pay. Ben quickly changed his mind. Money talks. He happily cut his hair and looked great as a country boy from the South.

All the kids except for Michael required voice coaching, since none of them were from the South. Our dialect coach, Jessica Drake, wore headphones and listened carefully to every word they spoke on the set. This proved to be frustrating for Bob, since it was difficult enough to get the performance he was looking for, let alone the correct accent along with it.

Passing by all the filmmakers' relations, young Forrest finally finds a seat.

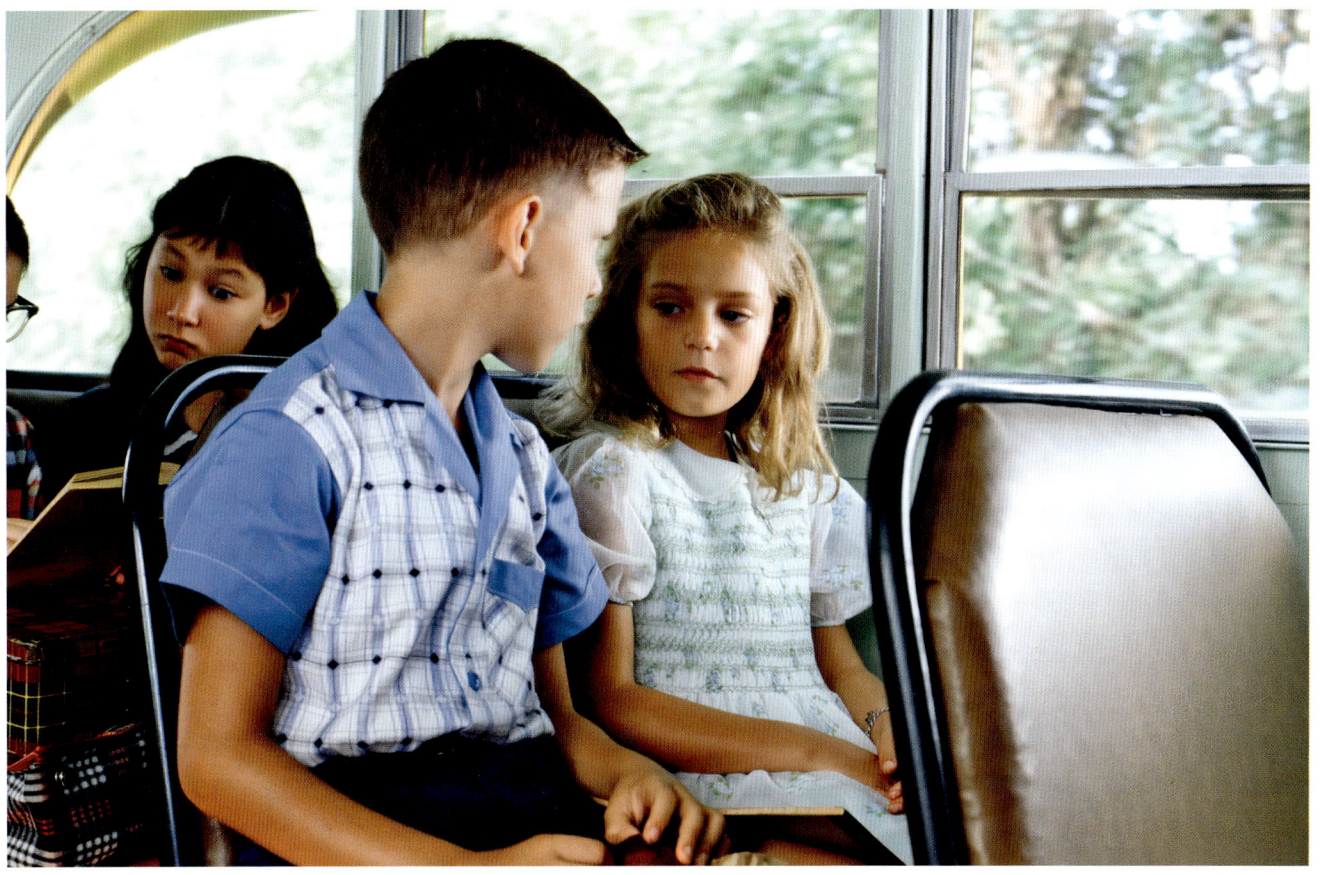

                  GIRL (V.O.)
  You can sit here if you want.

He turns. A little GIRL with curls pats the seat next to her. In Forrest's
eyes, she's a vision. He's speechless, his mouth agape.

             FORREST (V.O. from the bench)
  I had never seen anything so beautiful in all my life. She was like an angel.

He stares at her. JENNY CURRAN.

                JENNY
  Are you going to sit down, or aren't you?

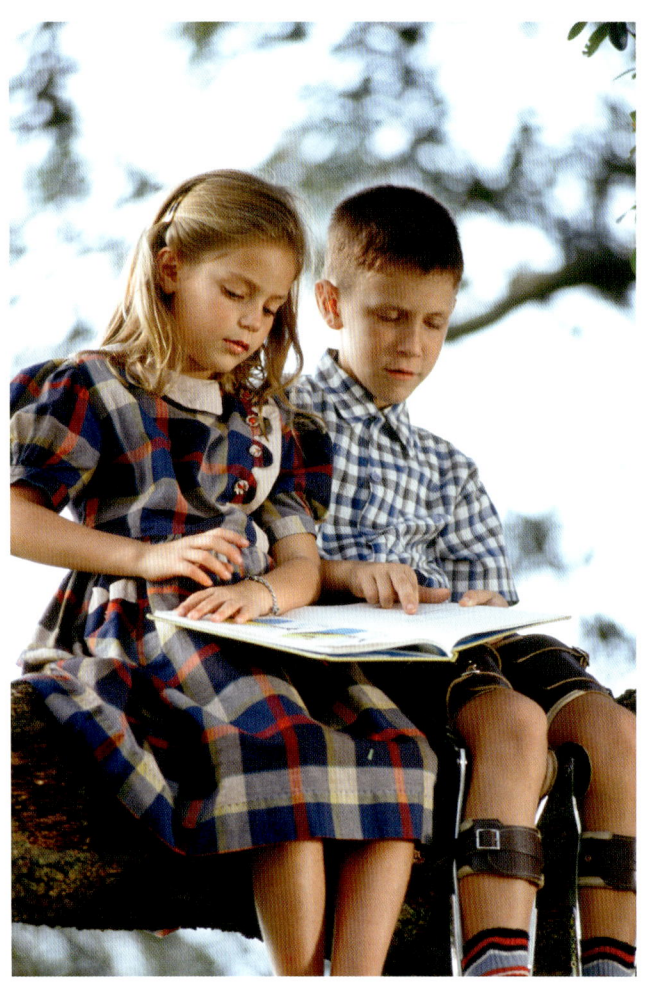

Jenny and Forrest sitting in their tree

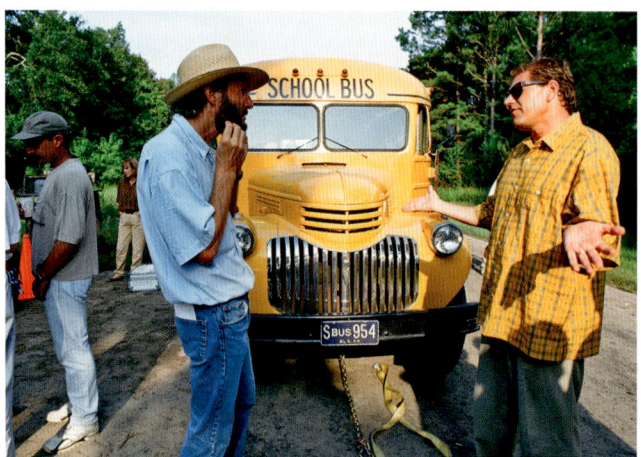

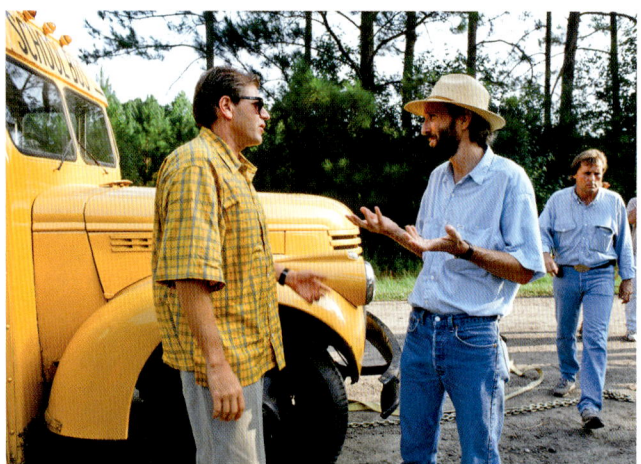

Bob and me wondering how we were going to
finish the unending list of shots

Voice coaching was also required for Hanna Hall, our young Jenny, although her performance was often spot-on.

The days were long, and the shooting was difficult. There were so many short scenes to film, with inexperienced kids in every one of them. We were shooting efficiently, but there was no way we were going to keep up with the schedule we had laid out for the studio. Days 1 and 2 had gone according to schedule, but by the end of the week, the number of small unfinished scenes started to add up. The studio called and said we had fallen behind, and we should show ourselves a day over. The adverse effects of my shortened schedule were already starting to show. I tried to put off confirming that we were falling behind, but at this point, we had no choice.

Hoping to quicken our pace, we decided to start a splinter unit. I would take our "B" cameraman, a few grips, and anyone I could spring from the first unit and get the next setup ready for the first unit to shoot. In this way, we would leapfrog through the day. There would be no waiting. Bob and the cast could show up and immediately start shooting.

For example, I would head out to the oak tree location and set up a shot. Then, as soon as Bob finished with the first unit, he would head over and finish his day with young Forrest and young Jenny sitting in the tree.

Or he might grab a shot I had prepared of young Forrest running—running over a bridge, through town, or to Jenny's farm. This was the only way we could put a dent in the day's work and pick up some of the pieces left behind from previous days.

But even with all the leapfrogging and the help of the splinter unit, we still couldn't finish all the shots with young Forrest before principal photography with Tom Hanks and Robin Wright began. We would have to devise a way to get those scenes done, perhaps without Bob at the helm. With his frustration building, he couldn't wait to work with the adult actors.

The transition, as scripted, from the young Forrest and Jenny to the older characters was the largest section of the film that did not make the final cut.

EXT. A RIVER—GREENBOW, ALABAMA—DAY

We're looking at a river, like a Monet painting, running so slowly, it doesn't seem to be moving at all. We see in the water the reflection of little Forrest, stupidly smiling, holding a fairly large rock, Jenny standing beside him on the riverbank.

                    FORREST (V.O.)
        Watch this, Jenny...

We see the reflection as he hurls the rock. It makes a big SPLASH, disturbing the reflection.

The splash subsides, the water becoming calm again. We see in the water's reflection now, Forrest, a high school senior (the star of our movie, now).

Standing beside him, a high school senior (a star of our movie), still the best of friends, Jenny. We pan over to them.

                    FORREST
        That was the best splash ever.

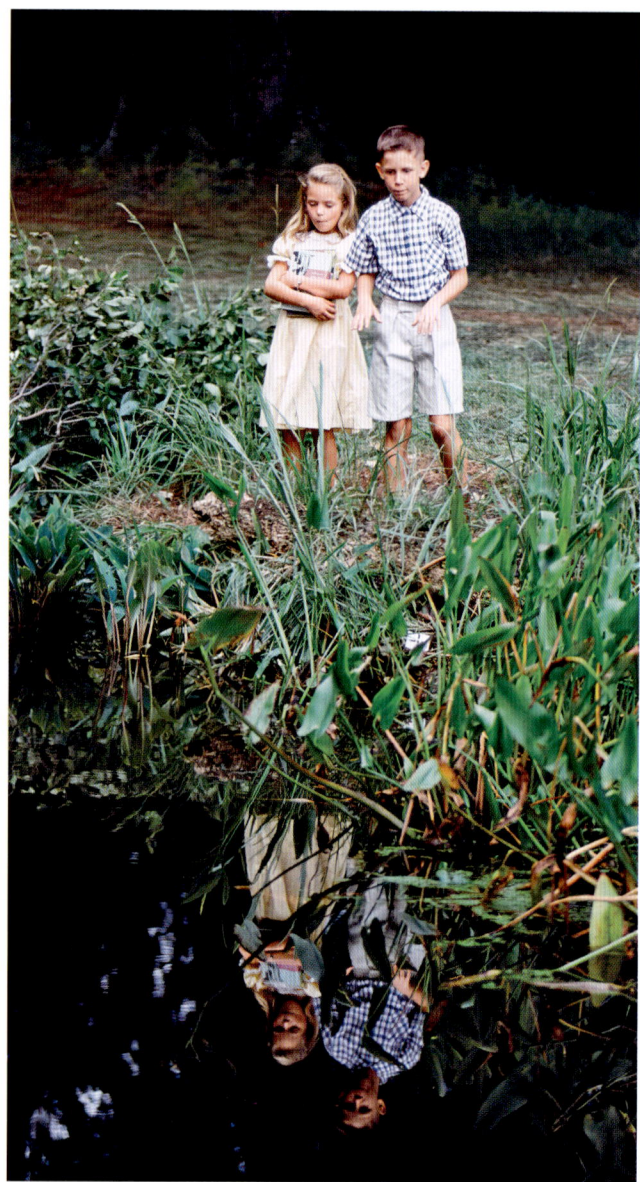

They move along the riverbank. Then Jenny reveals news to Forrest that breaks his heart for the first time:

JENNY
I want you to hear something, Forrest. I'm going to go away to college.

FORREST
(after a beat)
If you leave, who's going to be my friend anymore?

JENNY
(affectionately)
I'll always be your friend, Forrest...(a beat)...but I can't stay here the rest of my life.

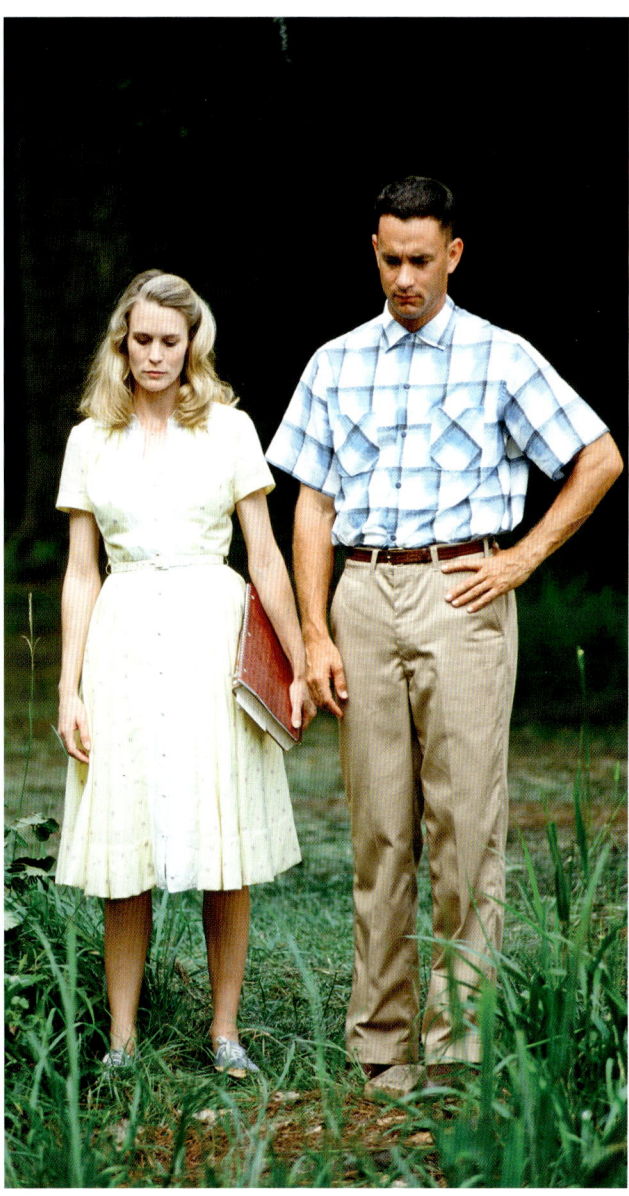

They both climb the riverbank and stumble upon a civil rights march led by none other than Martin Luther King Jr.

For a few reasons, this scene was cut. When Bob and Tom screened the film for the first time, Tom thought his body language as the grown-up Forrest had not yet taken shape and looked a bit silly.

Bob came up with a better transition in the editing room. The sequence started in Oak Alley, when young Forrest is chased by bullies. Prompted by young Jenny, he takes off, shedding his leg braces, and sprints to freedom.

```
                    JENNY
             Run, Forrest, run!


As he runs like the wind into the distance, completely and utterly free...


                 FORREST (V.O.)
    From that day on, if I was goin' somewhere, I was running.
```

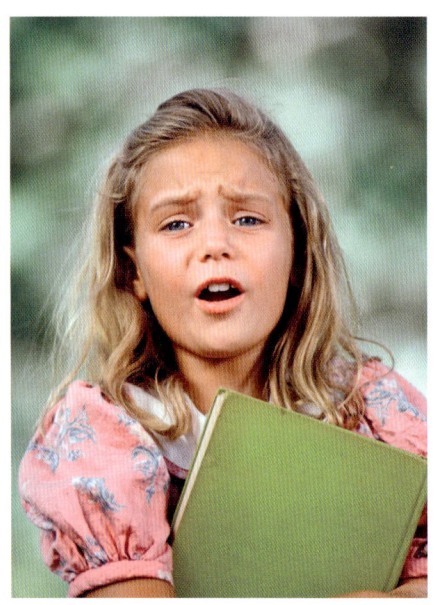 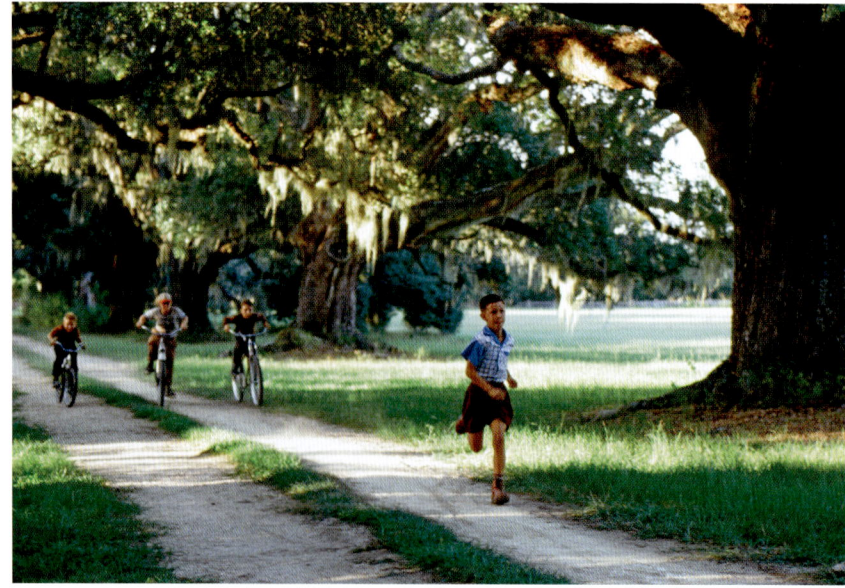

The sequence continues with Forrest running by fishermen on a bridge, past a chain gang on the side of the road, and up the drive to Jenny's farm, where we learn of Jenny's abusive childhood.

At the end of this series of scenes, we finally return to Oak Alley and encounter Tom Hanks as Forrest and Robin Wright as Jenny, now high school teens. Forrest is hit in the head by a rock and chased by grown-up bullies in a pickup truck while Jenny yells at Forrest.

```
                    JENNY
        Run, Forrest, run!
```

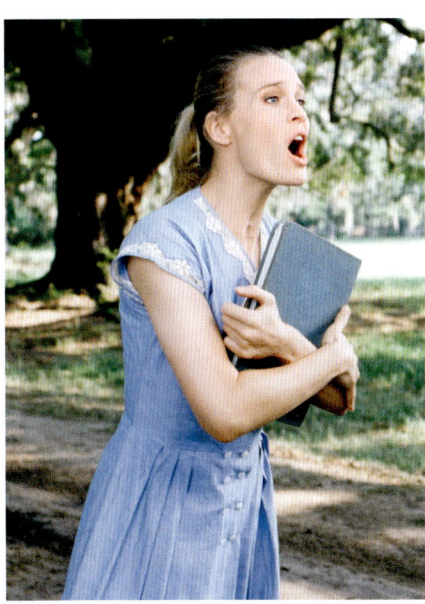 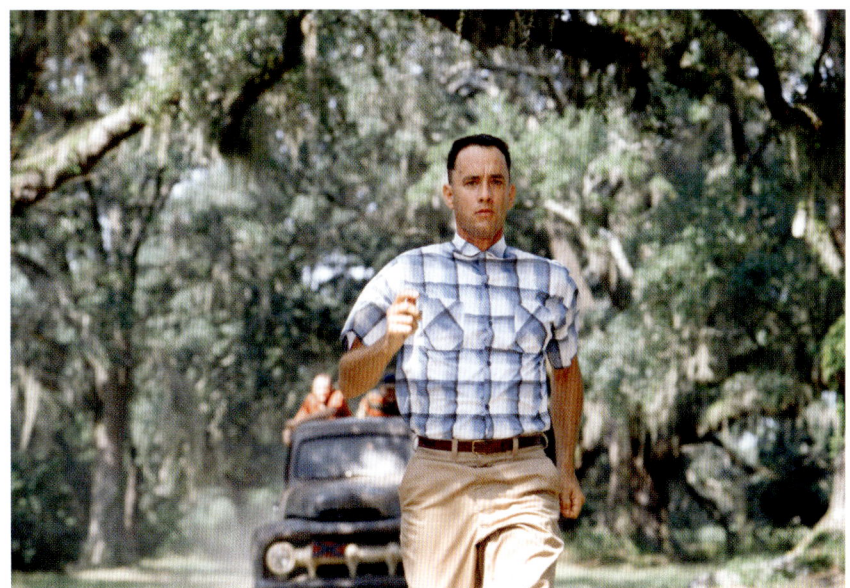

This unscripted transition from Forrest and Jenny as kids to teenagers worked seamlessly.

But the filming of all scenes with Jenny had to wait. On August 6, just about a month before she arrived in South Carolina, Robin had given birth to her son, Hopper. When she finally arrived, we were already filming, and she needed to have her wardrobe fittings, meet with the dialect coach, and do some "look" tests before her first day on camera. To buy ourselves a little more time, we decided to fill up the schedule with the shrimping sequences and the arrival on set of Lieutenant Dan.

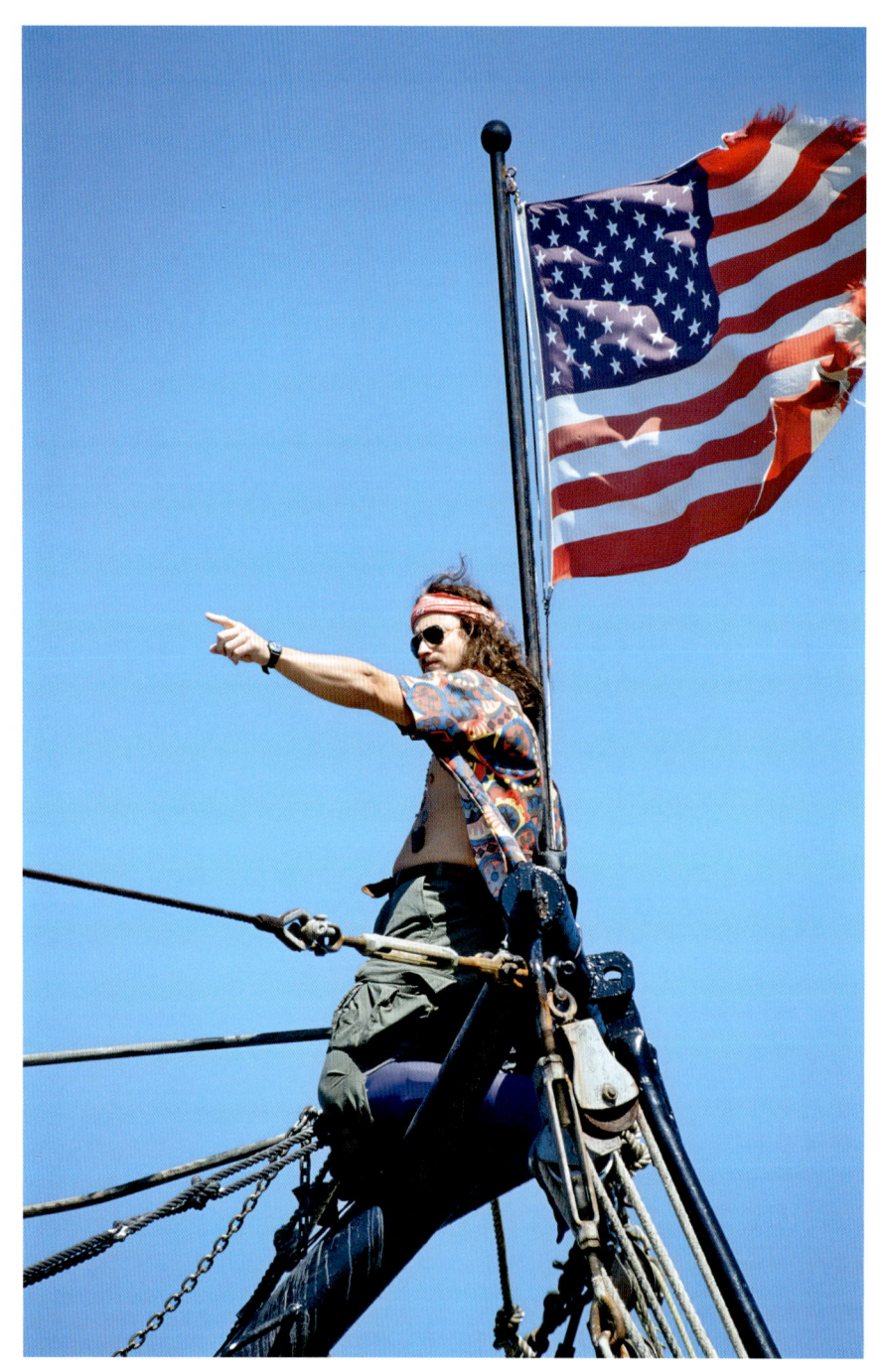

7 | Saved by a Hurricane

PLUNK. THE SHELL from the clam hit the bucket centered in the middle of the table. Next came an oyster. *Clang.* The top of the bucket was even with the tabletop, so it was an easy toss. Then came the tail of a shrimp. Bob Zemeckis, Gary Sinise, and I were at Steamer's on Lady's Island, going through the entire script and reviewing Lieutenant Dan's scenes one by one, from beginning to end. We needed to order more seafood. This was going to be a long night.

Gary was set to appear on camera for the first time in a scene where he reconnects with Forrest at a boat dock in the bayou. This was in the middle of his character's arc in the film, so he needed to map out his journey in order to play his first scene on camera correctly.

We first meet Lieutenant Dan at base camp in Vietnam, when Forrest and Bubba arrive as FNGs (f. . .ing new guys). He is a tough, cynical officer. Shortly thereafter, in the heat of battle, Lieutenant Dan is shot and is saved by Forrest. But Lieutenant Dan's destiny has been shattered. His dream of an honorable death on the battlefield, following in the footsteps of his heroic forefathers, has been ruined by Gump.

```
                LT. DAN
...We all have a destiny. Nothing
just happens...It's all part of a
plan, a scheme. I was supposed to
die in the field with honor and now
I'm a cripple! A legless freak!
```

Lieutenant Dan becomes an angry drunk. Sometime later he reconnects with Forrest, offering to be the first mate on Forrest's shrimp boat. While on the boat, a change comes over Lieutenant Dan, and after a violent hurricane at sea, he puts his anger behind him and thanks Forrest for saving his life.

As often happens, we had to shoot Lieutenant Dan's scenes entirely out of continuity. In a perfect world, a character's scenes would be shot in the order they appear in the film. The actors would be happier, as would the director. When we shoot out of continuity, the actors must have an intimate understanding of where their characters have traveled in the story up to that point. We had the meeting at Steamer's in anticipation of the upcoming work.

Likewise, all the departments—hair, makeup, and wardrobe—had to do the same work. It was crucial for each of them to break down the script to understand the character's changing looks throughout the film and be prepared for any scene we were shooting.

Gary seemed to be satisfied after our meal, and the departments were also prepared. But before shooting the scenes with Forrest and Lieutenant Dan at the shrimp dock, we scouted one last time. There are always logistics and safety protocols to review when shooting on a boat, particularly when going out to sea. Life jackets are a must, and safety personnel are required.

Among the first scenes we planned to shoot was Forrest's return to the dock on his boat, the *Jenny*. He sees a figure in the distance:

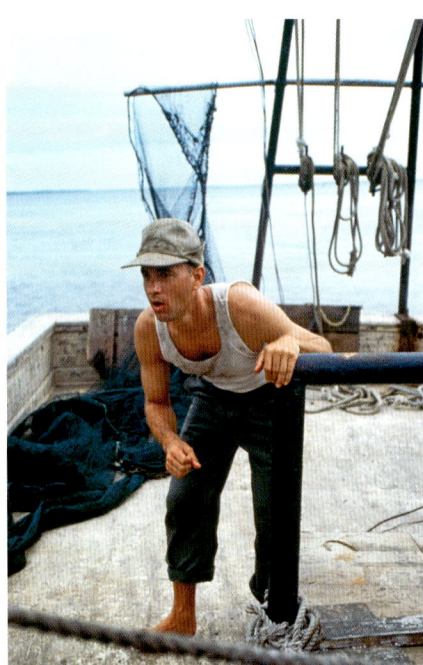
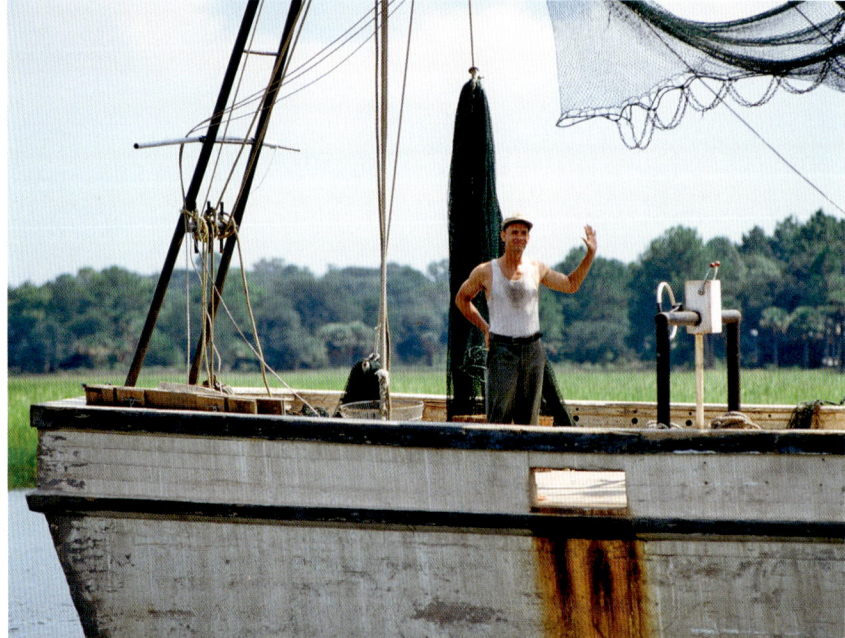

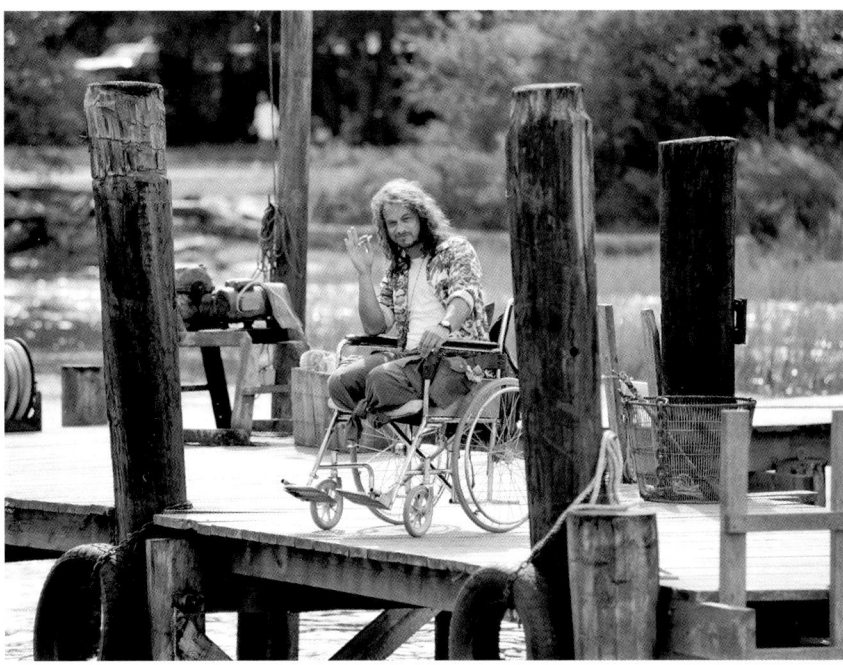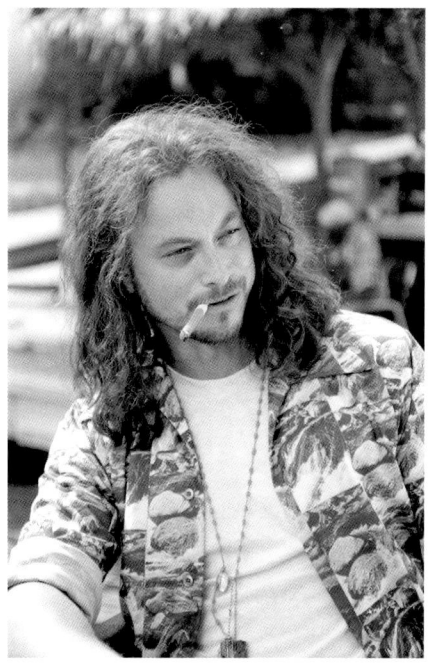

And we see the "Jenny" with Forrest standing at the helm, looking like the idiot he is, coming in from the day's work...And we see a FIGURE in the distance waiting on the dock. And as the boat comes closer, we can see, sitting in his wheelchair, it's LT. DAN.

And without thinking, he stupidly jumps into the water, swimming to the dock. As he climbs onto the dock:

FORREST

Lieutenant Dan. What are you doing here?

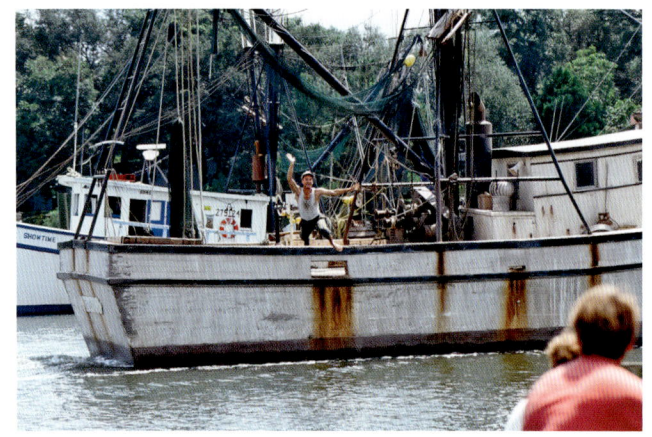
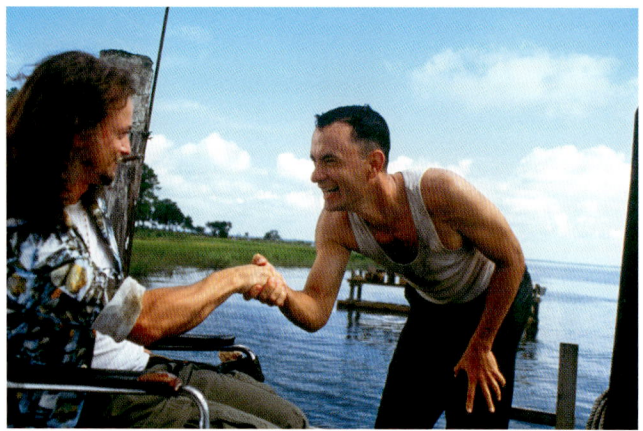

LT. DAN
I thought I'd try out my sea legs.

FORREST
You ain't got no legs, Lieutenant Dan.

LT. DAN
Yes, I know that...

Forrest's boat crashes into the dock.

FORREST
That's my boat.

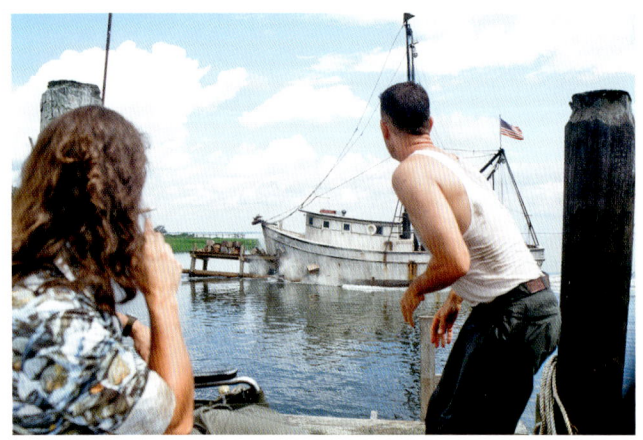
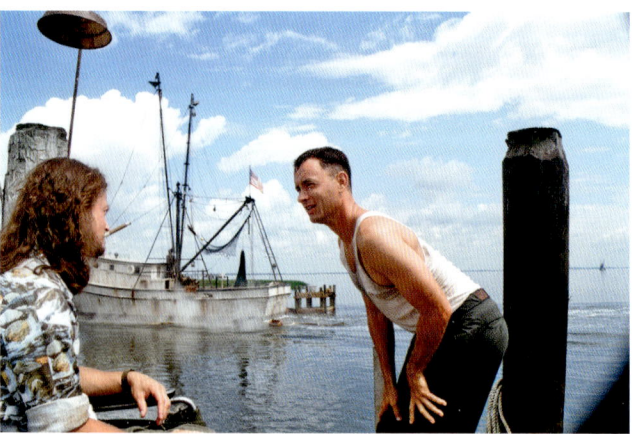

But Forrest has left his boat without a captain, and it's still heading toward shore.

On our final scout, Bob decided it would make a better joke if, after Forrest jumps off, the boat crashes into a neighboring dock, punctuating the end of the scene. I had to admit it was a good joke. Could we afford it? Of course not. Could we get it ready on time? I wasn't sure, but I knew I had to make it happen. I needed someone to supervise a crew of effects guys to prepare the dock for the crash. And it would have to be done perfectly, in one take. Allan Hall, our special-effects supervisor, was swamped with upcoming scenes. But our script supervisor, Susie Malerstein, piped up that her husband was in town visiting, and coincidentally, he was an effects supervisor. He happened to be standing next to Susie and said he was willing to step in. Once we got his start papers in order, we were off and running.

After a few days of additional prep, it all came off without a hitch. Forrest, startled by the crash, turns to Lieutenant Dan and says, with perfect comedic timing, "That's my boat."

Adding to the complexity of the scene was that we had to show a legless Lieutenant Dan in his wheelchair. That would prove to be tricky on the dock, but it was even more so in a different scene onboard the shrimp boat, when Lieutenant Dan jumps into the sea.

On the dock, we used a wheelchair designed by Ricky Jay, the master illusionist. We had hired him early on to design a wheelchair that could hide

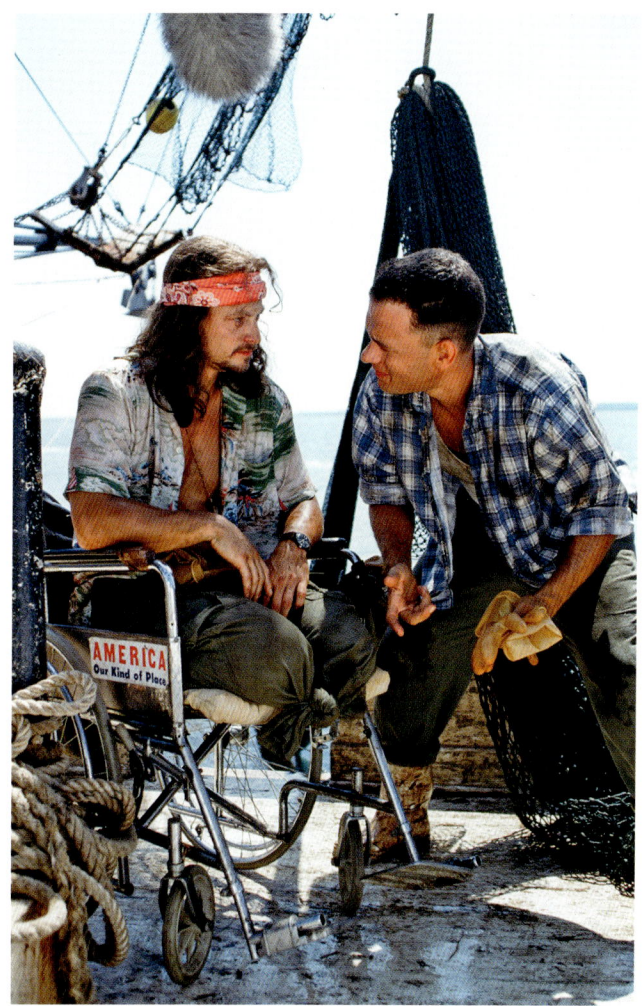

Legless Lieutenant Dan in the magical wheelchair

Gary's legs. The chair he came up with used mirrors to make it appear that you could see underneath the chair and through the bottom. While sitting in the chair, Gary could bend his legs and tuck them under the seat.

67

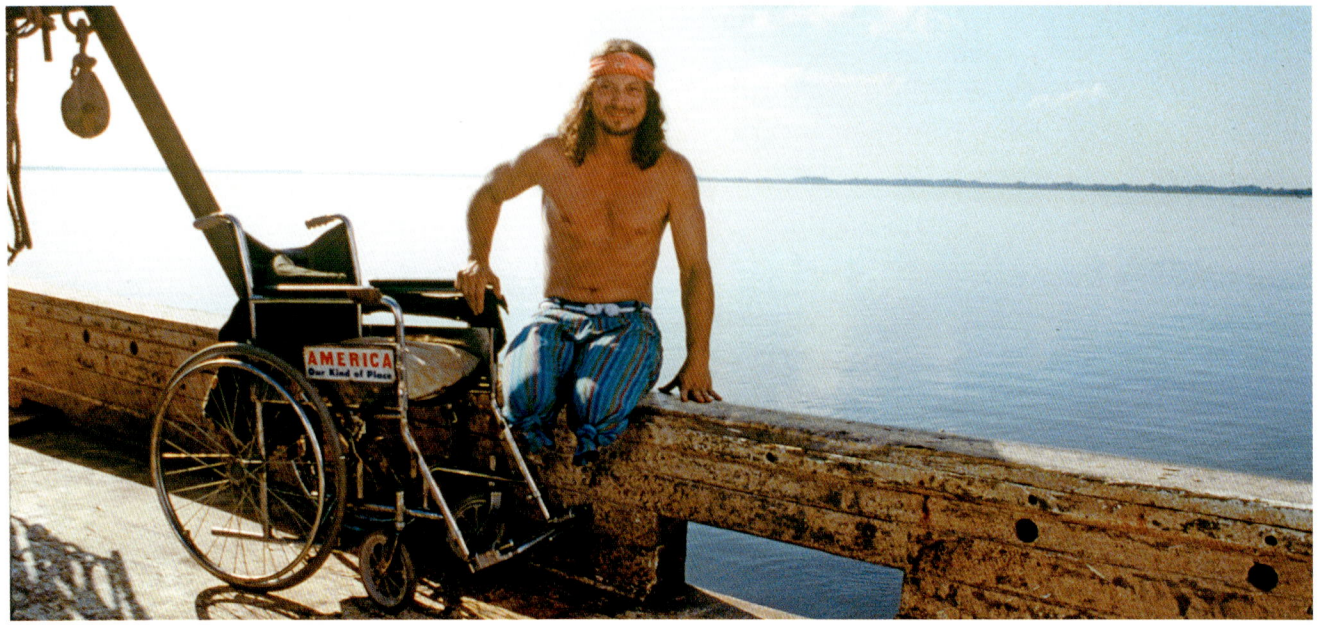

Lieutenant Dan prepares to leap into the water

Using this wheelchair, we were able to eliminate a good number of visual-effects shots, saving time and money. While this was both economical and efficient, Bob wanted a next-level effect that would make audiences say, "Wow! How did they do that?" This type of shot had to surpass the simple sleight of hand that viewers were expecting.

We see Lieutenant Dan sitting on the boat rail and then swinging his body to jump into the sea. It would be next to impossible for a person with legs to do that. To pull off the shot, we turned to Ken Ralston and visual effects. He wrapped Gary's legs in blue screen, then had a piece of the boat removed so Gary could swing his legs freely while pivoting on the boat rail before making his leap. The missing piece of the boat was digitally replaced later. Quite ingenious, and it kept the suspension of disbelief going.

Meanwhile, I was acquiring a feel for Low Country living, and shrimping was getting under my skin. Driving to and from my rental house on Dataw Island, I passed a lovely salt marsh. Birds were in abundance, and the green of the grasses was blinding. A small bridge arched over an estuary, and I always noticed a group of locals fishing for shrimp there. They tossed their nets into the water and pulled them up, hand over hand, to check their catch. One day I stopped and took a closer

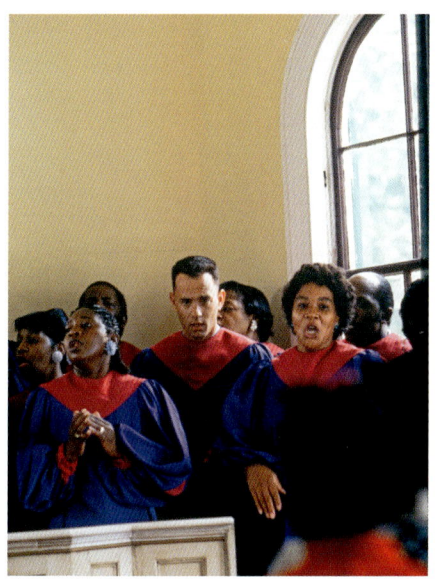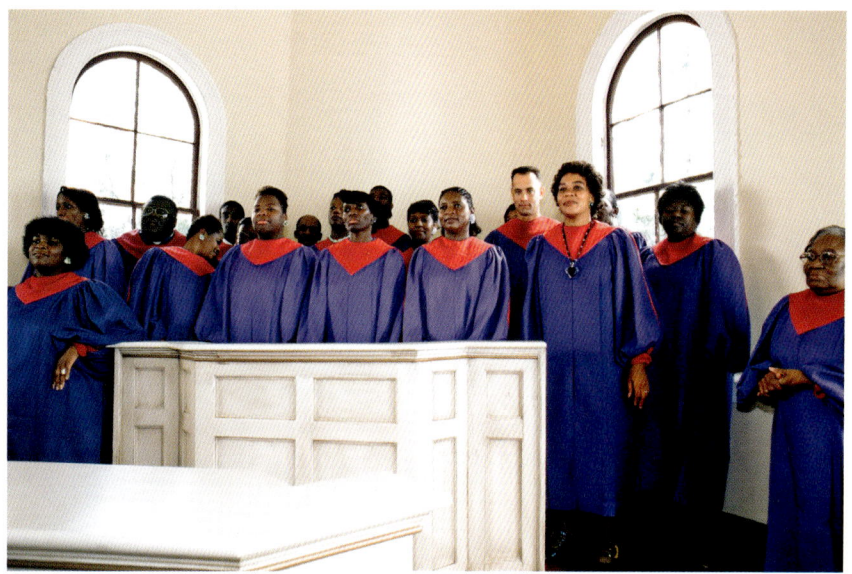

Forrest joins the Hallelujah Singers

look. The top of the nets had lead weights spaced evenly around the circumference and attached to a thin piece of nylon rope that was a drawstring. The tightly woven net tapered to the bottom into a cone shape. The shrimpers grabbed the top of the net with both hands, spread their arms wide, and put a third section of the net in their teeth. Then they flung the net into the marsh. As it flew, the top of the net fanned over the surface of the water, and the rest slowly sank to the bottom. Holding on to the drawstring, the fishermen pulled the net back to the surface with shrimp and odd debris trapped inside.

Shrimping without a boat. I could do that, I thought. You just had to be careful not to pull your teeth out. I told Liv about my discovery, and lo and behold, she found a net for me. That evening when I came home, I cast the net off the dock behind our house, fishing the incoming tide, as the guys had told me to. We had wonderful linguine with fresh shrimp that night.

After work one evening, we paid a visit to the local Presbyterian church in the small town of McPhersonville and were treated to several rousing hymns and spirituals by the Hallelujah Singers. They would end up in a scene where Forrest joins a choir, singing and praying for better luck shrimping.

I should have done the same. But rather than praying for better luck shrimping, I would be praying to stay on schedule. That was the only way to keep the studio from breathing down our necks.

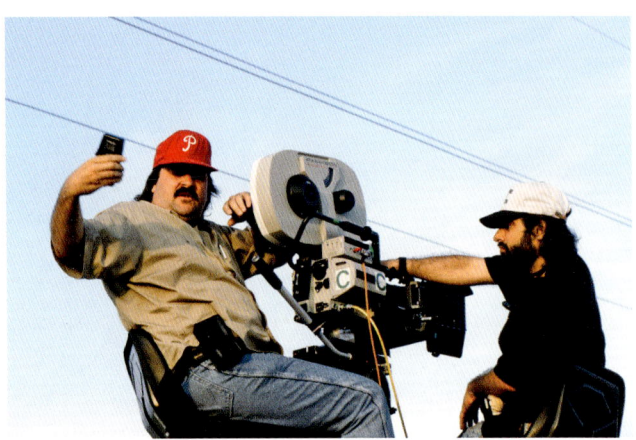

Dave Dunlap, riding the camera crane
and reading his light meter

The splinter-unit idea had helped, but it did not solve the problem. There were still many incomplete scenes from the first few weeks that needed to be shot before we left the South. The only way to complete the missing pieces and continue to leapfrog ahead of the first unit was to start a full-time second unit.

I had great respect for second-unit directors. I had watched director Frank Marshall pull a rabbit out of his hat on *Who Framed Roger Rabbit.* I stood in the background as Max Kleven set up death-defying stunts on *Back to the Future II* and *III.* I had never really thought of doing this work myself, even though I had got a taste for second-unit directing on a Steven Spielberg episode of *Amazing Stories* years earlier.

Now, while going through the shooting schedule, Bob, first assistant director Bruce Moriarty,

and I determined that the only way we could make it through each day of filming was to expand the splinter unit into a second unit. This unit would continue to be centered around Dave Dunlap, the second camera operator on the first unit, who was required to be on our crew by union regulations. We thought, why not really put him to good use, since Bob did not use two cameras very often. He thought that shooting with two cameras compromised each of the setups by getting in each other's way.

It turned out that Dave was more than a good camera operator. He could also help set up the shots and do the lighting.

I would "splinter off" with his camera crew and a few dedicated grips and electricians and a few effects guys when needed. I would bring along whatever props were called for. I had an assistant director to run the set and a production assistant to take notes and keep up with the continuity of what I was filming. When we were not needed to prepare a shot for the first unit, I would work on a shot that Bob was comfortable delegating to me.

We started the process with young Forrest's scenes. Not surprisingly, our boy Michael was less interested in acting than he was in chasing lizards, and Bob didn't want to deal with him. So those shots were added to my list. I had to become a motivational therapist to get Michael excited about the day's work. The motivation to run came in the form of bribes.

If he ran through town, he could go chase some lizards.

If he ran to Jenny's house, I promised him snacks.

If he ran up Oak Alley, he could take the rest of the day off and go play.

A few of my shots were immediately cut out of the movie, which would normally give a second-unit director an inferiority complex, but not me. I was having fun and learning. I might have to do a shot two or three times before getting it right. Often it wasn't until Bob looked at my attempts in dailies that I understood what he really wanted.

For one shot, Forrest swings across a stream on a rope tied to a tree, then races across the back lawn of the Gump house. Since Michael could not do the swing effectively and get into a quick run, we did a "Texas switch": I had a stunt double swing across the stream on the rope. Then young Forrest, hidden in the trees, took off running on my cue. I thought the shot looked okay, but Bob didn't. I tried it over and over again, but it never made it into the movie.

My favorite shot with the young Forrest was when he loses his leg braces running up Oak Alley toward the Gump house. It was a difficult shot that required perfect timing from everyone involved. As such, it was too time consuming for the first unit. But I had all day to get it right.

We mounted the camera on a four-wheel off-road go-cart and paced it just ahead of the boy as he ran up the dirt road. When both Forrest and

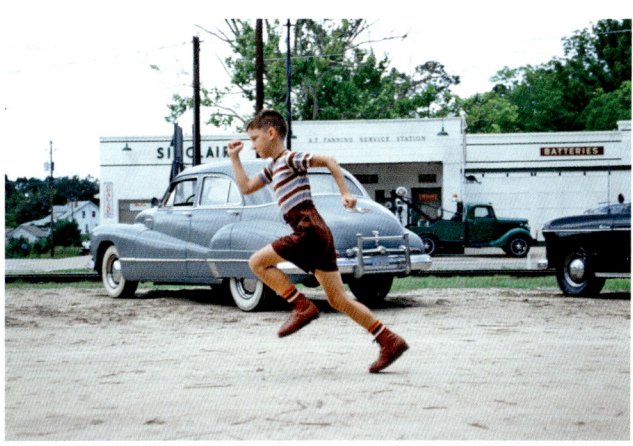

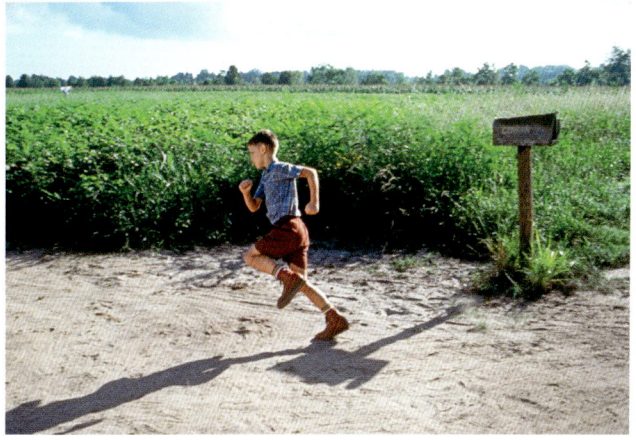

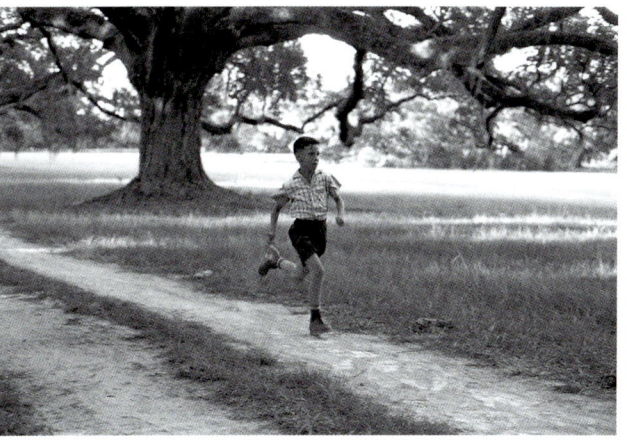

71

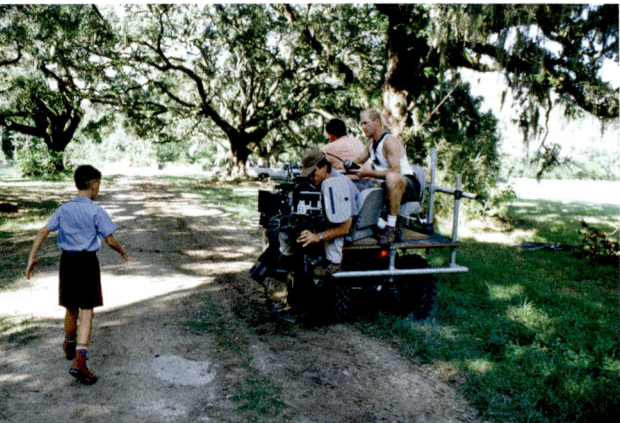

Lining up the camera on the ATV

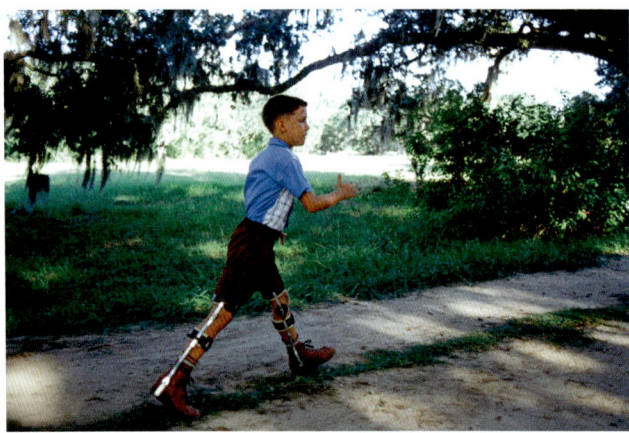

Young Forrest starts his run

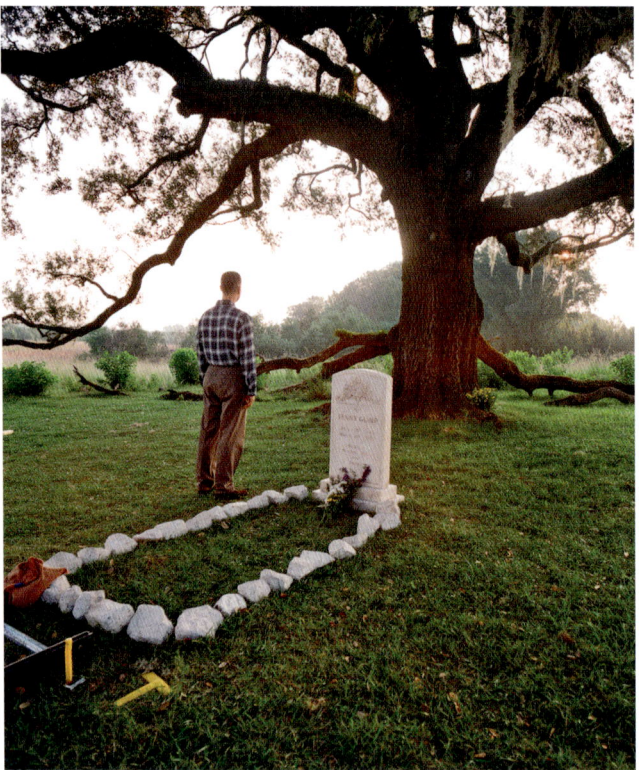

Forrest speaks to Jenny at her grave

the vehicle were up to speed, I gave the cue, and the effects man released the leg braces. Then the camera tilted up to Forrest's face to catch his jubilant reaction to his newfound freedom. Getting the timing right was tricky, but it finally all came together.

After filming most of the day at Oak Alley, I went back to check in with the first unit, which I always did at the end of my day. They were shooting at the iconic oak tree. The set was eerily quiet. The crew generally circled the set, watching a scene unfold, never knowing if they might be called in for some final touch-up. But this was different. I stepped in closer. Forrest was standing at Jenny's grave, speaking to her. Some of the crew had tears in their eyes. I quickly forgot what I had been doing and stood and watched. Tears were soon running down my cheeks, too.

I continued to leapfrog ahead of the first unit to keep things moving. One day we set up a shot near the Gump house, where Jenny comes running out of her grandma's motor home, climbs into a VW van, and slides the door closed. Following Bob's instructions, I had the camera on a crane. The shot started at the door of the trailer and pulled back as Jenny got into the van. We did some rehearsals with Robin's stand-in, and then Robin said she was ready to try a few herself. We were rehearsed and ready. I called the first unit on the walkie-talkie and asked when they were planning to join us. "Soon," they said.

Well, the sun was going down, and we were still sitting around waiting. I called again. "We're still shooting," was the reply. Then the first unit came back on and said, "If Robin's game, why don't you shoot a few, warm it up for us, and we'll see the shot when we get there."

Robin was fine with that, so we shot a few takes. After a while, I was happy, as was Robin. I called back again and reported, "We're pretty happy with what we have." They came back, "We're on our way."

The sun had dipped behind the trees by then, and the light was dropping fast. Bob raced in, jumped out of his golf cart, and asked to see what we had. I played back the video of my favorite takes. "Looks good to me." He turned and said, "Robin, you happy?" She nodded. Bruce called for a wrap. Just like that, we were done.

I was happy but insecure. Although I figured if Bob was happy, I should be happy too. Bruce bumped my shoulder and said, "You did great." Everyone was glad to have the shot in the bag.

The next morning Bruce, Don Burgess, and I were shooting the breeze around the camera, waiting for Bob to arrive on set. We met every morning to review the day's work and figure out if there was anything I could do, outside of my production responsibilities, to help the first unit.

Bob arrived, walked up to the group, and asked me, "So what're you going to shoot today?"

"I don't have plans to shoot anything at the moment," I said. "Just jump ahead and help out first unit."

Bob turned to Bruce and said, "Let's all look at the list and see what Starkey can do." Bruce and I exchanged looks, and we realized that this was what we needed to do to reduce our looming shot list. In addition to overseeing an advance camera team for the first unit and knocking off shots with young Forrest, there might be more pickup shots and small vignettes that I could handle. Bob went down the list and circled the shots he was willing to let me do.

From that day forward, when Bruce was preparing the call sheet for the following day, he listed shots for my unit, ran them by Bob, then published it and made it official. As my shot list grew, so did my unit (which I christened the Steve Starkey, or SS, unit), and it eventually included every department. I even got a motor home to use as a mobile

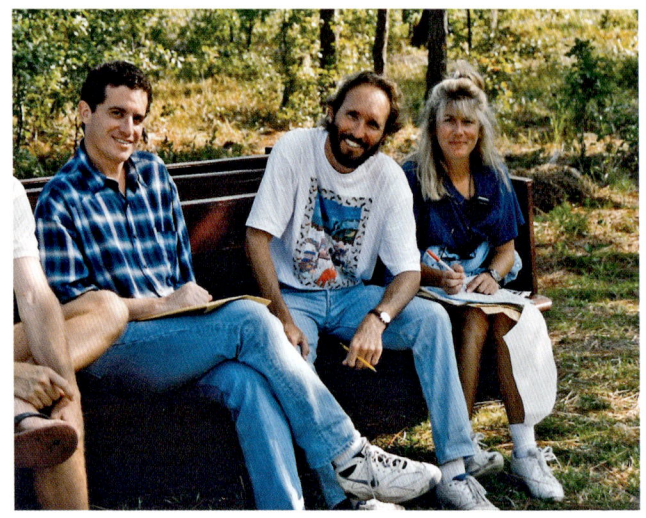

Charles, me, and Cherylanne

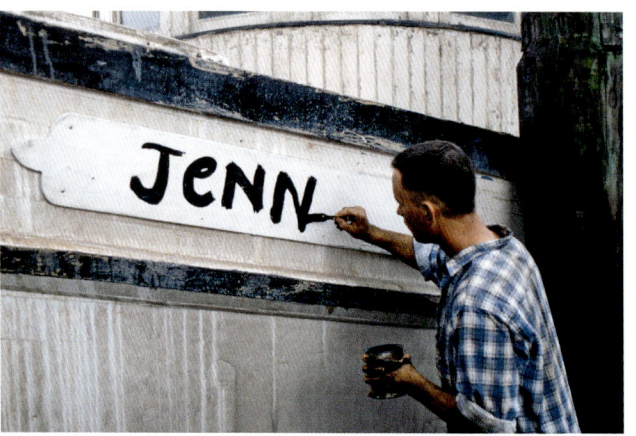

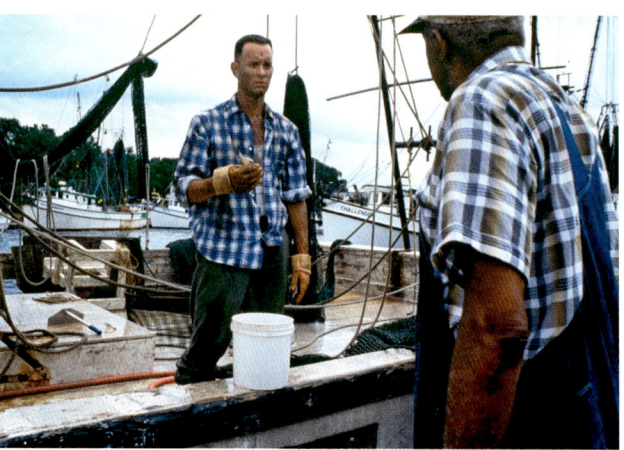

office. Thereafter, the SS unit filmed shots almost every day. My days were carefully planned so that I could be wherever I could help the most.

By this point, the movie had seeped into my system. Bob had set the style. I would do my best to emulate it. I wanted my shots to flow seamlessly into the first-unit shots; I wanted them to feel as if Bob had shot them. He would carefully go over with me what he needed and how to shoot it, even suggesting the camera lens to start with. I was fearful of the task, but I knew I could always reshoot anything that Bob rejected, which, putting on my producer's hat, I hated to do.

Even though my second-unit directing experience was limited, it felt logical for me to step up. I hated the idea of hiring a full-time second-unit director, who would end up sitting around too much and bothering Bob with questions I knew the answer to. Also, I could do my other work while moving around.

I grabbed Cherylanne Martin, the second assistant director from the first unit, to work alongside me. She could organize the crew and my days, and the two of us could work together on upcoming

74

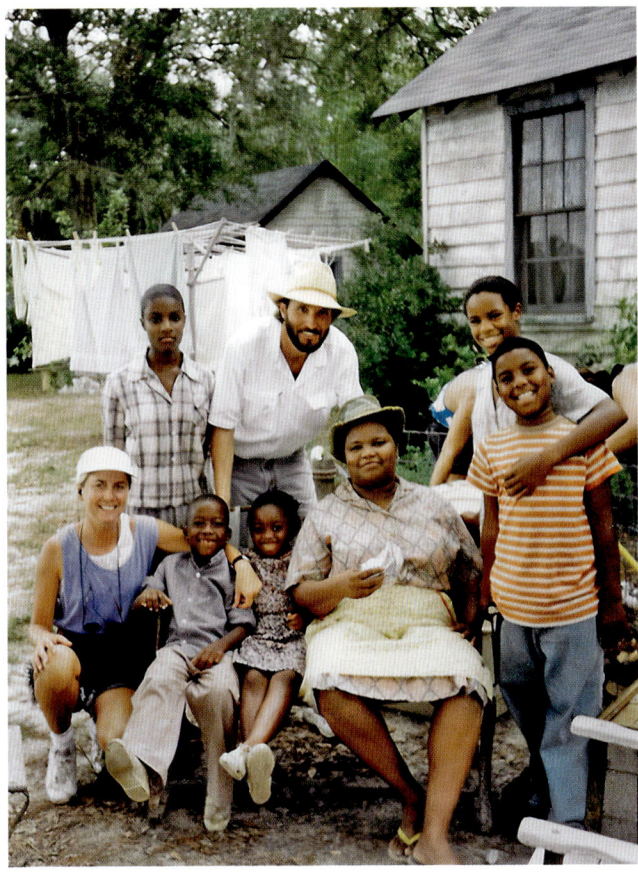

Me and Bubba's family

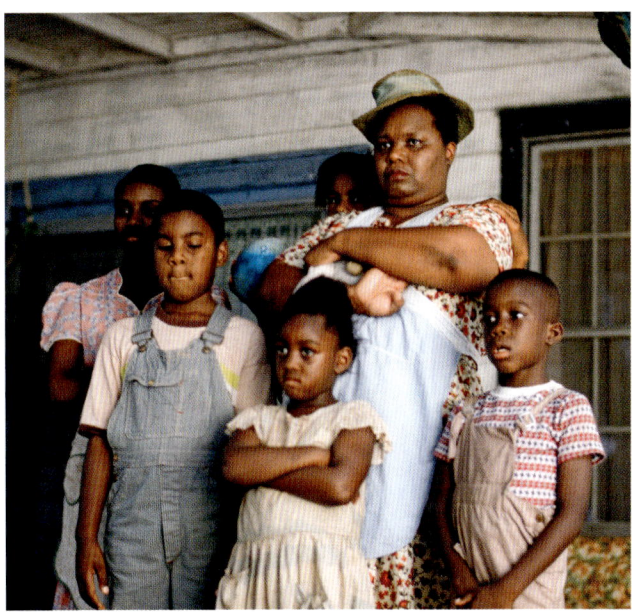

Bubba's family on the front porch

prep. At this point in her career, she was ready to assume more production management responsibility, and Charles Newirth could use all the help he could get.

I needed to join the Directors Guild of America, not only to get paid but also to make my new position legit. Some days would be eight-hour second-unit days; others might be only two or three hours. When I accumulated my first forty hours, I filled out my application to join the DGA and got Bob and Tom Hanks to sponsor me. I was officially a member of the guild.

I was off and running. After the first unit shot Forrest on the dock buying his boat, giving it a name, and showing his meager catch to a seasoned fisherman named Stanley, they left me behind to shoot Stanley fishing.

My daily shot list increased in both size and complexity. After Bob ended his day shooting Forrest meeting Bubba's family, he left me to shoot Bubba's mom opening the letter with a check from Forrest. Bob had already set up the front porch of the house and the family, so it was easy for me to build on what he had done.

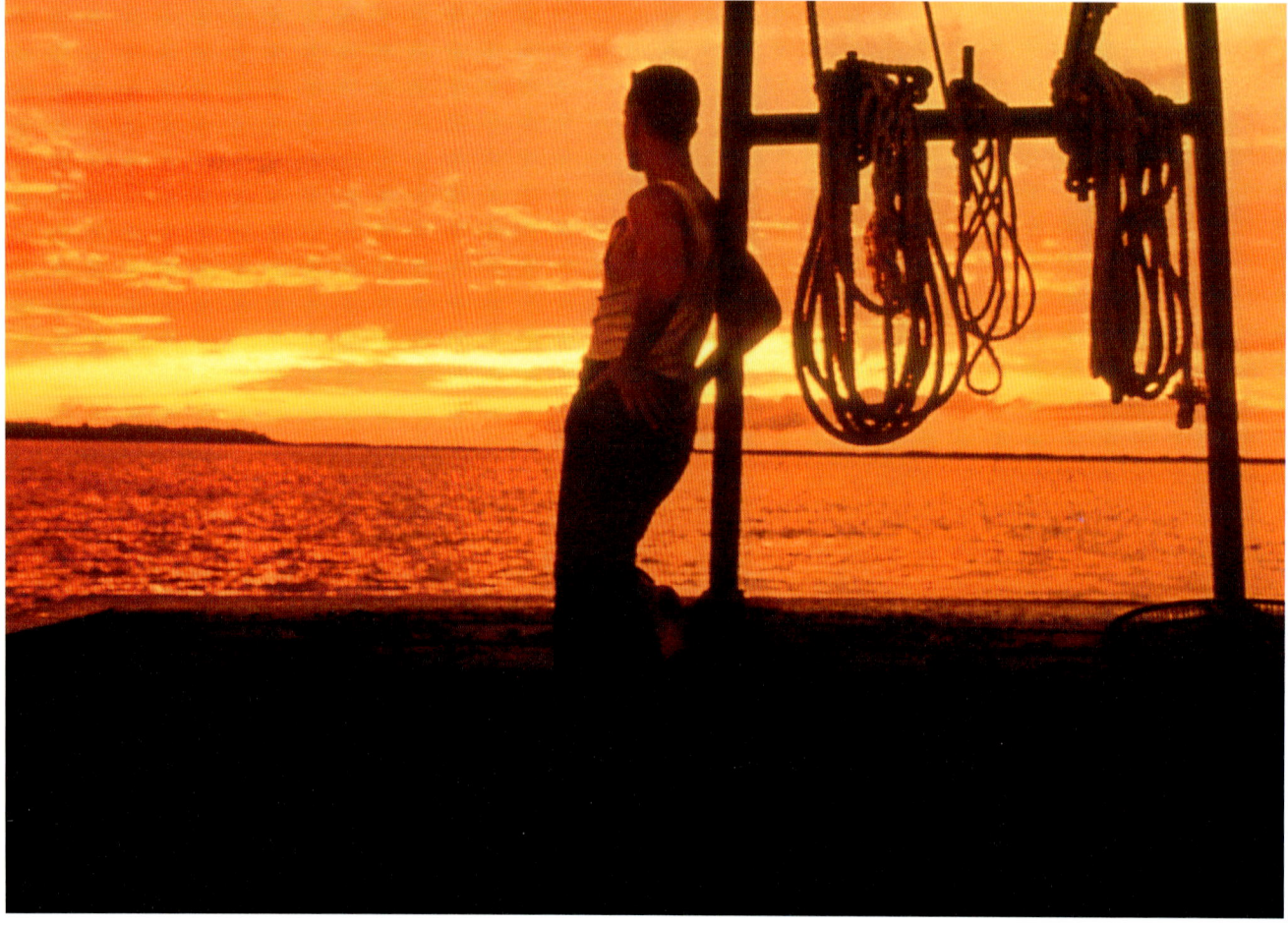

We did the same with a scene at the church. Bob shot Forrest singing in the choir, then I shot the raising of the cross after the church was renovated. These two shots were among a trio illustrating Forrest's philanthropy after he got rich from his shrimping business. The third was the ribbon cutting at the new Gump medical center.

On another day, when the first unit was doing a shot on the ocean, I set up a camera on a separate fishing boat, allowing Bob to run over at the end of the day and shoot Forrest standing on the stern of the boat at sunset. That shot was part of a sequence late in the movie, when Jenny is dying.

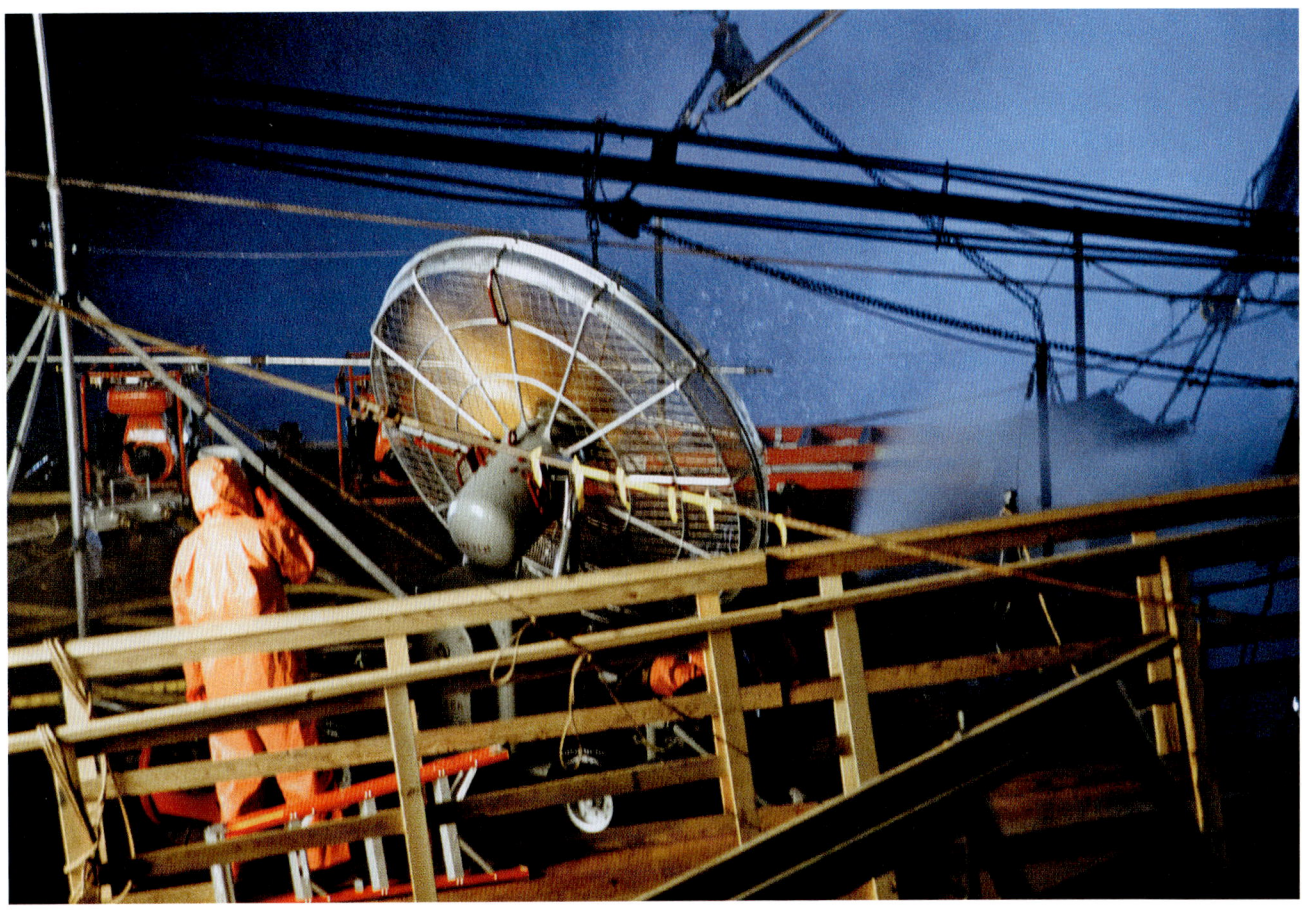

Forrest's boat getting blasted by wind and rain effects

The plan seemed to be working—my unit setting up shots and getting some on our own. It helped, but it was still not enough. We were barely keeping up. And then came the hurricane scene.

Bob wanted one day with all the bells and whistles for the hurricane, so we gave it to him. Working into the wee hours of Sunday morning, we shot Forrest's boat getting blasted by a hurricane. We had rain towers overhead. Surrounding the boat, the effects technicians manned several fire hoses stationed in front of powerful jet engines that blew the water onto the set. The crew fanned additional fire hoses back and forth to fill in the scene with waves. The boat, tied to the dock, was rocking and rolling throughout the scene. Lieutenant Dan yells,

77

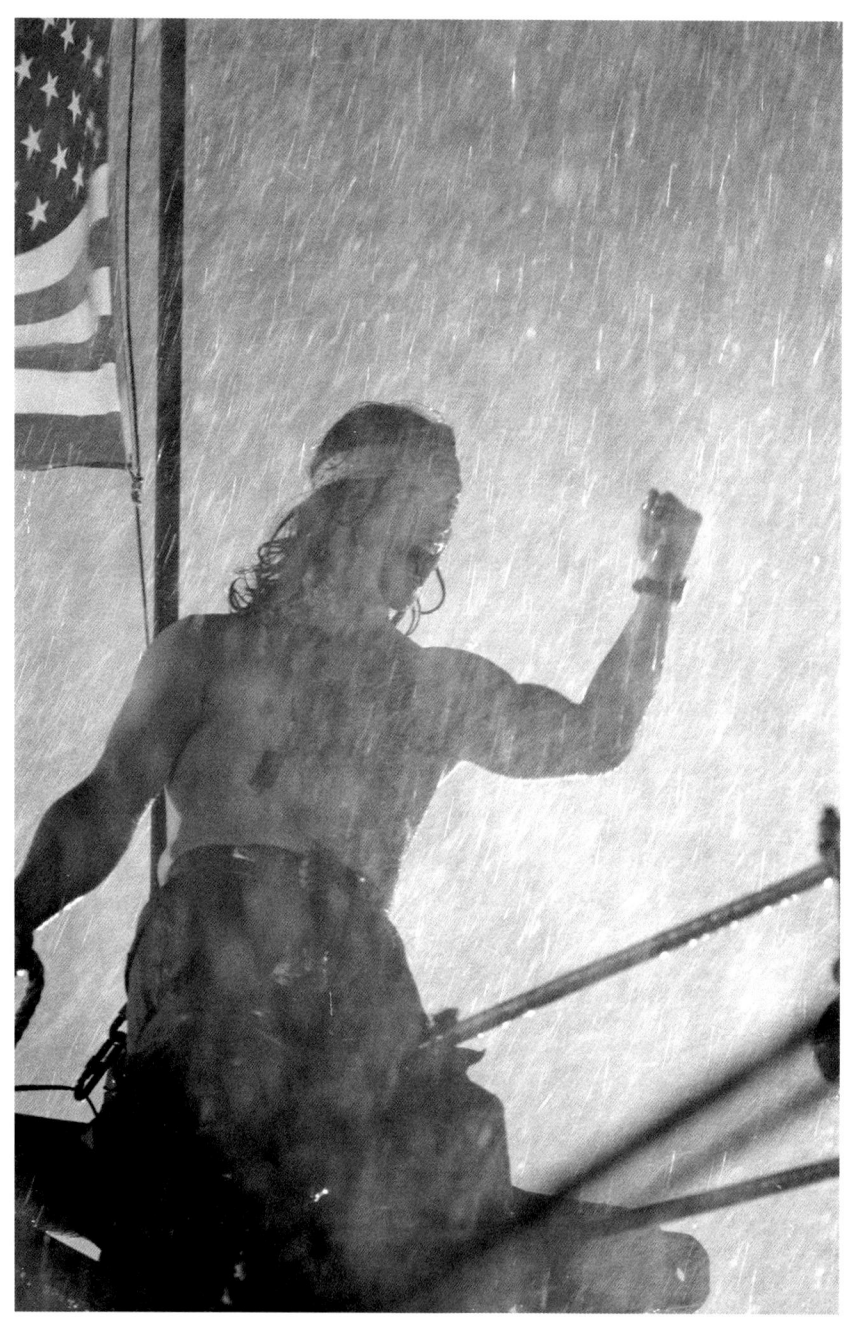

"You call this a storm? Blow, you son of a bitch! Blow!"

"You call this a storm?" and Forrest holds on to the ship's wheel for dear life.

More wind-driven rain was added in post-production at Industrial Light & Magic (ILM). All this for a scene that had been cut from the budget. I was not sure how to explain that to the studio.

We had started principal photography on August 27 and had given ourselves two weeks of shooting with Mama Gump, young Forrest, and young Jenny, followed by the shrimping sequence and the hurricane. By the time we finished this work, we had to declare ourselves two days over schedule. Not good. I had cut ten days from the shooting schedule to hit the budget number, but I did not think we would be over by two days so soon. We had accomplished a lot, but our daily hot costs revealed excessive overtime and departmental overages. The studio did not take this well. They started to watch the production like hawks. The executives at Paramount began to think they had an out-of-control movie on their hands.

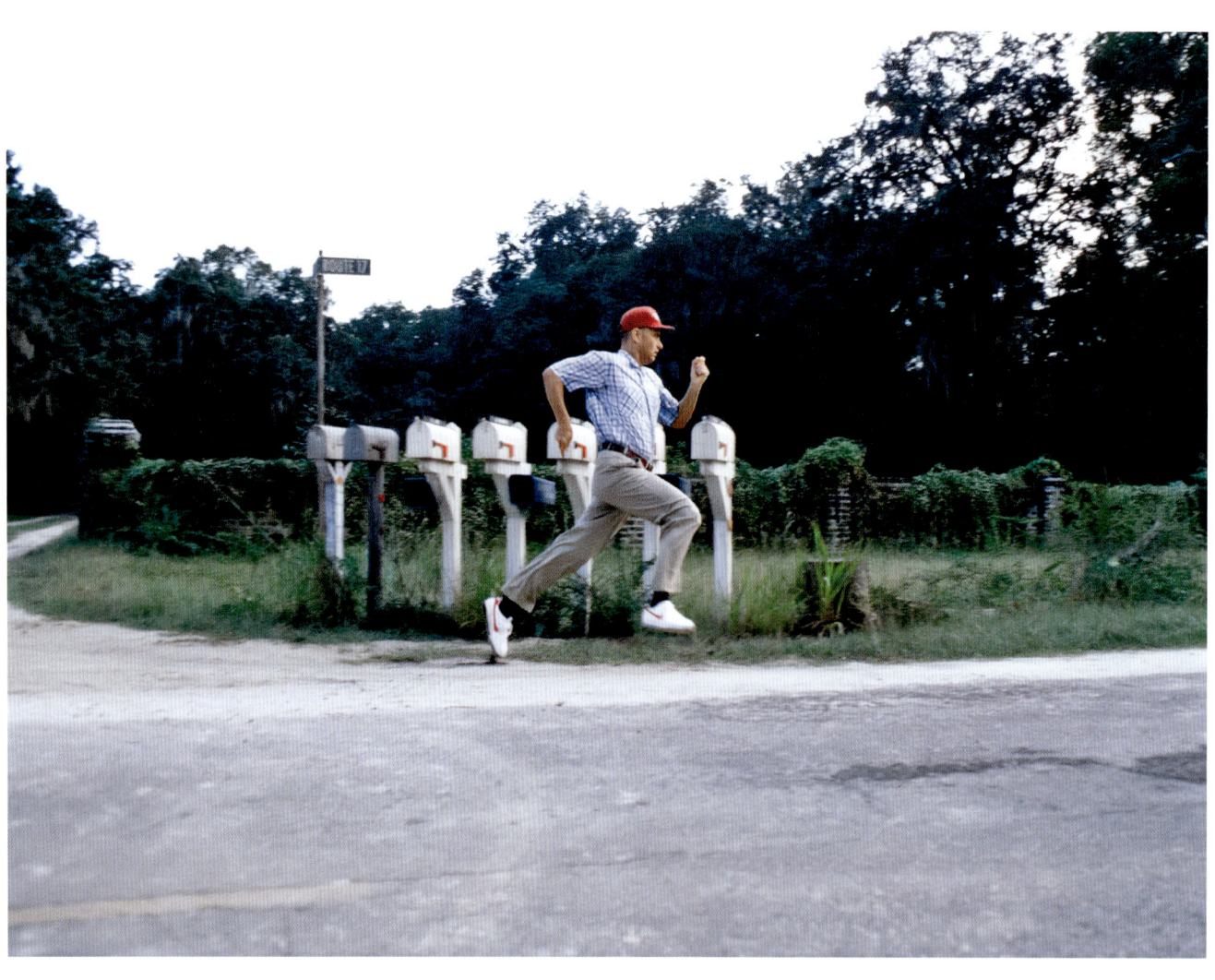

8 | A Production on the Run

THERE WERE 275 SCENES in the script for *Forrest Gump.* That's a lot of scenes by any standard. As we bounced from location to location and scene to scene, we were humming. We were knocking off shots left and right. The crew was fast, and we were shooting like the wind. But with a movie of this size and scope, it is never enough. And I started to feel guilty. In our shooting frenzy, I had lost sight of Tom and his workload on the film. It was easy for us to make demands on him without thinking of the man behind the shots. I hated to take advantage of his good nature.

On one of the first days of shooting, I drove Tom from base camp to the set in my golf cart. I knew he was going to be working on the film every day after we finished with the kids. I also knew he would be working long hours. SAG rules required me to ask him each day to waive his short turnaround and come back to work without sufficient rest. So rather than pose that question every day, I left it up to him. All he had to do was tell me—give me a wave or something—to indicate that he needed some extra time before returning to work the next day. I would then adjust the call for the following morning so he could get a few more hours of precious sleep. Throughout the entire shoot, Tom never asked for a break. He merely asked what time to report. Even I didn't know how bad it would become.

We were shooting one scene after another, from all over the script, never in continuity. This didn't seem to bother Tom. He might start his day singing in the church choir and then run past the barbershop at the beginning of his cross-country run. He started another day as a teenager by the riverbank and ended up at the Gump house for a going-away party as Forrest heads off to Vietnam. On the day we shot Forrest crying at Jenny's burial site, we also shot him happily sitting in the same oak tree with Jenny at his side. Tom simply asked us where and when to report for work.

The shooting schedule was not easy on Robin Wright either. She always had to remind herself where she was in the film. She was fortunate that we started filming her as she first appears in the movie, as a teenager yelling, "Run, Forrest, run." We were fortunate as well. In her youthful scenes she was glowing from having recently given birth.

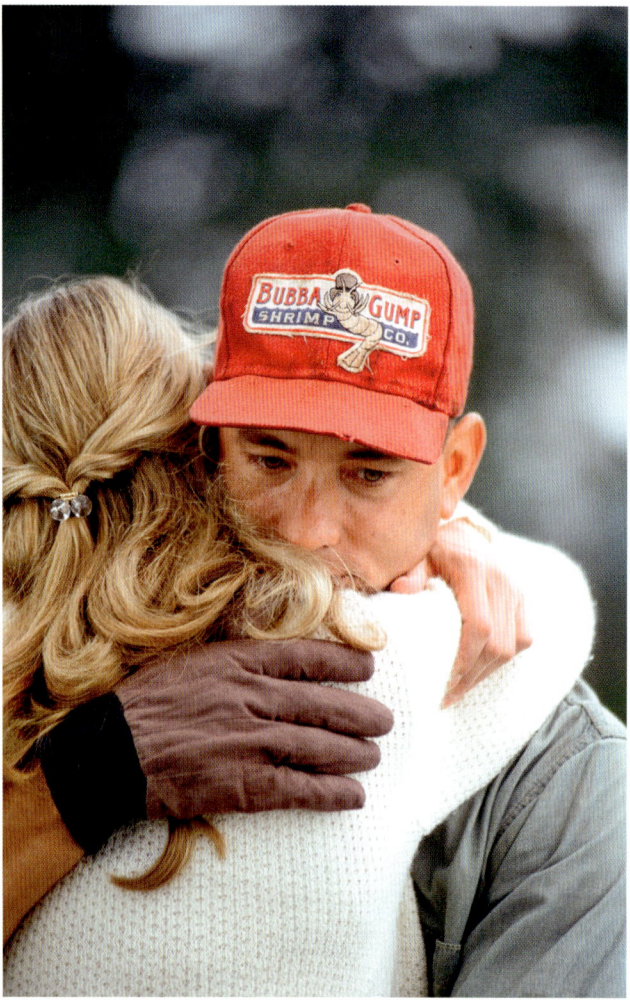

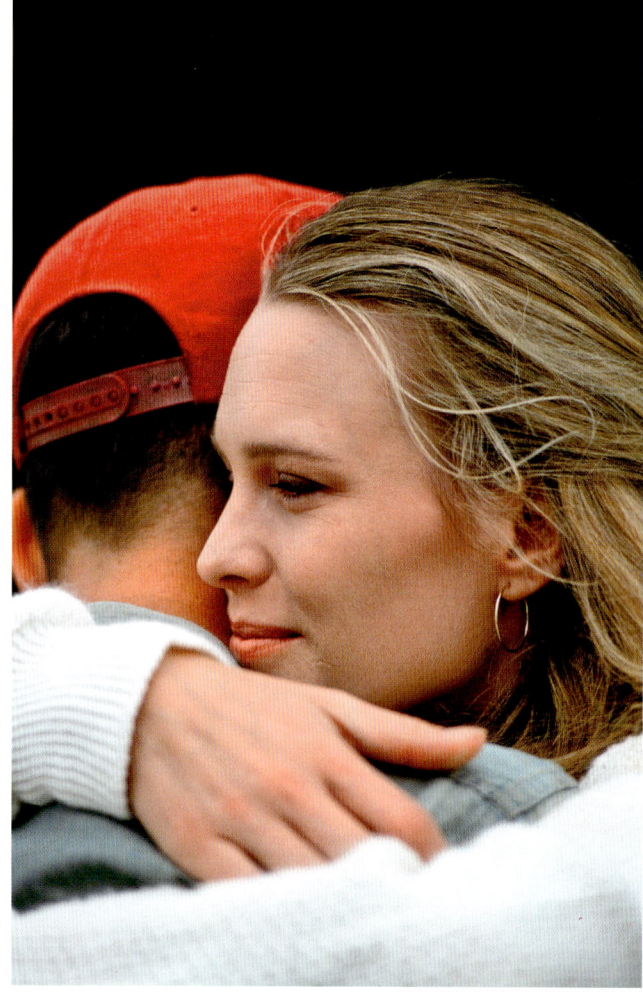

In other scenes that we shot early on, including Jenny's wedding to Forrest much later in the film, Robin looked as beautiful as ever, despite what her character had been through. But what a mental jump it was, from one of her earliest scenes to one of her last. It must have taken serious preparation to keep it all straight.

The bulk of Robin's scenes in the South took place in and around the Gump house, but that didn't simplify the leaps we took when scheduling them. When she returns to the Gump house after living through the darkest period of her adult life, she is lovingly welcomed back by Forrest.

82

FORREST (V.O.)

I never really knew why she came back. But I didn't care. It was like olden times. We was like peas and carrots again.

EXT. THE OLD OAK TREE—DAY

We see Forrest and Jenny, just like kids, sitting in their tree.

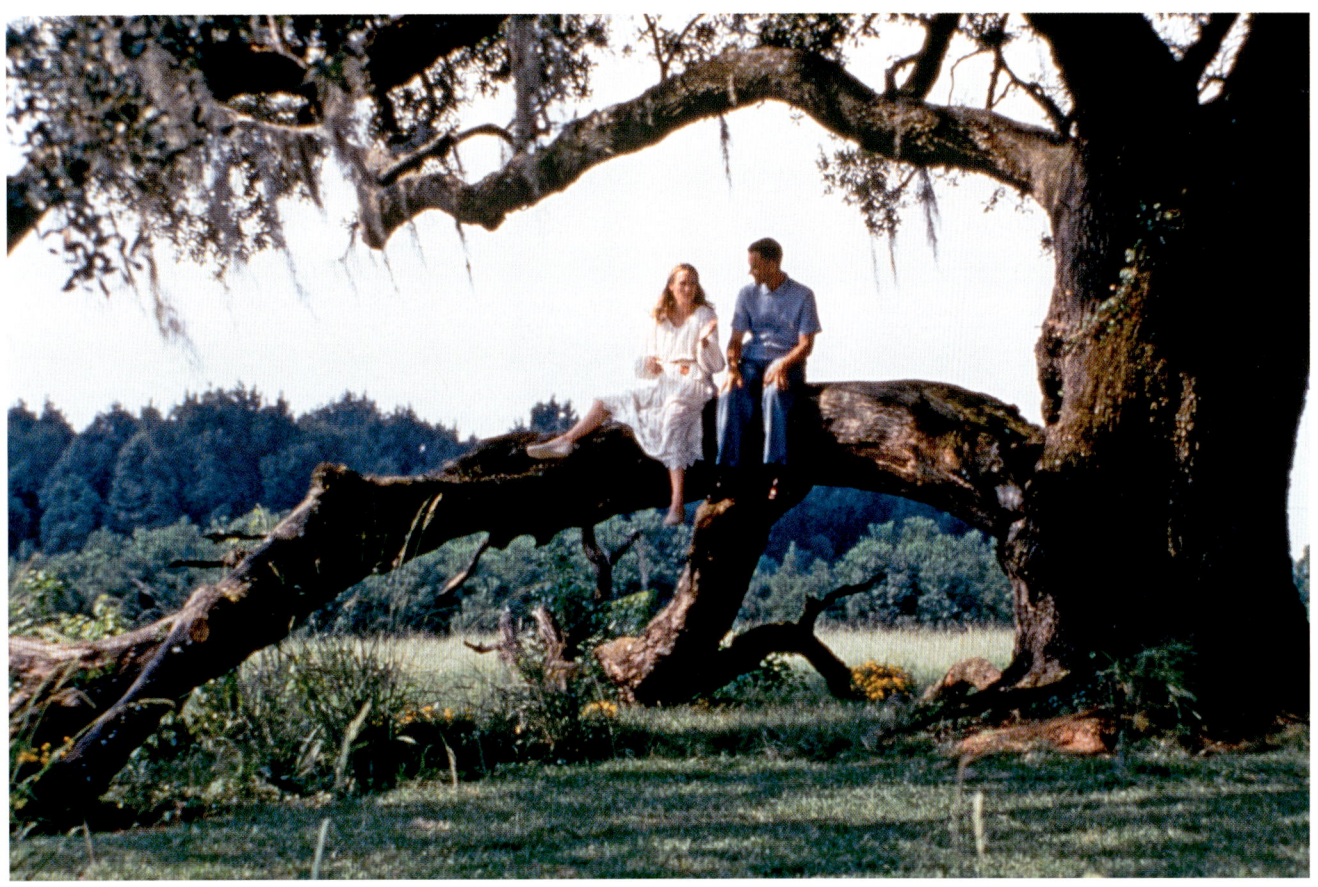

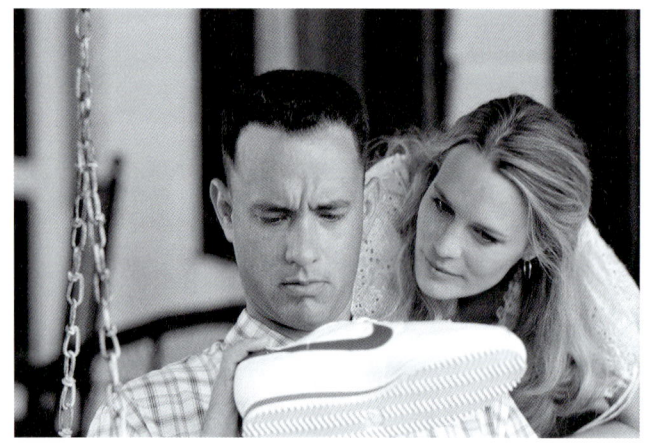

FORREST (V.O.)
And she gave me the best gift anyone could ever get in the wide world.

EXT. THE GUMP HOUSE—FRONT PORCH—DAY
We see Jenny watching Forrest open a box of running shoes.

FORREST (V.O.)
And she even showed me how to dance.

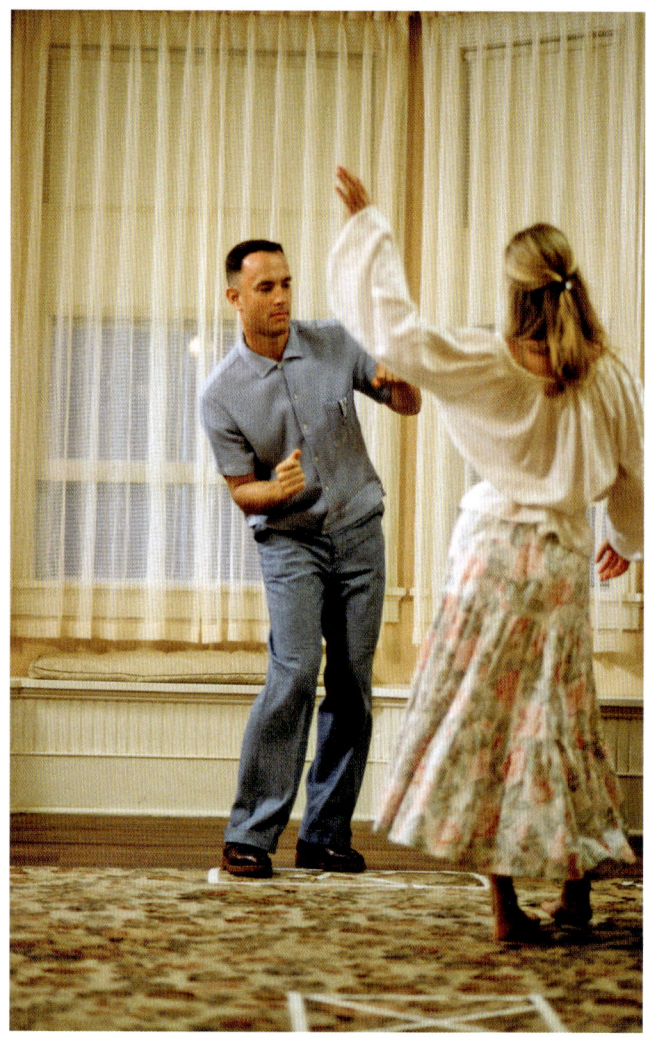

But when Forrest asks Jenny to marry him, she doesn't accept his proposal. Defensively, in the face of her rejection, Forrest says, "I'm not a smart man, but I know what love is." And then he steps outside, letting the screen door close behind him. Later that night, Jenny gets into bed with Forrest, tells him she loves him, and kisses him affectionately. Then they tenderly make love.

Early the next morning she leaves him once again. This devastates Forrest, who has already lost his mama and his best and only friend, Bubba Blue. Jenny's sudden departure only makes things worse. Lonely and grieving, not knowing what to do, he puts on his new magic shoes, the pair of Nikes from Jenny.

> FORREST
> That day, for no particular
> reason, I decided to go for a
> little run.

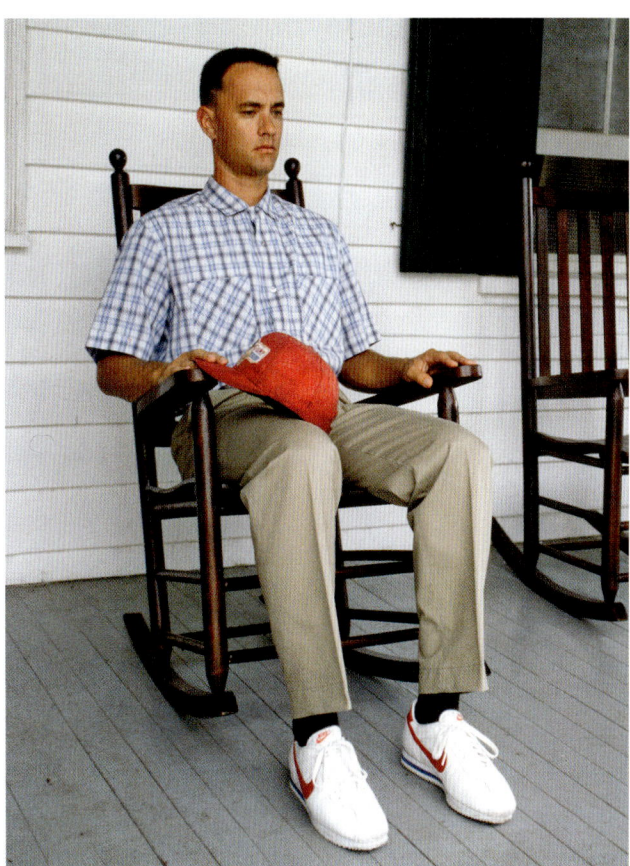

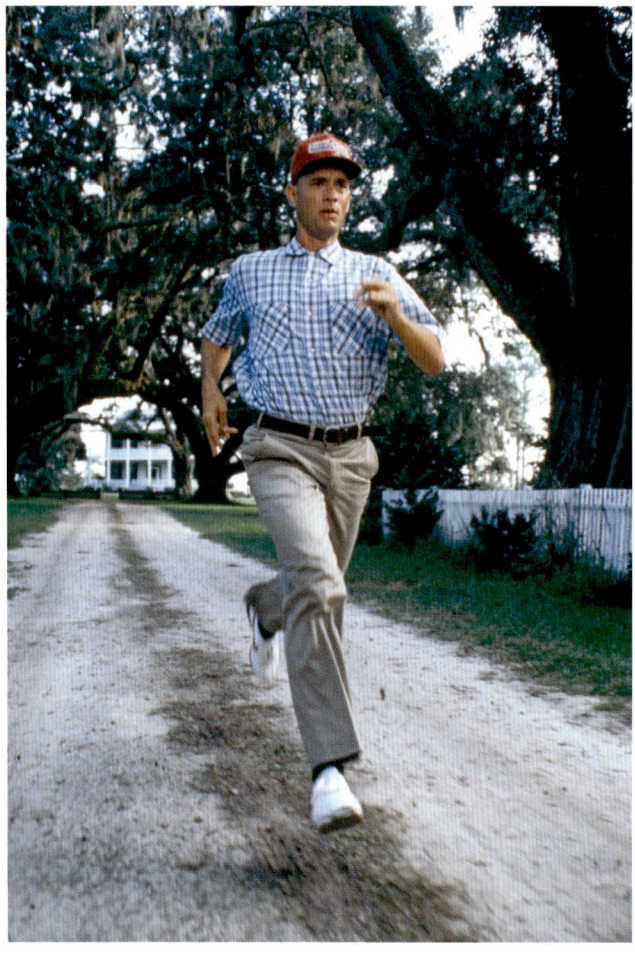

Forrest begins his run on Oak Alley

And from that day on, Forrest was running. And we became a production on the run. Shooting the cross-country run became part of our life. How to pick up all the vignettes was a puzzle and, ultimately, a challenge. We grabbed shots whenever and wherever we could in the most imaginative ways possible.

This was a part of the movie the studio executives did not understand, which had become clear during our initial budget crisis. They repeatedly pointed to the run as a potential cost-saving area. "Cut it down" was their mantra. I said we would take a look, but we stuck to our guns. Bob and I were going to shoot everything in the script and then some. All the pieces added up to a poetic journey for Forrest, and we wanted to decide in the editing room what felt right. After all, when a person has suffered so much loss, where does grieving end and life begin?

The run started on the porch of the Gump house, with Forrest properly dressed, wearing his special shoes. He gets up from his chair, jogs across the lawn, then picks up the pace and heads down Oak Alley. Making a turn by Mailbox Corner, he keeps on running. His route takes him along the main street of Greenbow, Alabama, and across the fishing bridge marking the end of the county. But he doesn't stop there. He runs clear across Alabama, finally passing the sign that welcomes him to the great state of Mississippi.

This particular shot was handed off to the Starkey unit. As it turned out, that day of filming proved to be a traumatic one for me. It was the day I lost my temper.

I have a reputation for having a very calm disposition, but not on that day. The morning got off to a good start when I stopped by the location to check in with my crew. I met with the art department and placed the Welcome to Mississippi

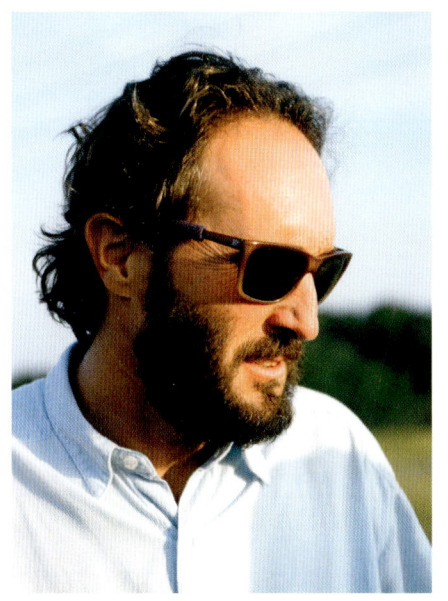
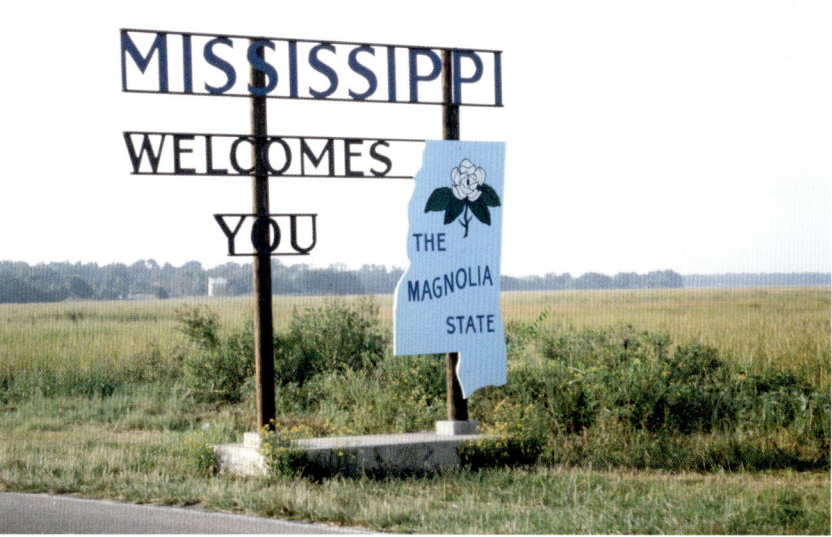

Me placing the welcome sign on the road outside of Beaufort, South Carolina

sign on the shoulder of the road, just before the Chowan Creek Bridge, which links Lady's Island with St. Helena Island in the beautiful open marshland just outside of Beaufort.

I told the cameraman to mount the camera on a crane and have it ready to go. I described the shot to him. We would start with a medium shot of Forrest passing by, then the camera would rise and pan to reveal the Welcome to Mississippi sign as Forrest runs down the road. Everyone seemed to be clear. I told Cherylanne, my trusty unit supervisor, and Dave Dunlap, the cameraman, that I would head to town where the first unit was filming. When it seemed like Tom was about an hour away from finishing his work, I would head back to the set, and we would prepare for his arrival.

It all went like clockwork. Bob finished shooting the scene with Tom and was preparing to continue without him, so I took off. All Tom had to do was go back to base camp, change his wardrobe, hop in his car, and head to my set. I would be fifteen or twenty minutes ahead of him, so it would be perfect. This would be the first shot I did with Tom and my second unit, and I wanted it to go just right.

I drove away from the set and headed down the road to the location, anxious and excited. No

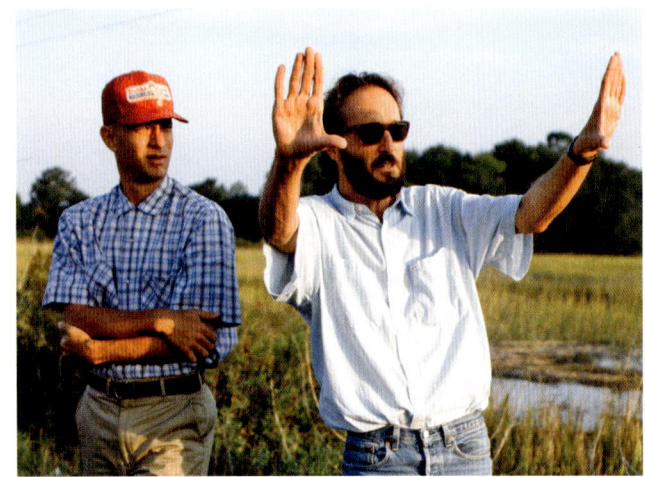

Framing the shot with Tom

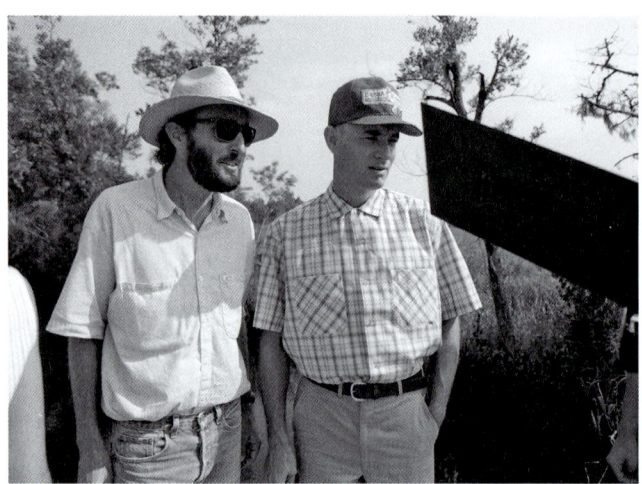

Tom and me watching the video playback

sooner did I cross the bridge outside of Beaufort than the traffic came to an abrupt halt. I was about a mile from the set. What the hell is this all about, I wondered? I sat there, getting a bit worried. Was there an accident? I hoped that was not the case. Then I noticed that there was no traffic on the two-lane road heading in my direction. That's strange, I thought. I started to creep out onto the other side of the road to see what was going on. But I couldn't see anything.

Then it dawned on me. The company—my shooting company—had probably stopped traffic. That would be necessary when we actually filmed the shot, but not now! How was I supposed to get to the set? How could I rehearse with the camera before Tom arrived? How was Tom going to get there? The more I thought about it, the more confident I was that this was the problem. I pulled out

into the oncoming traffic lane and sped down the road, past all the stopped cars lining the highway. As I got closer to the set, I could see that I was right. The crane was out in the road, blocking traffic in both directions, and the cameraman was rehearsing the camera move without me. Damn them!

I pulled up to the location, left my car on the shoulder of the road, and ran up to the set, yelling at whoever I saw. "Get the crane off the road! What are you thinking? The traffic is gridlocked all the way back to Beaufort! There is no way Tom can even get to the set!"

Cherylanne tried to calm me down, which she eventually did, but she ended up taking the brunt of my tirade. "Release the traffic!" I screamed.

Once the crane was off the road, the cars slowly started to move past the set. Surprisingly, since we were in the South, only a few of the drivers raised a fist at us. At the end of the dwindling flow of cars, Tom arrived. By that time, I had composed myself, and my anger had passed. After a quick rundown of the shot, we were ready to go.

We did a few takes, looked at the video play-back, and decided we had the shot. If Tom was happy, I was happy.

The traffic jam was even reported in the local newspaper the following day!

But I could never forgive myself for losing my temper. It's only a movie, after all.

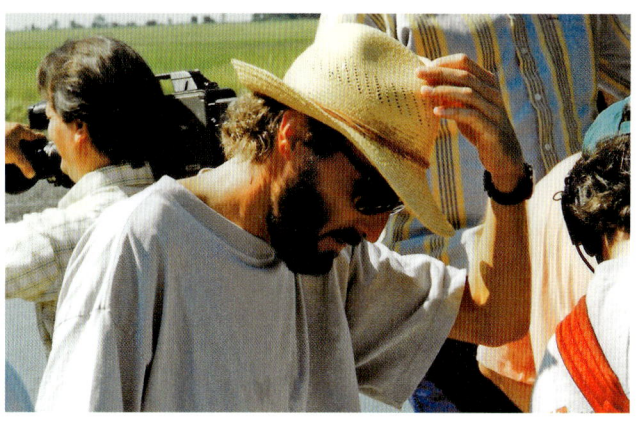

Me, feeling bad for yelling at my crew

Filming snarls U.S. 21 traffic

By CATHY CARTER HARLEY
Gazette assistant lifestyles editor

Traffic was jammed along U.S. 21 for two hours Wednesday afternoon during the filming of *Forrest Gump* on the Chowan Creek Bridge.

The public was not notified of the scheduled closure from 5-7 p.m. and some motorists had to wait from 45 minutes to an hour near the bridge, which connects Lady's and St. Helena islands.

Traffic was backed up from the bridge to the signal at Sea Island Parkway and in the other direction as far as the St. Helena Post Office. The bridge is the the only route to St. Helena, Harbor, Fripp and Hunting islands.

Cpl. Gary Maule of the S.C. Highway Patrol said Wednesday night that he was alerted of the situation when he began getting telephone complaints about traffic congestion. Maule immediately radioed officers on the scene with orders to stop the filming and let traffic pass.

He said a fire department dispatcher also called with concerns about the traffic holdup. Clayton Ellis, Lady's Island/St. Helena Island fire chief, said he was not offi-cially notified of the closure, but found out about it through an Emergency Medical Services employee who was working on the set of the movie.

"It was the wrong time to close it off because of all the traffic at that time of the day," Ellis said. "But one of the lanes was open for emergency traffic. But I had no prob-lem with it."

Maule said patrolmen from other parts of the state are handling operations for the film, which likely caused the confusion

Motorists bound for Lady's Island reported seeing a sign that read 'Mississippi Welcomes You' at the end of the bridge. Actor Tom Hanks was also spotted in the area.

Forrest Gump officials were unavailable for comment Wednesday evening.

Filming also will close the Woods Memorial Bridge to vehicular traffic from 6 a.m. to 3:30 p.m. Sunday. The closure will affect U.S. 21 from King Street in downtown Beaufort to Meridian Road on Lady's Island.

The bridge will be open to navigational traffic as usual, with possible slight delays, according to a news release from the S.C. Department of Transportation.

Local news article covering the traffic jam

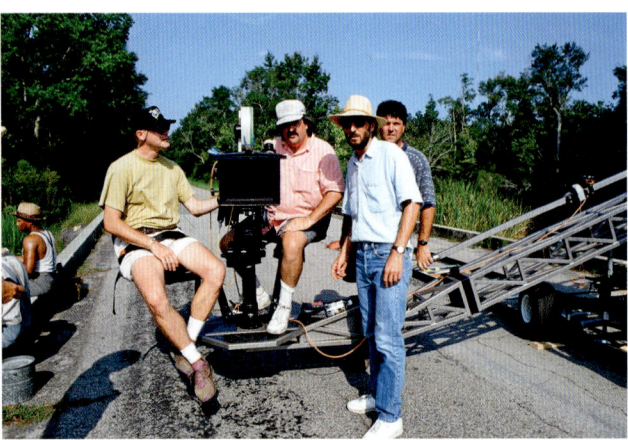

Lining up the shot

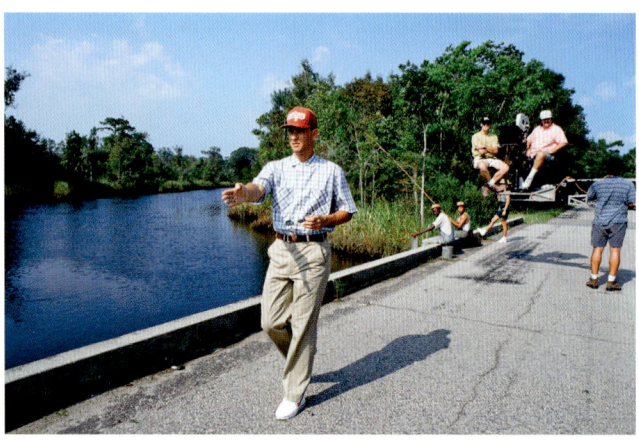

Tom as adult Forrest runs across the bridge,
re-creating young Forrest's run

I followed up that shot with one of Tom running across the same bridge that young Forrest had run across. Bob said to duplicate the shot as closely as I could. Tom knew much more about lining up a shot than I did. All I had to do was yell "Action," and the rest was done by Tom and Dave Dunlap.

In all the running shots we had done thus far, from Forrest leaving his front porch to crossing the state line into Mississippi, he was running alone, wearing the same clothes as when he left home. No wear and tear. But then the sequence jumped ahead in time. The next time we see Forrest on his journey, he has crossed the entire country, all the way to the Pacific Ocean. Then he turns around, heads east, and crosses the country back to the Atlantic.

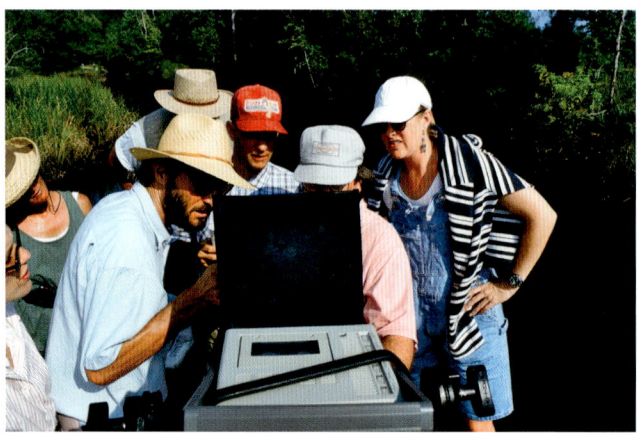

Checking the shot

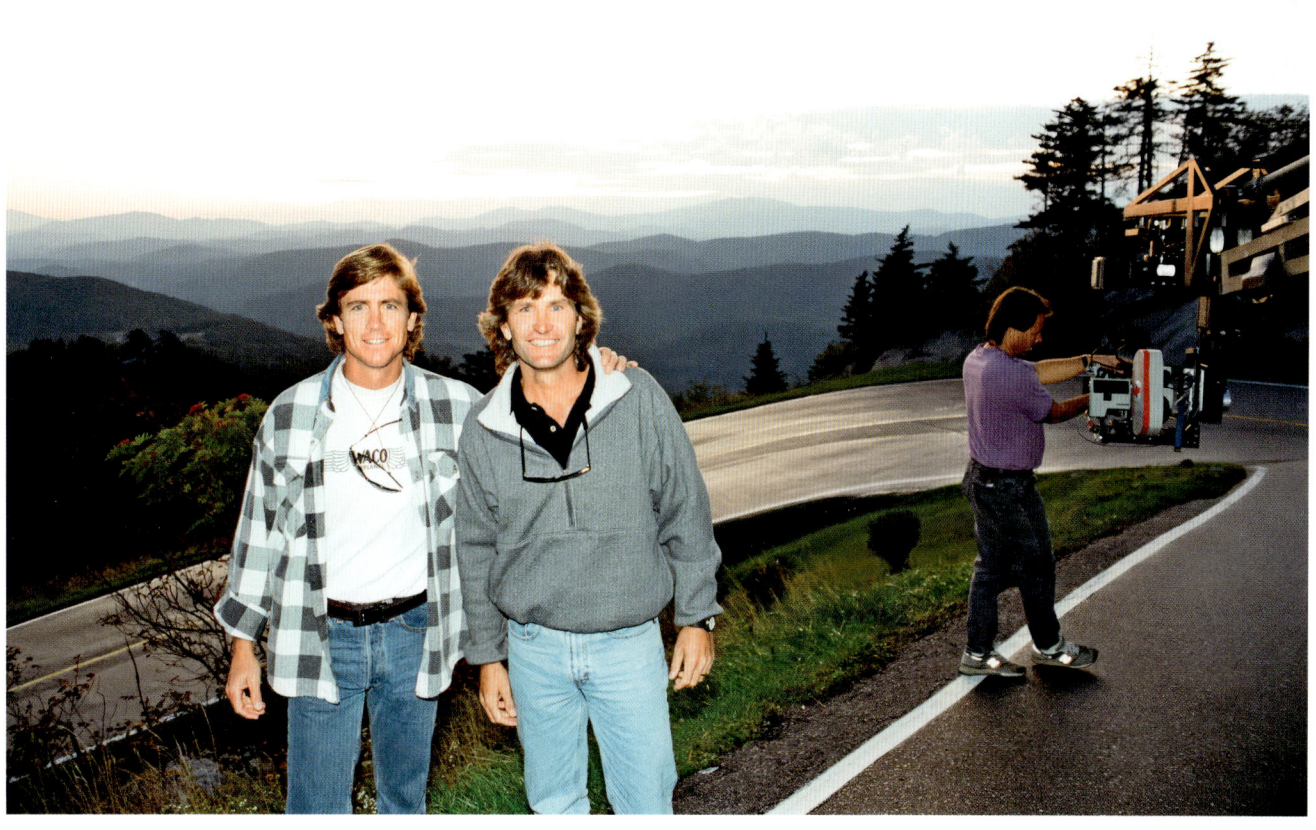

Chris Woods of Momentum Films with Don Burgess

We were completely unprepared to jump around during the shooting of this sequence, catching shots at various stages throughout his run. In addition, we had to start a special film unit—dubbed the Fantasy Unit—for the run, and the crew needed to know how Forrest looked wherever they were using Tom's "running double." We needed a meeting, and we needed it fast.

I assembled makeup, hair, and wardrobe along with the assistant directors and had Bob oversee a breakdown of the entire run, beginning to end. It started with Forrest reaching the West Coast for the first time. How long should his hair and beard be? What would his clothes look like? How long would it take him to get back to the East Coast, and what would he look like? He picks

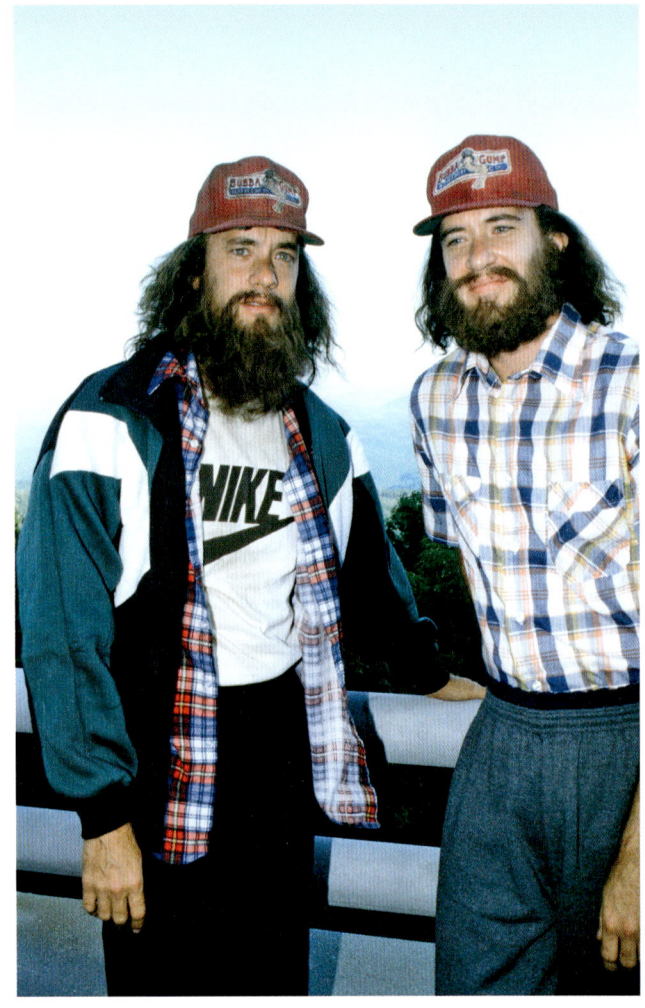

Tom, on the left, with his brother, Jim

The meeting became quite spirited. The group asked me how long it took to grow my beard. "I haven't shaved since 1972," I said, "so I can't remember." What about hair? Bob asked how long it would be in three months' time, or in a year or two years. When it came to wardrobe, the questions were more difficult. Does Forrest ever wash his clothes? Or does he simply stay in the same clothes until they wear out and then discard them and change into something else? What about when he gets cold? Where does he get a jacket? All these questions had to be answered, and right away.

The company we hired to shoot portions of the run, Momentum Films, normally produced commercials—most often car commercials in gorgeous landscapes. We needed the beauty shots the company was known for, but with a runner rather than an automobile. Don Burgess had recommended them, so we felt confident about the outcome.

Momentum was willing to cut its usual fee, since working in film was new to the company. But we needed to act fast. They would be heading out soon to the wheat fields of Nebraska and the towering peaks of the Rocky Mountains before the seasons changed. We also wanted to hit New England at the peak of the fall colors. We could not leave the meeting until we had all the answers.

A series of these shots would be done without Tom. For his running double, Tom decided on his brother, Jim. I recall standing outside the door to Tom's motor home, listening as he very carefully described Forrest's running style to Jim. Tom had

up an entourage along the way. When do these people start following him, and what are they wearing? And if they run with him for a number of months or years, how do their appearances change? We needed to know the answers to all these questions.

established the style, and he wanted perfection. His brother listened and watched Tom. Jim did a short run in the parking lot. Tom wasn't satisfied, so Jim did it again. Tom made corrections until Jim got it right.

Tom wished his brother well, but I knew he would have liked to do all the running shots himself. Tom did do most of the shots, but it nearly killed him. Combined with his other scenes in the film, he worked every minute of every day, often seven days a week.

We couldn't let ourselves get consumed by the cross-country run, however. We had a lot of other shooting to do. We were looking down the barrel of a gun at our work on Vietnam. The running shots would have to be slipped in as we dodged the bullets on the battlefield and those from the studio back home.

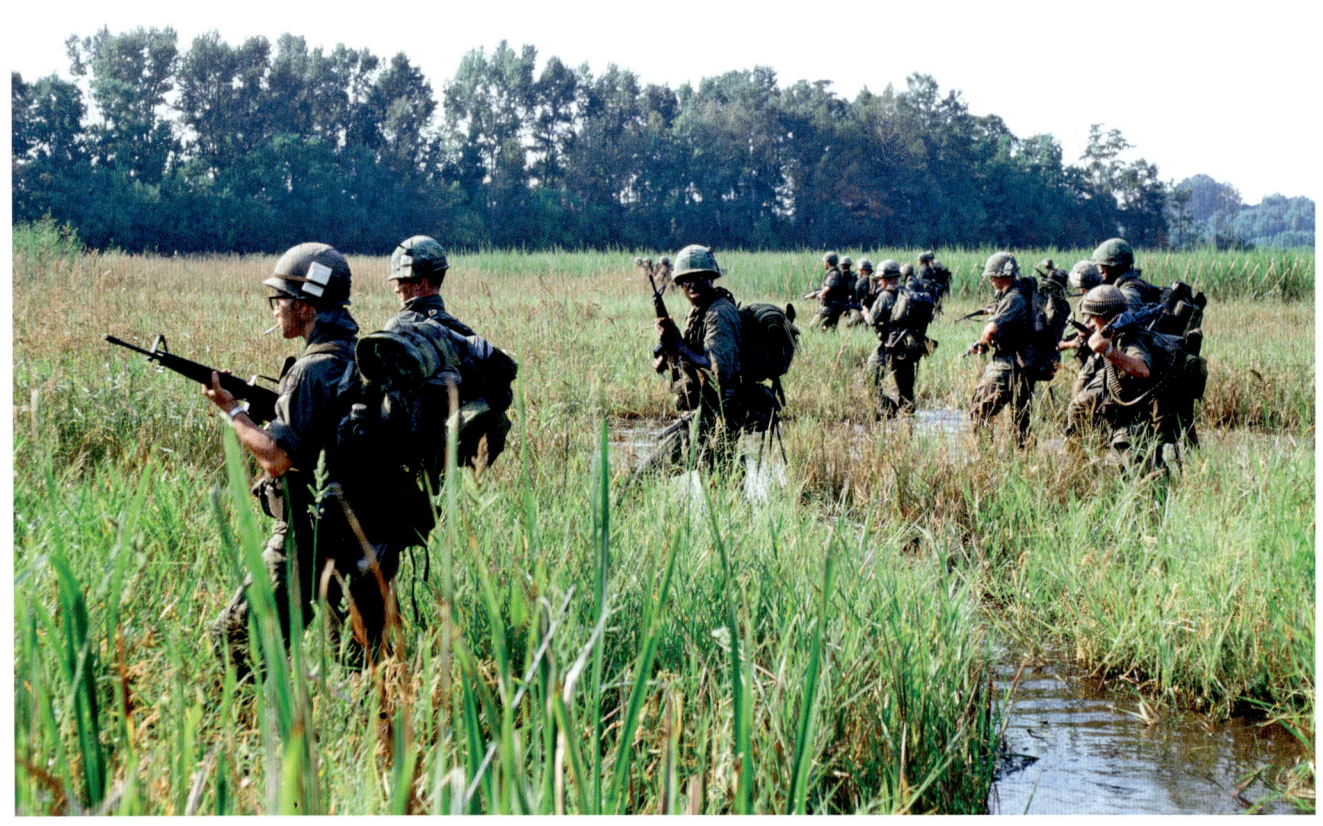

There's something happening here
But what it is ain't exactly clear
There's a man with a gun over there
Telling me I got to beware

I think it's time we stop,
Children, what's that sound?
Everybody look what's going down

FOR WHAT IT'S WORTH,
STEPHEN STILLS

9 | Vietnam

WHEN I ENTERED THE production offices in Beaufort, South Carolina, I felt like I was facing an insurrection. I was surrounded by cast members who had been hired to play marines in Forrest's troop in Vietnam. They were visibly upset, and some of them were ready to quit. These shell-shocked, sleep-deprived young men feared for their lives. It was not surprising. They had just spent a few days and nights going through basic training with Dale Dye.

Dale was a military man who learned about movies in the school of Oliver Stone, which is where we got his name. He had worked on *Platoon* and *Born on the Fourth of July,* to name a few of Oliver's films. As an enlisted marine, Dale had risen to the rank of master sergeant, and he never let the troops forget his rank.

He took the cast through a condensed boot camp, preparing them to act like soldiers in the field. They would learn how to wear their uniforms and keep them in top shape. They were trained to patrol in an orderly line and hold up or stop on command, carefully watching the hand signals of their platoon leader. The actors became experts

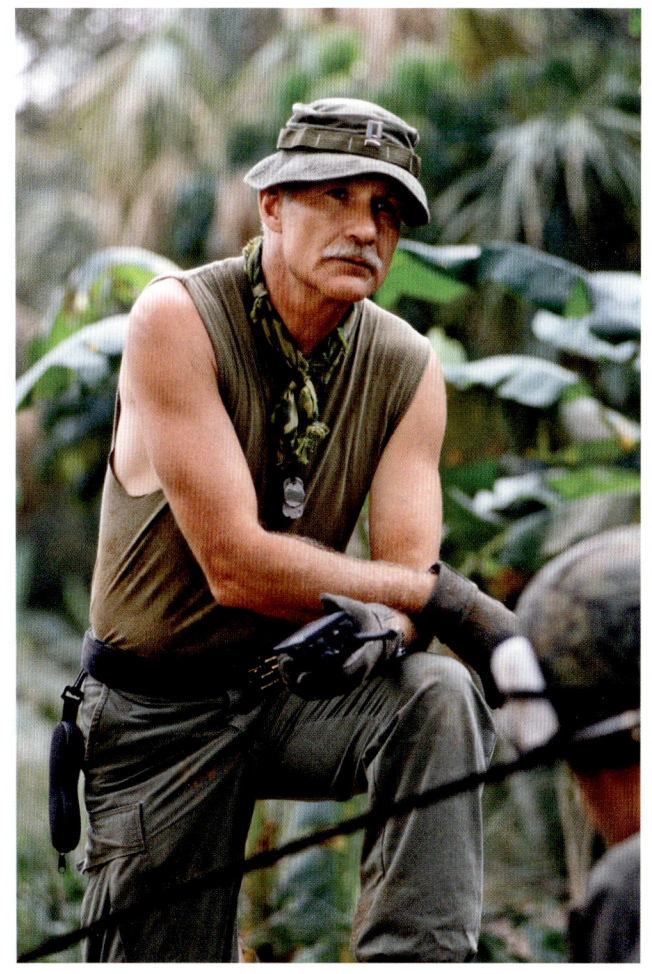

Dale Dye

95

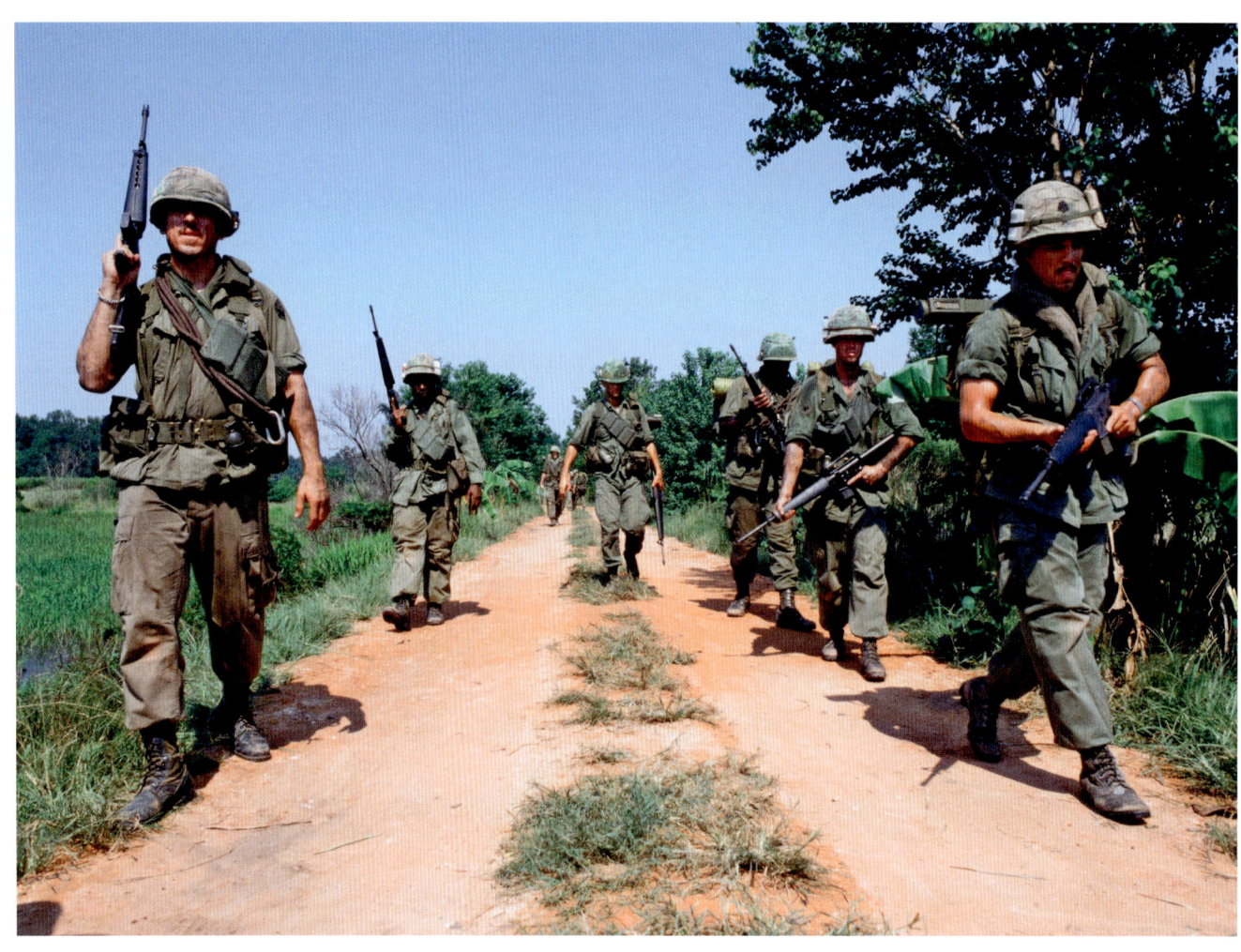

Actors marching following boot camp with Dale Dye

in how to handle and clean their weapons. Dale wanted them to appear on-screen as if they had gone through basic training and knew what they were doing. The cast had agreed to the training because actors generally like to understand their characters so they are believable. However, they did not expect Dale's brand of education.

We hired Dale after the army turned us down for support on the film. They found aspects of the script shed an unfavorable light on the military. Having the army as a partner would have had many advantages. Access to weapons, equipment, and uniforms would have made life easier for many departments and certainly for me. The transportation department would have had a place to acquire tanks and heavy machinery. Costumes would have been easier to rent. Props, including guns, would have come our way. All these things could be found elsewhere, but having the army working with us would have made the process smoother.

On the flip side, the army would have been looking over our shoulder every step of the way, watching every action and listening to every word, telling us, "You can't do this; you can't say that." Everything would have been spelled out in the contract, and we would have had to do things the army's way. And that would have driven Bob crazy. We were better off without them.

Instead, we had Dale Dye. He was the captain in command. The troops respected him. So did I. They also feared him, and now many of them wanted to go home. According to the young actors in my production office, Dale had set off gunshots and explosives, torn them from their beds, and scared the shit out of them. They hadn't signed up for this, they said. Of course, most of the kids who went to Vietnam didn't either.

I had told the actors and their agents that the cast would be training to become real soldiers. And I made it clear that if they did not want to go through the work, they shouldn't take the job. Now a few wanted out. One or two may have left, and I seem to remember that some grievances were filed. In any case, the actors' "boot camp" was worth it. When I saw the troops marching down the road, weapons at the ready, they looked good.

Tom, Gary Sinise, and Mykelti Williamson went through training as well, though not as intensely as the others. Still, their training was thorough. One day, on the way to lunch, Bob picked up Gary in his golf cart. As they approached base camp, Gary jumped off the cart and walked the final steps. He feared he might lose the respect of "his men" if they caught him taking a ride. And Dale had told him that he could *never* lose their respect.

Gary's first scene with Tom and Mykelti began with a joke.

LT. DAN
So, where you boys from in the world?

FORREST / BUBBA
Alabama, Sir...Alabama, Sir...

Lt. Dan stops and stares at Forrest in the eyes.

LT. DAN
Are you twins?

FORREST
(stupidly)
We're not relations, sir...

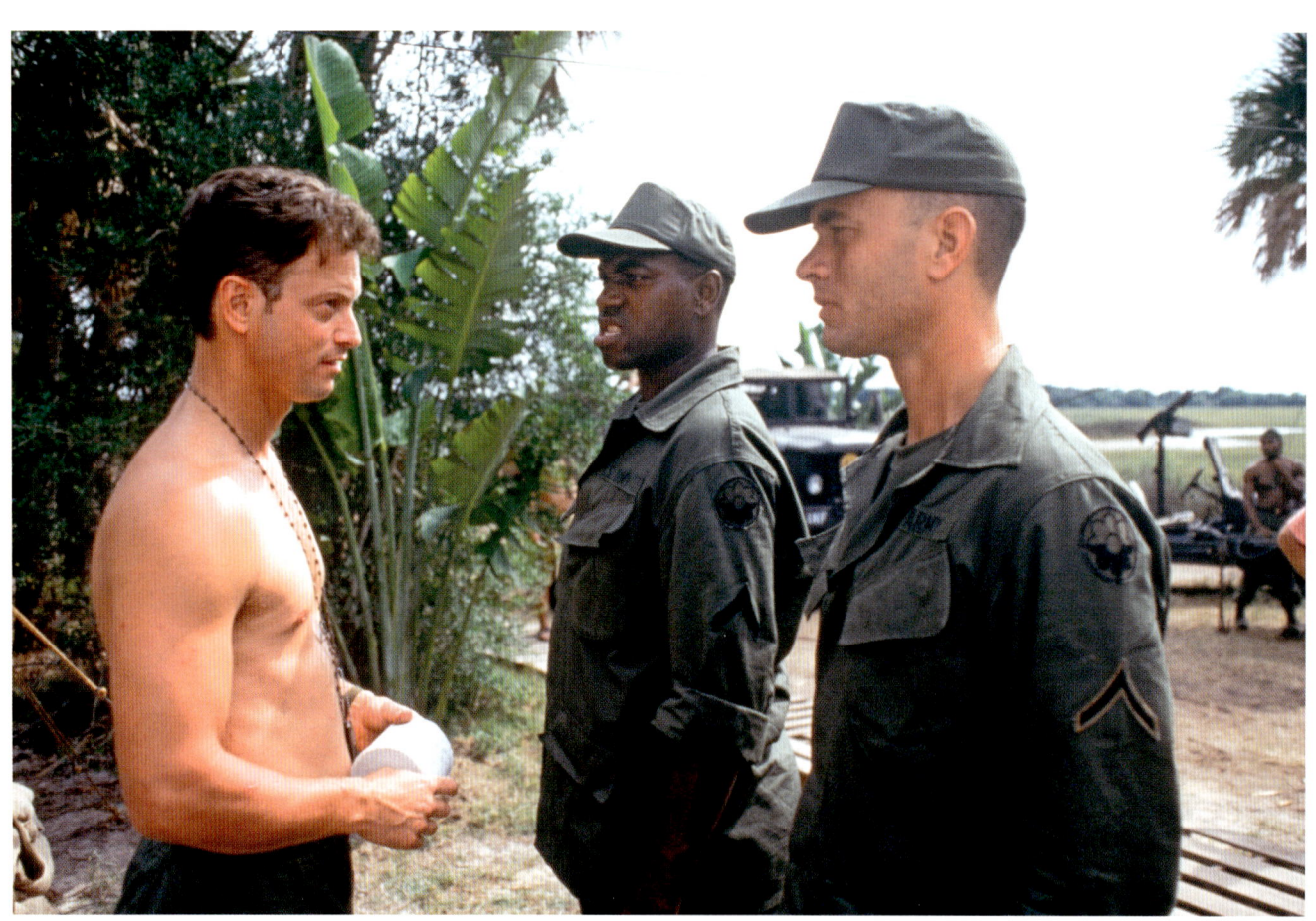

I enjoyed the deadpan exchange. What had preceded the joke wasn't a laughing matter, though, at least not for me. During the shooting of Forrest and Bubba's arrival by helicopter to the firebase, I was nervous. Picture a real helicopter almost touching down so its skids are about a foot off the ground. With the props still whirring, Tom and Mykelti step down, hold on to their hats, and cross to camp. I was terrified. Who was this pilot, anyway?

"Highly skilled," Dale reassured me. "Done countless missions in Vietnam." But one tiny error, and that would be that.

I had worked around helicopters when doing second-unit work on the *Back to the Future* films, and I had never felt safe then. Helicopter shots usually don't involve having actors inside the craft. The actors—or stunt persons—are typically on the ground doing the scene as the helicopter flies into position while the cameraman, peering through the open door, films the action taking place below. Now *that* can be hair-raising enough, even though the guys have done it countless times. But actors stepping out of a helicopter while it idles? That was a whole new ball game.

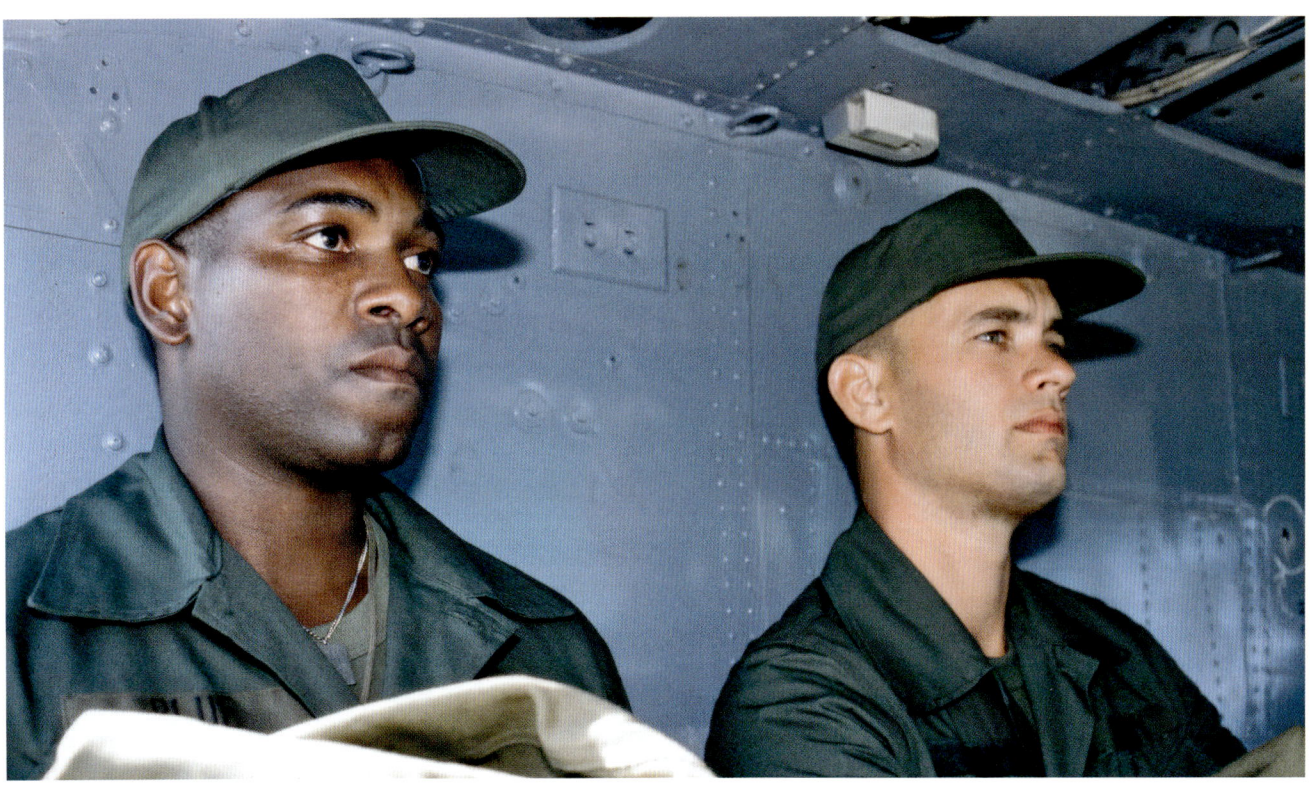

Bubba and Forrest in the cabin of the helicopter, ready for takeoff

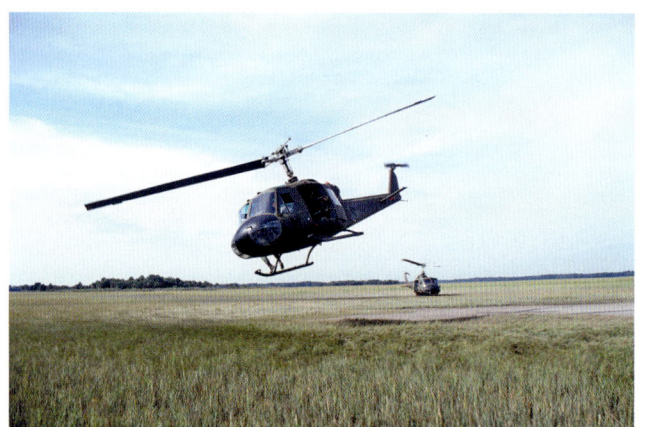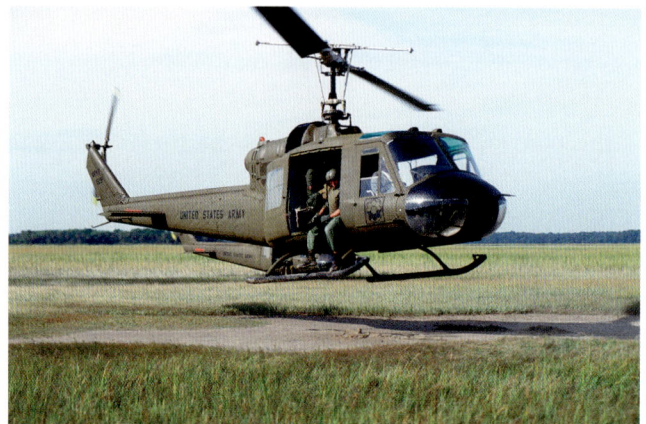

The helicopter lands in the marsh with the cast on board

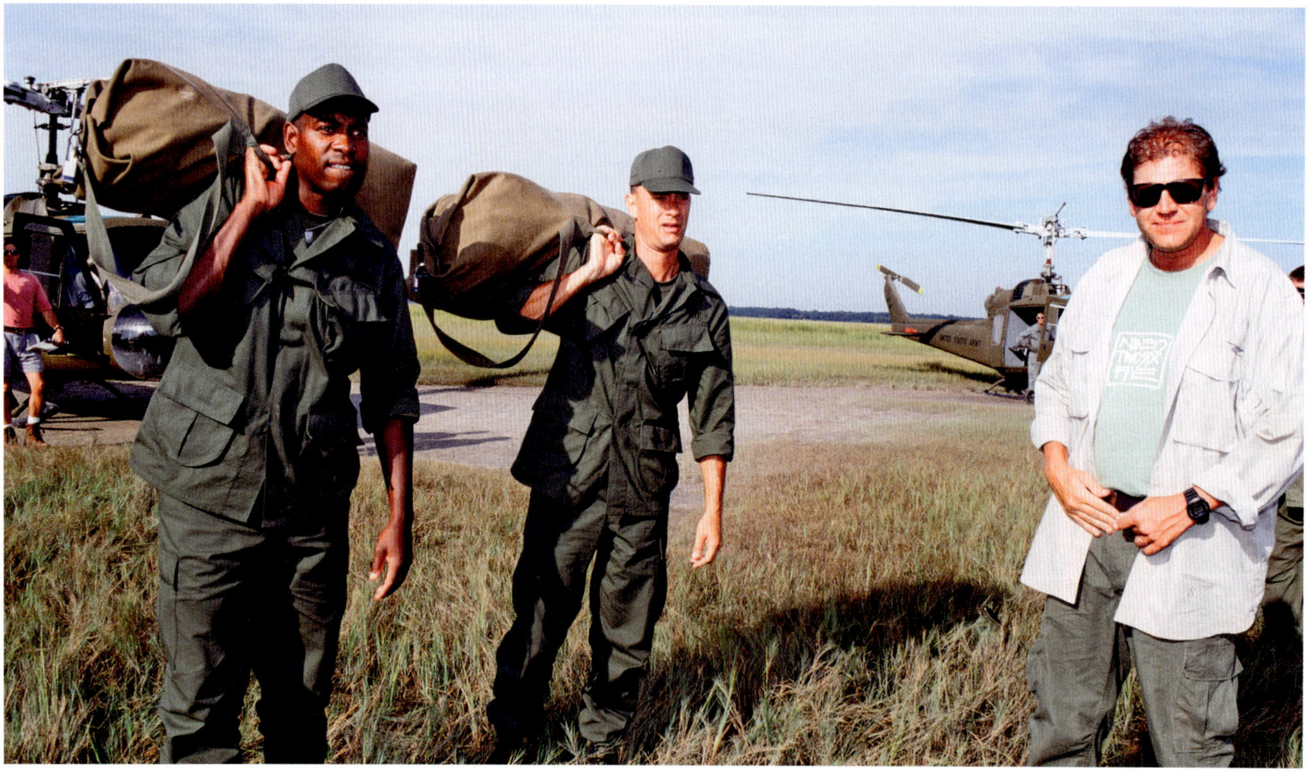

Mykelti, Tom, and Bob prepare to shoot

In this case, the pilot could not even set the helicopter down because the ground wasn't firm enough. I watched a few run-throughs done to perfection with stand-ins, and finally it was time for the principal cast to do a take. They got into the helicopter, and it spun away into the sky for the approach and landing. With absolute precision, the pilot set the bird down as close to the ground as possible, and just like clockwork the actors jumped out, held on to their hats, cleared the prop wash, and ran to base camp. Looked good to me.

Then Bob said, "Let's do another."

Generally, you like to have a few good takes to work with in the editing room. This time, though, I thought one good take was enough. We had dodged a bullet. I couldn't believe I had to stand there and be terrified as we did it again. I have never been happier than when I saw the helicopter fly off into the distance for the last time.

As the troops left base camp, it started to rain, with additional help from the special-effects guys.

```
...big old fat rain, rain that flew
sideways, and sometimes rain that
seemed to come straight up from the
ground.
```

To protect the actors when they crossed the swamp in the rain, we set off explosive charges so no dangerous snakes would remain hidden in the marsh. We even wrapped wire mesh around the actors' legs to prevent snakebites.

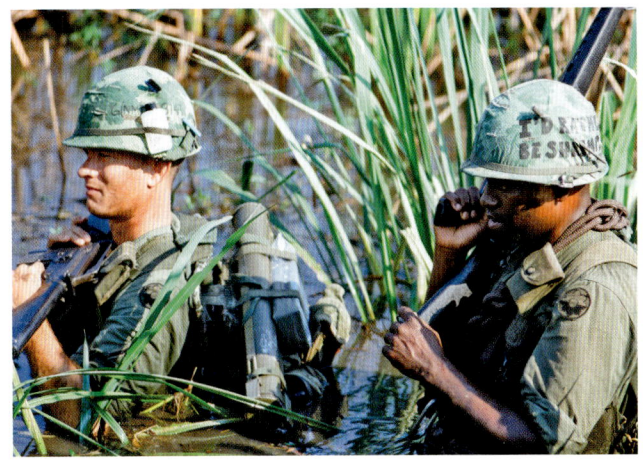

```
And we see the rain just suddenly
stop on a dime. Afternoon sunlight
bathes the Boys. They start taking
off their rain ponchos...And sud-
denly, they're hit with tremendous
FIRE, rockets and machine guns, from
the surrounding jungle.
```

While the enemy fire poured in, Bob decided we would never show the Viet Cong. Instead, Bob shot the entire scene from Forrest's point of view. This came as a big relief to me. It saved the production from having to cast, outfit, and film the enemy's side of the story. In fact, Bob maintains the main character's point of view in all his films. In scenes like this, that has a terrifying effect.

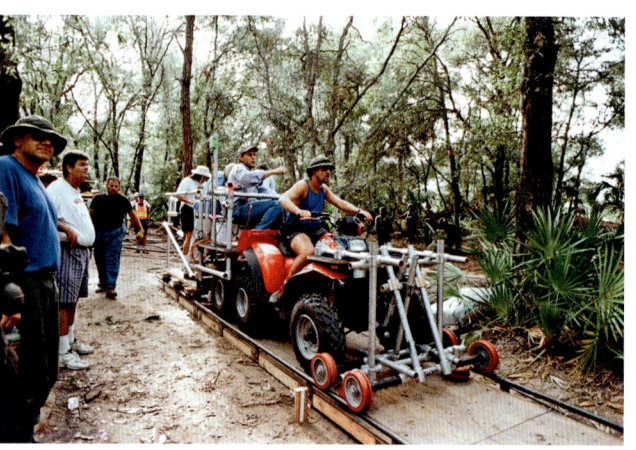 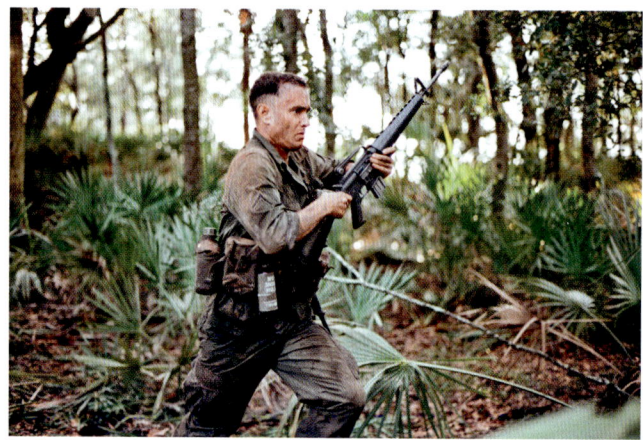

Camera on a dolly filming Forrest running through the jungle

When the shelling began, all the troops could do was run.

                    LT. DAN
              (shouting to the boys)
         Pull back...! Pull back...!

And we see Bubba and the Boys begin running back through the clearing toward the mango grove for safety. Lieutenant Dan sees Forrest still standing there, frozen. Continuing to fire, Lieutenant Dan moves over to Forrest and screams into his face:

                    LT. DAN
         Run, Gump! Goddamn-it, run!

And just as Jenny once told him to, Forrest runs like hell. Until he suddenly stops and, facing enemy fire, returns to look for his friend Bubba. While searching for Bubba, he rescues one injured soldier after another. To shoot these vignettes economically, Bruce Moriarty and I had met the preceding Sunday to pinpoint the location of each injured soldier that Forrest would pick up off the jungle floor. We selected spots close to one another along the same dirt road, which got us through the day quickly. We also had a Forrest stunt double do some of the heavy lifting along with Tom.

Bob had designed the shot of Forrest emerging from the jungle with Bubba in his arms running straight toward the camera. Bombs were exploding close behind them. Since Mykelti was too heavy for Tom to carry while running, we did the scene in two parts. First we put Mykelti in a harness and suspended him on wires from a construction crane. As Forrest runs, cradling Bubba's body, we moved the arm of the crane forward. This way, Tom wouldn't have to bear Mykelti's body weight. It was a bit tricky to get the arm to move at the same pace as Tom, but it worked.

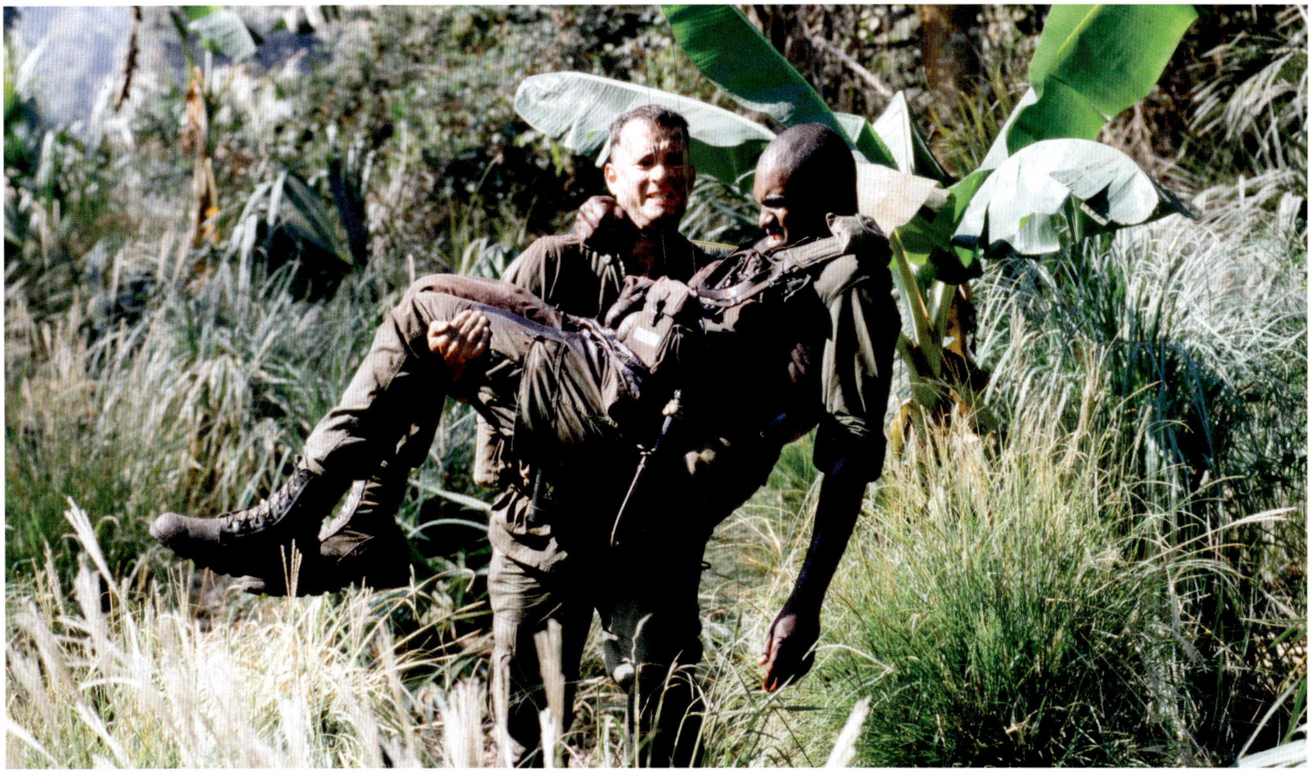

Tom carries Mykelti, who is suspended by wires from a crane

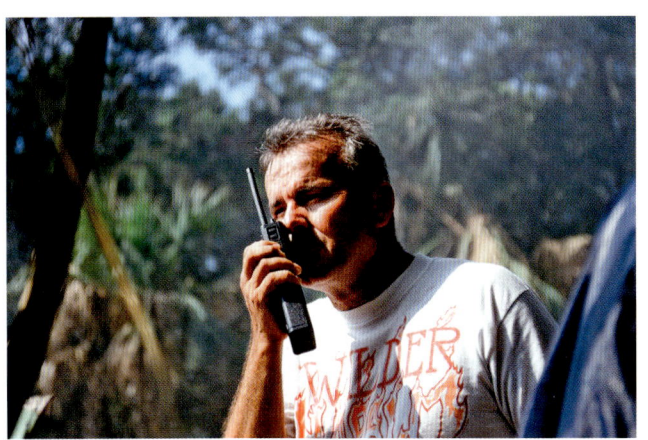

Alan Hall, communicating by walkie-talkie with his crew

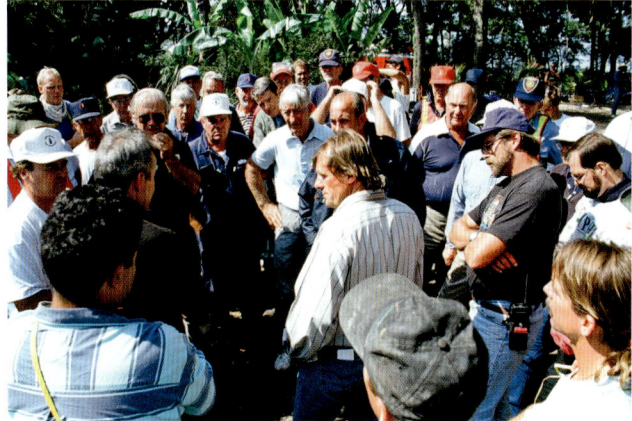

Bruce Moriarty, back to camera, leads a safety meeting

After that shot, we set off a giant explosion without anyone in the frame. We'd been granted permission to do that in an area designated for a future golf course. Before we detonated the explosion, we had a safety meeting led by Bruce Moriarty. Alan Hall, the effects supervisor, was given specific protocols before pulling the trigger.

However, when the explosion went off, Bob was nowhere in sight. None of the assistant directors around the camera had double-checked to see if Bob was in his viewing tent, a safe distance from the set. The rest of us were much further away from the action, so we didn't notice his absence. When Bob heard the explosion, he raced back to the set, thinking there had been an accident and the explosion had happened prematurely. The fire from the explosion was quickly doused by the volunteer fire department on Fripp Island.

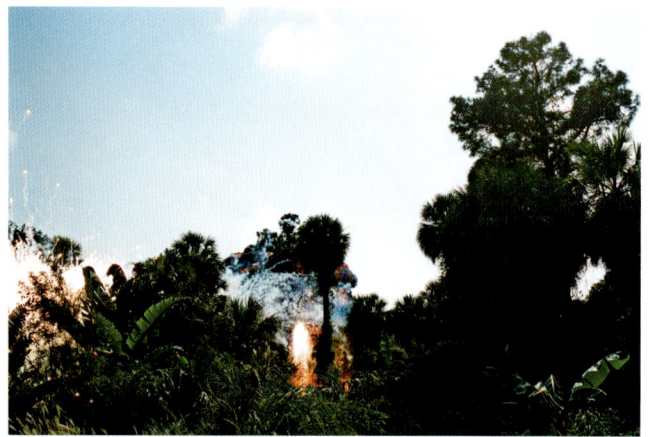

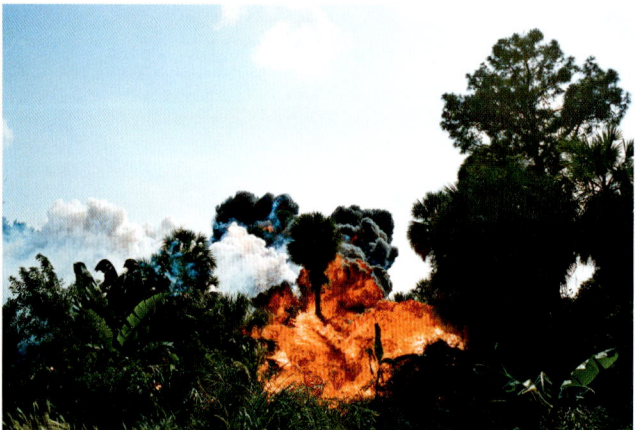

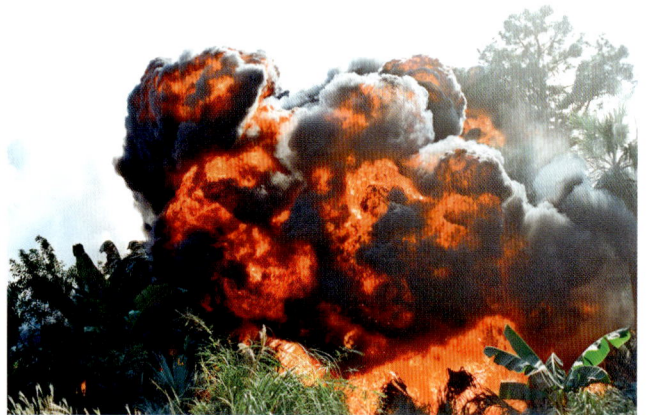

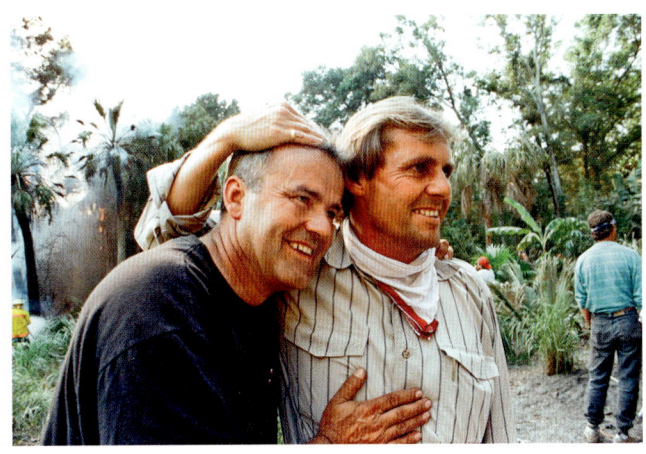

Bruce Moriarty, on the right, congratulates Alan Hall, the effects supervisor, after the explosion

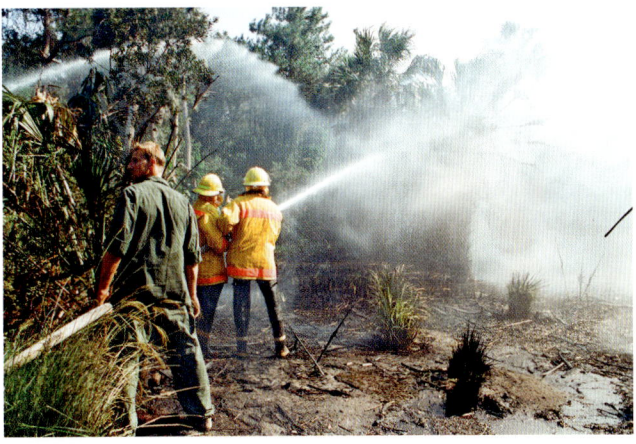

Volunteer firefighters extinguish the flames

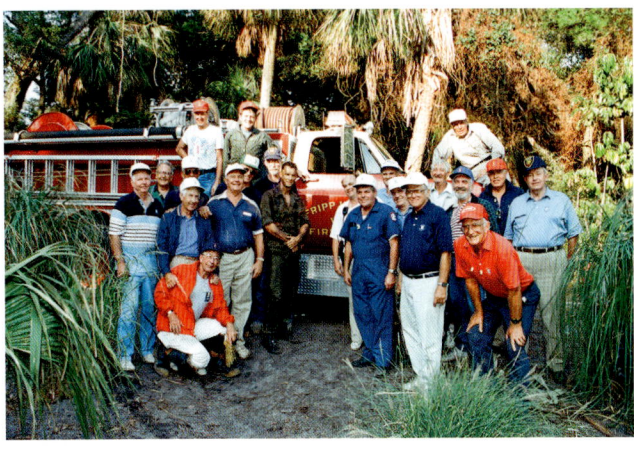

Fripp Island volunteer fire department with Tom Hanks

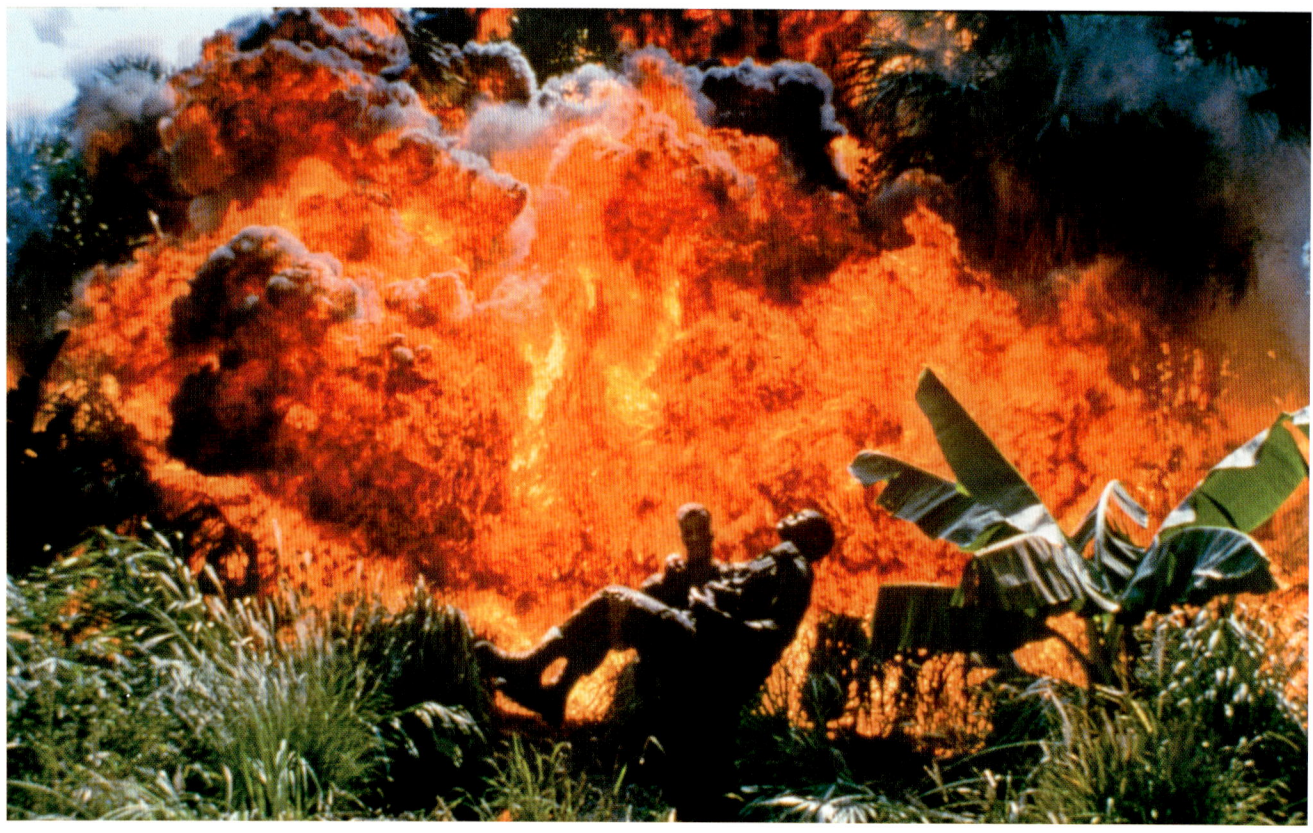

Everything was fine, and in fact, the scene came off without a hitch. It all looked perfect when Ken Ralston put the two parts together at ILM, adding planes strafing the jungle and appearing to set off the explosions.

Dale Dye approached me after filming the final shots in the jungle and said this location was exactly like the Mekong Delta. He thought it was the most accurate filming of the Vietnam experience he had ever seen.

I don't think he was simply patting himself on the back. The scenes had unnerved him. His steely expression had vanished. He looked as fearful as a young recruit.

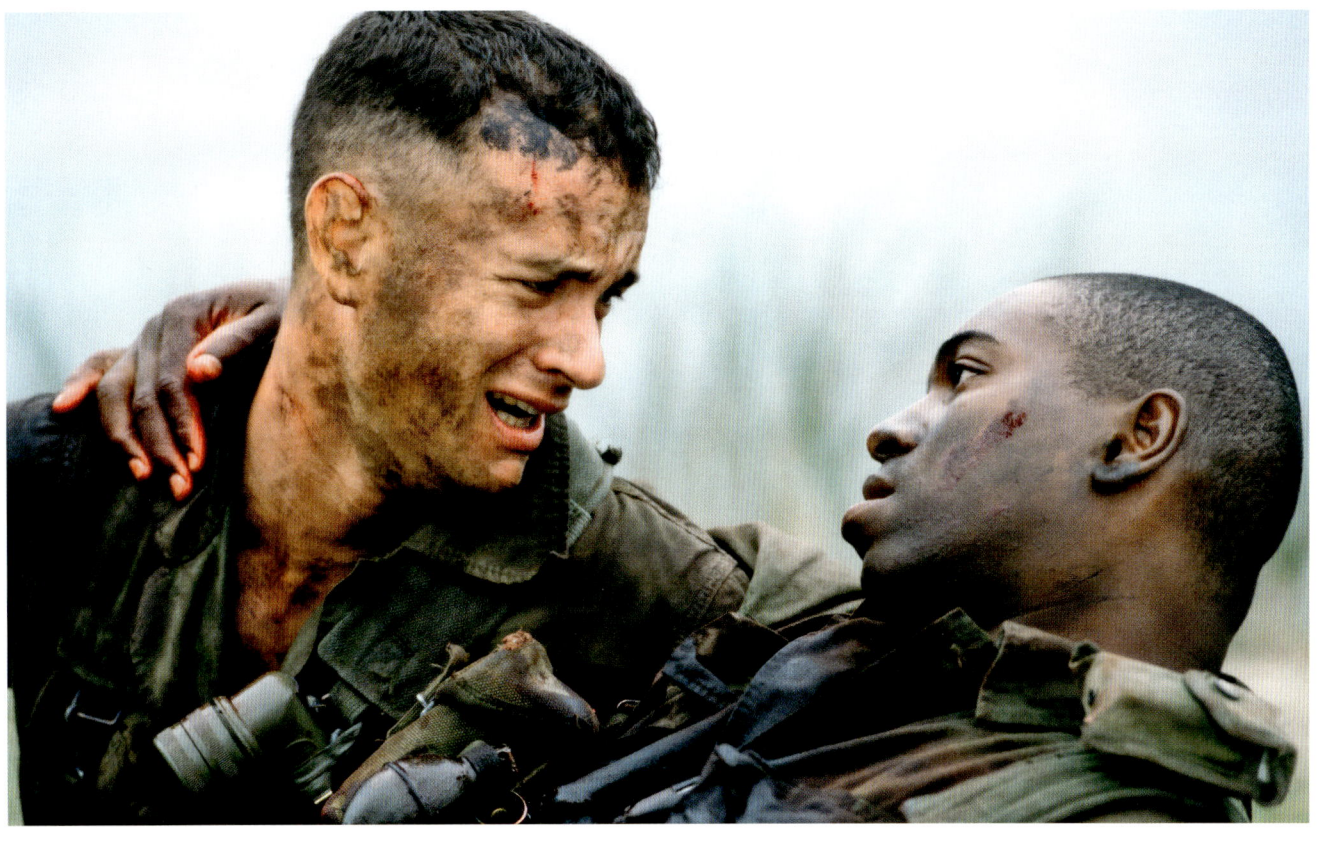

                              BUBBA
              Forrest, why'd this happen?

                          FORREST (V.O.)
              Then Bubba said something I won't ever forget.

                              BUBBA
                            (poignant)
              I want to go home.

        Bubba squeezes Forrest's hand.

                          FORREST (V.O.)
              Bubba was my best good friend. And even I know that's
              something you can't just find around the corner.

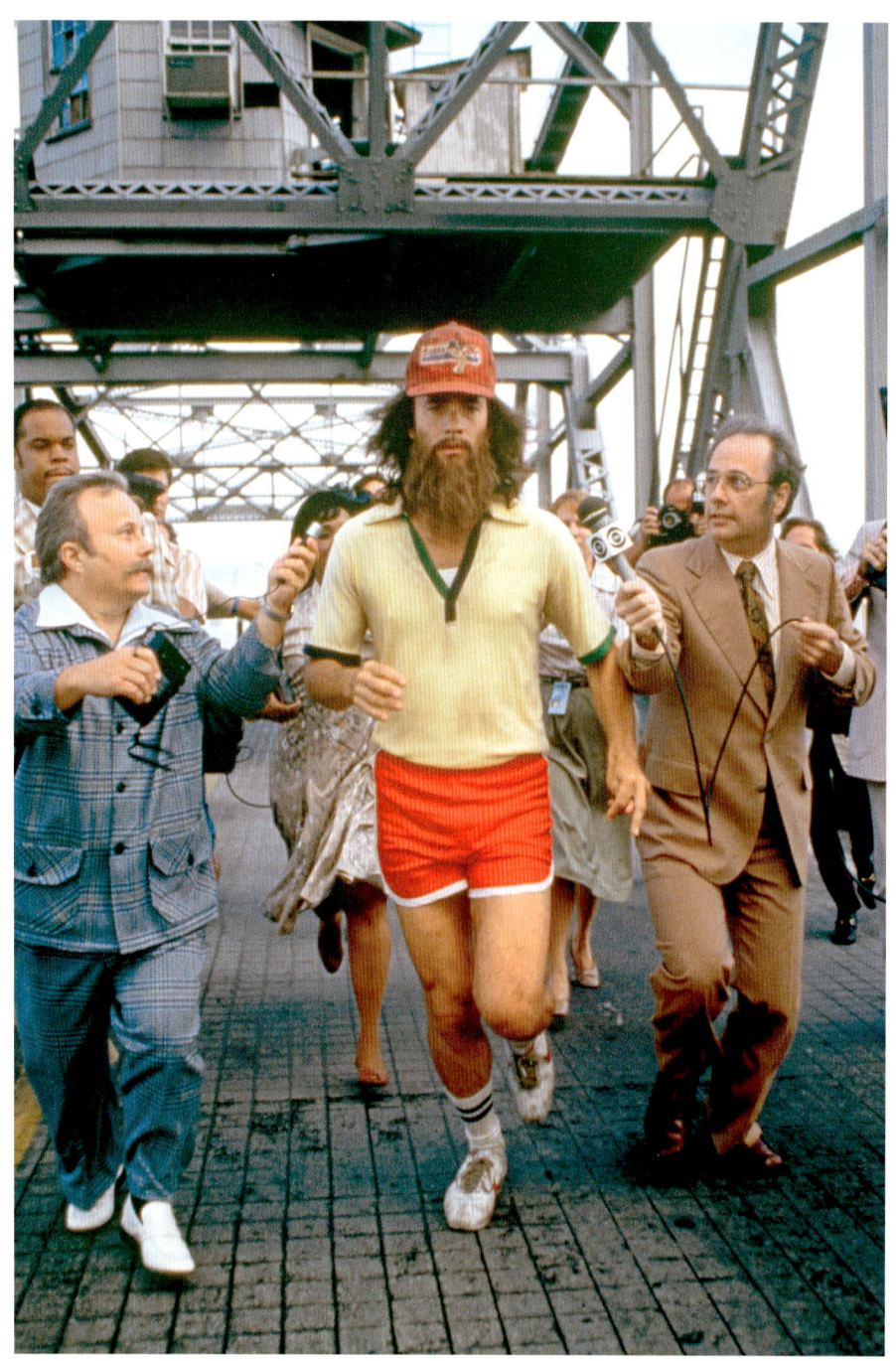

10 | Runnin' on Empty

"CAN'T YOU JUST LET ME DIE and go home?" These were not the words of a young recruit in Vietnam. This is probably what Sally Field was thinking. She was done. She was tired of waiting. We had kept her locked up long enough. Much to her dismay, Sally still had a few scenes left, including her dying scene, which prevented her from wrapping up her work and going home. We'd extended her time in South Carolina by almost two weeks, much longer than she expected, while we finished the Vietnam sequence. When you have a scene that provides cover for bad weather in the South in the summer, you have to take advantage of it. We'd found that out the first week, when we narrowly escaped Hurricane Emily. I felt terrible about it, but Sally would have to wait.

We had already done a makeup test for the look of the dying Mama Gump, so we would be ready to shoot on a moment's notice. We hired one of the best prosthetic artists to fabricate and apply the character's final look. When Sally appeared in front of the camera for her test, though, everyone was speechless. Sally's face was gone. We couldn't see her expressions. The prosthetic had killed her character.

Bob didn't know what to say or do. Neither did I. I had never been in this situation before. I felt a tap on my shoulder. Danny Striepeke, Tom's legendary makeup artist, had come up behind me and whispered in my ear. He discreetly said that the prosthetic was destroying Sally's look and her ability to act. He asked for a chance to try his own aging makeup on her. His solution would be simple. He just needed an afternoon to make a few little pieces that he would apply to her eyes and around her mouth. He would do the rest with traditional makeup. "Trust me. I know what to do," he said.

We had no choice and were relieved that Danny was confident he could solve the problem. He not only solved the problem, but it looked completely natural. All of Sally's emotions came through beautifully.

In addition, Sally's time in the makeup chair was reduced from many hours to the usual hour plus. We said good-bye and thanks but no thanks to the initial makeup designer and planned to shoot the scene with Danny in charge. Danny was one of the many excellent crew members on the

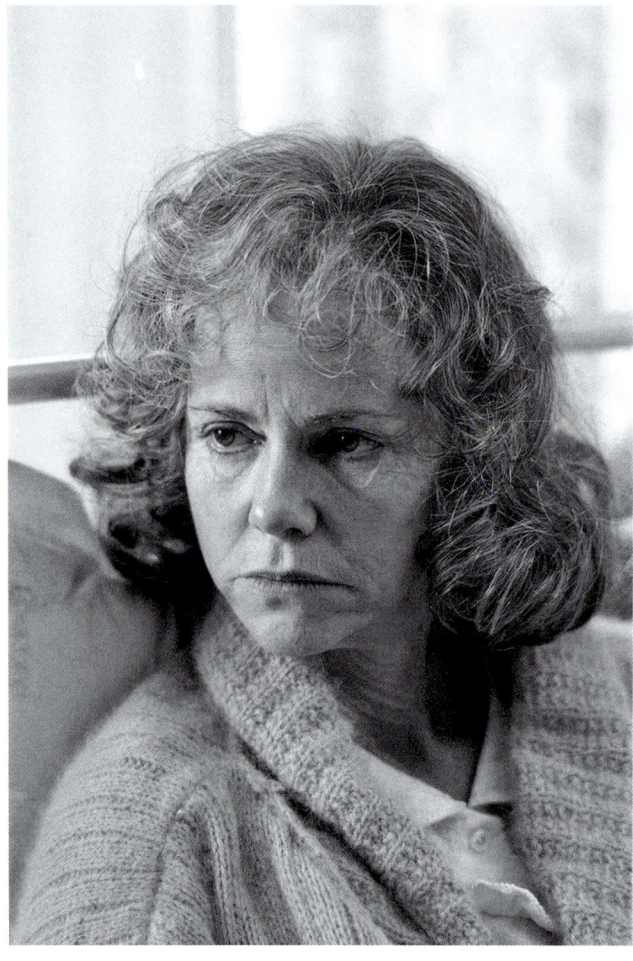

Sally Field, with aging makeup by Danny Striepeke

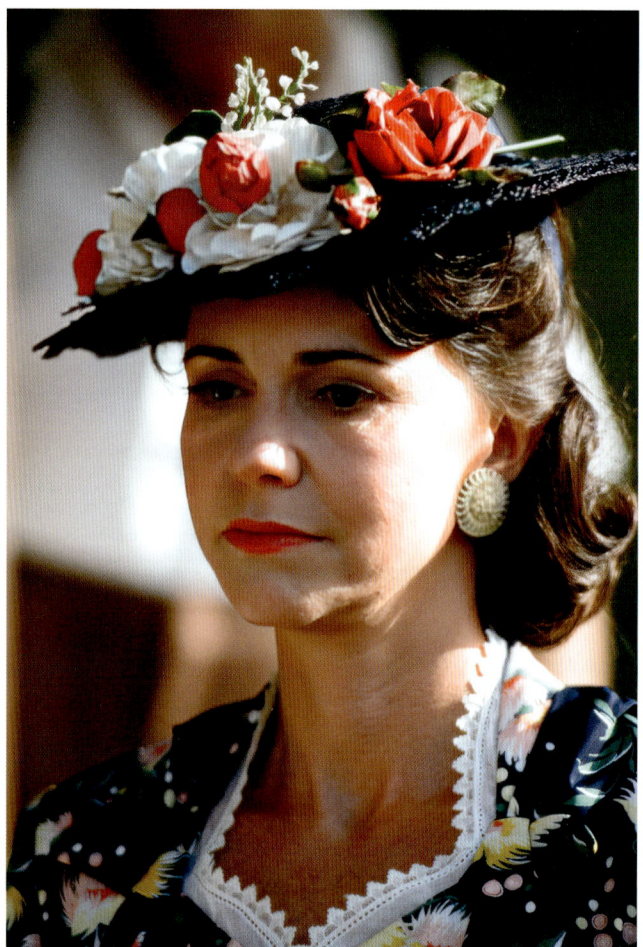

Young Mrs. Gump

film. And we needed them all to accomplish what we set out to do because the schedule was becoming more grueling by the day.

———————

The Vietnam scenes had taken their toll, and we had gone another day over schedule. We were now up to sixty-eight days, four more than we had budgeted for. The costs were really starting to mount. Long days could not be avoided. We stepped up the intensity. We had been shooting six days a week, but that was about to change. A Sunday shoot was looming, the first of a string of working Sundays.

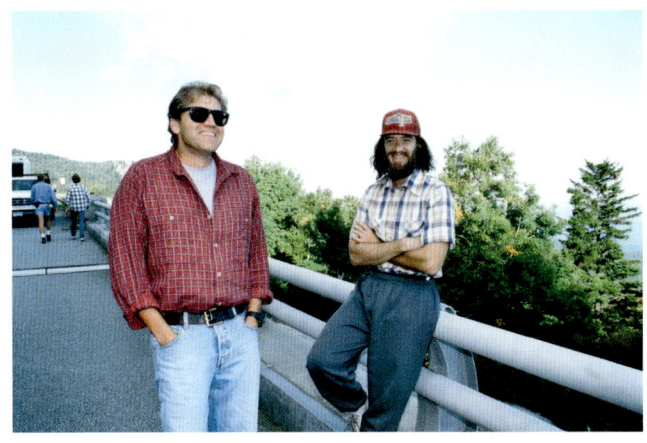

Bob and Tom on the Blue Ridge Parkway, waiting to shoot

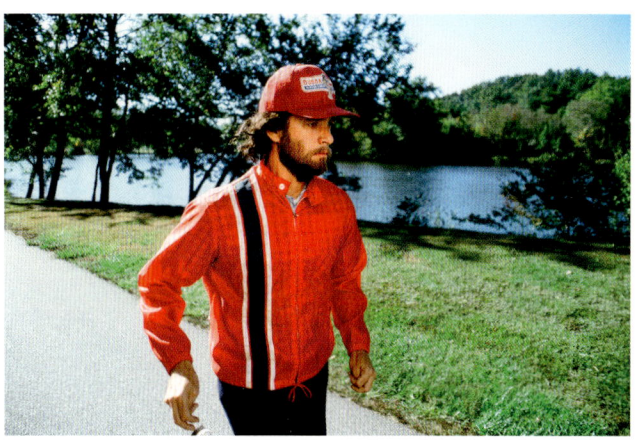

Forrest runs by a lake at the Biltmore Estate

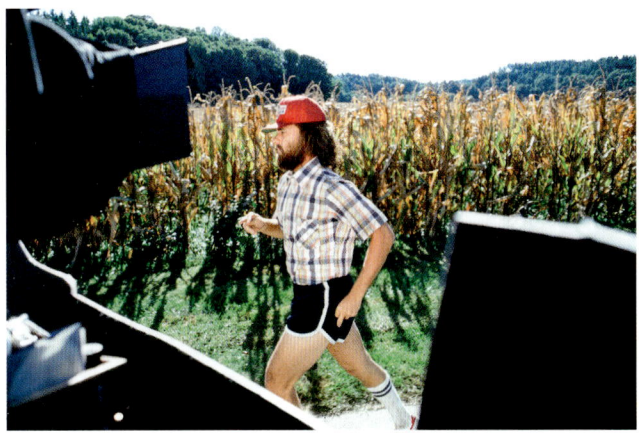

Filming the run past a cornfield at the Biltmore Estate

We planned to travel to Asheville, North Carolina, and shoot some of Forrest's run in the Blue Ridge Mountains and at the Biltmore Estate. This work was assigned to the SS unit, despite the fact that Bob and Tom; Tom's hair, makeup, and wardrobe team; the first assistant director; and Don

Burgess would all be with us. They were essential. The rest of the crew would be provided by Momentum Films. The scope of that company's work was growing, but we had no choice. And all this Sunday work was for scenes the studio didn't even want in the film!

We chartered a plane. Bob, Tom, and the selected crew would leave after work on Saturday, shoot all day Sunday, and return to South Carolina on Sunday night, ready to work again on Monday morning. The question was, how could I reconcile this with the budget? My small allowance for the entire run was dwindling fast. I had used some of the money to pay for the beauty shots throughout the country with Tom's brother as his double. And I still had a long way to go. The good news was that we got a lot of bang for our buck. There were wheat fields and vineyards at the Biltmore Estate, and the Blue Ridge Parkway, which Momentum

111

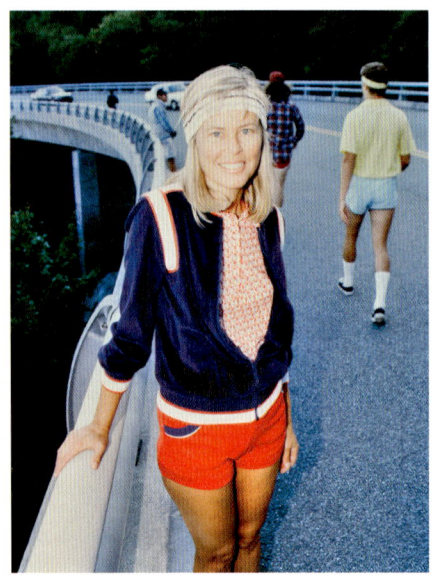

My wife, Liv, as an extra

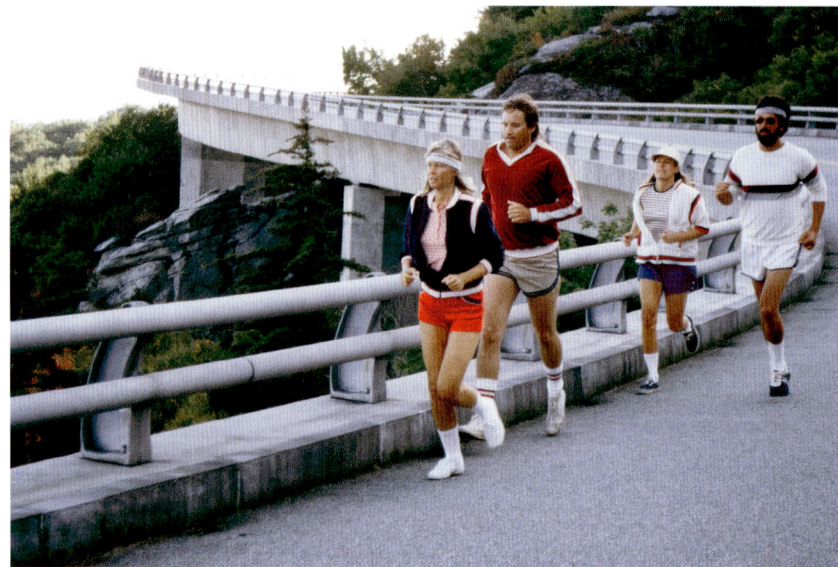

Liv in a shot that was cut from the film

Films had used for some of its car commercials, was spectacular.

I felt sorry for my wife, Liv. Our costume designer, Joanna Johnston, thought Liv would make a great addition to the short line of runners trailing behind Forrest. Take after take, she ran up around a bend in the highway. The shot was used, but not the piece with Liv running. That was cut from the film.

Years earlier Liv had worked as an extra alongside Bob Hoskins in a scene from *Roger Rabbit.* She was cut from that scene, too. Liv said that was it. Her days as an extra were over.

Back at work on Monday morning, we fought our way through the final scenes in Vietnam. We may have made it out of the jungle, but, as often happens when making movies, we had to shoot the beginning of the sequence last: Forrest meeting Bubba on the bus to boot camp. This was followed by Forrest going through basic training with his overbearing drill sergeant in the barracks.

In the meantime, I was plotting the next excursion for the Starkey unit to shoot more of Forrest's run. I had been tracking the changing colors of the fall leaves in the Northeast. A band of color had crossed the Canadian border and was moving south, approaching New England. The trees were expected to hit their peak color in Vermont at the end of the week.

We quickly set our sights on another Sunday day trip for the crucial shots of Forrest running among the beautiful autumn leaves. The trip would also give us an opportunity to film Forrest reaching a lighthouse on the East Coast after crisscrossing the country. Not only did I need to figure out how to piggyback the two; I also had to plot how to pull off yet another unbudgeted Sunday of work.

I thought if I left South Carolina toward the end of the shooting day on Thursday, I could fly to New England and start scouting and setting up the locations early on Friday. The Marshall Point Lighthouse in Port Clyde, Maine, would be our first stop. Momentum Films would meet me in Maine to get things started. From there we would fly to Vermont and take a day and a half to find and secure the locations for Forrest's run with the fall leaves in the background. Then Saturday night Bob and Tom and the rest of the group would join us; we would shoot on Sunday and then fly home. With that plan set, I could turn my mind to finding the money for the weekend work.

Late Thursday afternoon I headed to the airport for my New England adventure, leaving Bubba and Forrest scrubbing the floor of the barracks with toothbrushes, while Bubba counted the ways to prepare shrimp.

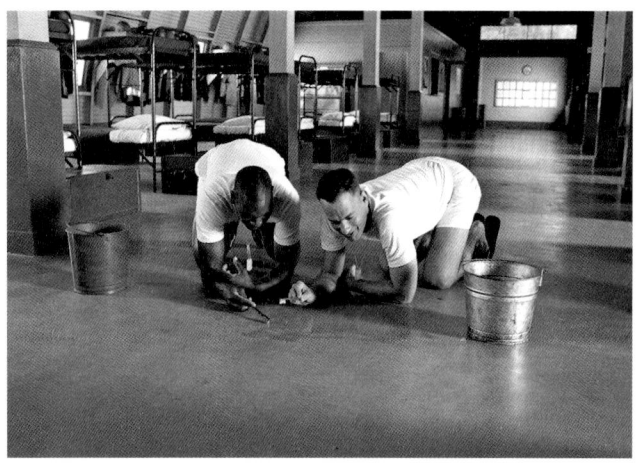

                    BUBBA
          (dreams about shrimping)
     ...like I was saying, shrimp is
     the fruit of the sea...You can
     barbeque it, boil it, broil it,
     bake it, saute it...

Similarly, I started to count the ways I could fund the trip. The extras account, the wardrobe account, the props account, and the set-dressing account all had allowances for purchases and rentals. I could take a bit from each.

                    BUBBA
               (continuing)
     There's shrimp kabobs, shrimp
     creole, shrimp gumbo...pan
     fried, deep fried, stir fried...

There were the overtime accounts. I could pinch each department for unspent overtime and extra Saturdays and Sundays not yet worked.

                    BUBBA
     There's pineapple shrimp, lemon
     shrimp, coconut shrimp, pepper
     shrimp, shrimp soup, shrimp
     stew, shrimp salad...

I could tap into the above-the-line travel and living expenses to charter the plane and pay for hotels.

```
            BUBBA
shrimp  and  potatoes,  shrimp
burgers, shrimp sandwiches...
That's about it.
```

That was about it for me too. I had exhausted all my ideas for diving for dollars. Did I really think the studio wouldn't notice my shenanigans? Studio executive Michelle Manning seemed to be looking the other way. I was feeling fine about the plan, so I forged ahead, not worrying about the possible consequences.

I spent the night in Boston, woke up early, boarded a small chartered plane, and landed in Rockland, Maine, a short distance from the Port Clyde lighthouse, which we had seen only in photos. I stood along the path leading to the lighthouse and imagined Forrest running as far east as he could. The location felt good.

E. J. Foerster, the producer from Momentum Films, had arranged for a grip crew to meet me at the location. They were armed and ready to build camera platforms, and we reviewed what we were planning to shoot. Bob and I had gone over the storyboards for the shots before I left town. He had two setups, one wide and one closer, both following Forrest as he ran out to the lighthouse, turned around, and headed back west. Using a viewfinder,

I made my best guess and marked the spots where to set the platforms. We could change the locations of the cameras when Bob arrived, but this would save time later.

———————

We jumped back on the plane and headed to Rutland, Vermont, to scout for the perfect fall leaves. Hitting the ground running, we passed through the town of Woodstock and aimed for Jenne Farm, an idyllic property nearby. Along the dirt road leading to the farmhouse, there was a beautiful stand of trees on the right and a grassy slope rising on the left. It was easy to imagine Forrest running under a blaze of orange, red, and yellow leaves in all their glory. Not a bad start. An old codger owned the place, and we made a deal to shoot on Sunday morning. With that in our hip pocket, we headed to Killington, where we had rented a condo.

The following day we searched the back roads of Vermont from morning to night. The scenery was so beautiful that I felt as if I were on vacation. In addition to the hero shot of Forrest against a backdrop of autumn color, we were trying to find trees that could make a canopy over Forrest as he ran. It turned out that the best locations were at Jenne Farm and along a nearby country road. We took mountains of photographs to show to Bob when he arrived that night.

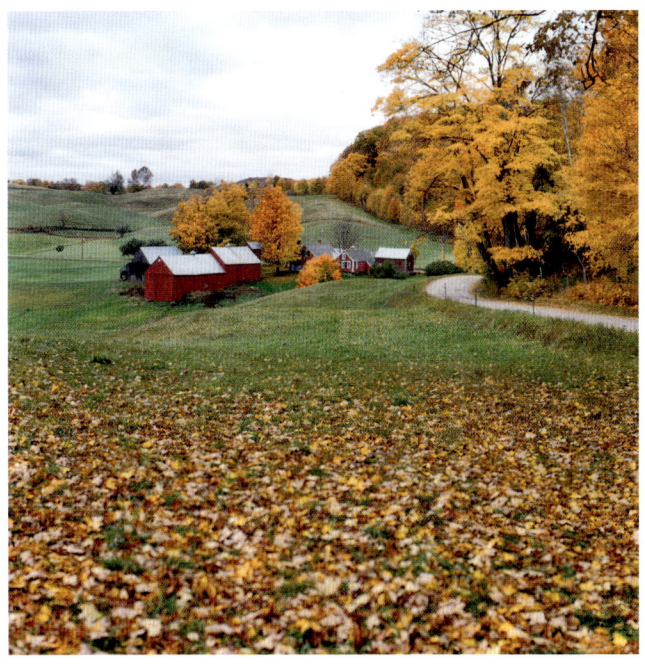

Jenne Farm in Rutland, Vermont

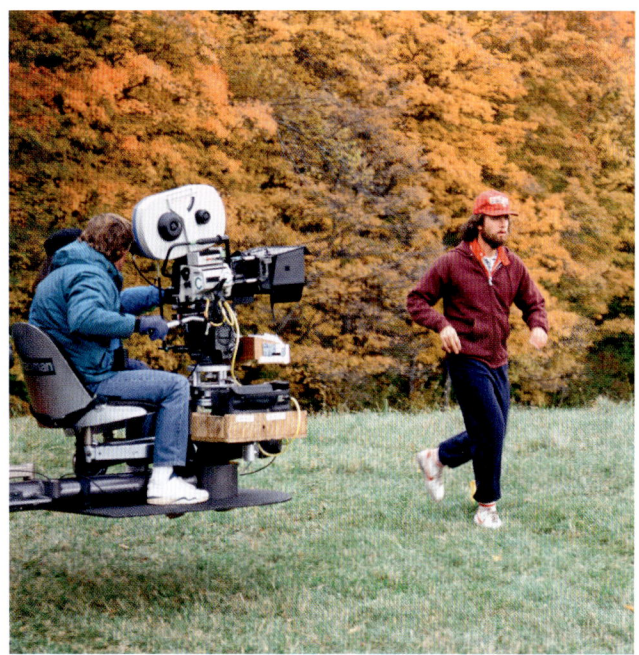

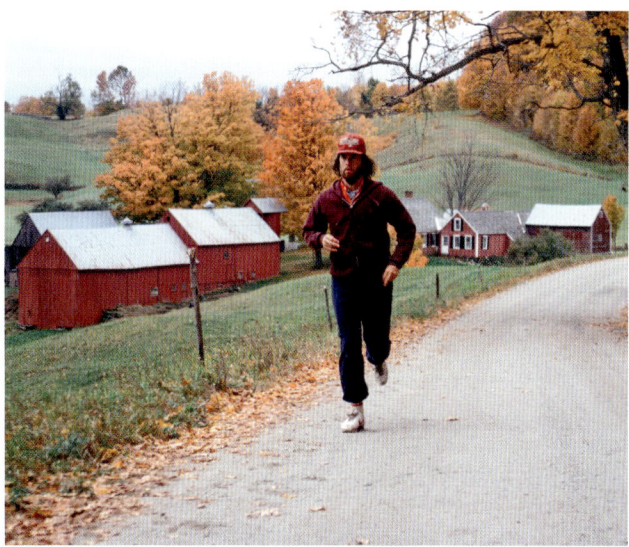

At about 11:30 p.m. Bob showed up at the condo, and we did a quick review of our favorite locations and the plan for the following day: after getting the shots in Vermont, we would board our charter plane and head to Maine and the Port Clyde lighthouse. "Sounds like a plan," Bob said as he headed off to bed.

When I arrived at Jenne Farm the following morning, E. J. came rushing up to me with a panicked look on his face. "We've got a problem. The old man has a shotgun and some alcohol on his breath. He is threatening to kick us off his property unless we make him a better deal."

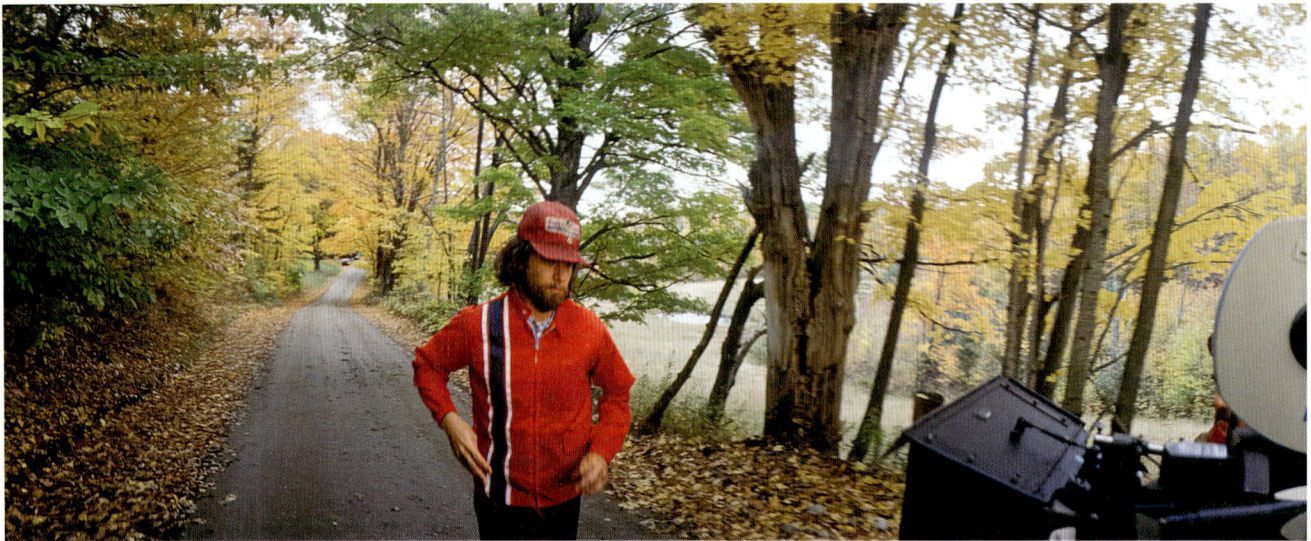

"You're kidding. Can we reason with him?"

"Not in his present state of mind. He doesn't look like he's had any sleep. He wants more money."

"How much does he want?"

"$150 cash."

"That's it? Pay him. Then let's shoot as quickly as we can and get the hell out of here before he changes his mind!"

Now I was in a hurry for the wrong reason. Bob was ready to shoot, and Tom was on his way, getting his makeup done on the road. I don't think the old man liked the fact that we'd driven the Chapman crane up on the hill to get a sweeping shot of Forrest running against the backdrop of trees. But we were out of there in an hour, with our country boy sitting on his front porch in his rocking chair, watching us leave.

The caravan of vehicles drove to the second location, and we got a perfect shot of Forrest enveloped in fall color.

Then we were off to the airport. We arrived on the Maine coast on a crystal-clear autumn day. After a quick picnic lunch by the lighthouse, everything went like clockwork, and we got the setups Bob was looking for.

As we flew back to South Carolina, we chuckled among ourselves about another Sunday of work accomplished under the studio's radar. We all felt good about the day. Then there was a bit of turbulence. Tom jokingly said, "Plane goes down en route to South Carolina. Tom Hanks and other unnamed passengers were on board." It got a good laugh. Finally in bed sometime after midnight, I wondered what was in store for me that would burst this bubble.

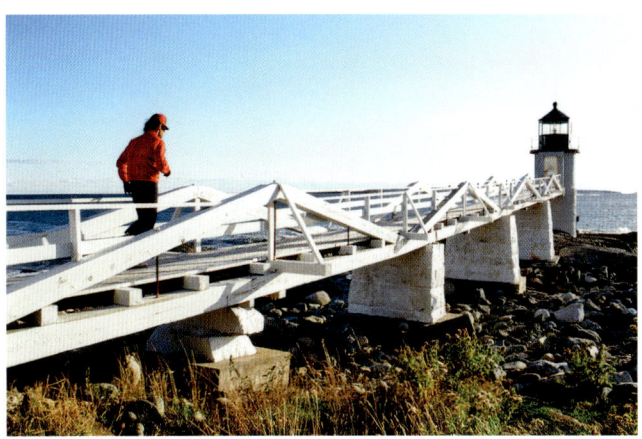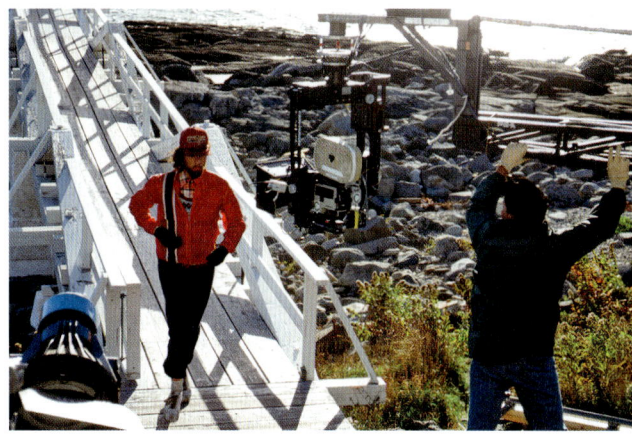

Filming at Marshall Point Lighthouse in Port Clyde, Maine

It was all going too well. I would soon find out.

We were down to our last eight scheduled days of shooting before heading to Savannah. There was no stopping us now. The first unit was on fire, shooting Forrest returning from his epic run on one day and Jenny throwing rocks at her old farmhouse on another. The SS unit was leapfrogging with the first unit, doing what we could to accelerate the process. Everything was going according to plan—my plan, that is. But not so much the studio's. I spent the end of each day reassuring the studio that we knew what we were doing. They needed a lot of reassurance. "Going over schedule and budget will not be the norm," I told them. "We have the rest of the shoot under control." I knew otherwise, but I exuded confidence, and it seemed to keep them at bay.

Finally, Sally Field got her wish. We were ready to shoot her final scene. Boy, was she happy. The happiest dying actress I ever met.

Then the time had come for Robin to shoot Jenny's final days.

There was too much dying going on for my taste. Maybe it was an omen. In fact, it *was* an omen. The next day was hot and humid, and I was standing in the shade of one of the stately oak trees on the road to the Gump house when Charles Newirth pulled me aside. He had heard some scuttlebutt from LA: Paramount was looking to replace the producer on a big unnamed show in the South that was out of control and over budget. The studio was looking for someone else to take the reins and get it back on track.

Hmm. That was interesting news indeed. I looked down and checked my feet. Suddenly it

117

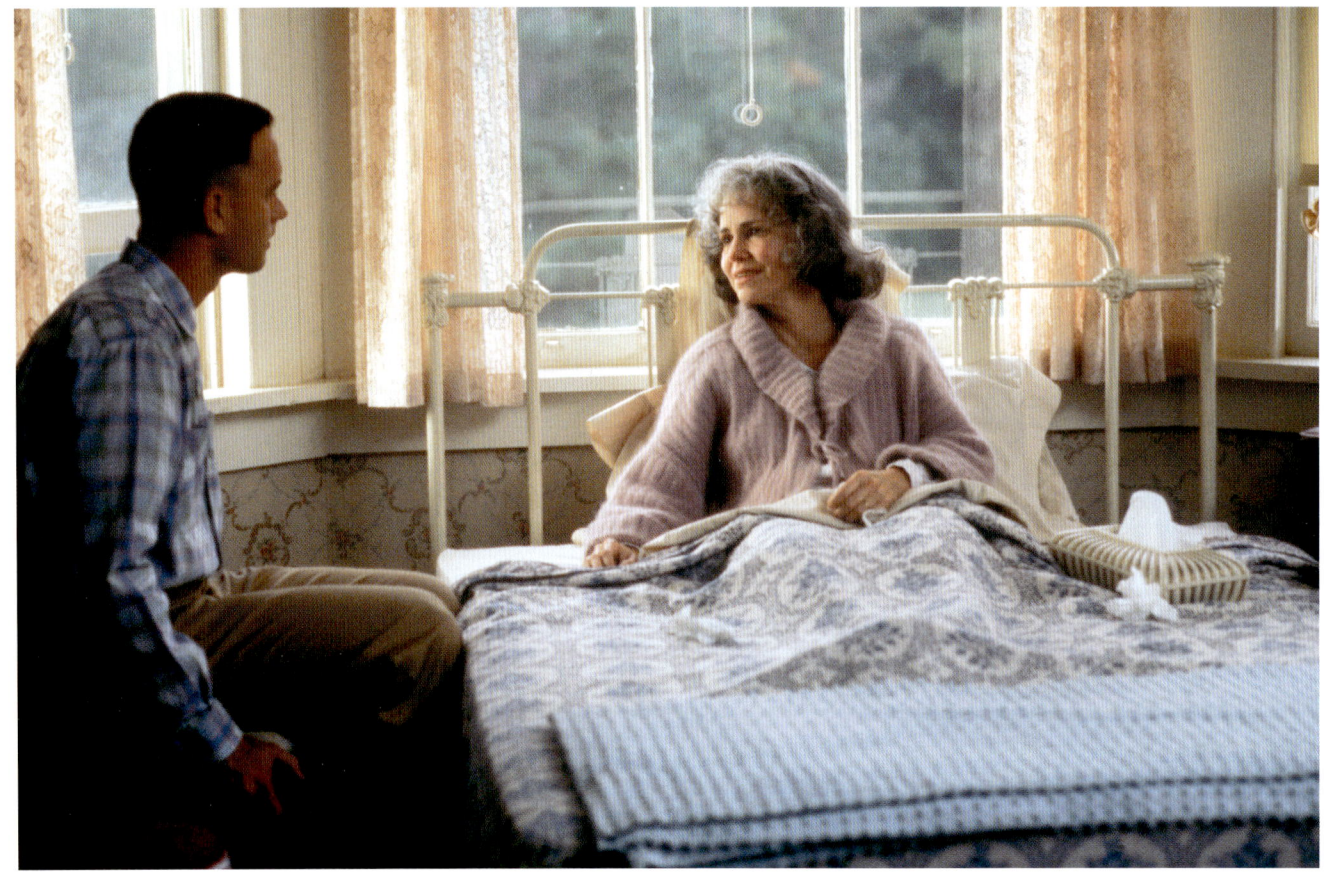

Sally Field finally shooting her last scene as Mama Gump

felt like there were fire ants crawling up my pants. Then I heard more interesting news. Michelle Manning and a representative from physical production, Larry Albucher, were flying out to the set. Evidently they were coming to rescue our show from its escalating costs. This was starting to feel uncomfortable.

During the day I mentioned to Bob that the studio execs were planning a visit. He asked if I thought the ruse was up. I told him I didn't know, but they were certainly aware that we were over schedule, and they had to know that the cost overages were adding up. We'd just have to wait and see what happened. I hesitated to say anything about the hunt for a new producer. That might have derailed him.

By the time the Paramount folks arrived, we were yet another day over schedule, adding fuel to

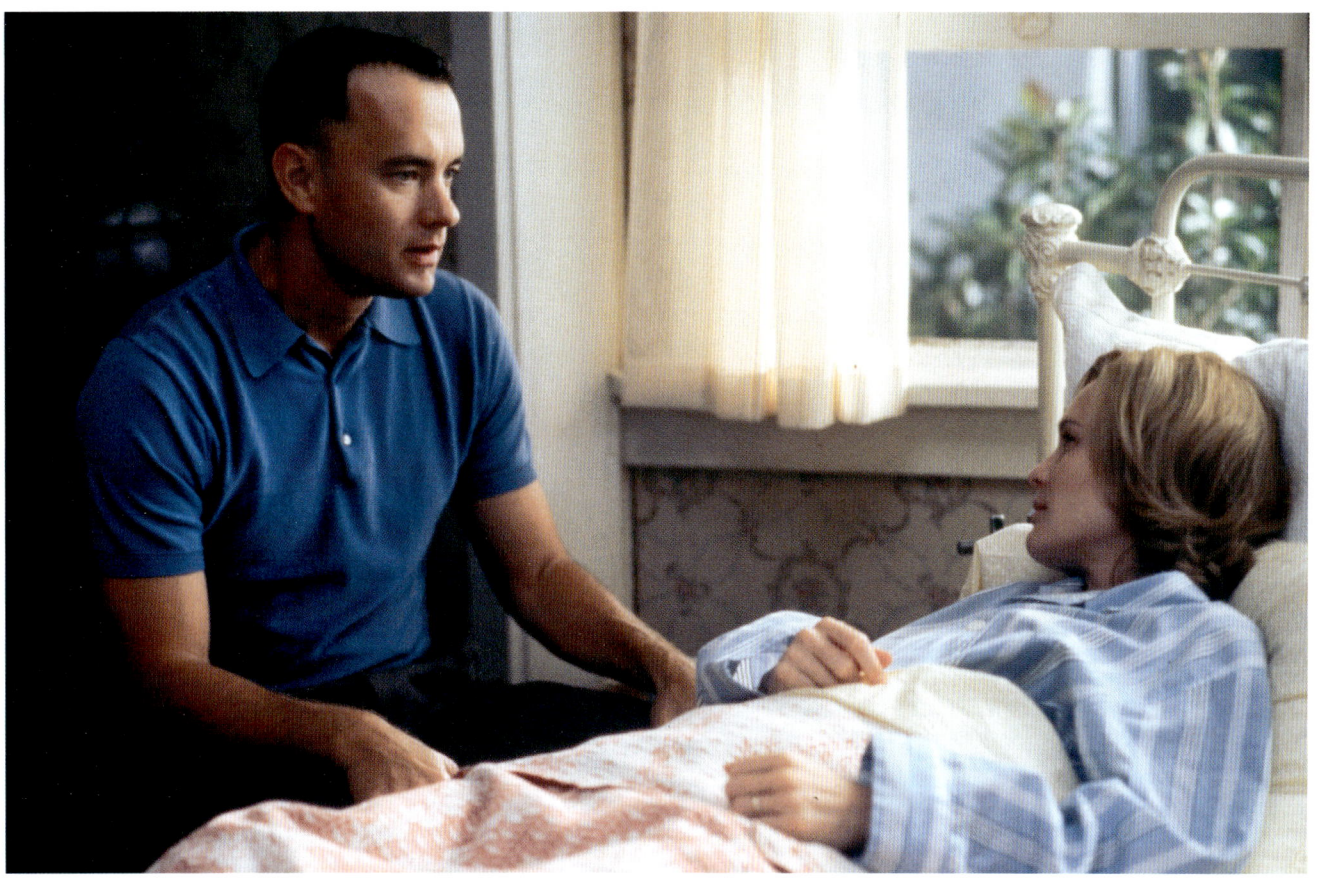

Filming Jenny's final days

their fire. I had not revealed that we were planning another day of shooting on the upcoming Sunday. That surely would have raised eyebrows.

When Saturday rolled around, I asked our visitors to join us for an SS-unit shot on the bridge in Beaufort the following morning, explaining that this was the only day of the week we could shut down traffic. There we were, coffee in hand on a Sunday morning, making small talk on the Beaufort bridge, with all the bells and whistles of a movie crew. Bob was directing with the full staff of assistant directors. Don Burgess and his camera crew were shooting. We had a gaggle of extras, some of whom were holding video cameras or microphones, running along with Forrest as if they were filming, yelling questions at him.

The extras required makeup, hair, and wardrobe. The video equipment had been provided by

119

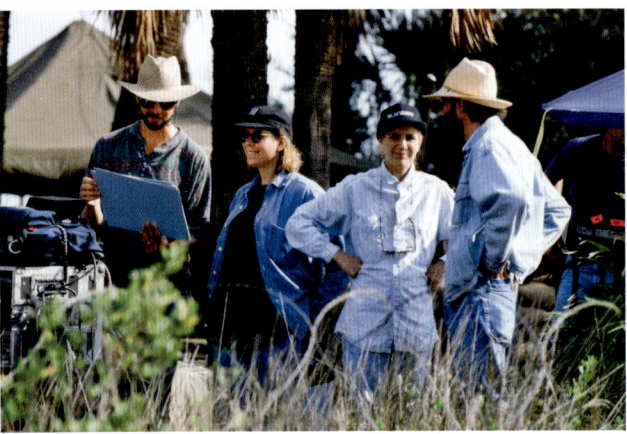

Paramount executive Michelle Manning, producer Wendy Finerman, and me, on the right

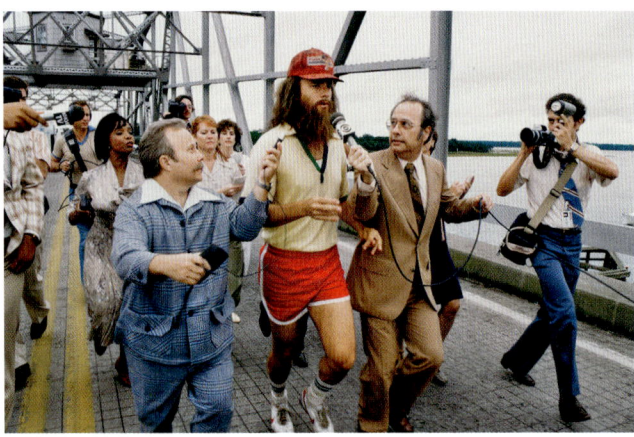

Video engineer Ian Kelly (on the right) runs alongside the actors, shooting footage for another scene

the prop men, who carefully distributed it to the actors and extras. Ian Kelly, our video engineer, ran alongside the reporters with a live video camera, shooting footage that would be played back in another scene—on a TV set in a diner where Jenny was working. In other words, this was a full-blown crew, not a second unit. The Paramount execs had to realize that. Or did they? I continued to stand around shooting the breeze with them. The question never came up. Nor did the fact that we were working on a Sunday on a scene the studio had wanted to shorten to begin with. What were they thinking? It was a mystery.

During our usual after-work cocktail hour, I finally told Bob about the search for a new producer, suggesting that the studio execs wanted to see firsthand what was happening on our troubled film. Bob became incensed. How dare they come

down here and spy on us! We were doing good work. They had no idea what they were getting. "I want her out of town now," he said, referring to Michelle. "Do you know where she is?"

We drove into town and stopped by the back door of a restaurant, a regular crew hangout. Bob jumped out of the driver's seat and asked me to wait in the car. He went inside and quickly emerged with Michelle close behind. He was enraged.

"You can't do this to my movie!" I watched him yelling at her, face-to-face, while pointing down the road. Essentially, he told her to get out of Dodge. I think he would have stayed and watched her leave if he weren't confident that she would follow his orders. Sure enough, Michelle left town.

I heard a rumor that she went to Hilton Head, tripped off a curb, and sprained her ankle. I felt bad for her. She was probably so shaken up that she lost

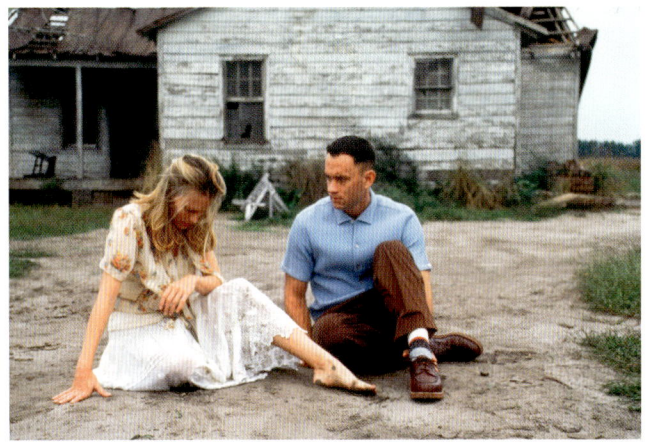

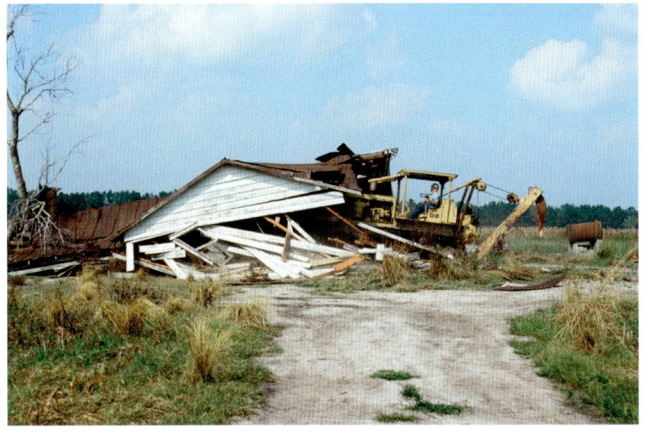

her step. Or maybe she had a drink before calling her superiors to tell them she was coming home.

But after that display of protective behavior, I felt safe. I knew that Bob had my back. He also had the backs of the crew. We could take on any challenge that came our way.

After shaking off the visit from Paramount, we returned to Jenny's farm and filmed the scene where she tries to bury her past and Forrest attempts to comfort her.

After double-checking that we had nothing remaining to shoot at Jenny's farmhouse, we set up the final shot, where it is bulldozed to the ground.

Before leaving the location, and to provide a bit of levity, we staged a photo with Tom Hanks, Charles Newirth, and me being admonished by Don Burgess because we had leveled the wrong house! It was all part of celebrating the completion of principal photography in South Carolina.

We were ready to head to Savannah, Georgia, where we would finally shoot the beginning of the movie: Forrest Gump sitting on the bus bench.

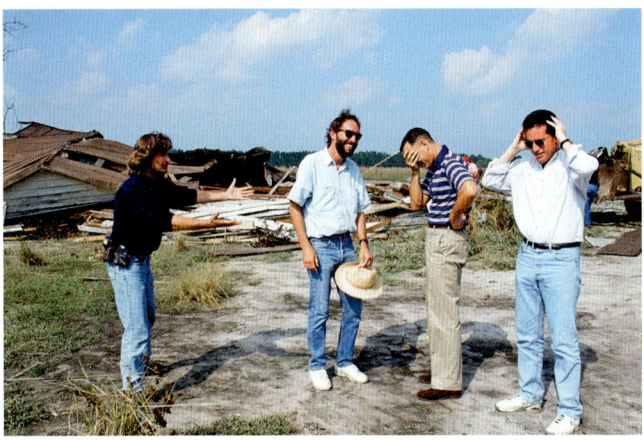

Top: Jenny buries her past at the old farm

Middle: Jenny's farmhouse is bulldozed

Bottom: Oops, wrong house! (Just kidding)

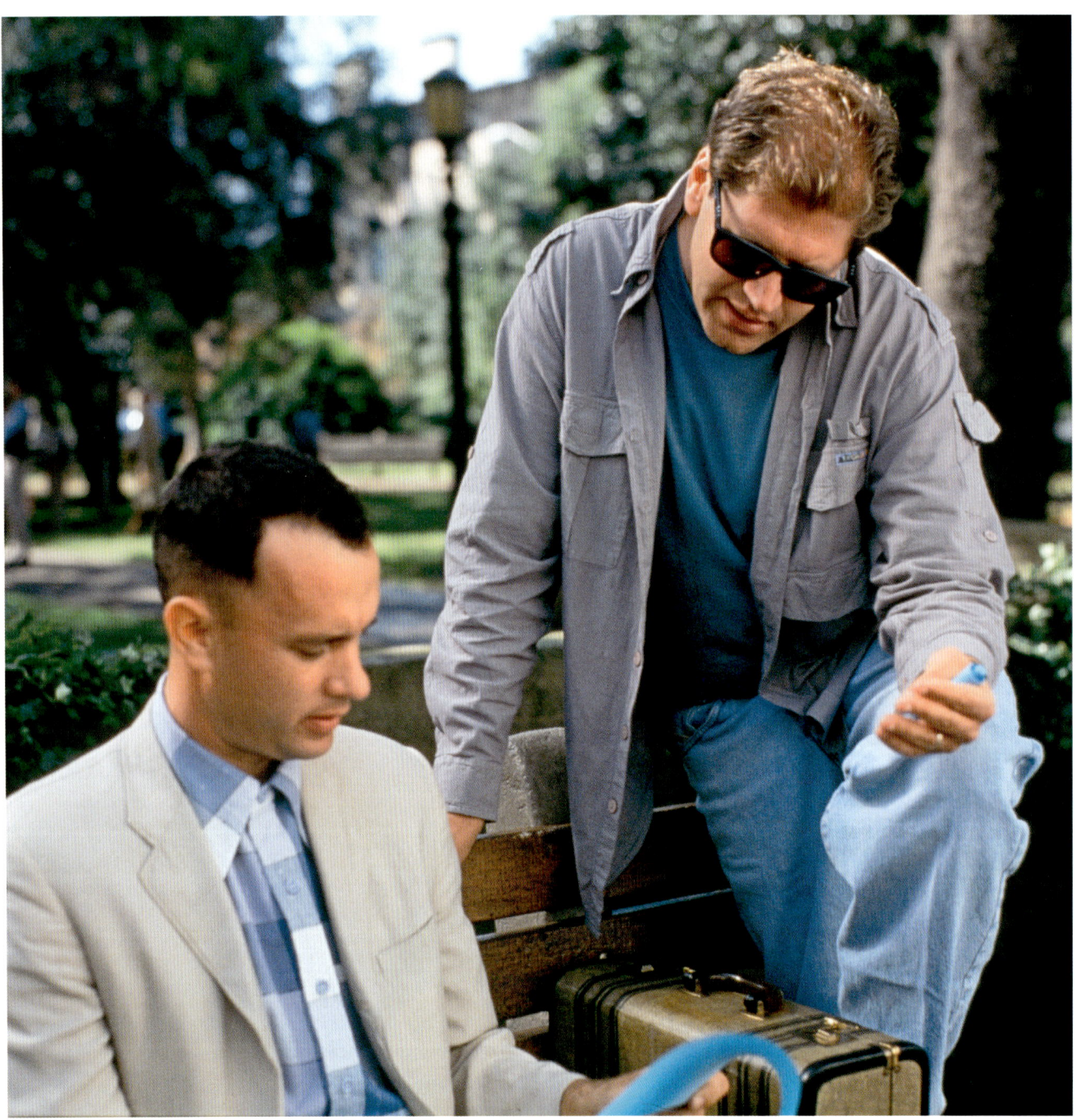

11 | Floatin' on a Breeze

"WHAT'S THAT SMELL?" I asked.

"It's the paper mill," the innkeeper said. "When the wind blows in our direction, the odor covers the entire town." Liv and I had checked into our bed-and-breakfast, the Kehoe House, and were dismayed by the unpleasant aroma. "Don't worry, the wind will probably change later this afternoon," he assured us.

I could only hope that the wind was blowing in the right direction when we filmed our first shot on the bench in Savannah, Georgia. That feather needed to land at Forrest's feet!

Bob hates to make a location move on a film and not shoot anything. He considers that a wasted day. When he is in shooting mode, he wants to shoot, shoot, shoot! So that's what we did. We completed the final scene in Beaufort during the day and then traveled to Savannah that same evening. The crew followed early the next morning and headed straight to the location. They would check in to their accommodations after work.

———————

We had a full day of shooting, beginning with a very loving scene between Forrest and Jenny on a park bench at Forsyth Park:

                              JENNY
            I'm sick, Forrest.

                              FORREST
            Is it something you ate?

                              JENNY
                        (shakes "no")
            I have some kind of virus. The doctors don't know what it is.
            There isn't anything they can do.

A breeze ruffles through their clothing. She looks into his sweet eyes for the
longest time. And she asks him:

                              JENNY
            Forrest, will you marry me?

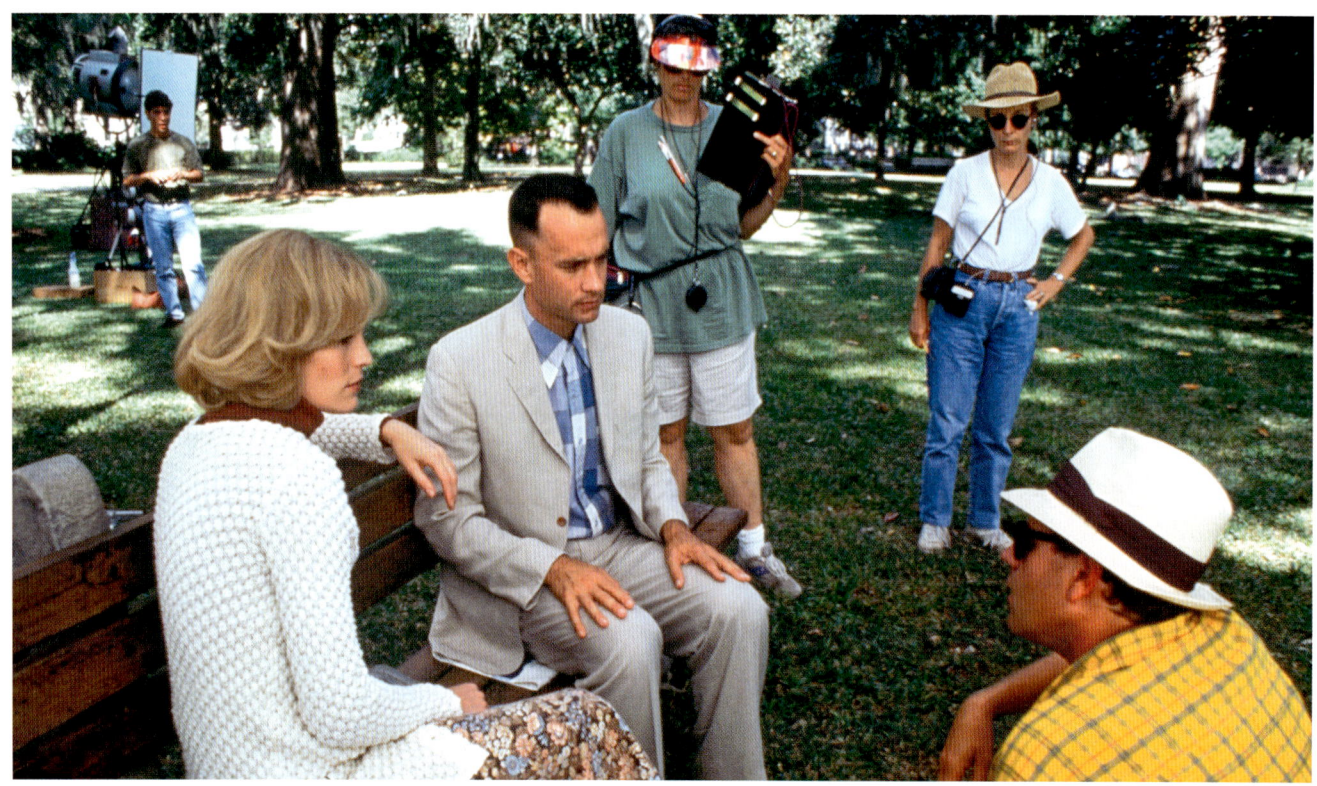

Shoot, shoot, shoot, as Bob would say. No rest for the weary. We arrived in Savannah with little sleep and then shot in three locations there on the first day! After the work in the park, we moved to shoot Forrest arriving outside Jenny's apartment.

We ended the day with a shot from the run. It was hard to go to a new city without shooting something from the run. On this particular day Forrest picks up his first follower, who has an almost religious awakening when he meets Forrest:

```
                 YOUNG MAN
...It's you...I can't believe it's
really you...I mean it was like an
alarm went off in my head, you know!
I said here's a guy who has his act
together...! Here's somebody who
has it all figured out...! Here's
somebody who has the answer...I'll
follow you anywhere, Mr. Gump...
```

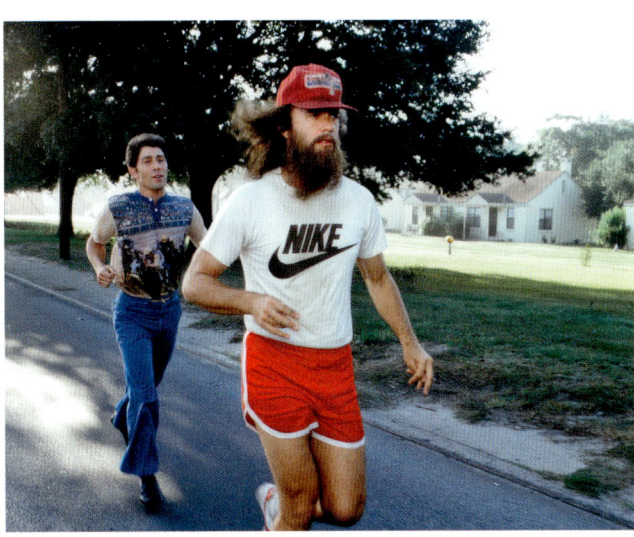

We'd follow you anywhere, Mr. Zemeckis. All of us were like Forrest's new adherent, following our fearless director.

The setting for the meeting between Forrest and his disciple needed something unique—more than the row of yellow houses the script called for. Something inexplicably special, and I knew just what it was. I called the set decorator, Nancy Haigh, and asked a particular favor, something I normally wouldn't do, especially with an overworked department on a very demanding show. But I did it anyway. I asked for mirror balls. Mirror balls? Yes, I wanted a ball placed in front of each of the identical houses on the street where Forrest meets his follower.

Mirror balls—gazing balls, reflecting balls, orbs, whatever you might call them—mean something special to Bob and me. Growing up in the Midwest, Bob had seen these gleaming reflecting balls gracing his neighbors' lawns. I encountered them when I visited my wife's family in Dubuque, Iowa. In addition, during a trip we had taken to the northern Midwest, Bob and I noticed a beautiful ball on a pedestal next to a pretty white farmhouse. We decided to approach the owner and ask if we could buy the orb. He said that normally he would have loved to give us his ornament, but it had been his wife's favorite, and he couldn't bear to part with it since she had recently passed. As you can imagine, we felt embarrassed, sad, and stupid after that. Soon afterward I bought an orb and set it on a pedestal in front of our office at Universal.

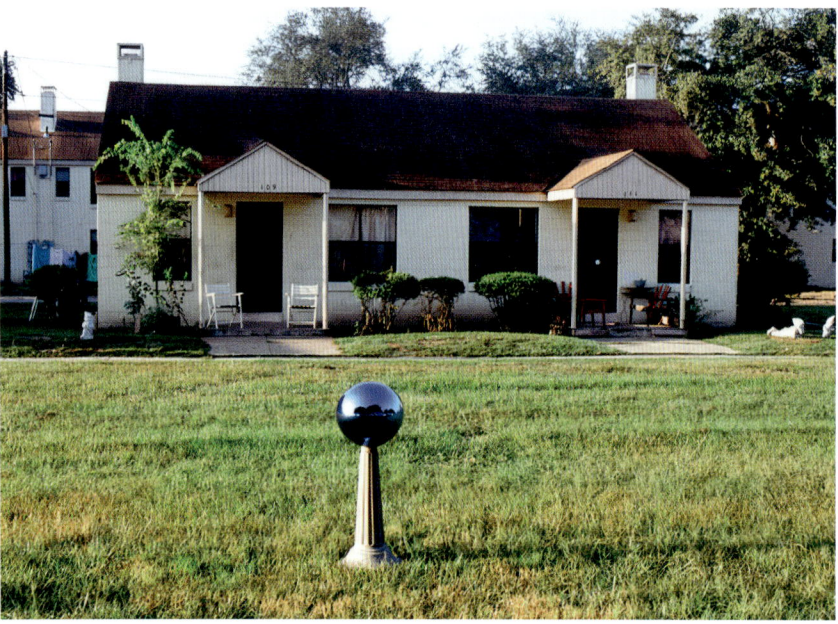

A mirror ball adds flair to an otherwise bare front lawn

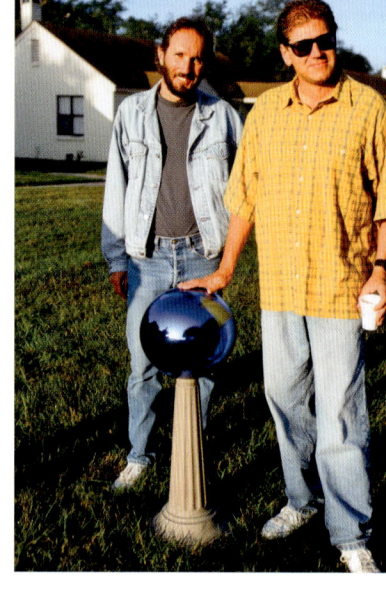

Bob and me with one of the orbs

Those darn balls continued to hold a very special place in our world.

So here we were. I had asked Nancy to place an orb in front of each of the identical houses, and she came through the morning before we arrived at the location. I think she had to scour every nursery in Savannah. They may not be noticeable and have little meaning to most viewers, but they added the necessary flair to the scene.

The next day, Friday, we shot an all-nighter on the Houlihan Bridge outside Savannah, where Forrest tells Jenny he is going to Vietnam. The following day, Saturday, I had the day off, something I was not accustomed to on this show. And Tom finally got a day off, too! After twenty-seven straight days of shooting, on that Saturday he was able to sleep in. Of course, his day of rest may have started at noon, since he'd been shooting all night. But it was a day off nonetheless. I thought back to that early conversation I had with Tom, asking him to let me know if he needed some additional rest. Never, not once, did he approach me about that. We just gave him his call time, and he reported to work without complaint. And after that partial day off, he went right back to work on Sunday.

Finally came the scene we'd all been looking forward to, the reason we had come to Savannah in the first place: Forrest sitting on the bus bench when a feather, gently floating on a breeze, comes to rest at his feet.

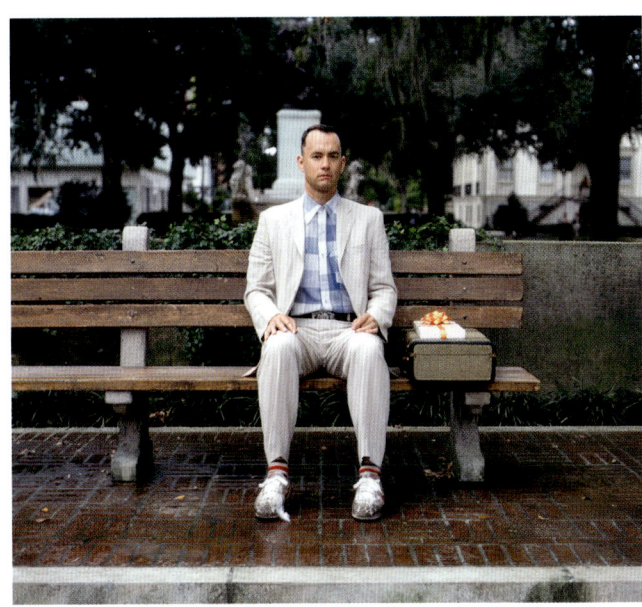

And taken by a small breeze, it (the feather) lightly falls, and silently lands, by "chance," at this time, at this place, on this street, at a MAN's feet, wearing a pair of dilapidated running shoes, sitting on a bus bench, in Savannah, Georgia.

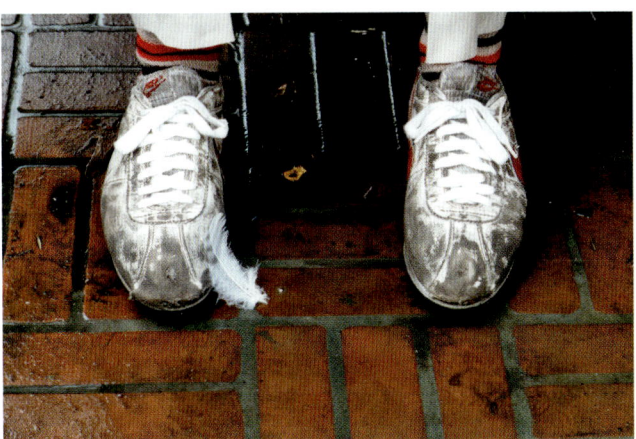

Of course, the falling feather was not there at all. It would be added later. For now, what we saw was a camera hanging on a crane, making a serendipitous descent and following an imaginary feather, all guided by our effects guru Ken Ralston.

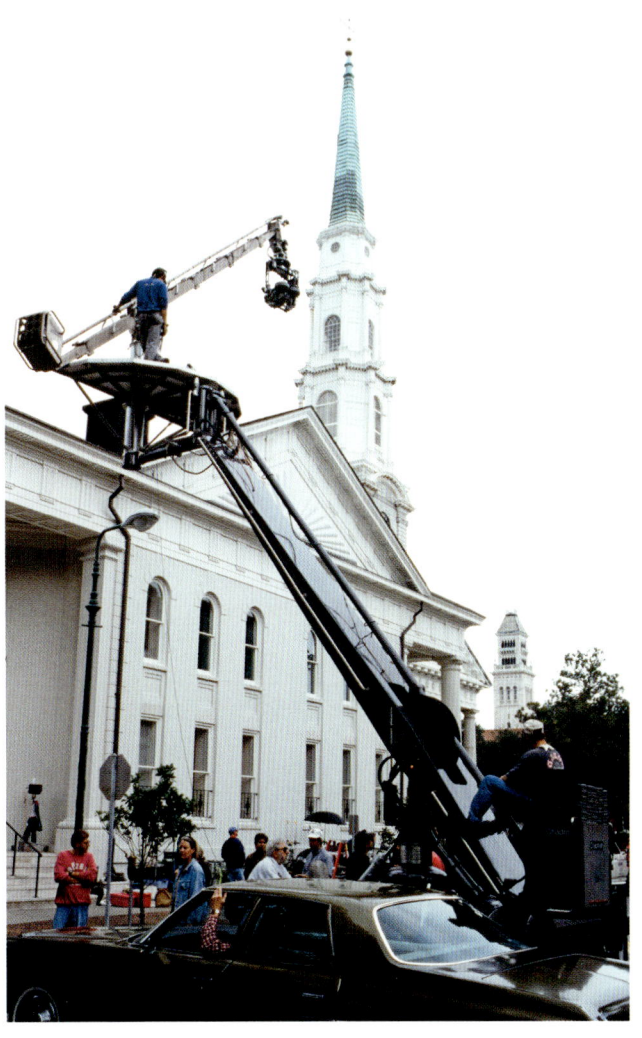

The camera hangs from a crane, filming a feather that isn't there

127

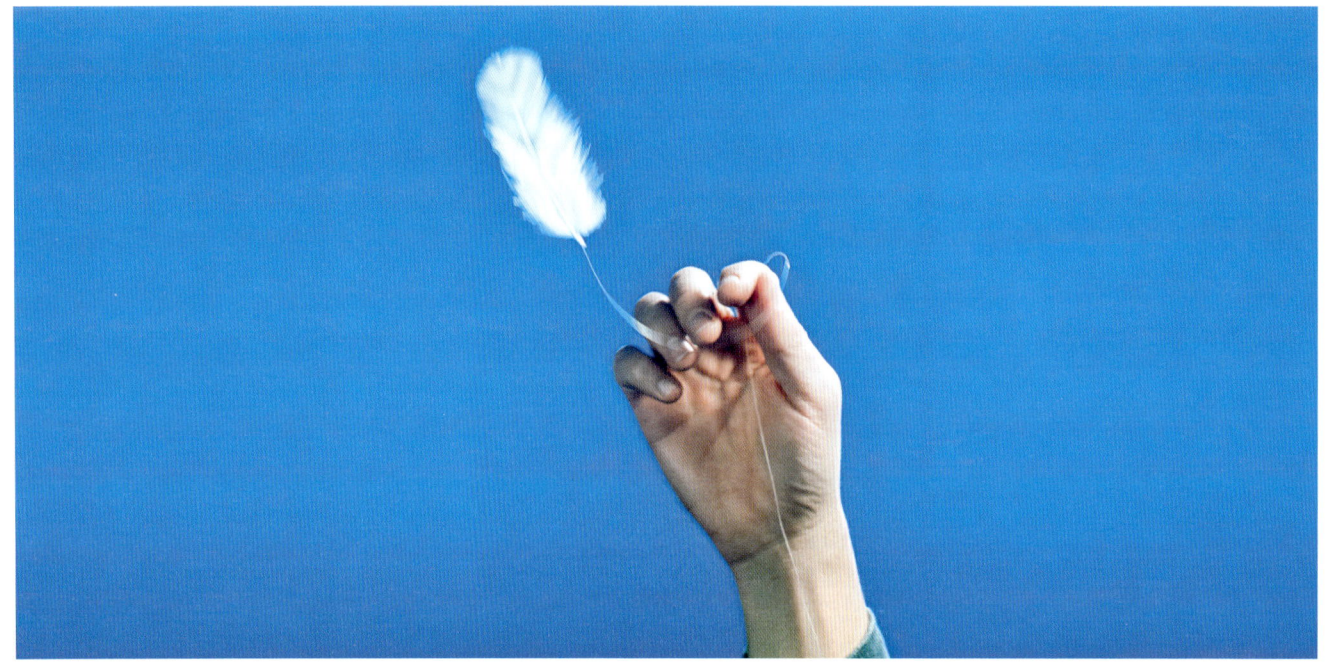

Filming the feather against a blue screen

Ken later performed his magic, filming the feather against a blue screen, matching the movement of the camera. Then he seamlessly blended the falling feather with the one at Forrest's feet, making it appear that the feather had lightly fallen and landed, only to be picked up by our hero.

The bench had been placed on Chippewa Square, just where we had imagined it many months before, on our initial scout of the South.

What a welcome moment it was to hear Forrest telling his story on the bench. As he narrated his adventures and reflected on his life experiences to complete strangers, we relived many of the days we had recently spent filming in the South—the Gump house and Oak Alley, the oak tree, Jenny's farm, the town of Greenbow, shrimping, Vietnam, and a good portion of the run.

Surprisingly, the final scene on the bench had changed from my first reading of the screenplay:

FORREST

...I am supposed to go on the number nine bus to Richmond Street, and get off and go left one block to... (showing her the letter) 1947 Henry Street, Apartment 4.

THE ELDERLY WOMAN

Why, you don't need to take a bus (and motioning). Henry Street is just five or six blocks, down that way.

FORREST

Down that way?

THE ELDERLY WOMAN

Down that way.

He looks up to where she is motioning. And he suddenly grabs up his stuff.

FORREST

(in a hurry)

It was nice talkin' to you.

And jumping up, he starts to run off.

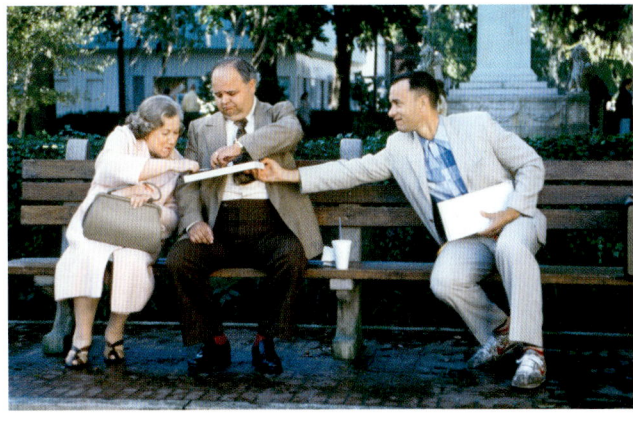

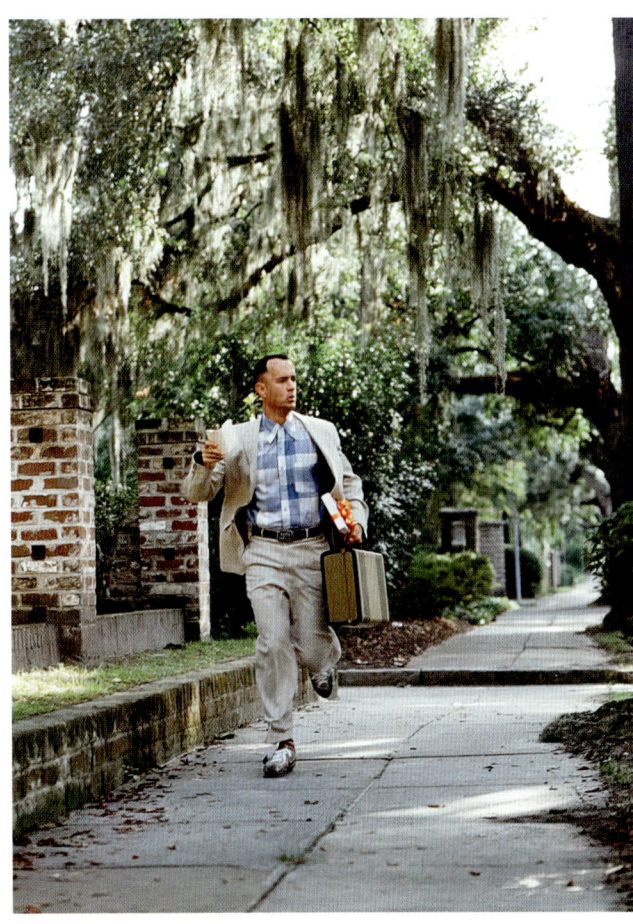

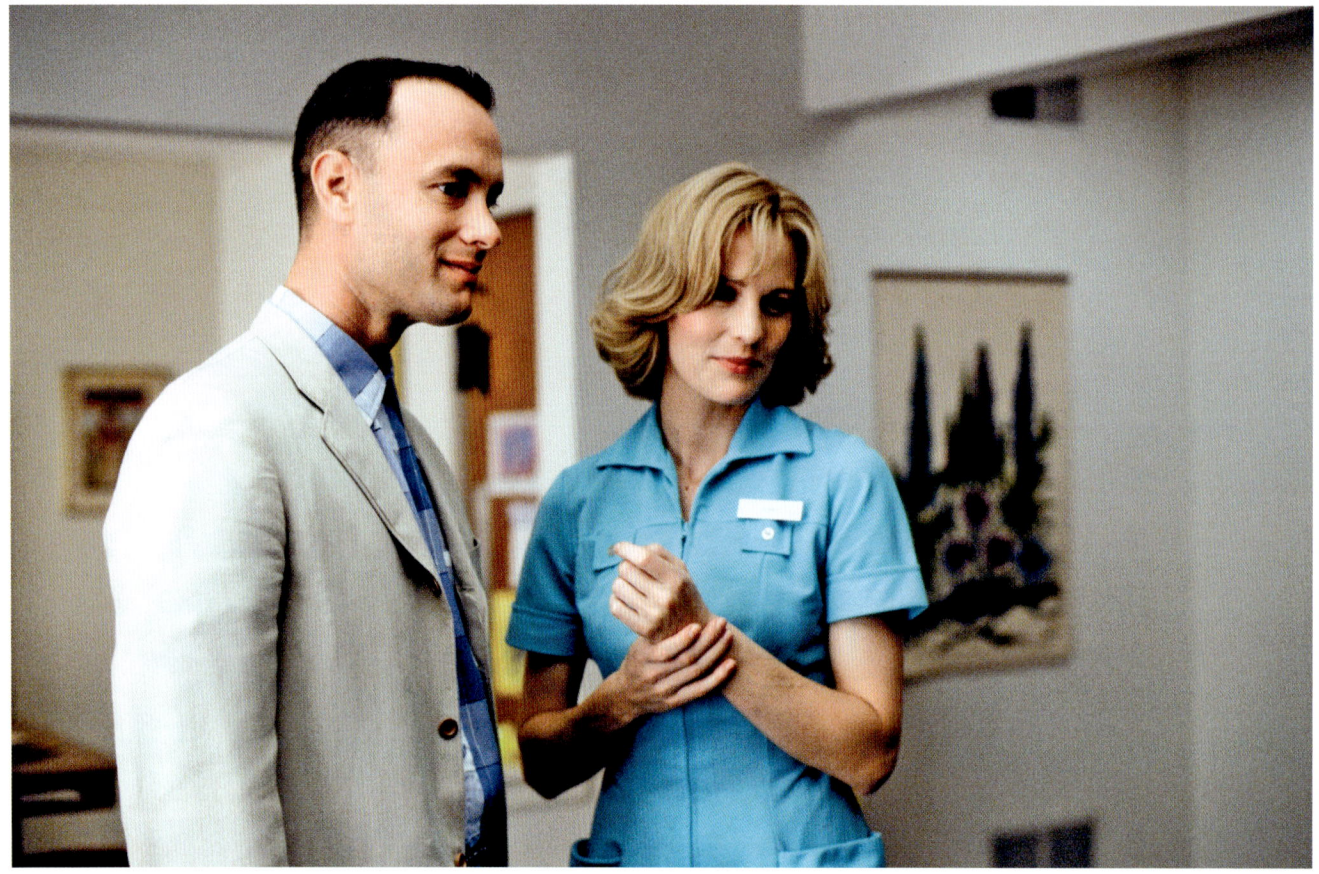

Forrest reunites with Jenny

In that early draft of the script, Forrest never got up from the bench. He remained there to tell the end of his story. At some point before shooting, Eric Roth and Bob Zemeckis changed the scene so that Forrest realizes he doesn't need to take the bus to get to Jenny's apartment after all. It's only a short run down the street. What irony. In the revised script (and in the finished film), we follow the end of Forrest's story in real time—beginning with Forrest reuniting with Jenny and meeting his son.

Then they return home to the Gump house, where Forrest and Jenny marry, sharing precious time together before she dies. The drama was intensified by watching Forrest's life as it unfolded. In a sense, he actually narrated the end of his story at Jenny's gravesite, by bringing her news of their son, Forrest Jr.

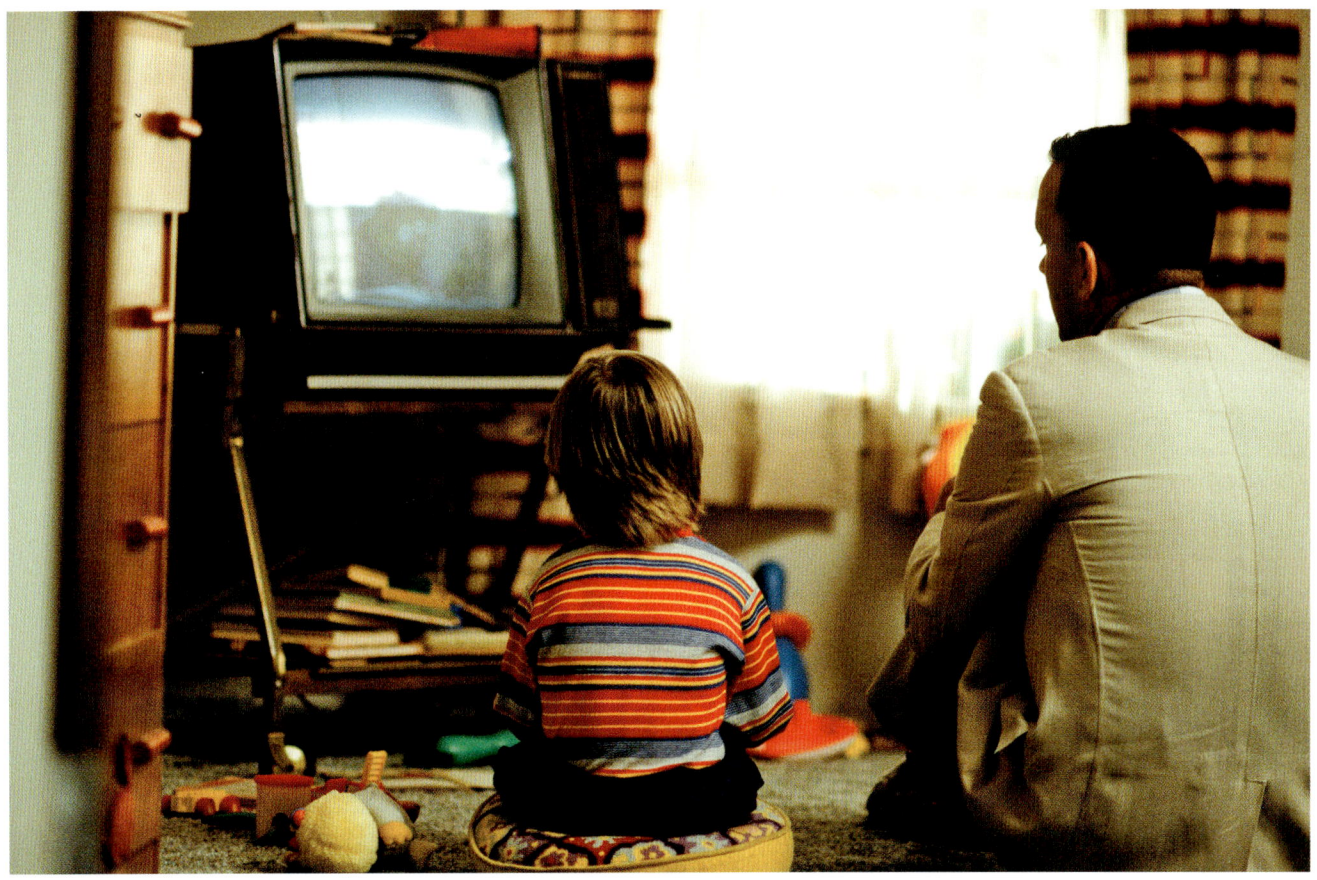

Forrest meets his son for the first time

The drama that had surrounded us in South Carolina seemed to drift away on our arrival in Savannah. The studio was not as crazy as it had been. When we arrived, we revealed that we were an additional day over schedule, and by the time we left town, we had added another. We were fifty-one days into our shooting schedule and still had twenty to go. Instead of our original sixty-four-day schedule—at least the one the studio had—we were now looking at seventy-one days, seven days over.

I knew we would add even more days before we finished shooting. In addition, the overall costs were mounting. Could we make it through the Washington, DC, scenes without a skirmish? I was starting to feel more confident that we would finish our location work before the proverbial shit hit the fan.

131

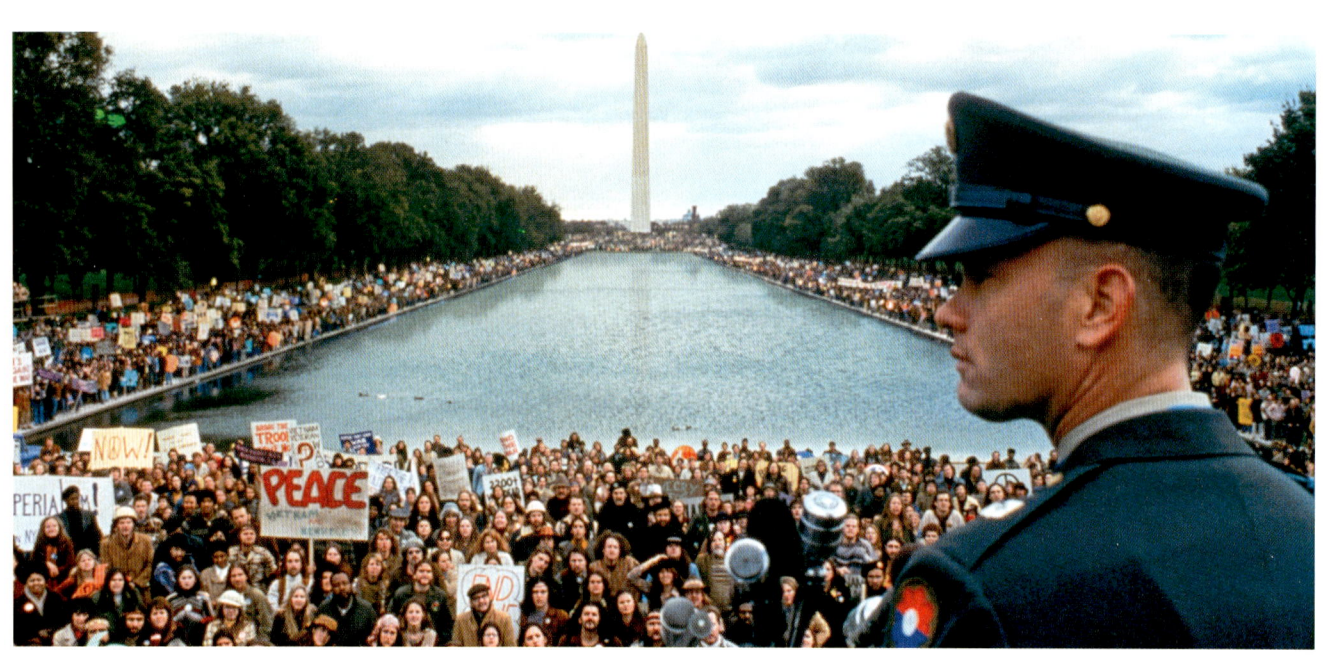

12 | Tiling? What the Hell Is Tiling?

STANDING IN FRONT of the Lincoln Memorial, gazing out at the Reflecting Pool and the Washington Monument, Mary Morgan, our location scout, told us we had received our permit from the National Park Service just a few days before we arrived. It was the worst bureaucracy she had ever faced. Then she quipped, "Clint Eastwood was here yesterday and stole a few shots without a permit."

"Where? Here at the Lincoln Memorial?"

"Yes, just Clint and a few of his crew."

Leave it to Clint to grab a freebie. I guess he figured, what's the worst that can happen? Fine me? Close my movie down? After all, he was Clint Eastwood. The officials probably would have asked him for his autograph before kicking him off the Lincoln Memorial. I'm not sure we could have done that. Not that Tom Hanks couldn't sway whatever officials were in charge, but because we had brought in a virtual army for filming.

The weary soldiers working on our show had just come off a grueling shoot in the South and had one day to settle in, regroup, and prepare for one of the biggest days on the film. The day after their arrival, on Sunday, we rehearsed and scouted, which only increased my fear of the daunting amount of work that lay ahead. Every department had grown in scale to meet the requirements for the coming week, starting at the Lincoln Memorial, where Forrest addresses an antiwar rally and reunites with Jenny. While tourists paraded around us, unaware of our preparations, I was looking for reassurance—reassurance that each department would be ready bright and early on Monday morning. When faced with a supersized location like the National Mall and the Washington Monument, the stakes seemed higher. If even one department faltered, the day could fall apart.

Although there were many individual pieces to worry about, I was focused on the multitude of extras that would surround the Reflecting Pool and achieving the right period look. But then again, I was paid to worry. As the crew psychiatrist, like Lucy in the *Peanuts* comic strip, I mostly just listened. That usually did the trick.

Today, though, the roles were reversed. The crew would be consoling me. I was quickly put at ease. I watched the set being assembled while we were rehearsing. No worries about that. We had done a prop show-and-tell, so the period micro-phones to be used on the dais had been checked. Period buses were in place, carefully parked to camouflage any evidence of present-day Washington. What about those darn tourists? We could not keep them off the Lincoln Memorial. Those were the rules set down by the National Park Service. What if they drifted into a shot and screwed it up? We had carefully arranged fences to delineate where we would be shooting, but still.. . .

What about those extras? Would they look right? I had full faith in costume designer Joanna Johnston. She was painstakingly hands-on. Perfection was her working style. She personally approved the look of every actor or extra that walked onto the set. I didn't want anything to look phony either. I had been to a demonstration the year before ours was meant to take place, so I knew what it should look like. I would be checking everything. Plus, set decorating, props and wardrobe, and the hair department were just as exacting as Joanna. They had seen countless photos for historical reference. Rick Carter, prop man Robin Miller, and Nancy Haigh were about my age, so they had firsthand knowledge of the period as well. They all had a vested interest in their work.

Many of the extras had been recruited from a Renaissance festival in nearby Maryland. These revelers loved to wear the period dress of the fif-teenth and sixteenth centuries, some of which resembled the clothing of late 1960s hippies. Many had the long, flowing hair of the era. Of course,

many aging hippies also answered the call; they were always looking for an excuse to pull their old clothes out of the closet and relive the days of their youth.

"Joanna, there are so many extras to look at," I told her. "You really don't have time to see them all." Her response was that one bad extra could ruin the scene. When I said we could push the sore thumb to the back, she replied, "What if Bob pushes that one lousy, imperfect extra to the foreground?"

When I asked when she planned to get started, she said, "I'll probably get in around 1 a.m. and be ready for the first group of extras arriving at 3 a.m."

"Wait, that's only ten hours from now."

"I know," she said. "I won't be getting much sleep tonight."

I knew that somehow she would make it work. She always did.

After the relative calm instilled by Joanna, I had to face my greatest fear about the extras: How were we going to fill the entire National Mall sur-rounding the Reflecting Pool with tens of thou-sands of protesters when we had only fifteen hun-dred extras over the two days of filming?

"Tiling? What the hell is tiling?" I asked Ken Ralston, our effects guru.

"It's like a quilt," he explained. "A repetition of squares of extras, filmed one grid at a time. When these are stitched to one another, the entire area will fill up with people screaming and yell-ing and waving their signs." Would they appear

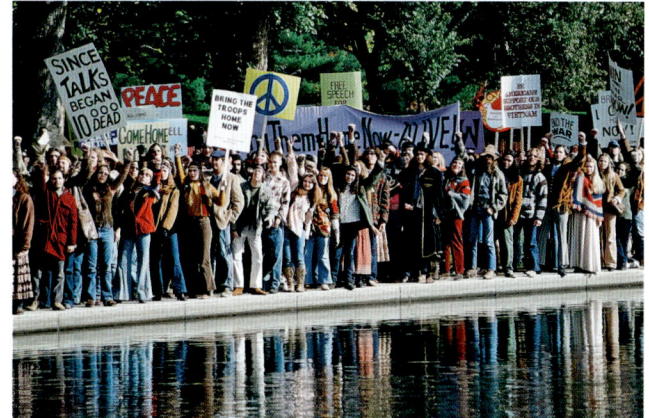

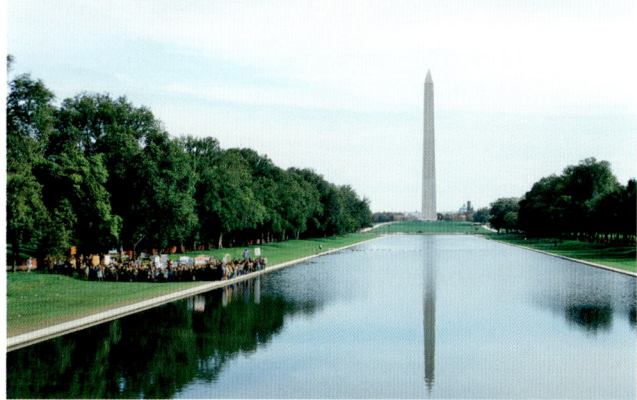

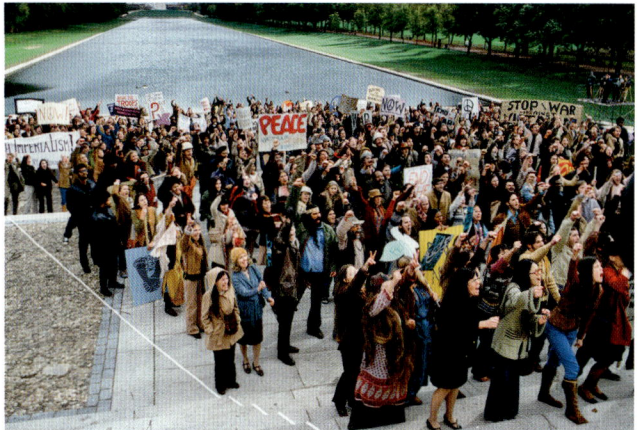

Filling the National Mall with protesters using tiling

to be different if the same groups of people were standing next to one another? "We'll mix them up along with the signage, and no one will know the difference. Trust me."

The shots from the stage, where Forrest addresses the crowd, were going to be Tondreau shots. I remember using ILM's Tondreau system on *Back to the Future II.* That system allowed us to do a computer-controlled, repeatable move with the dolly and camera in order to multiply the people, or extras, in the frame. In *Back to the Future II,* we added three characters into the same shot, all played by the same actor, Michael J. Fox. In this case, we would be tiling extras—thousands of them. It could be great, or it could be a disaster. If the Tondreau system failed, we were done for. I'm not sure what we would have done.

It was November 1, and the days were getting shorter, adding to the pressure of getting everything finished. We didn't rehearse with the extras until around 9:00 a.m., and to make matters worse, the extras needed a lunch break, since they had started at 3:00 a.m. Finally, we began with the master shot of Forrest walking up the platform stairs, joining Abbie Hoffman onstage to speak to the multitudes. Then the first unit left us behind, moving to another area of the Lincoln Memorial with a good group of extras of their own.

I stayed behind with the tiling group, wrangling extras all afternoon long, helping Ken get what he needed. We marked off the first grid where the extras had been standing, then moved them

135

to the adjacent grid. We played back the master take of the scene on a loudspeaker, and the "new" group would listen and react, much the same way they did when we shot it the first time, yelling and screaming and waving their signs on cue. Then we moved them to the next grid and repeated the same exercise over and over again. All afternoon. Until all the squares of the "quilt" were completed.

And then there was the F-word. Who could shoot a scene with Abbie Hoffman without having him use the F-word multiple times? As Forrest says:

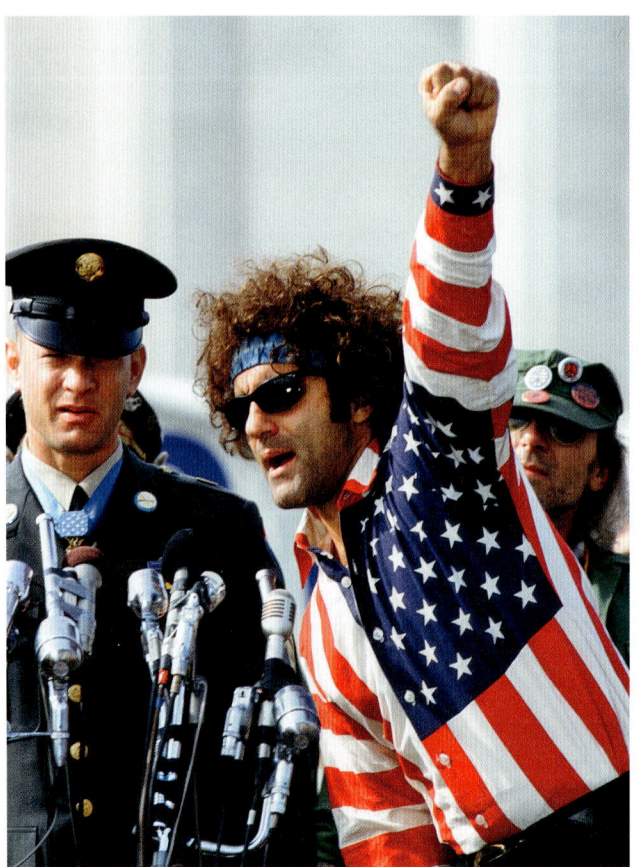

FORREST (V.O.)
There was this man givin' a little talk, and for some reason, he was wearin' an American flag for a shirt. And he liked to say the F-word, a lot. F this and F that. And every time he said the F word, people for some reason, well, they'd cheer!

For a movie to keep a PG-13 rating, the Motion Picture Association allowed only one use of the F-word. That was our goal. Two F-words would trigger an R rating, and we didn't want that. Many other issues—nudity and drug use, to name a couple—also would have guaranteed an R rating, but for this scene, the F-word was what we had to worry about. Our solution was to have a faulty sound system. This would allow our Abbie Hoffman to scream the F-word throughout his speech, but we'd hear only one, with the others carefully disguised by an audio squelch or feedback. No one was the wiser.

After leaving the Lincoln Memorial, we filmed Forrest and Jenny around all the sites in Washington, DC, morning, noon, and night. We began with a candlelight vigil in front of the White House at night, followed by their stroll past the Jefferson Memorial at dawn. We ended by looking through a window at the US Capitol, but not in the way one might suspect.

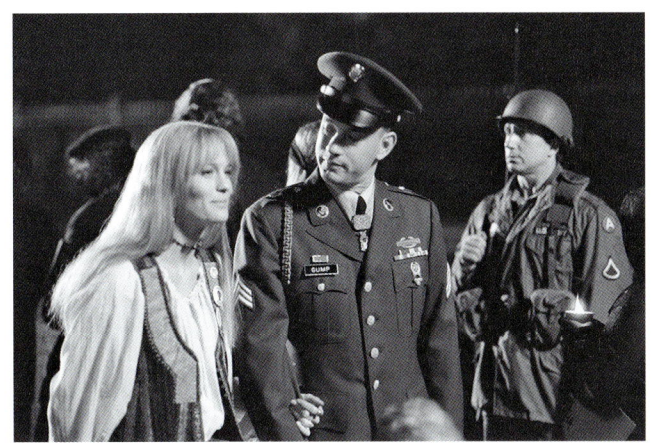
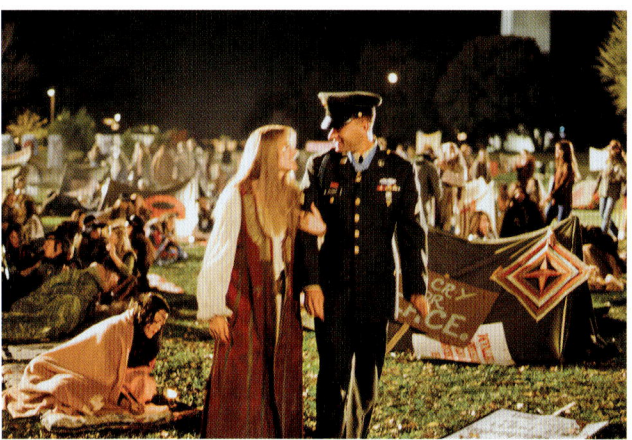

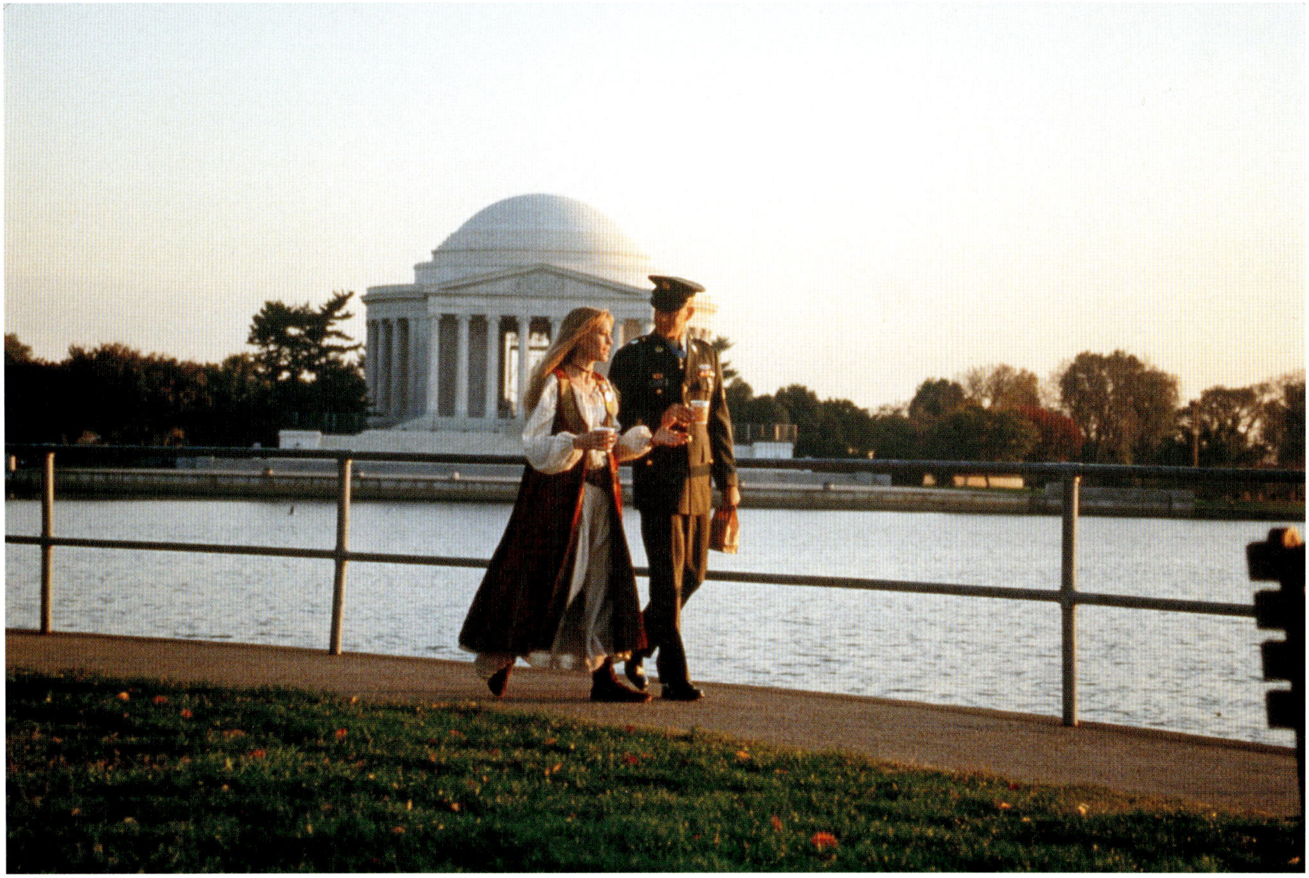

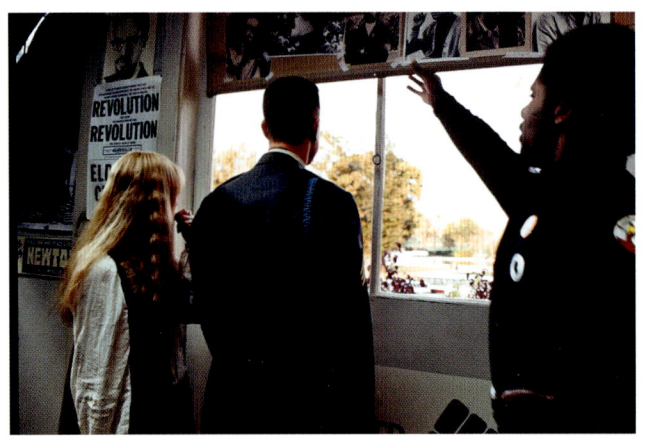
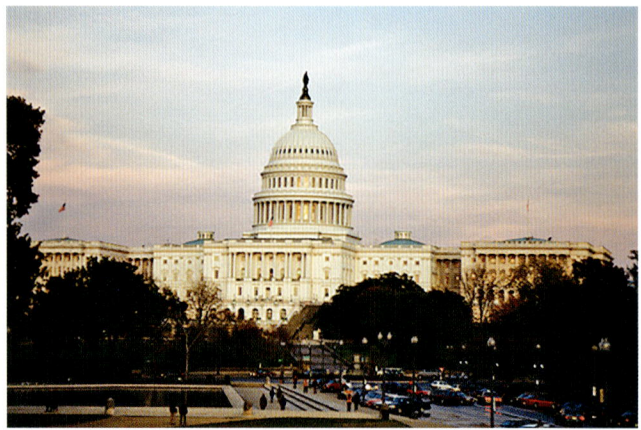

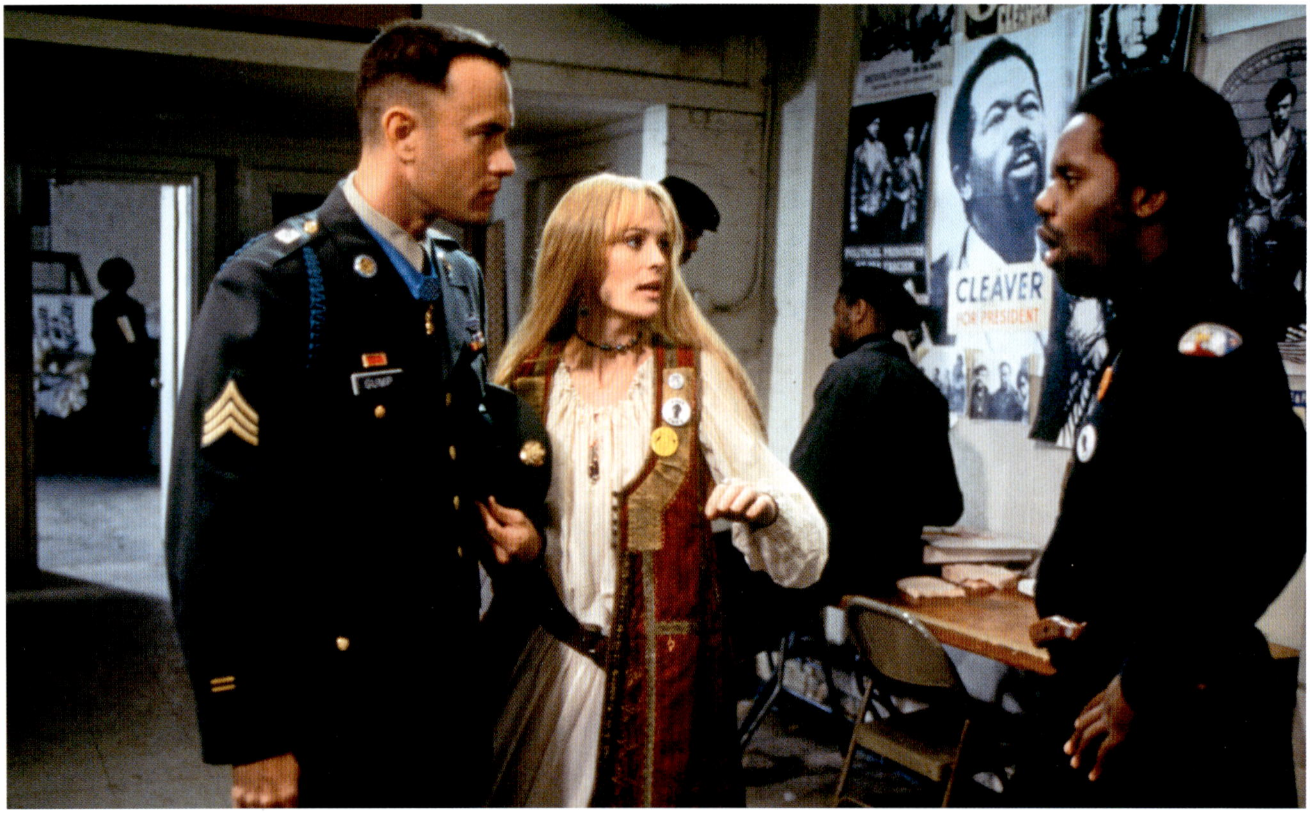

Forrest and Jenny at Black Panther headquarters

Bob wanted to show the proximity of Black Panther headquarters to the Capitol building. We built a single wall on a platform in an open field, so you could look through a window straight at the Capitol dome. Only three characters—Forrest, Jenny, and the Black Panther Masai—were in the scene:

> MASAI
> Shut that blind, Man, and get your white ass away from that window. Don't you know we're in a war here!!

As he speaks, Masai shuts the window blinds. For the next shot we moved to an interior set, where the blinds remained closed.

As the scene continues, Forrest gets into a fight with Jenny's abusive boyfriend and is kicked out of Panther headquarters.

After a loving reunion with Forrest, Jenny waves good-bye, leaving him alone again.

We had an incredibly long and busy week, and it was time for the production to leave Washington, DC, and head home to LA. While we were shooting in DC, a fire raged through Topanga and Malibu Canyons, and Robin Wright lost her home. Her life was upended. On our return to LA, our life on the film would also be upended in a way I could not have imagined. As it turned out, the studio was awaiting our return, eager to question us in person about our dubious behavior and runaway production.

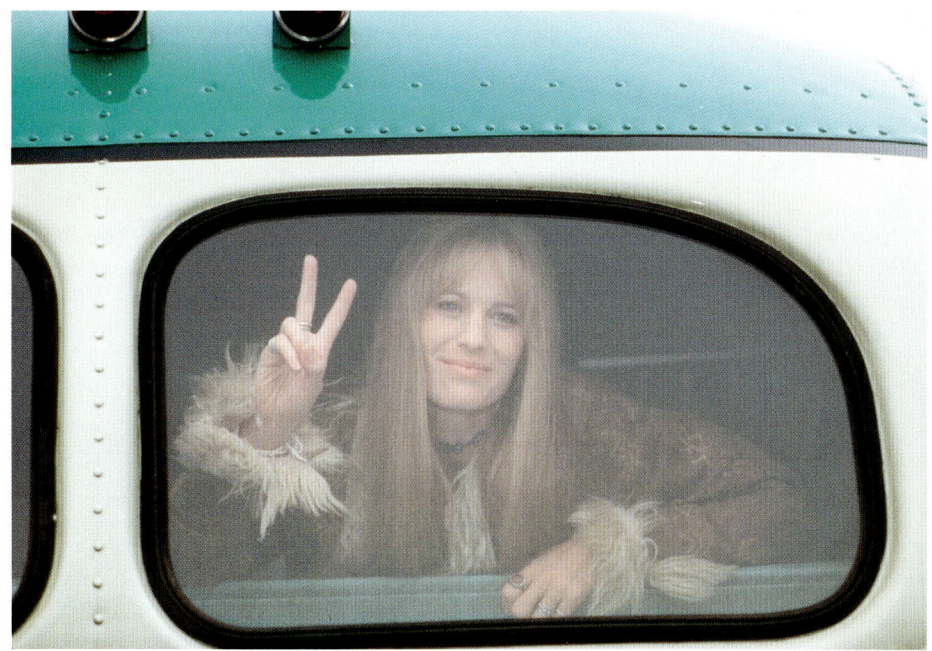

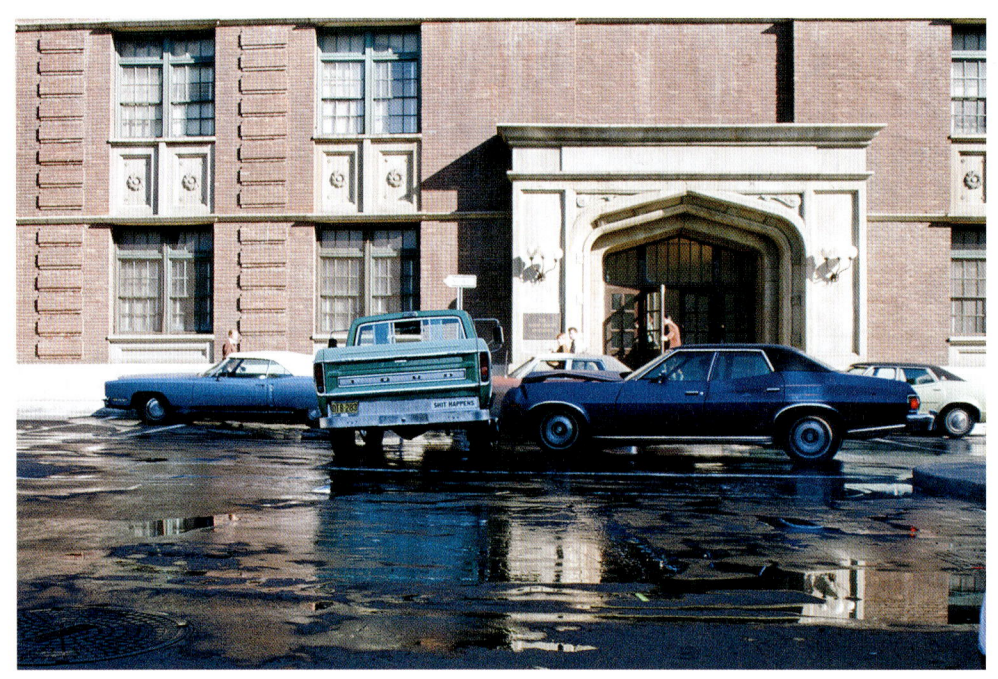

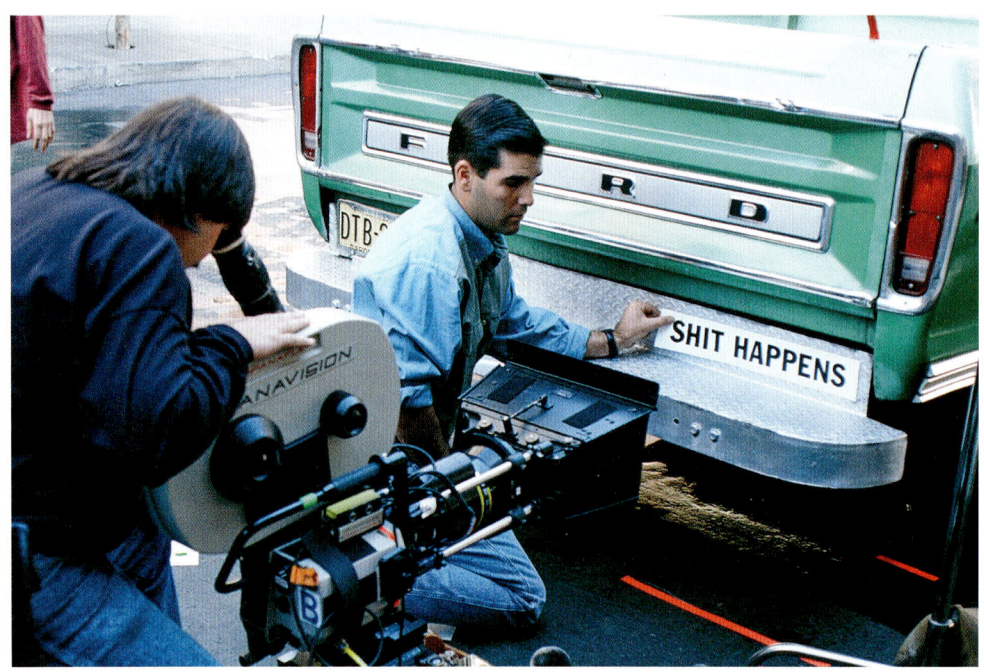

13 | A Day of Reckoning

EVERYONE KNOWS where they were on November 22, 1963, the day President John F. Kennedy was assassinated. I was on the playground of my elementary school when our sixth-grade teacher gathered the class together to break the news. Thirty years later, in November 1993, it was my day of reckoning on *Forrest Gump.* I remember the day well. We were shooting on Stage 31 at Paramount Studios. Forrest, as a member of the collegiate All-American Football Team, would be meeting with President Kennedy in the Oval Office of the White House. On that day I was called on the carpet in the office of the head of production at the studio. I had known this was coming. They hadn't wasted any time. I had told Bob I thought we could pull off our budgeting and scheduling ruse until we returned to LA. As it turned out, I was right. But I didn't even make it through the first day of shooting before I was summoned to the meeting.

The head of physical production who had showed me his golf swing and approved the budget was no longer at the studio. We had never spoken again after our meeting in his office. He had been replaced by Fred Gallo, a very firm and savvy production guy. Even though this was only my second feature film as a producer, I knew of Fred and his reputation. My coproducer, Charles Newirth, was also present at the meeting, but the finger-pointing focused on me. As we sat around in a circle, I could feel the tension in the room. I tried to act friendly, as I always did, but there was little time for small talk before the showdown got under way, with Fred leading the charge.

"Steve, you must know why you're here. The film is over budget and over schedule, and the costs are escalating by the day. We are hoping to get some clarity from you, both on how we got here and where you think this is going to end up."

I nodded my head, waiting to see what would happen next.

"Let's start with the extras. The account seems to be depleted. According to your breakdown, you have quite a few days remaining, which require a significant number of extras. How were you planning to finish the film without any money left for extras?"

"That's a good question. I don't know. I guess we will be over budget in that account."

"Yes, you will. For starters, let's look at the upcoming day at the East Los Angeles College football stadium, where Forrest runs across the field during a game. How many fans or extras did you think you would need to fill the stadium?"

"As many as we can afford."

"You can't afford any."

"Well, then, we'll have to figure out how to do the scene with as few as possible."

"You don't seem to understand. You don't have *any* extras left in the account. Maybe you can use cutouts or something. But we won't be giving you the extras you planned on."

"Just tell me how many I can have, and we'll make it work."

"That's admirable of you to try to minimize your overage. But you need to understand, we are not in the overage business. We like to come in on budget. And when we see a problem, we speak to one another and come up with a solution. Does that make sense to you?"

"Yes, it does."

Department by department we went through the budget and reviewed the estimates to complete the film. Most departments lacked the necessary funds to make it to the finish line, and that was just on paper. I knew it was worse.

"Steve, these accounts have been depleted. You are out of money throughout the budget. I am not

sure how you planned to finish the show. What were you thinking?"

That was a question that had not been asked until now. And I didn't have an answer, at least not one I could share. But I believe the studio knew what I was thinking: I would keep up the charade until I was caught. I just didn't think it would be with my pants down.

"It seems like you were spending with reckless abandon."

"We will plan to keep a closer eye on our spending from this day forward," I promised.

"It seems like we will have to keep an eye on your spending for you."

I was stunned into silence. Everyone was looking to me for answers, and I didn't have any. Embarrassed and not knowing what to say, I just sat there. I started to wonder what was going to happen. Shut the show down? Could they do that? Would they do that? Fire me? I had no idea. And the inquisition was not over.

"Do you have any cuts you can make?"

"Do you mean scenes?"

"Yes, scenes or days. You are going over schedule."

He didn't know that everything in the schedule was going according to plan—just not the studio's plan. "I will review the scenes we have remaining with Bob and see what we can cut."

"I will tell you right now, you won't be ending the run in Monument Valley. I suggest you stay

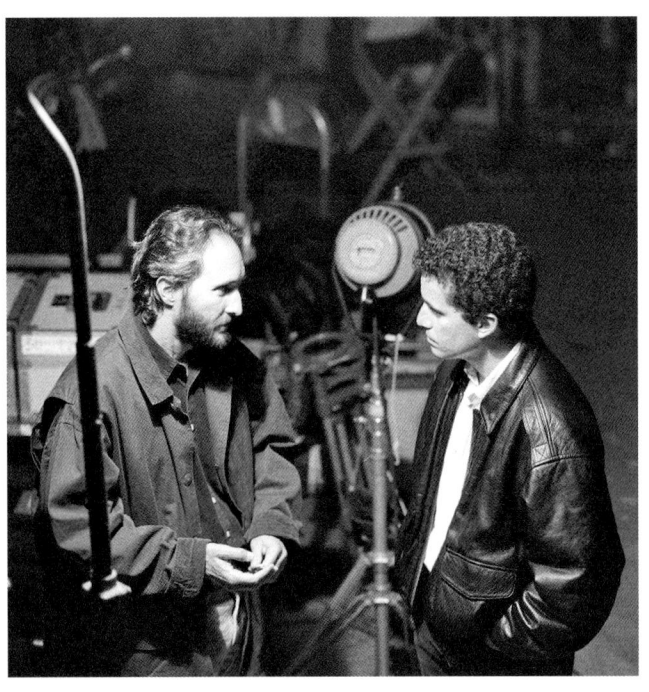

Charles Newirth and me, licking our wounds

what I planned to do. "Nothing, I guess. Let's take it one day at a time and see what happens."

I was glad the meeting was over. At the end of the day, it seemed like nothing more than a good spanking. Strangely, I felt protected. Protected by the film. Few scenes were vulnerable to getting cut. Every scene we had left to shoot was tied to something we had already shot. Anything we cut would unravel the story. At least, that's what I believed. The studio should have made cuts before we started shooting, not now. So, despite the studio's bravado, I thought they had little recourse other than making me feel bad and responsible. I would not let the studio damage the picture. I knew that much. I still wasn't sure what they could or would do. We would have to wait and see.

in LA. Take a look at Canyon Country, maybe Vasquez Rocks. Many TV shows have made it work there. Scout the locations and let me know what you think."

"Will do." I could see where this was going. Deep. Very deep. With that, the meeting ended. We had been put on notice. Now that we were back in LA, the studio was in charge. They were tightening the purse strings. I had no idea how this would play out. I had never been in this position before. Yet I still planned to finish the movie we had set out to make. As we left the meeting, Charles asked

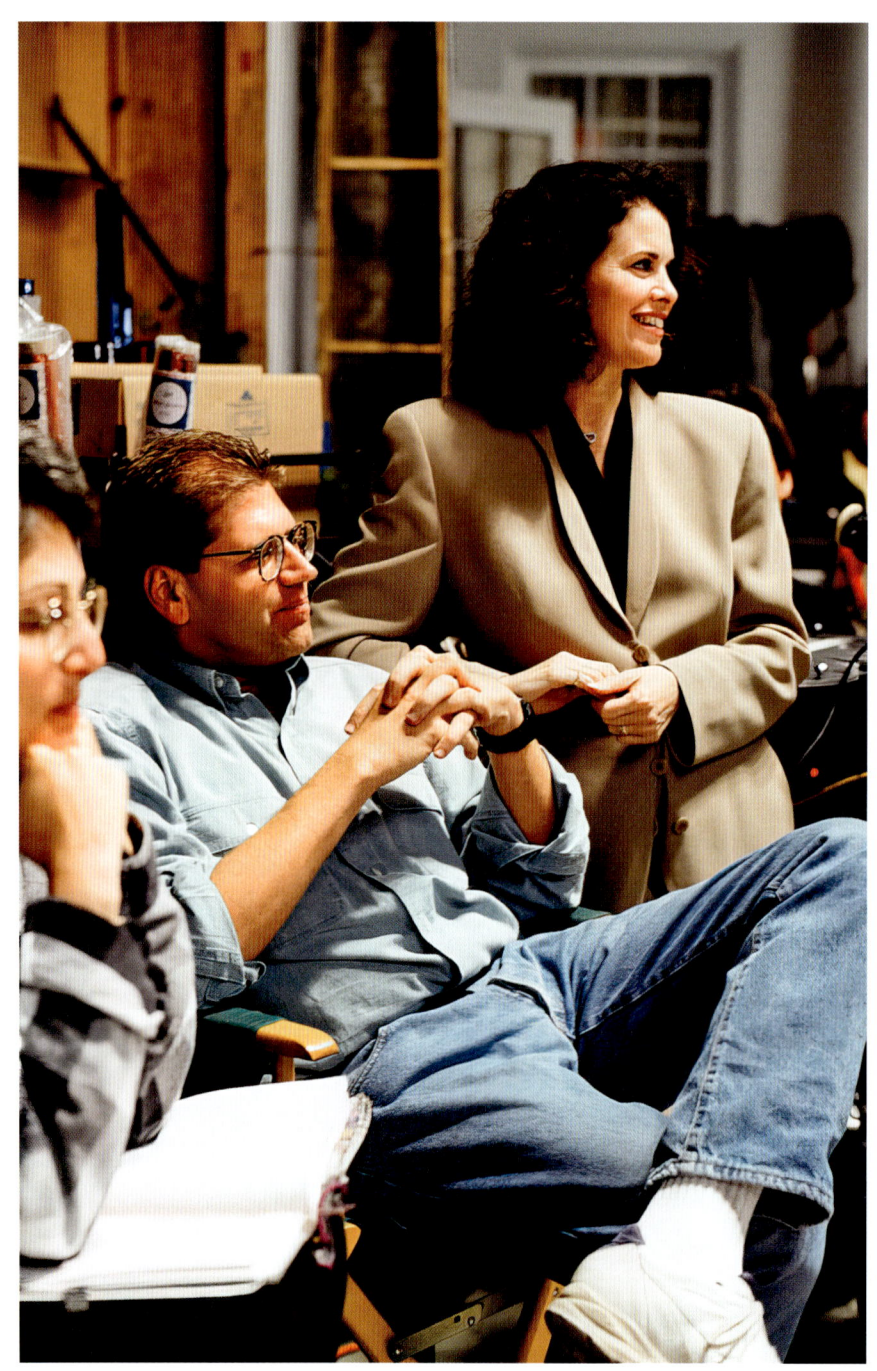

14 | Meeting the Presidents

WHEN I RETURNED TO the stage, Sherry Lansing, the chair of Paramount Pictures, came by for a visit. I felt awkward. I knew she must have been aware of my meeting with Fred Gallo, but nothing was said.

I was just happy to get back to shooting the movie. I felt like I had dodged a bullet. While Bob was getting ready for his first setup in the Oval Office—where Forrest would meet with President Kennedy—I drifted into the adjoining bathroom set and caught a glimpse of a photo of Marilyn Monroe next to the sink. It was signed. I chuckled at Bob's humorous addition of the picture to the set dressing. The audience would get the joke when Forrest washed his hands after he excused himself to go pee.

I was starting to feel human again after the tense studio meeting. The Oval Office set looked like the real thing, and the extras for the scene resembled the football players in our licensed stock footage of an actual collegiate team meeting Kennedy. Most of the scene was shot on the set with a stand-in for the president. Then we moved to the blue-screen stage to shoot Tom Hanks shaking hands with an imaginary Kennedy. With a sound-alike voicing the

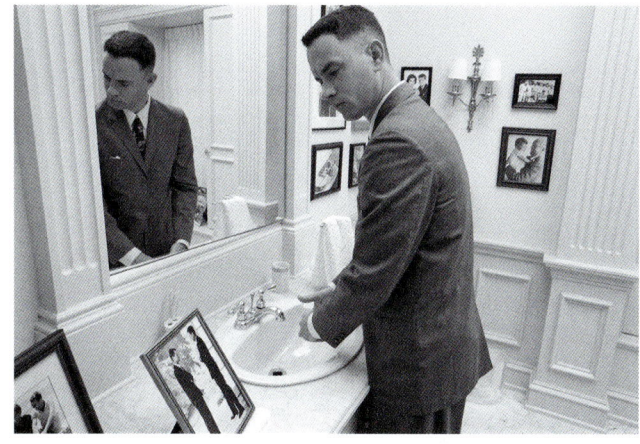

Forrest washes his hands in the White House bathroom

president, a little manipulation of Kennedy's lips, and clever cutting, it would appear that Forrest had met the president of the United States.

After we finished shooting that day, Bob and I had our usual Bushmills, and I told him about my studio meeting. It wasn't pretty, I admitted. "What do we do?"

"Let's just stay the course," Bob said.

"What about the cuts they want us to make in the script? Don't we need to throw them a bone?" I felt the only option was to agree with the studio's

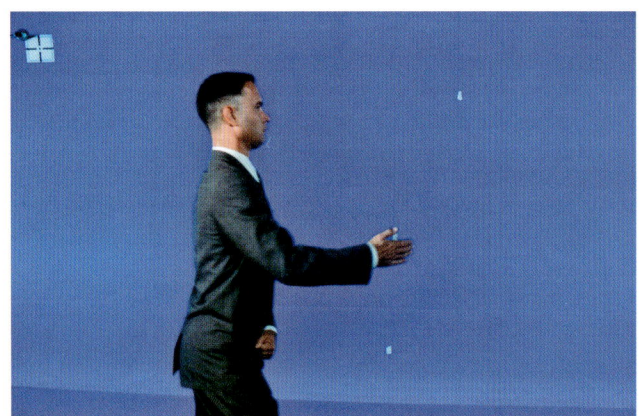 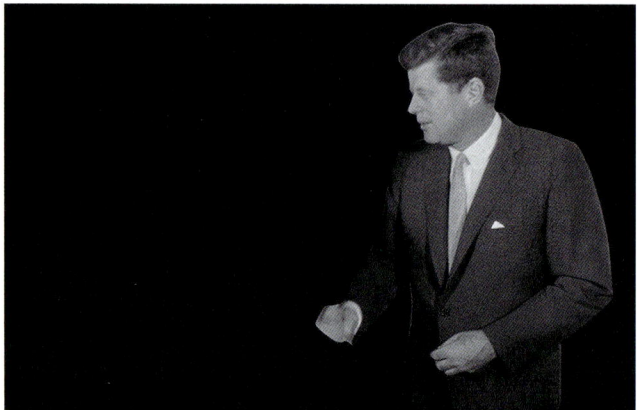

Tom acts against the blue screen to match the stock footage of President Kennedy

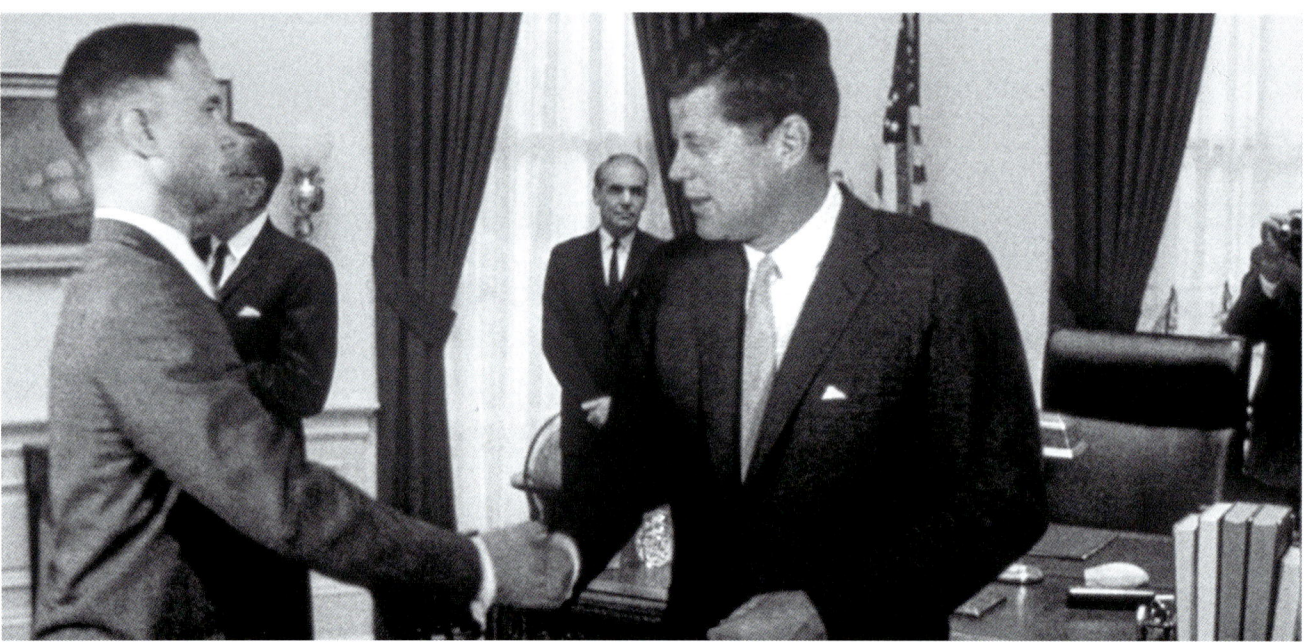

How the shot looks in the film

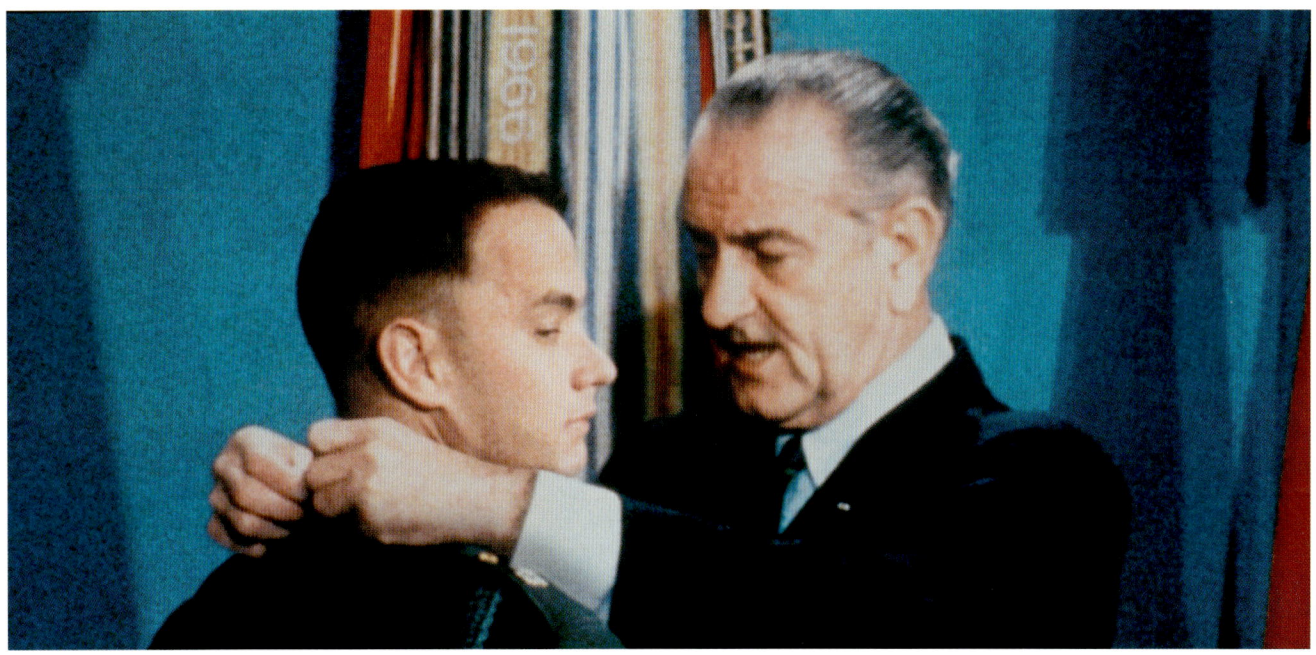

Forrest receives the Medal of Honor from President Johnson

suggestions and still shoot the movie our way—appear to be compliant, but do what we needed to do to finish our movie. That was the plan.

Following the scene with President Kennedy, Ken Ralston guided us through the scenes of Forrest meeting with Presidents Johnson and Nixon.

All the presidential encounters were laced with humor. During the encounter with Johnson, who was awarding Forrest the Medal of Honor for his bravery in Vietnam, Forrest reveals the wound on his buttocks to the president, which we filmed with a stand-in.

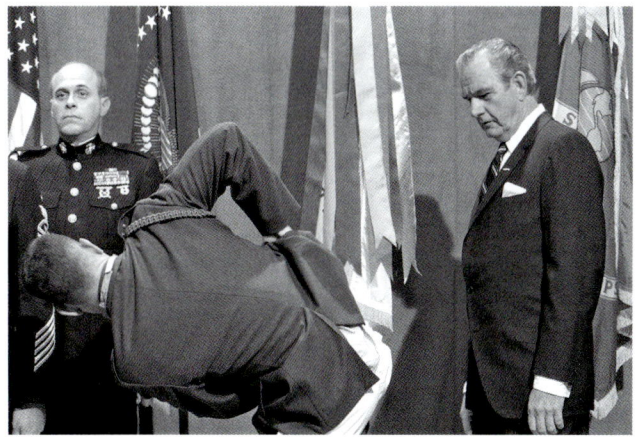

Forrest shows President Johnson's stand-in his war wound

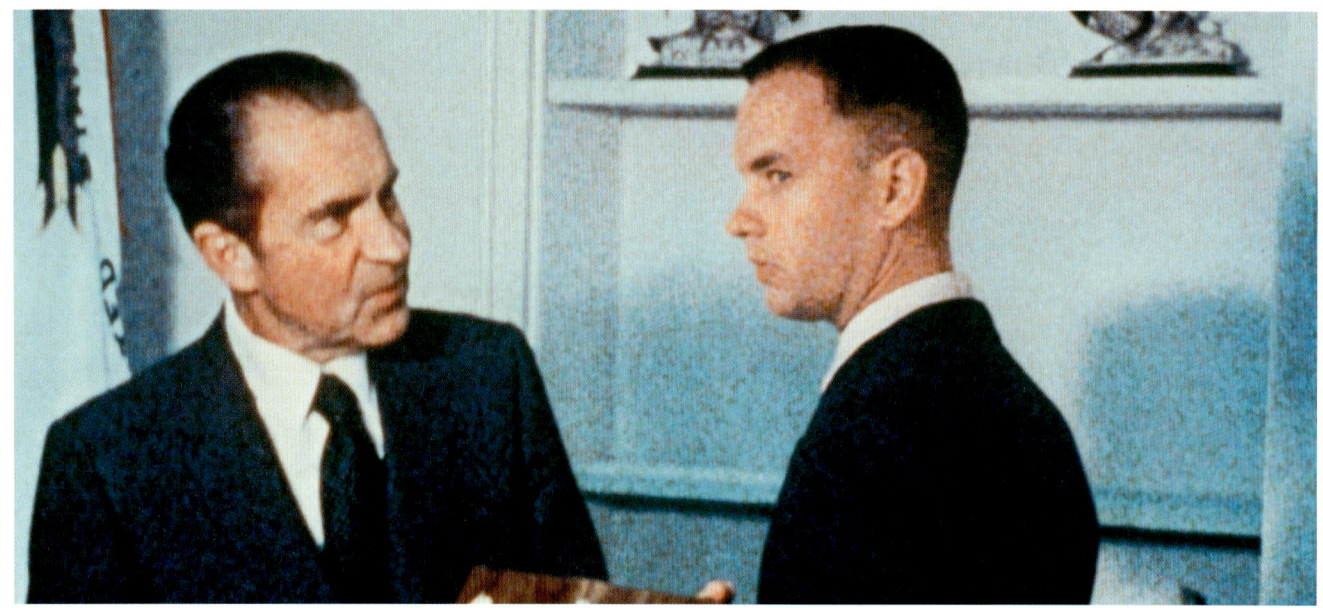

Forrest meets President Nixon

In the scene with Nixon—in which Forrest is part of the all-American table tennis team—the president suggests a nice hotel, the Watergate, in Washington, DC. Once he checks into his room, Forrest calls security when he observes a break-in taking place in the room across the way, leading to Nixon's downfall—a good joke, indeed.

Although shooting the scene with Nixon was difficult, the greatest challenge turned out to be shooting Forrest playing Ping-Pong in China.

At the end of the movie *Blow Up*, a group of university students pantomimes a game of tennis without a ball. Back and forth, back and forth, they wildly chase an imaginary ball. For our film, we asked a professional Ping-Pong player to

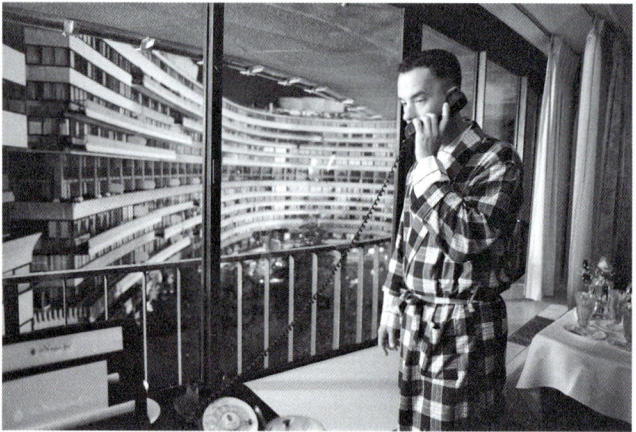

Forrest calls security from his Watergate hotel room

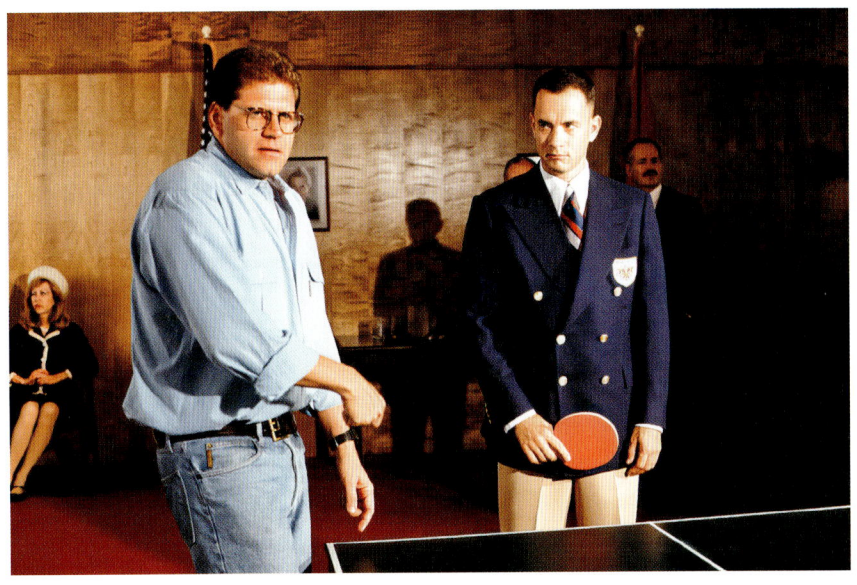

Bob gives last-minute instructions

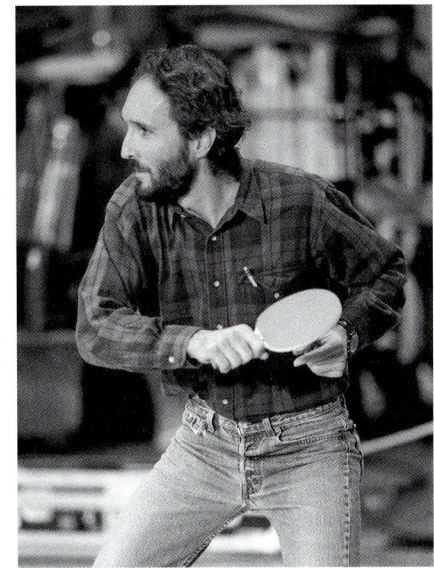

Me warming up our champion

pantomime the game with Tom Hanks. When I showed up for that shoot, I met our champion player for the first time. He didn't speak English very well. Centered in the set was a Ping-Pong table. In the background were seats for dignitaries to watch the match. I had played a bit of Ping-Pong in my youth, so I decided to break the ice and asked our "actor" if he wanted to hit the ball around. He held his racket upside down, or maybe in professional circles it's right side up. In any case, the handle was at the top, with the face of the paddle below. I could tell he was the real deal.

Considering the competitive level of play depicted in the film, our game couldn't be real. Tom was good at everything he did, but not that good. To re-create a game at the highest level, we explained to the pro that we'd be playing without a ball. That would be added later. He gave us a blank stare. He was completely confused. When Tom arrived on set, he took my paddle and got into position at his end of the table. He thought if he showed the pro what we meant by all this mumbo jumbo, what we needed would become clear.

They started slowly. Tom explained that it was all make-believe. "I hit, then you hit. I hit, then you hit," he said, as he swung his paddle at an imaginary ball, then pointed to his opponent to do the same. "Back and forth."

The pro fell out of sync immediately. It turned out that he was somewhat like Forrest Gump: Give him a Ping-Pong ball and a paddle, and he knew what to do. Take the ball away, and he was lost. The

149

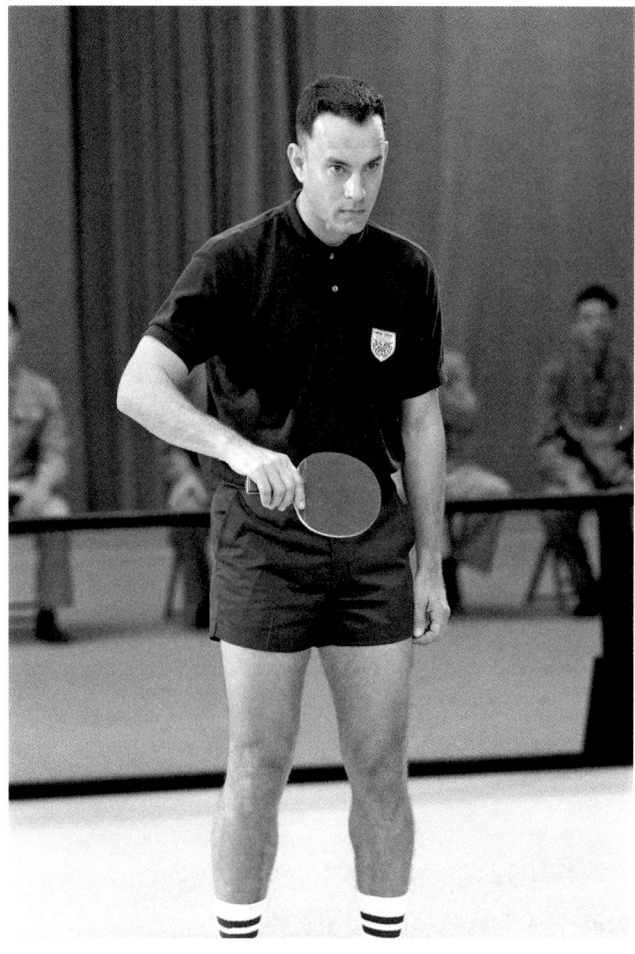

Playing Ping-Pong without a ball

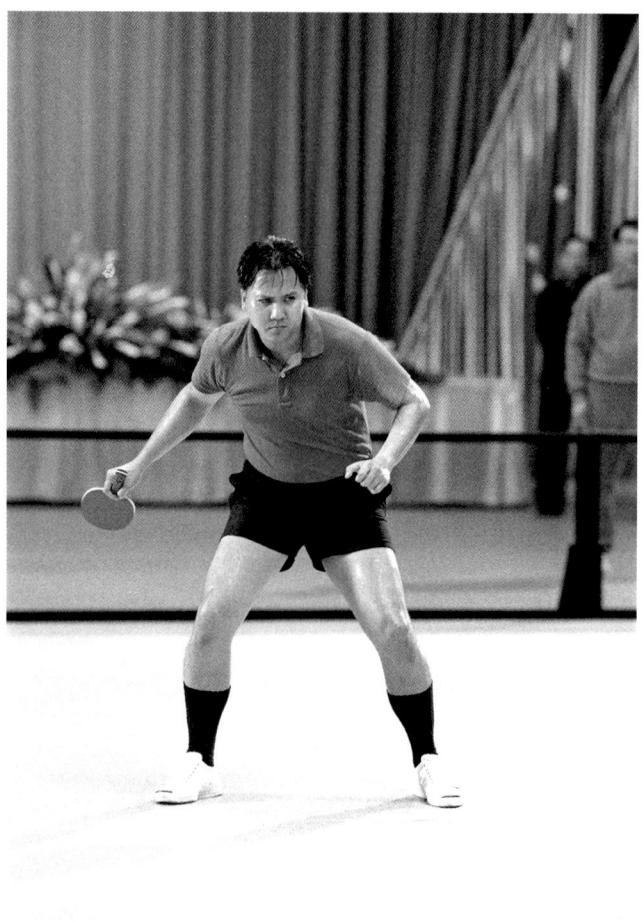

Forrest's opponent

notion of playing without a ball was impossible for him to grasp. Tom verbalized the hits he was pretending to make, mimicking the sound of the ball hitting the paddle. *Tick, tock. Tick, tock.* That didn't help. His opponent quickly lost the rhythm. No matter how hard Tom tried to get him in sync, the pro simply couldn't do it.

Bob was becoming frustrated. He decided we should have a click track broadcast on the set, so each time the ball supposedly hit the paddle, the sound would be heard: *tick, tock, tick tock,* like a grandfather clock. But the pro still couldn't match his stroke to the sounds. He either fell behind or swung too early. Finally, Tom said he knew what

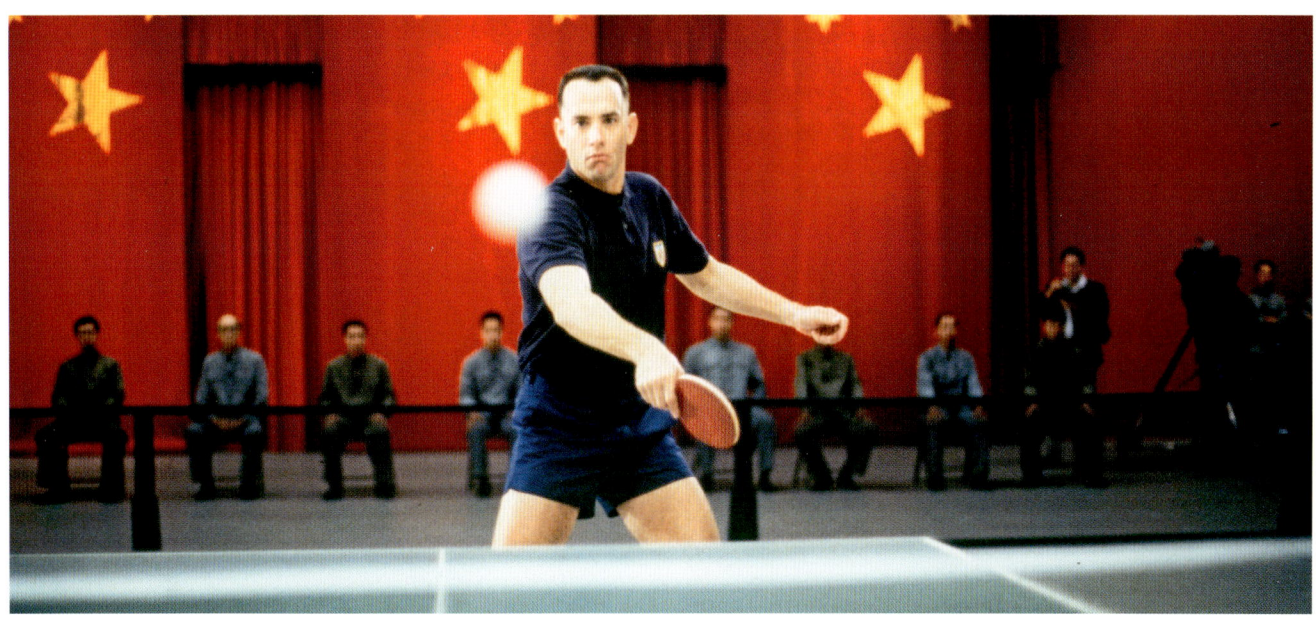

Forrest hits a winning shot

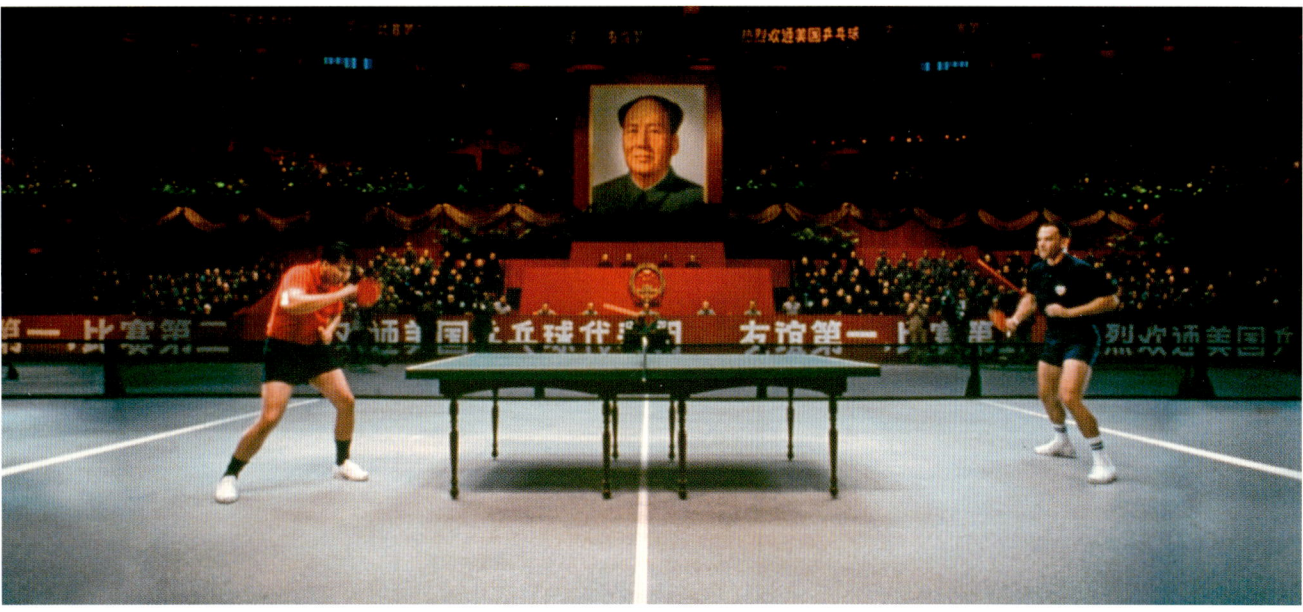

Forrest competes with his Chinese opponent

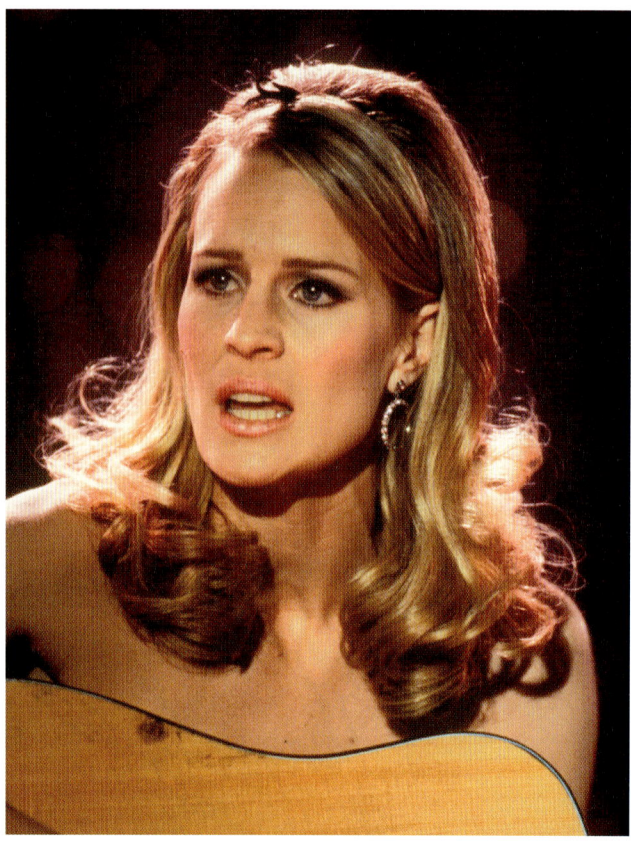

Jenny sings "Blowin' in the Wind"

Forrest's two remaining friends, Jenny and Lieutenant Dan, one had become a drug addict and the other a drunk. The scenes with Jenny taking drugs at a disco and a musician's low-rent apartment were both shot at the Ambassador Hotel, as was a sequence at a topless club where she sings "Blowin' in the Wind."

This was the same hotel where Robert Kennedy had been shot. The building was shuttered and derelict, only a shadow of its former self. The same could be said for Jenny in many of her scenes in LA. Her character's beauty had diminished, and, as it turned out, Robin was also going through a rough patch after losing her home to a fire. She had rented a place close to our home in the Pacific Palisades, with her toddlers in tow. But I was starting to worry about her. I feared she wasn't eating properly.

I called Goldie Hawn, who had become a friend on *Death Becomes Her,* and asked if she knew of someone—a cook or a caterer—I might hire to prepare some dinners for Robin and her family. Goldie offered up her own cook. A few days a week, I had dinner prepared for Robin and dropped it off on my way home from work. I was worried about her well-being—not her acting. That didn't fall off one bit.

Meanwhile, Lieutenant Dan had become a lost soul who had turned to the bottle. After reuniting with Forrest outside the stage door of *The Dick Cavett Show,* Lieutenant Dan drags Forrest into his dark world.

to do. He would watch his opponent carefully, and whenever he hit the ball, Tom would adjust, so it appeared that he was on the receiving end of the shot.

Back and forth they went. Whatever the other guy did, Tom seemed to be hitting the ball back. He made our pro look like the champion player he was.

After completing that scene, we bounced back and forth, just like a Ping-Pong ball, from fun and games to the darker side of the film. Of

After celebrating the New Year in a bar, they go to Lieutenant Dan's hotel room with some hookers. It seems like fun, until Forrest rebuffs the ladies' advances:

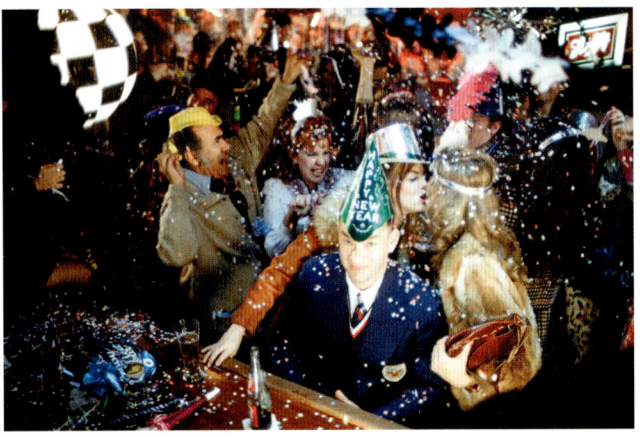 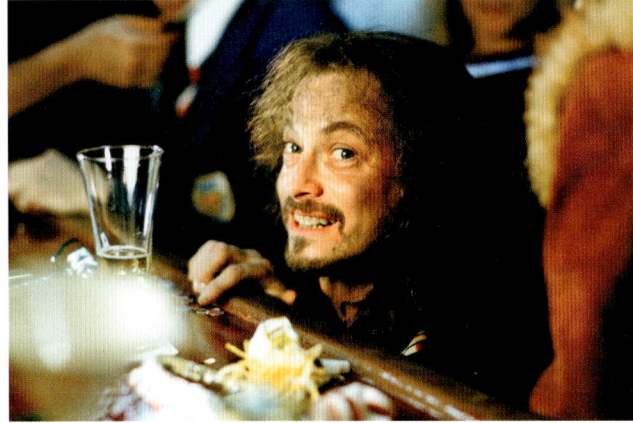

LENORE
(to Lt. Dan)
Is your friend stupid or something?

CARLA
Yeah, what's his problem? Did he lose his pecker in the war or something?

Lieutenant Dan comes to Forrest's defense and throws the girls out.

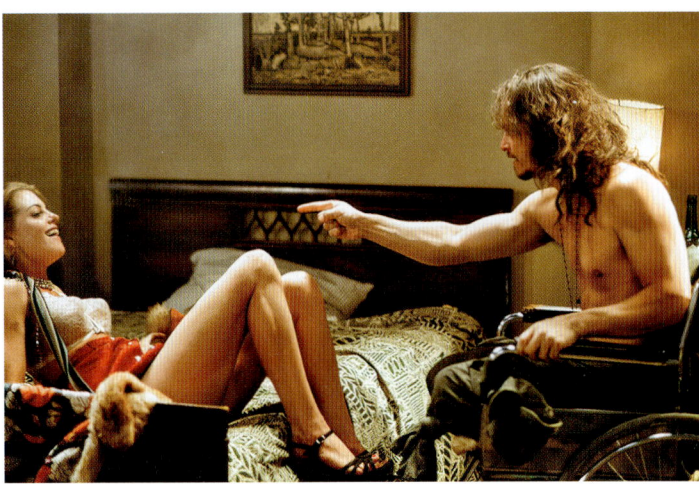

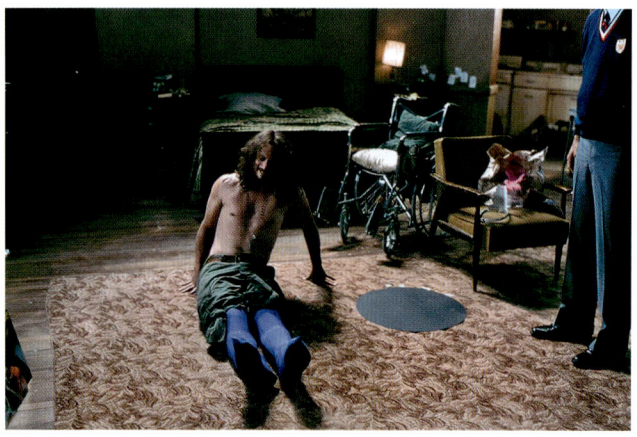

Gary Sinise's legs wrapped in blue for special effects

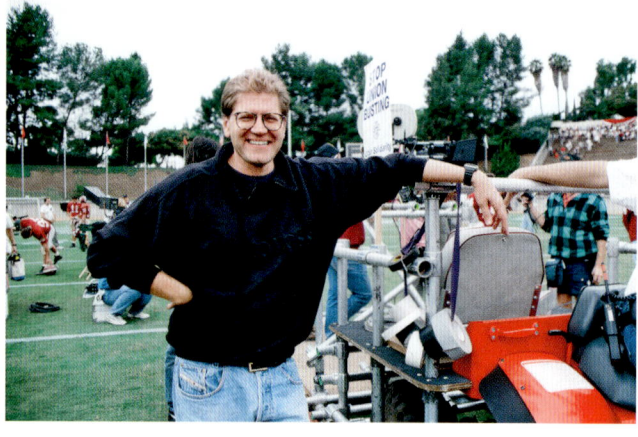

Bob on the set of the football field

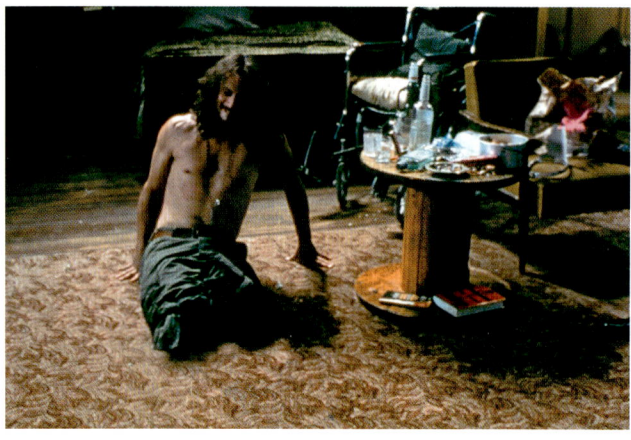

A legless Lieutenant Dan with table added

After falling from his wheelchair, he struggles to get back up. Bob designed a shot with Lieutenant Dan swinging his hips past a table and positioning his body to pull himself back into his wheelchair. Only a legless man could make a move like that.

Once again Ken Ralston worked his magic, doing the shot without the table and then replacing the table in post-production. It would keep the audience on their toes. They might even wonder if Gary Sinise was an amputee.

After working with Gary and Tom on the bar scene all night Friday and into Saturday, we reported to the football stadium at East Los Angeles College early Monday morning on very little rest. With a little painterly help from Ken and ILM, the stadium would stand in for the University of Alabama, where Forrest's running had earned him a scholarship. We were huddled high up in the seats above the fifty-yard line, setting the first shot, when Tom came trudging up the stairs. Bob wished him good morning and asked how he was feeling. "Not so good, Bob. I'm pretty sick." Not skipping a beat, Bob replied, "That's too bad 'cause you have a shitload of running to do!" Despite how he was feeling, Tom ran his ass off all day long.

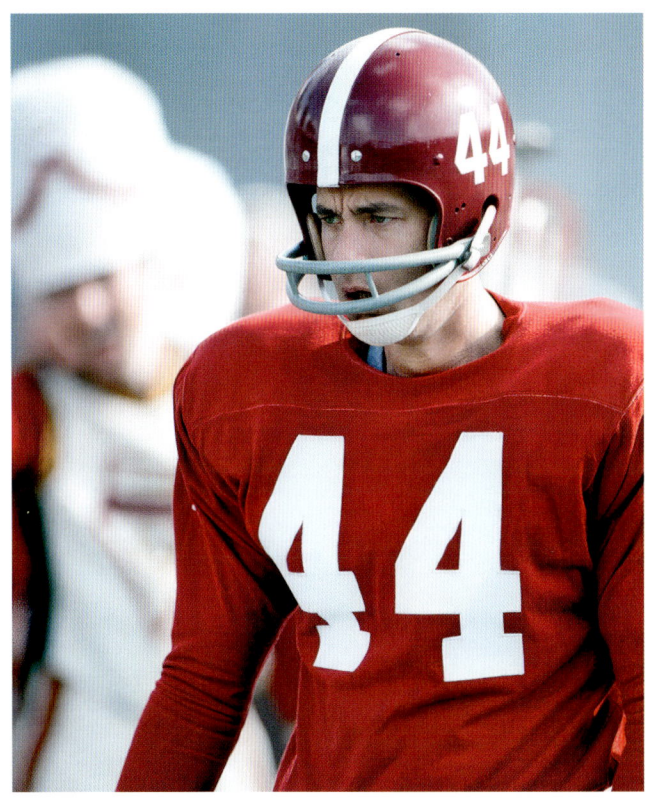

Forrest waiting for the kick-off

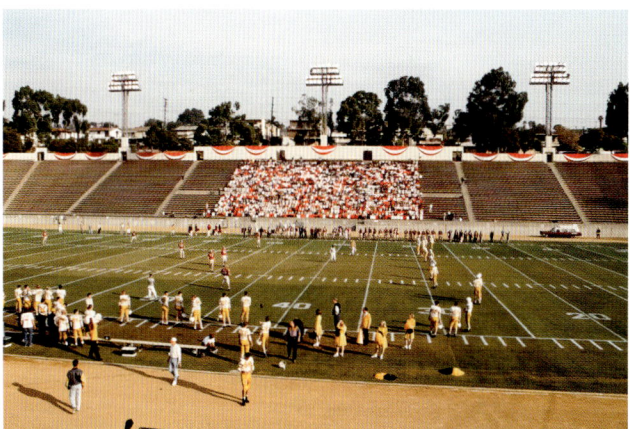

Positioning our extras at the fifty-yard line

Living up to their word, the studio had drastically cut the number of extras we could call on to fill the stadium. We didn't employ cutouts or dummies, as the studio had suggested. So in addition to using the few extras we had, we reverted to digital matte paintings to extend the stadium and fill it with fans. That bit of magic was put together in post-production. In a sense, we were kicking our financial problems downstream. We were spending a little less during shooting, but the effects budget wasn't getting any smaller. I figured I would face that problem later.

We made the scene work with the limited number of fans we could afford and filled the stadium with a little help from Ken Ralston and ILM.

The studio was getting more anxious by the day. At the end of the preceding week, we had to show that we were another day over. That was the first increase since our return to LA and the meeting

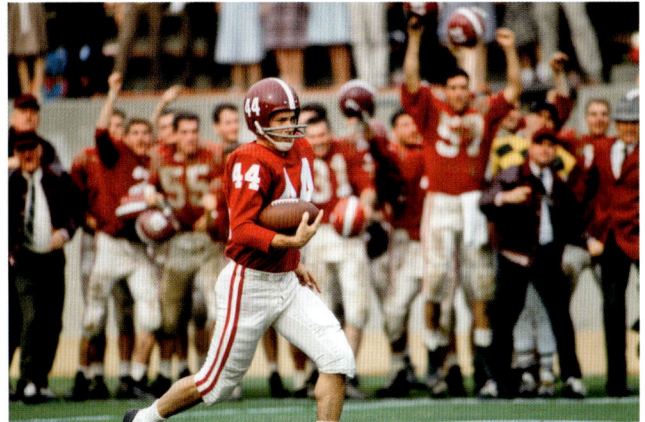

Forrest as a running back heads for the goal line

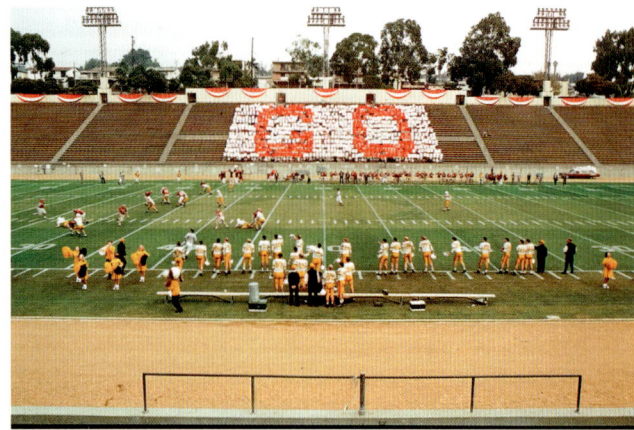

Filming with a limited number of extras

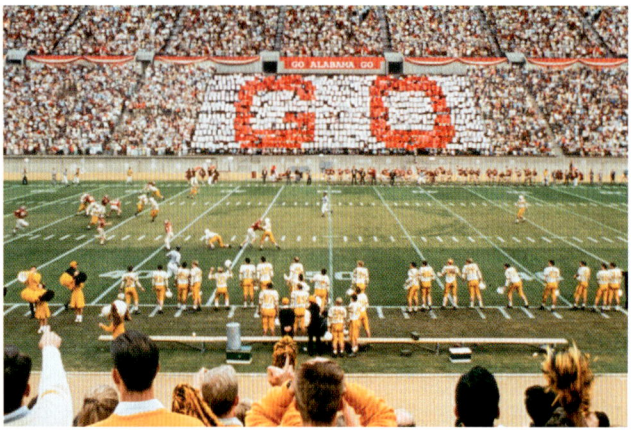

The final shot with help from Ken Ralston and ILM

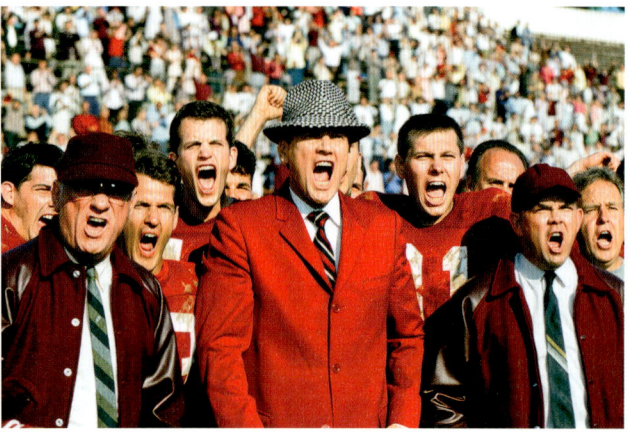

The Alabama coaches scream, "Run, Forrest, run!"

with the executives. Our total had now increased to seventy-two days, and the execs were not happy. Clearly I was not living up to their mandate of staying on schedule. But I was trying to dole out the bad news in small bites, knowing that the worst was yet to come. We had made the location shooting schedule more doable to get us back to Los Angeles alive. The more unrealistic days were stacked up at the end of the shoot. And although I knew that the "official" days remaining wouldn't get me to the finish line, I had some crazy optimism that we could overcome the lack of time. Boy, was I wrong.

After finishing work at the football stadium and the Wilshire Ebell Theatre—which stood in for a Saigon hospital ward and a hospital recreation room—shooting didn't get any easier. Scenes there with Forrest learning to play Ping-Pong and working with Lieutenant Dan took more time than we expected.

Over lunch Bob invited me into his trailer and had me read a couple of new scenes he had written for the run. More scenes for the run! You must be kidding. The studio would sooner cut the run entirely than allow us to add scenes!

"Just read the scenes," Bob said. He handed me the pages. As I read, I started smiling, then laughing out loud. Forrest had altered history throughout the film, and now he was the person who inspired both the "Shit Happens" bumper sticker and the happy face T-shirt. I shook my head in disbelief and told Bob, "You're nuts, you know that?"

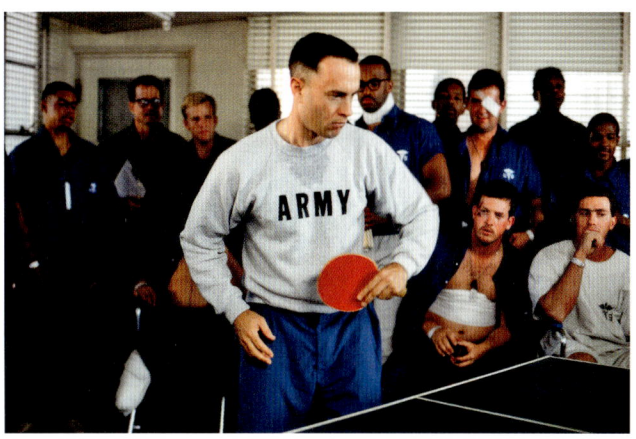

Forrest learns to play Ping-Pong

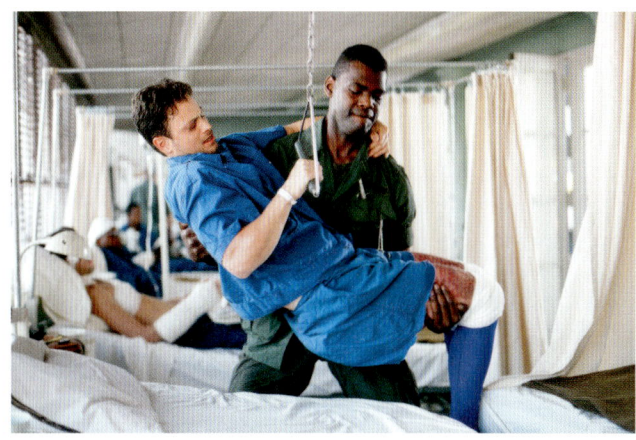

Blue-screen coverings on Gary Sinise's legs before removal in post-production

"The run needs a laugh," he said. "Something to offer relief to the audience. They need to put a smile on their faces. It's just an instinct."

I was sort of convinced, or at least convinced enough that it got me thinking. How could we squeeze these scenes in between now and the end of the schedule? We couldn't add any days.

157

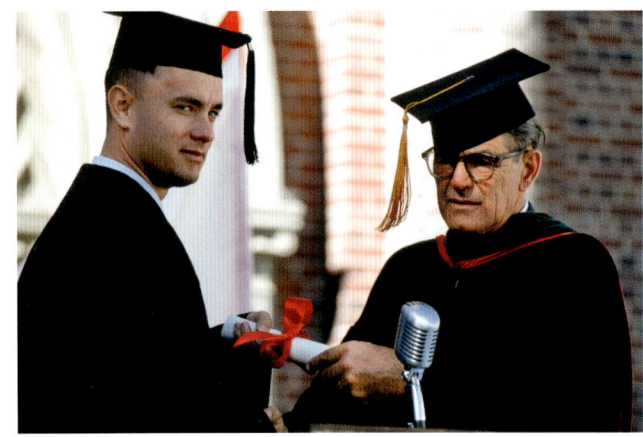

Forrest graduates from college

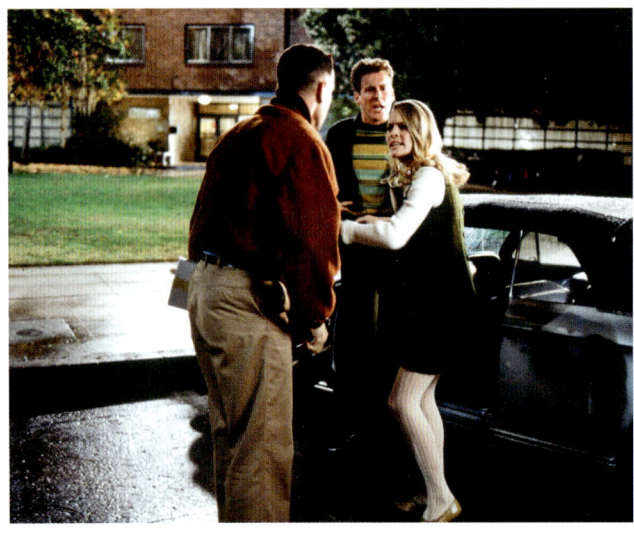

Filming in a parking lot at USC

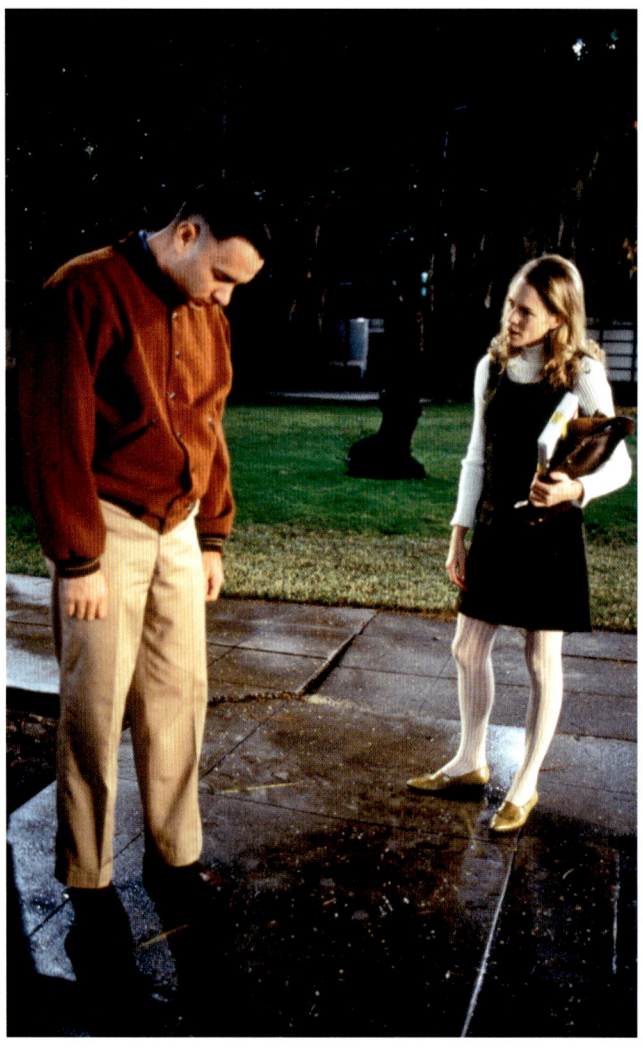

Forrest mistakenly rescues Jenny from a date

We certainly wouldn't be able to sell the studio on that idea. But if I could figure out a way to go to Monument Valley for the same cost as shooting the end of the run locally, why would they say no? If I got them to say yes, maybe I could squeeze these shots in, away from their watchful eyes.

Next we were off to the University of Southern California, standing in for the University of Alabama. Forrest received his diploma exactly where

Bob had received his from film school, an irony not lost on any of us.

The week ended at USC late at night, with Forrest mistakenly rescuing Jenny from a date in front of her dorm. As the work extended into the early hours of Saturday morning, I fell asleep in my director's chair. Fortunately there was no image of me to go viral.

With less and less work left on the show, reality set in. This difficult week added not one but three days to the schedule. Only a final, short week was left. Again I had to reveal to the studio where we stood. Ironically, we were at seventy-six days, just one day over our original schedule. But there would be no heroes by mentioning that fact now, only scapegoats.

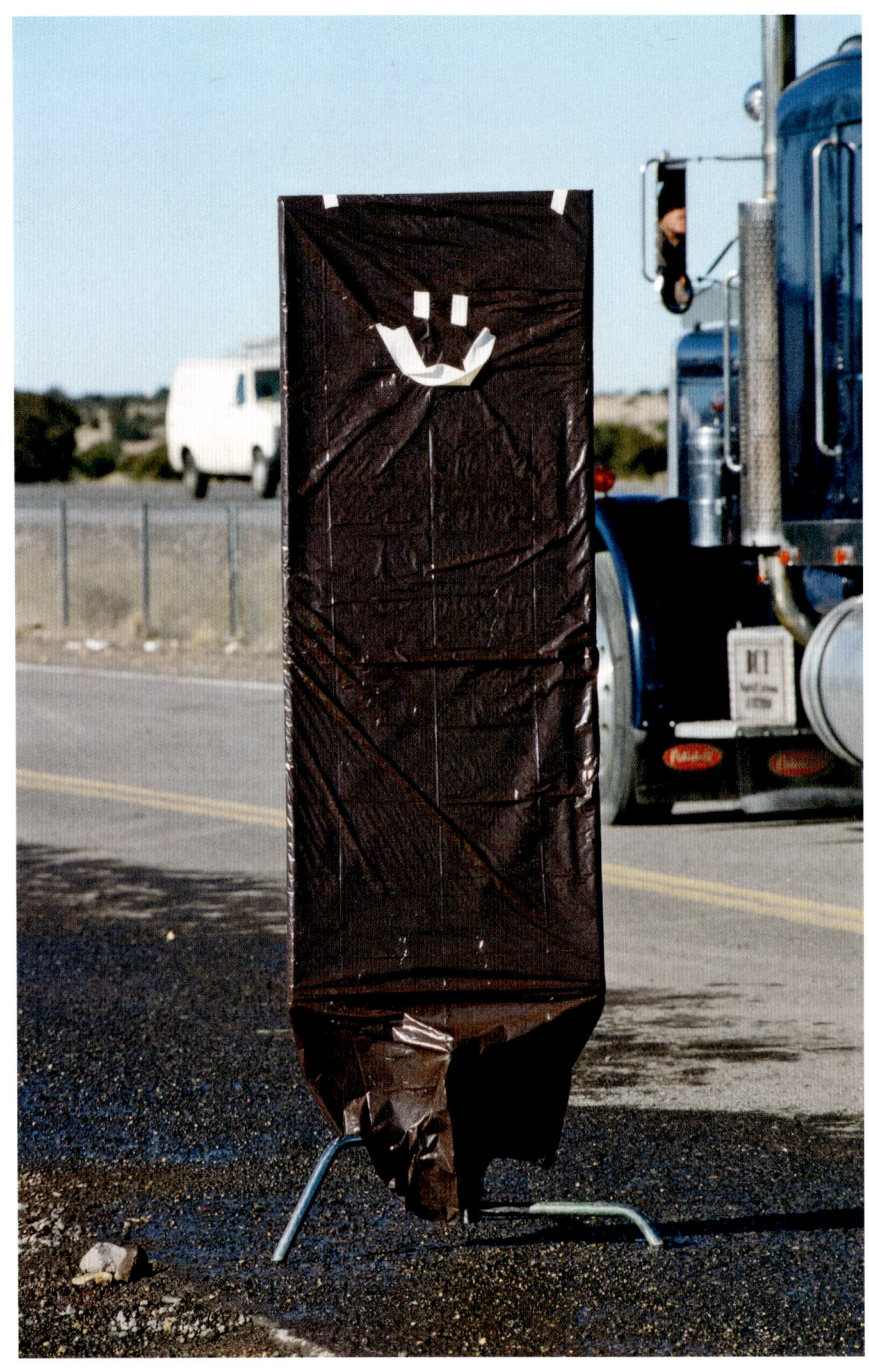

15 | We've Been Gumped

DESPITE THE OVERAGES piling up in both the budget and the shooting schedule, I was having difficulty giving up on the idea of Monument Valley. What more iconic place was there for Forrest to end his run and head home? In our fateful meeting, the studio had agreed that the location was perfect but still said no. Shoot it locally. Canyon Country or anywhere north of LA would work just fine.

But we refused to compromise after all we'd been through. Now I had an even greater incentive for shooting in Monument Valley: getting Bob's new running scenes into the film. I knew my only chance to shoot these new scenes was away from the watchful eye of the studio. I put together a plan and, with Bob's permission, took it to the studio: we'd charter a plane, fly early in the morning, shoot in the afternoon, spend the night in Monument Valley, shoot the next morning, and fly back that same evening. I had both budgets with me—the one for a local shoot and the one in Monument Valley. The studio executives looked them over. The numbers were the same. But going to Arizona and Utah was risky. There was no contingency plan. What if it rained? Where would the extras come from, and how would I fit them in wardrobe? Where would the cast and crew stay? I had all the answers. The execs seemed to think the plan was solid enough, but they needed to take it upstairs. At this stage, the studio was so upset that they wouldn't make any concessions to the filmmakers without higher-level approval. I left the meeting cautiously optimistic. At least they hadn't said no.

I told Bob where we stood. It was in the hands of the studio. In turns out the higher-ups were outraged that we had audacity to even ask for this allowance, considering what we had put them through and the overages we had already racked up. They called a meeting with Bob. From what he told me afterward, I was happy I wasn't there. With red faces and blood vessels swelling, they yelled and screamed at him. Due to the risky nature of the location, they demanded that he and Tom put up a bond for the insurance to cover any overages. Bob and Tom agreed, and once again we were off and running.

Transportation and equipment headed by road to Arizona in the early hours of the morning. The cast and crew took a charter plane and met the

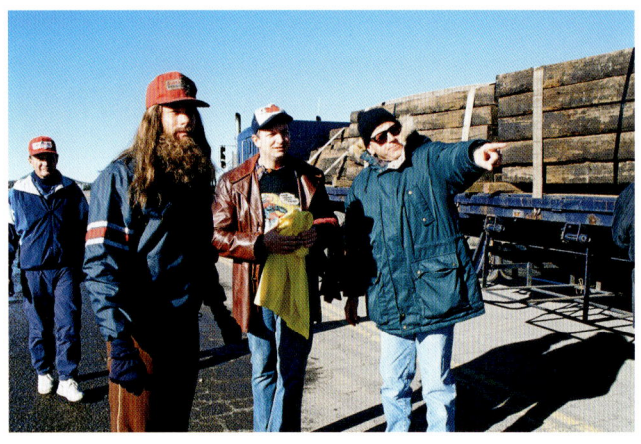

Bob lines up the Happy Face shot outside Flagstaff, Arizona

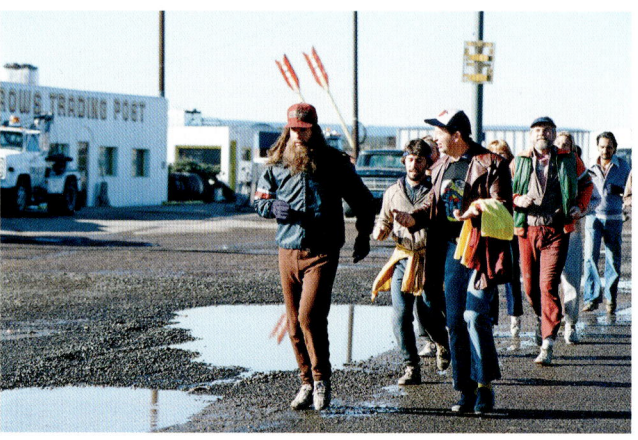

Forrest meets the T-shirt guy

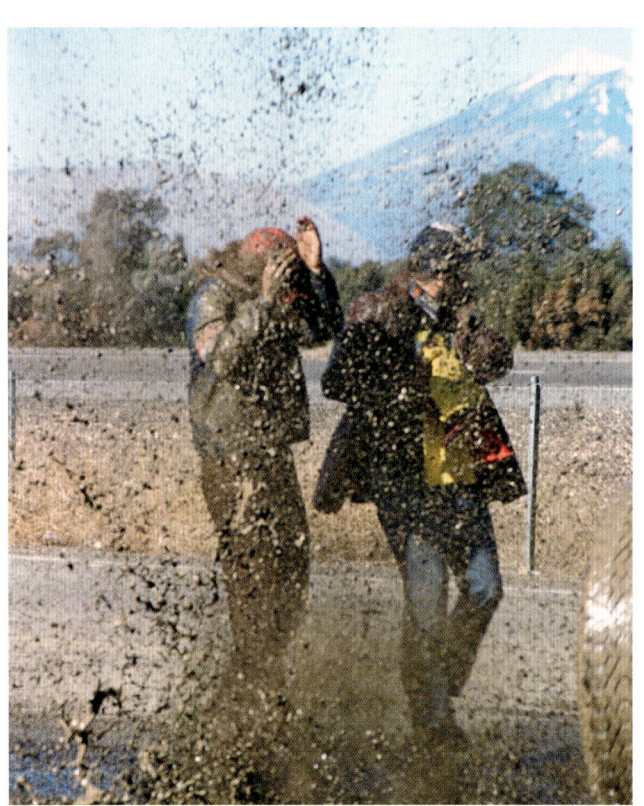

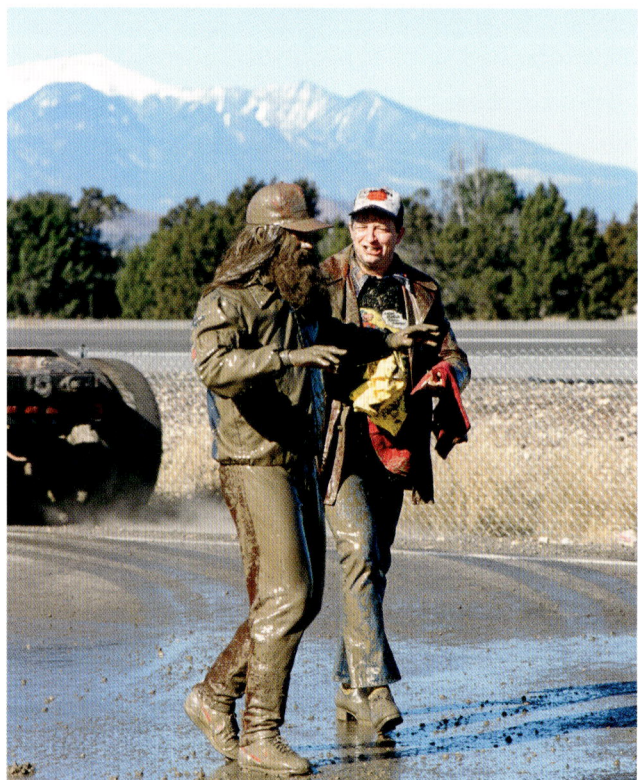

Sometimes you get the perfect shot in one take

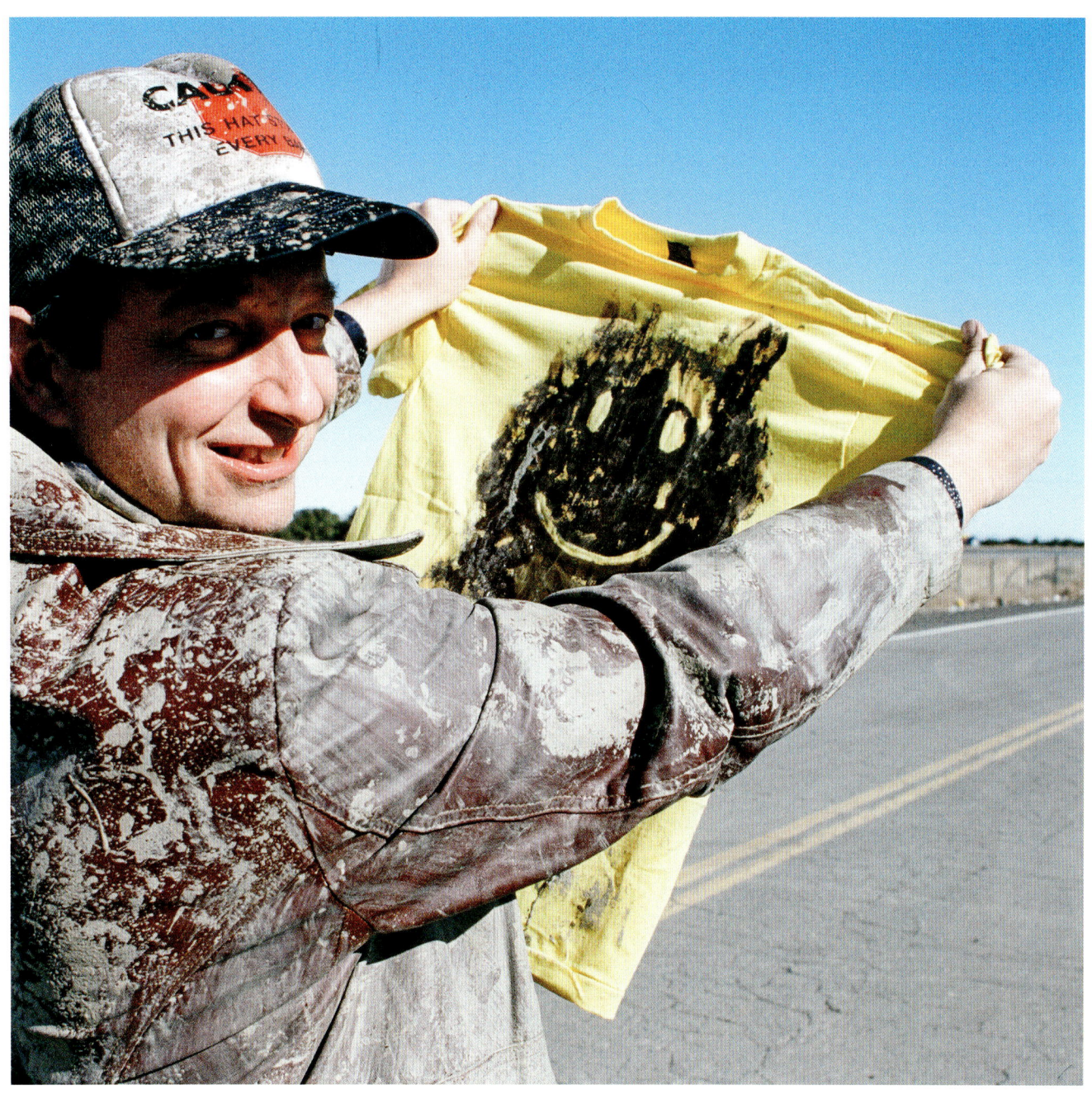

The iconic happy face T-shirt

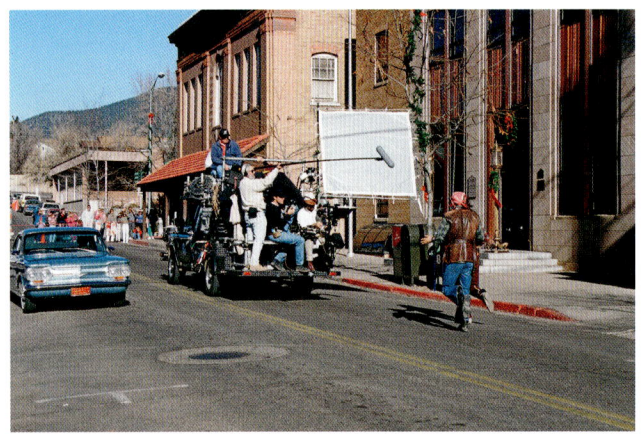

The shot maker in action

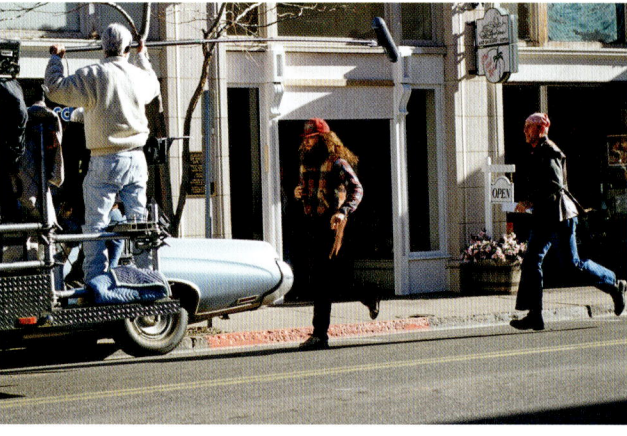

"Whoa, man, you just ran through a big pile of dog shit"

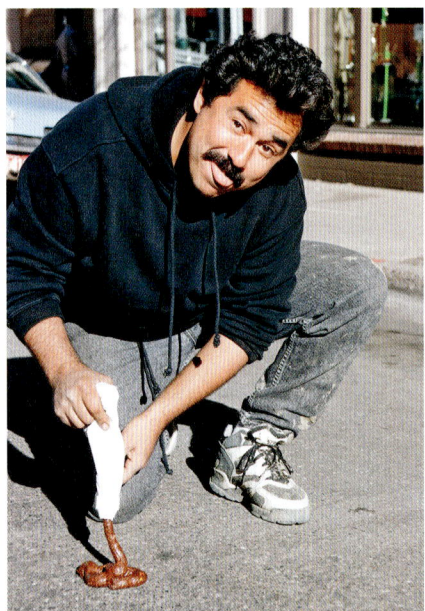

Prop man squeezes a pile of "poop"
from a pastry bag

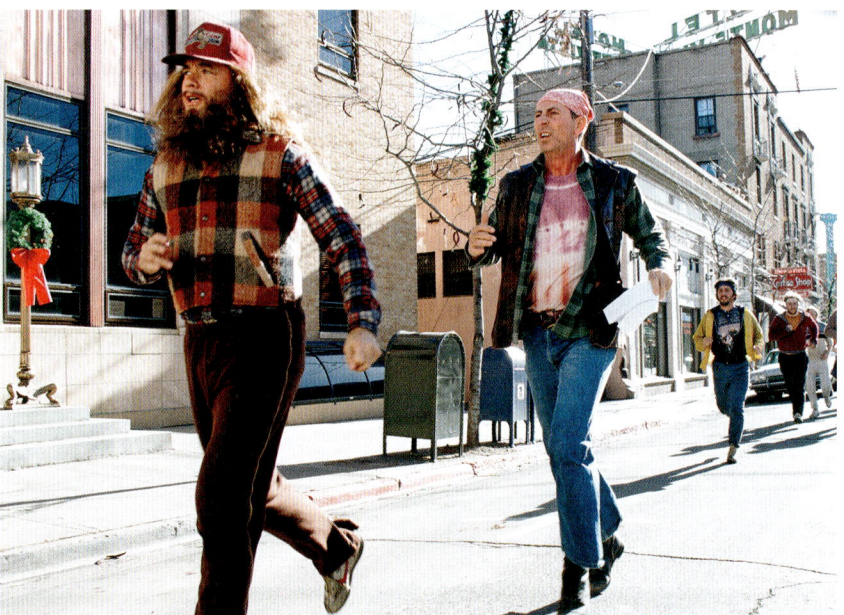

"It happens."
"What, shit?"

trucks outside Flagstaff. The crew jumped into action. We quickly mounted up the first shot along the road into town for what we called the "happy face" joke. Forrest is running down the road next to a guy carrying a bunch of T-shirts when a truck splashes mud all over him. The guy lends Forrest a T-shirt to wipe his face, and lo and behold, the iconic happy face is revealed. While they were shooting that scene, I was planning to leap ahead and get the next shot ready for Bob in downtown Flagstaff. I thought it would take forever for the truck to drive through a puddle and splash mud on our poor actor.

But while I was still sipping my coffee, they got a good take in the can. With no time to spare, I said a quick good-bye to Bob and raced to the next location to prepare for the "Shit Happens" shot. We mounted the camera on the shot-maker truck, and just as we got through one rehearsal, Bob drove up sooner than I expected. "We got lucky," he said. Bob started shooting right away, and once again we quickly got the shot we needed.

It was a miracle: a plane flight followed by two very tricky shots in two distinct locations in one afternoon. Elated, having "stolen" two bonus shots, we drove to Monument Valley to spend the night. Bob, Tom, and I, along with the key crew, stayed at Goulding's Lodge, a historic hotel overlooking the park. We went over our predawn plan and had dinner provided by our caterer, since the restaurant was closed. We unwound a bit by having a beer and playing a low-stakes poker game before bed. Setting out in the dark the next morning, we had no idea what the day had in store for us.

Our plan was to begin the day by shooting Tom running alone at sunrise in the desert. The shot would be used as part of a montage when Forrest recounts stories to Jenny as she lies in bed dying. We laid the dolly track, mounted the camera in place, and then waited for the sun to come up.

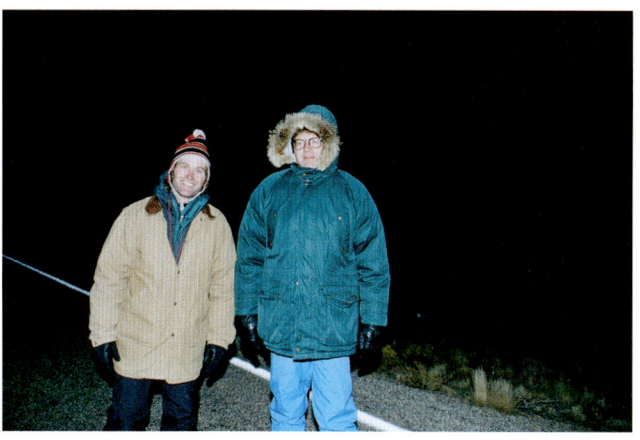
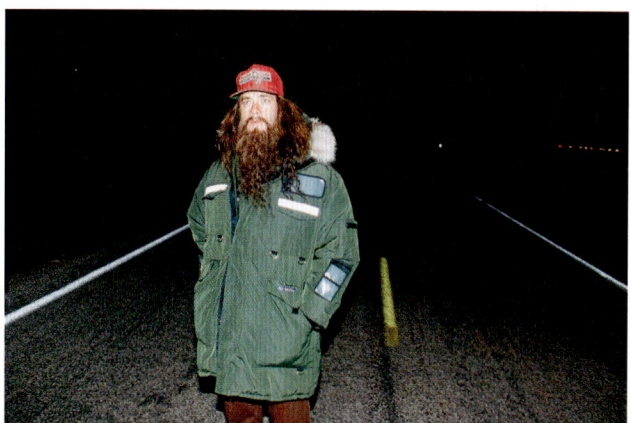

Don Burgess, Bob Zemeckis, and Tom Hanks awaiting the sunrise

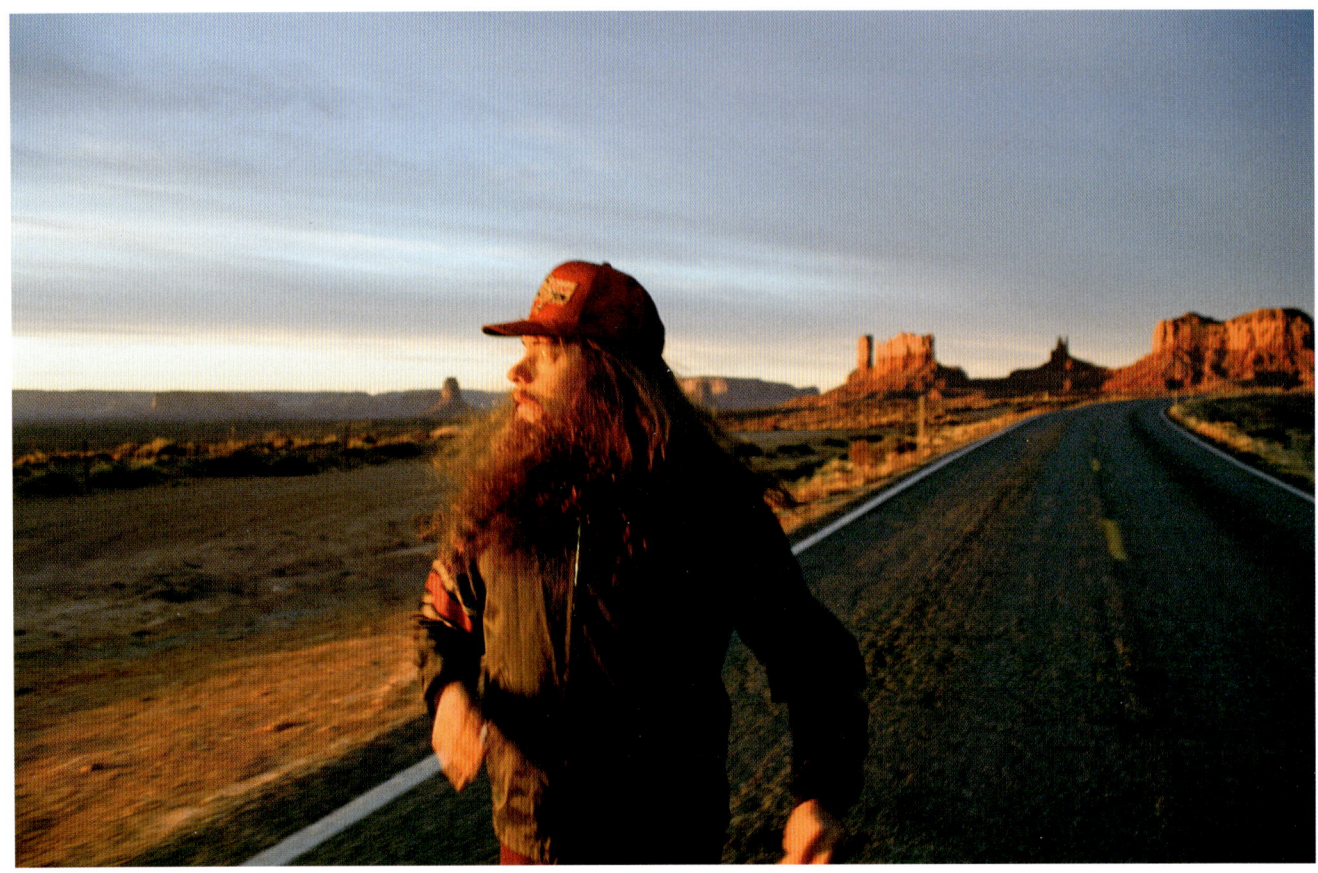

Forrest runs through Monument Valley at sunrise

What would this day bring? In the predawn light, the sky appeared to be bald, but then clouds started to form on the horizon—big, billowy clouds that took up most of the sky. At first light, when the camera was able to get a decent exposure, we started shooting.

Tom went back to his start mark, and we reset and shot again. On each take the sky seemed to lighten and become even more spectacular, saturated with rich oranges and reds. We couldn't believe our luck. We kept shooting, and Tom kept running, until the beautiful colors of sunrise faded away. But we still had a lot of work to do. We set some saguaro cactus alongside the road and grabbed another running shot across an unnamed desert landscape.

Another unscheduled shot was in the can. Meanwhile, the main crew was getting set for the big shot

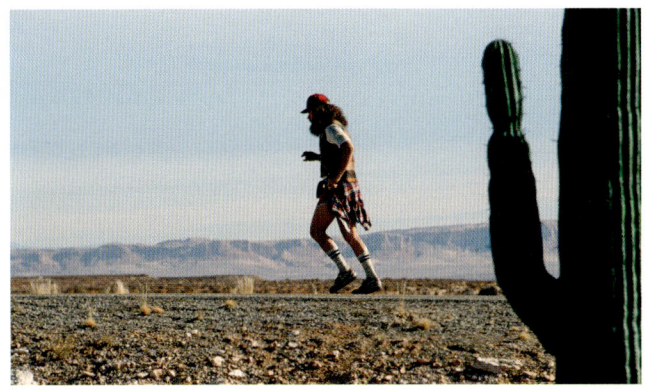 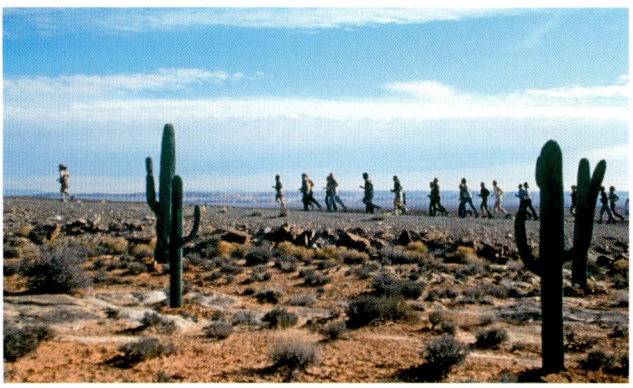

Forrest runs across a desert landscape dressed with saguaro cactus

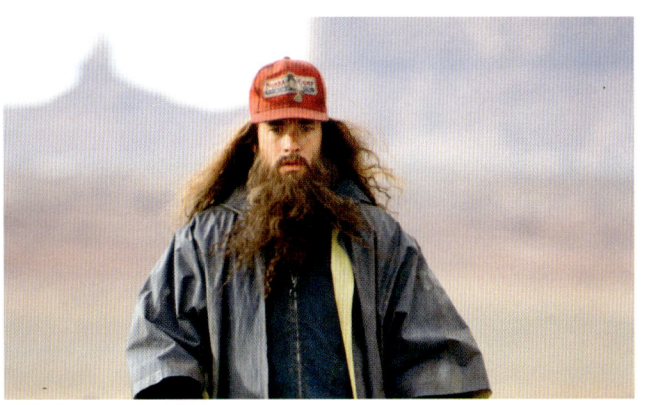 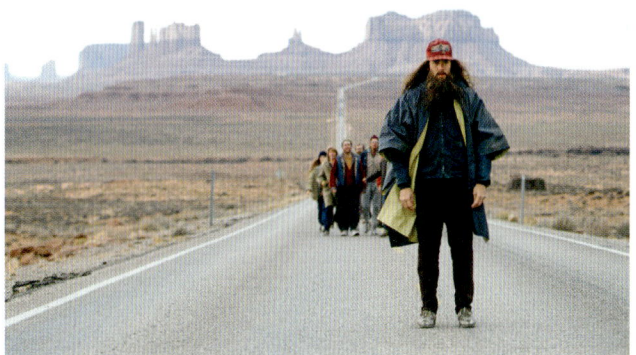

"I'm pretty tired. I think I'll go home now."

where Forrest ends his run. By starting with a solitary shot, followed by a shot with a small number of extras, we gave makeup, hair, and wardrobe a chance to get the background runners ready for the final shot. Once again the scene quickly fell into place.

I had expected to be there all afternoon, but shortly after noon we wrapped, and the crew packed up. We were on our way home, hours earlier than expected.

When I got back to the studio, I was happy to report that we had wrapped early, saved money, and come in under budget. "How do you figure?" the execs asked me. "You're way *over* budget!" My logic was that we were under budget for the Monument Valley shoot and therefore had not gone as far over budget as they had anticipated. They could only shake their heads at my twisted way of thinking.

167

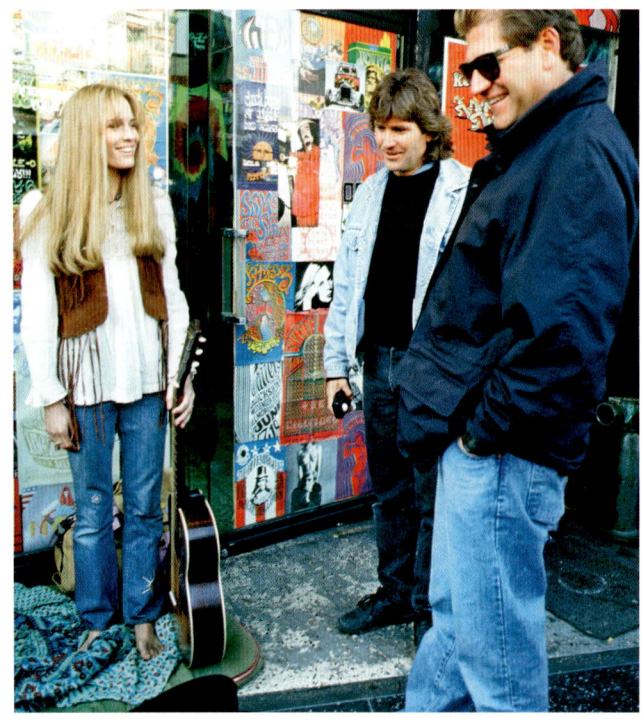

Robin Wright, guitar in hand, waiting to shoot
with Don Burgess and Bob Zemeckis

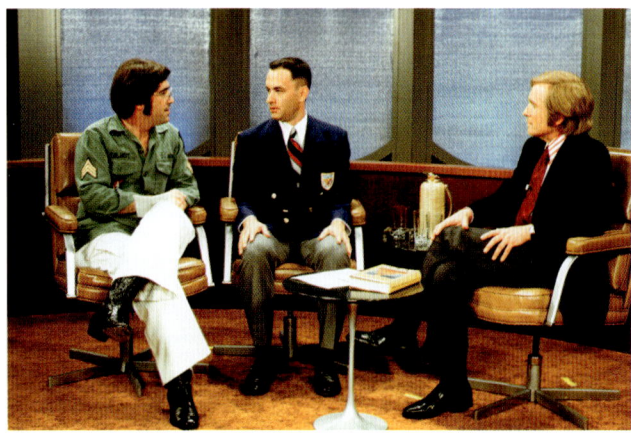

Forrest on *The Dick Cavett Show* with a
John Lennon look-alike

After the Monument Valley shoot we could see the finish line. Only three days to go. We started by shooting Jenny on Hollywood Boulevard playing her guitar and spontaneously jumping in a van to go to San Francisco. Since Robin didn't play the guitar, I briefly showed her the chords to "Get Together" by the Youngbloods. Talent that she is, she could play a perfectly acceptable version of the song in a matter of minutes.

Then we moved the company back to the studio for the *Dick Cavett Show* scene. We still weren't finished with our shenanigans. Inserting Forrest into the show with John Lennon was a risk. When we put Forrest in historical situations with public figures, such as the presidents, we were legally on solid ground. Their images were in the public domain. Not so with Lennon. More than likely we were fine, but it was a gray area. We were not using the footage in a derogatory fashion and were not showing Lennon in a bad light, damaging his reputation. The legal staff at Paramount gave us permission to move ahead. After all, everyone knows that Forrest Gump didn't really inspire John Lennon to write the lyrics to "Imagine"—or did he?

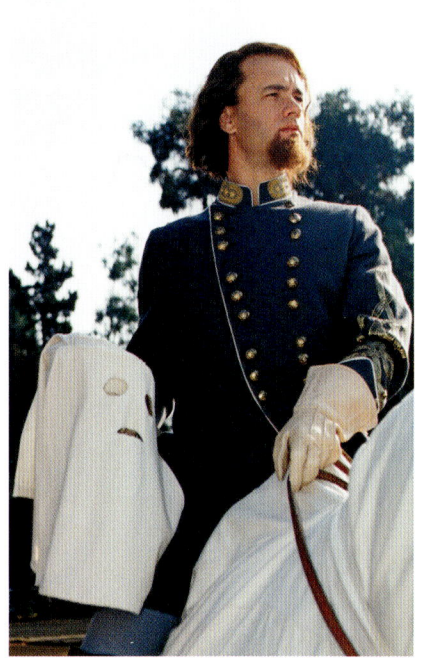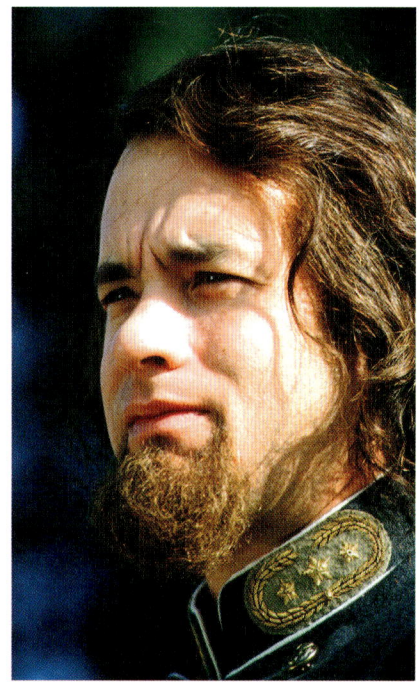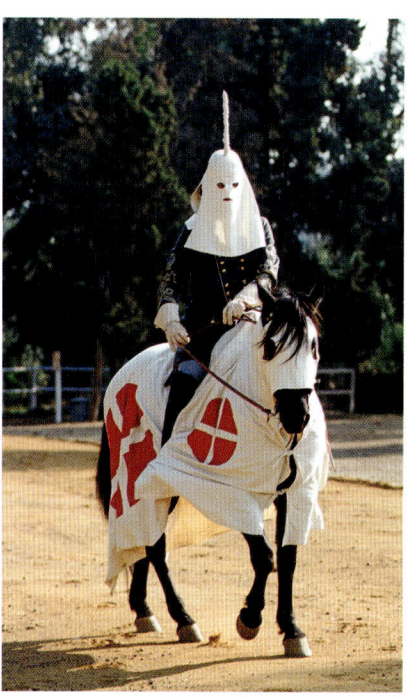

Shooting the KKK scene at Will Rogers State Park

The last day of shooting was a real mixed bag. The original plan was to start by filming Forrest at the Santa Monica Pier before he turns and heads east:

```
            FORREST (V.O.)
...I ran clear to the ocean...and
when I got there I figured since I'd
gone this far...I might as well just
keep on goin'...
```

Heading to the beach presented a perfect opportunity to grab a shot for the KKK scene at Will Rogers State Park, which was on the way to Santa Monica Pier. Although the studio had singled out that scene as something to cut from the film, we had a camera unit ready to grab the shot of Forrest on horseback riding toward the camera, depicting his namesake relative Nathan Bedford Forrest. Ken Ralston would later place it in a scene from *Birth of a Nation*.

169

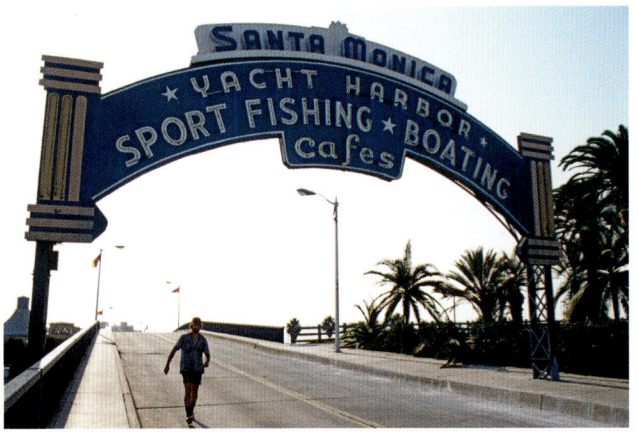
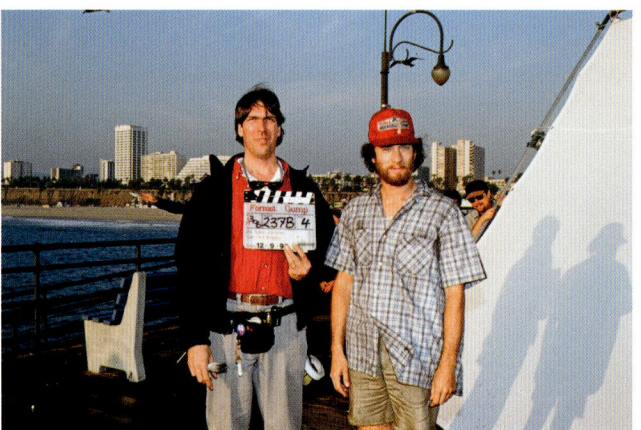

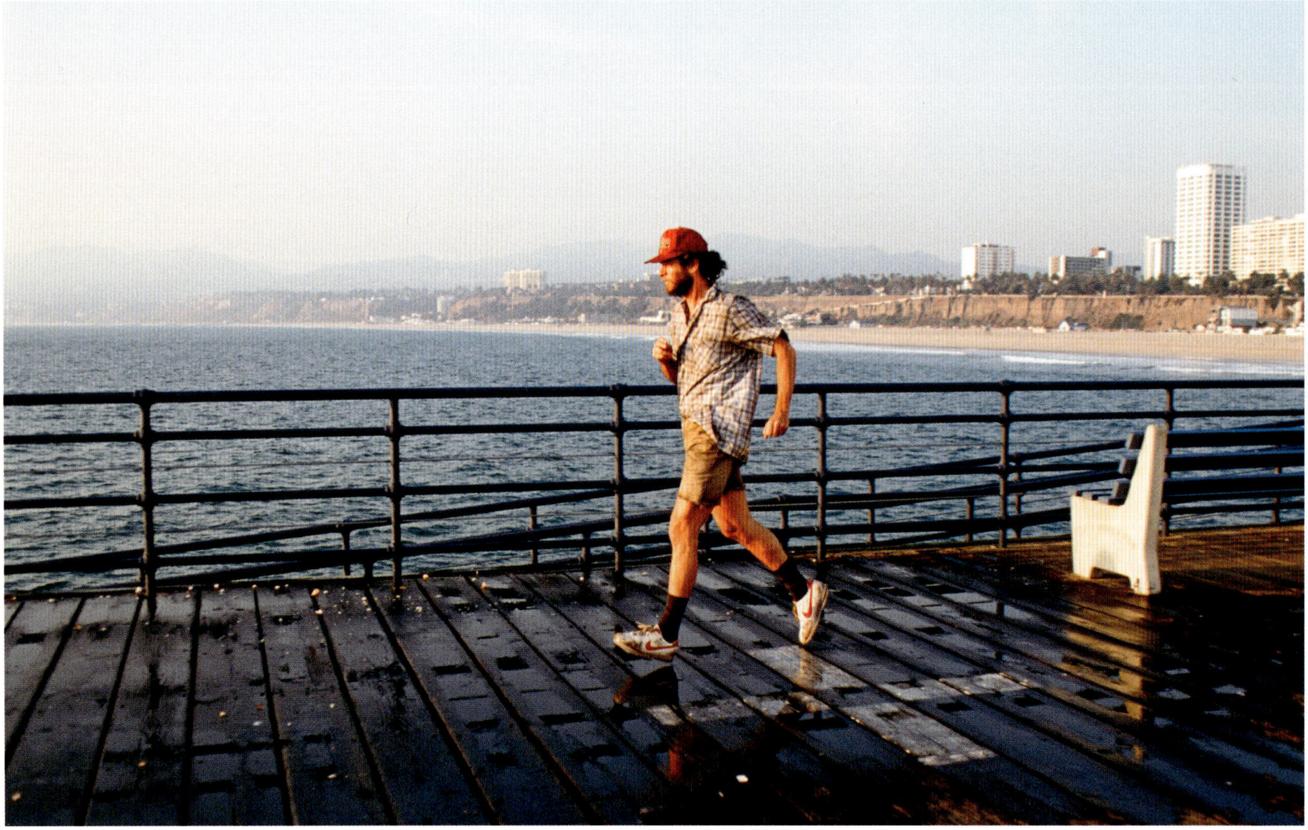

Tom's last shot in the film, at the Santa Monica Pier

Then we went to the pier to shoot Forrest reaching the West Coast on his cross-country run.

When we were done, Tom Hanks could have run straight home. He was officially wrapped on the movie.

What a long, strange, and exhilarating road it had been. We had gone through the war together and then some. Our good-byes were short and sweet. But for us, this long day was far from over. We still had work to do without Tom.

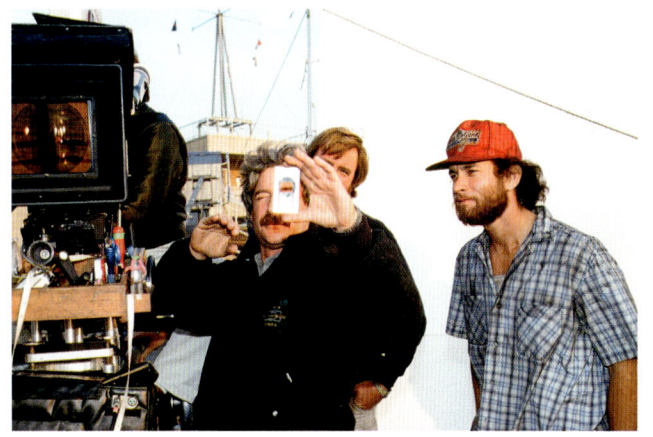

Checking the film gate to make sure it's clean

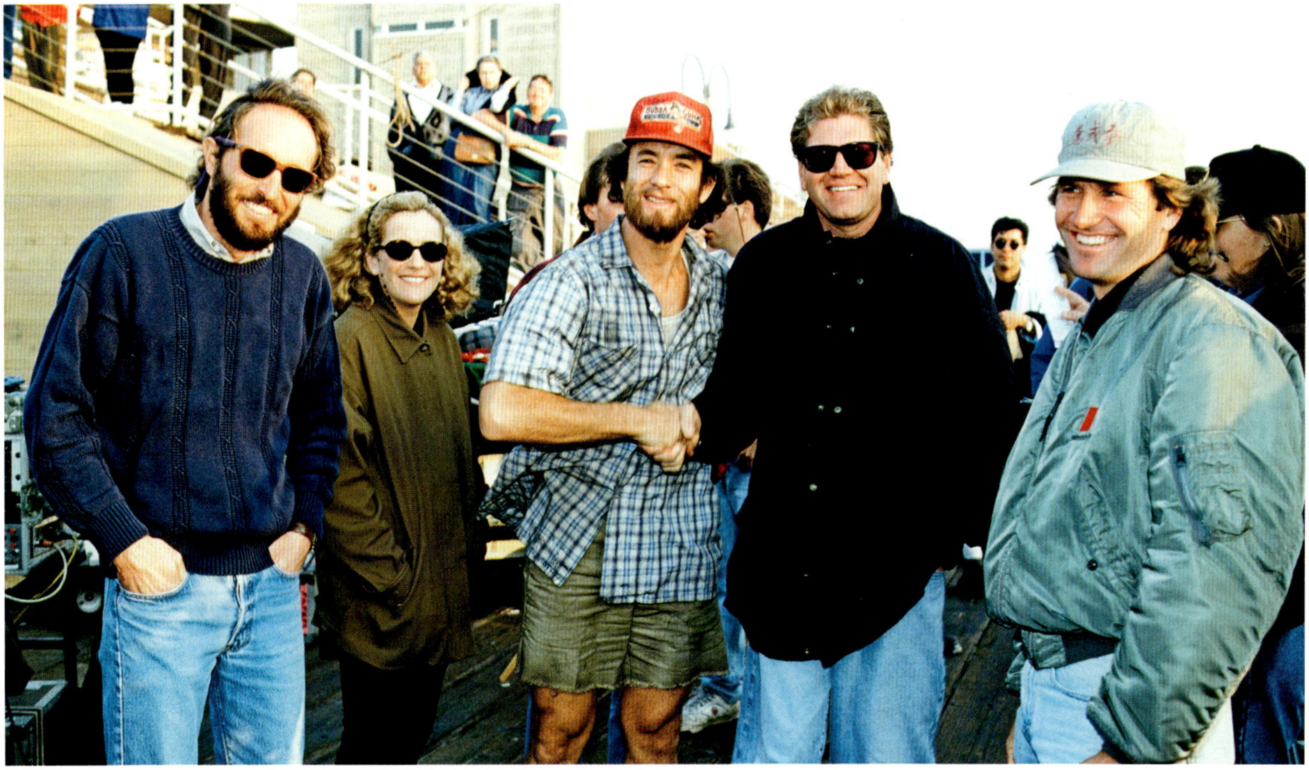

It's a wrap for Tom Hanks on *Forrest Gump*! Me, Wendy Finerman, Tom shaking Bob's hand, and Don Burgess

We moved our location to West LA, to the rooftop of a high-rise apartment building near Beverly Glen and Wilshire, where we prepared to shoot into the night with Robin Wright:

```
EXT. A BALCONY, THE HIGH-RISE APART-
MENT, SUNSET STRIP, 1974—NIGHT

She crosses outside to a balcony.
She's still, standing in the night
air. And suddenly she takes up a
small round balcony table, putting
it by the railing. She climbs on the
table. She looks below her at Sunset
Boulevard with its familiar bill-
boards. She looks up at the moon.
And it seems as if she is going to
jump, just "fly away." She press-
es her hands in her coat pockets,
stopping herself. She sits down on
the small balcony table. And pro-
tectively cradling her arms across
her chest, she starts to cry...And
she looks up at the moon again,
crying...
```

With that scene, we wrapped Robin on the film. In a strange way, all of us on the crew could have done the same thing Jenny did—look up at the moon and shed a tear. All those emotions that had been locked up were finally released. Despite all the obstacles presented by the studio, we had shot the film we intended to shoot.

In anticlimactic fashion, after saying good-bye to Robin, we had one last series of shots to accomplish. A few days before, we had filmed scenes of Lieutenant Dan's ancestors dying in wars, one by one, with Gary Sinise portraying all of his predecessors. But we had a problem with the small sets—eight- by ten-foot boxes filled with dirt—that Gary fell into. They didn't look like solid ground. They moved on impact when Gary landed in them. We had to reshoot the scenes. Can you believe it? On the last day and night of shooting!

We finished the scenes in the wee hours of the morning and finally wrapped Gary on the film. We hooted and hollered and let out screams of joy. We had completed principal photography on *Forrest Gump!* Despite what the studio thought, we had pulled off the impossible. They had no idea what they had or what we had accomplished. Everyone on the film had given it their all and had done spectacular work. We could not have been a tighter group on a singular mission. We would now head to the editing room. Who knew what would happen when the film was put together? But it was all in the can. And similar to what Forrest said at the end of his run: We were feeling kinda tired, and it was time to go home now.

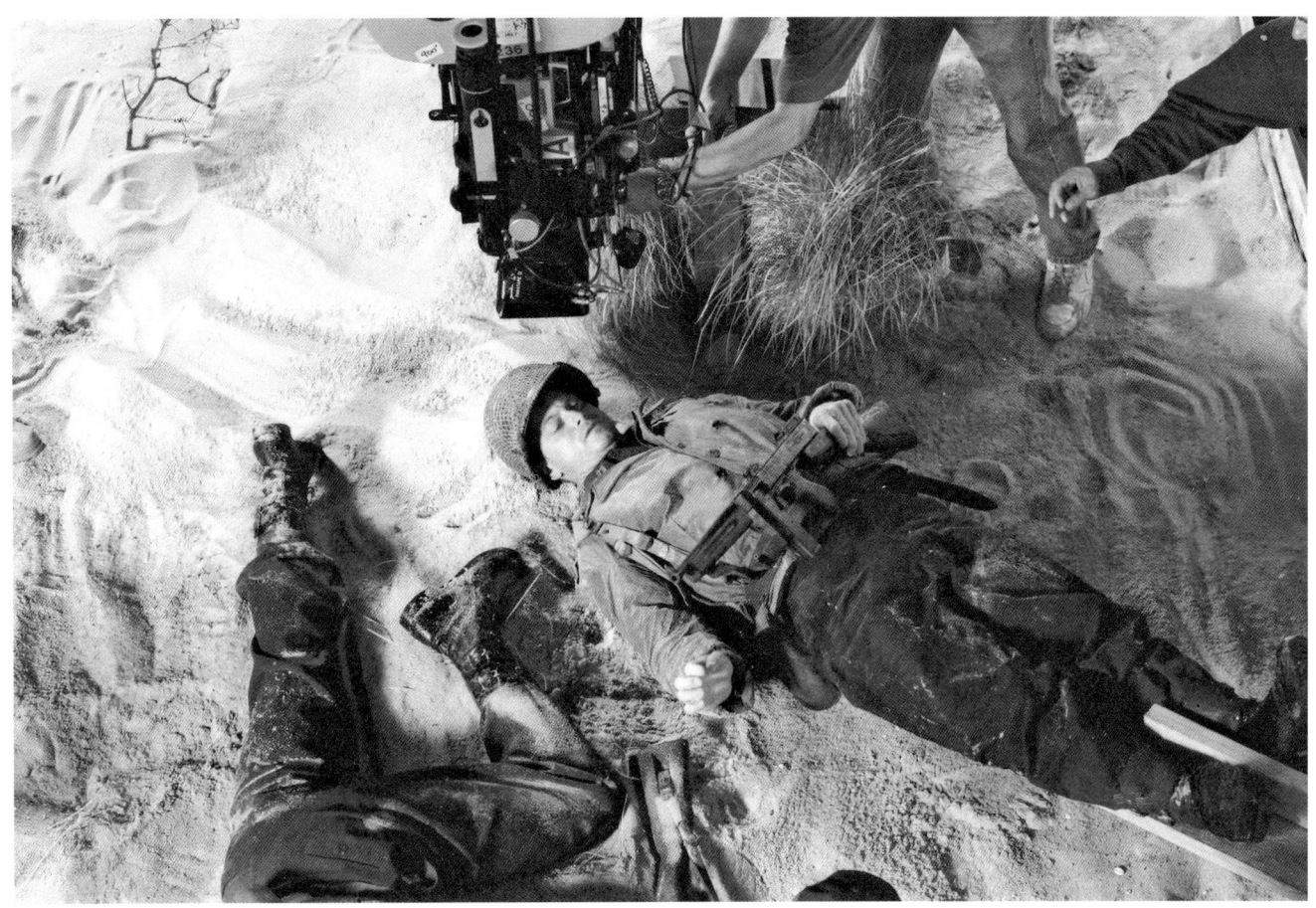
Gary Sinise portraying one of Lieutenant Dan's ancestors who died at war

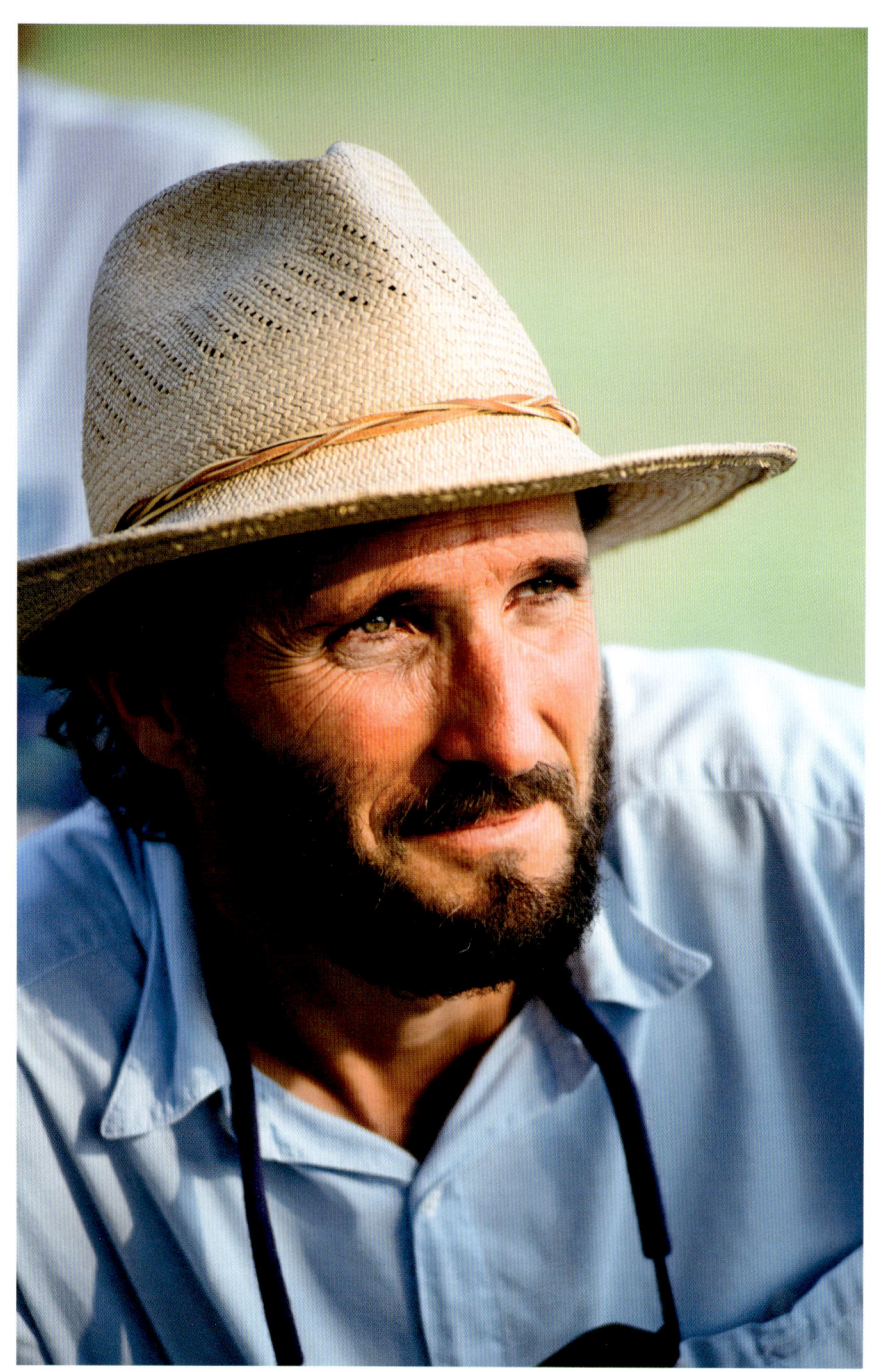

16 | The Silver-Tongued Devil

PAUL HAGGAR HAD SURVIVED more regimes at Paramount than anyone could remember, except Paul. He was the executive vice president of post-production at Paramount Pictures, and my first meeting with him, soon after we wrapped filming on *Forrest Gump,* was enlightening for both of us. He was tough as nails, but he carefully protected his films. Once they hit post-production, they were his babies. The key was to gain his respect. Paul also fiercely defended the wishes of the studio executives. It was a balancing act, just like producing.

Paul and I had started out as apprentice film editors, so we had firsthand knowledge of the editing room. I told him about rising through the ranks in the editing room on the *Star Wars* sequels before overseeing post-production and visual effects on *Roger Rabbit* and *Back to the Future II* and *III.* He was surprised. That was an unusual career path for a producer, and I think it warmed his heart. We felt an immediate kinship. I quickly understood that he would be my best ally in my quest to finish the film without any studio intervention. But he was not a softy. I still had a fight on my hands, and I

needed to prove myself. Paul would need a good reason to tell the studio to back off.

"Why are you editing the film in Santa Barbara?" he asked me. "We all love Santa Barbara, but come on, give us a break. Do you have to bring everyone up there, all the assistants, pay their living expenses and per diems? We have perfectly good editing rooms here on the lot."

"Zemeckis wants to edit up there," I said. "He lives there. The editor, Artie Schmidt, has a house there. Bob won't cut the movie in LA. And, by the way, do you want to pay living expenses for Bob to live in LA to edit the film? And Artie? Trust me, that would cost a whole lot more than bringing the assistants up there. By the way, I found a house to rent for the editing rooms, and it's cheaper than the cost of your rooms on the lot. I checked."

He looked at me in disbelief. "Not since working with Warren Beatty have I met a silver-tongued devil like you."

I took it as a compliment, whether it was intended that way or not. We each had met our equal. But Paul had the upper hand. No matter what I said, he could say no. But he didn't. I don't think he wanted to fight the director over this. He was willing to fight with me but not with Bob. He respected directors. He still had to clear it with the executives, though.

"What about Skywalker Sound? Why go there?" Paul was questioning why we wanted to take the film to George Lucas's post-production facility in Marin County.

"Because Zemeckis wants to go there. They do good work, and it's cheaper." At this stage in the game, I knew I could mix the sound up there only if it was cheaper than mixing in Los Angeles. We had mixed our last few films at Universal, and we were happy enough, but Bob and I were ready for a change.

I thought of using Randy Thom as a sound designer. He was one of the great sound designers in the Bay Area. I knew Randy since working with him on *Star Wars*. I told Bob that he would be a perfect fit for the film. Plus, it would get us out of town, away from the studio, and we would also be closer to ILM to finalize the visual effects.

Bob trusted my choice and agreed that Skywalker was the right place to mix the film, and he loved the idea of keeping the studio at a distance. Now I just had to convince the studio. I also had an ulterior motive. I had kept a house in Marin since my *Star Wars* days, and I was always eager to visit. I loved it up there. I desperately wanted to win this battle with Paul. I met with the general manager of Skywalker Sound and negotiated a price reduction, so the deal was competitive with the major

mixing facilities in LA, even with living expenses and per diems thrown in. Despite pressure from the studio to keep us in town, Paul argued on our behalf and shook the hand of the silver-tongued devil, giving us permission to go up north to mix, as long as we did the dialogue rerecording and music scoring in LA.

Nestled in our cutting rooms in Montecito, Artie and his assistants had a perfect place to work, far from the meddlesome studio. Not that the studio stayed out of our hair, but the distance made it more difficult to check on us. Soon after post-production began, Michelle Manning told me that the studio would not be covering my hotel and living expenses while I was working in Santa Barbara. I think this was how the studio chose to get back at me for all our budget issues. But that didn't stop me. The movie was more important to me than any personal cost I would have to bear. The studio may not have been aware of how close I was to the film or how closely Bob and I worked with each other. I felt my presence in the editing room was crucial.

I had been through some large-scale films—*Roger Rabbit,* the *Back to the Future* sequels, *Death Becomes Her,* and the *Star Wars* films before that. I knew what we were up against in post-production on *Forrest.* The visual effects alone were a challenge. It would take months to finalize each of the interactive scenes with Presidents Kennedy, Johnson, and Nixon, not to mention the one with John Lennon on *The Dick Cavett Show.* There was also a scene with Forrest and Governor George Wallace at the schoolhouse door. Plus we had the crowd duplications in Washington, DC, and the enhancements in the football stadium. We had to "remove" Gary Sinise's legs in quite a few of Lieutenant Dan's scenes. In addition, there were explosions, gunfire, and aircraft to put into the Vietnam sequence. Even the falling feather at the beginning and end of the film needed to be shot and inserted into its background.

The soundtrack and mix would also be very complicated. Sounds evoking the ambience of the South, Forrest telling his story on the bench, the Vietnam War, shrimping, and the running sequence all required a delicate balance. There were songs throughout the entire film to be selected and licensed. There was way too much work to do: I *had* to be there.

Bob and Artie had a field day with the songs. They paid no attention to the cost. They used any song that felt right. From the get-go, Bob had decided that all the songs should be written and performed by American artists. Even though many of the iconic songs of the era came from England, this was an American story through and through, so his decision made sense. And there were plenty of songs to choose from. The dilemma was how to pay for them. We couldn't possibly license the selected songs individually—not even close. Each artist's publisher and record company would want to make the most money they could. The total would be insane. When the studio got

wind of what we were up to, they made it clear that they would never agree to the soaring cost of the songs, even though they had not seen them in the context of the film.

That's when Joel Sill's advice came into play. We had hired Joel as our music supervisor, and although we couldn't afford his going rate, he agreed to do the film as a labor of love. He had his own music publishing company and knew everyone in the business. He told us the only way this would work was to create "favored nations" deals with anyone who wished to have their songs in the film. Each fee would be the same. We couldn't have a different price for every song. That would kill us. But if the license fees were the same for everyone, the deals would be simple. The Doors would get the same deal as Buffalo Springfield, who would get the same fee as Lynyrd Skynyrd. We took this approach to the studio, but they were not convinced. The studio wasn't the only roadblock; the musical artists weren't falling in step with the plan either.

When the Doors said no to the use of their songs, it hit us the hardest. We were shell-shocked. We had used a perfect medley of three Doors songs that built in tempo and intensity while Forrest was learning to play Ping-Pong in the infirmary, starting with "Hello, I Love You," followed by "People Are Strange," and ending with "Break on Through."

Faced with the necessity of replacing the Doors songs, Joel got us copies of every top-ten song list from each week of the same year. Bob, Artie, and

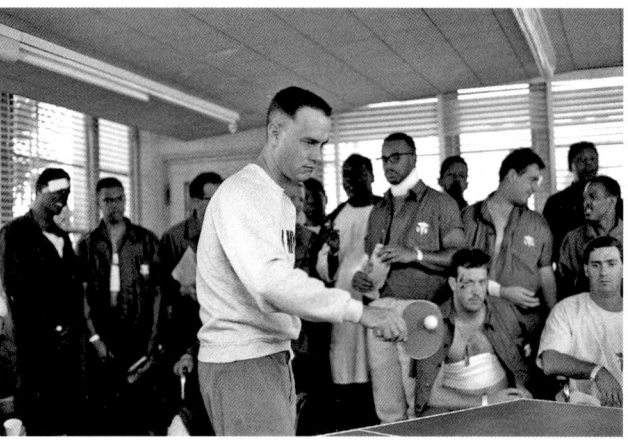

Forrest plays Ping-Pong, accompanied by the music of the Doors

I went home and tried to put together a different trio of songs. As hard as we tried, we could not come up with a good alternative. Nothing came close to the Doors.

Depressed, we called Joel. He said, "Screen the movie for the living members of the band. It's a gamble, but what do you have to lose?" Joel told us the greatest asset we had for selling the idea to reluctant artists was the movie itself. The idea made us nervous. We weren't ready to screen the film. It wasn't finished, and it seemed too risky. The temporary visual effects might be too confusing. The messy state of the film might cause the musicians to turn us down for the wrong reason. But we were between a rock and a hard place. We needed an answer right away so we could license the songs and finish the sound mix. We reluctantly agreed to follow Joel's advice.

We sent him as our ambassador to screen the film for the Doors. In the end, he was right. The film proved to be our most powerful weapon. Not only did the band members approve the use of the songs we had chosen for the film, but they also said we could use as many songs as we wished. They loved the film!

Now we had to conquer the studio. We needed their permission to move forward with the deal making. We hadn't taken no for an answer yet, and we weren't going to start now. Once again we decided to let the film do the talking. It was time to screen the film for the studio. We showed the executives the work print from the editing room—the only print we had—which included all the songs we intended to use. Bob asked me to check in after the screening and take the studio's temperature. I greeted Sherry Lansing and executives John Goldwyn and Michelle Manning as they entered the screening room and watched the doors close behind them.

I stepped away from the theater and wandered the studio lot while the film ran, not sure what to expect when it was over. The studio had doubted the unconventional nature of the project to begin with and certainly did not like the amount of money we spent to make it. I probably represented a lot of their fears and bore responsibility for the film's cost. I thought back to that day when Michelle showed up in Beaufort. If they could have gotten rid of me and hired another producer then, they would have.

I made my way back to the theater ahead of the film's finish and stood patiently outside the door. Sherry and the others took their time before exiting, so they must have given the film some thought. When they finally opened the doors, they still had tears in their eyes. Sherry composed herself and said to tell Bob that she loved the picture. They were all so emotional that it took me by surprise. The film had brought out a side of the executives I had not seen before. The gamble had paid off. They changed their tune. They could not imagine the movie without the songs, which were clearly part of the fabric of the film. They gave us permission to move forward and make our deals.

But their anxieties had not abated. They were still unsure how the film would play in front of an audience. They wanted to preview the film. And we know how that went: it ended with Sherry Lansing and me yelling at each other and a theatergoer claiming the film was the best he had ever seen.

I had to wonder if the studio's fears were justified or if our advocate at the preview had it right. It was time to let go of our baby and find out once and for all.

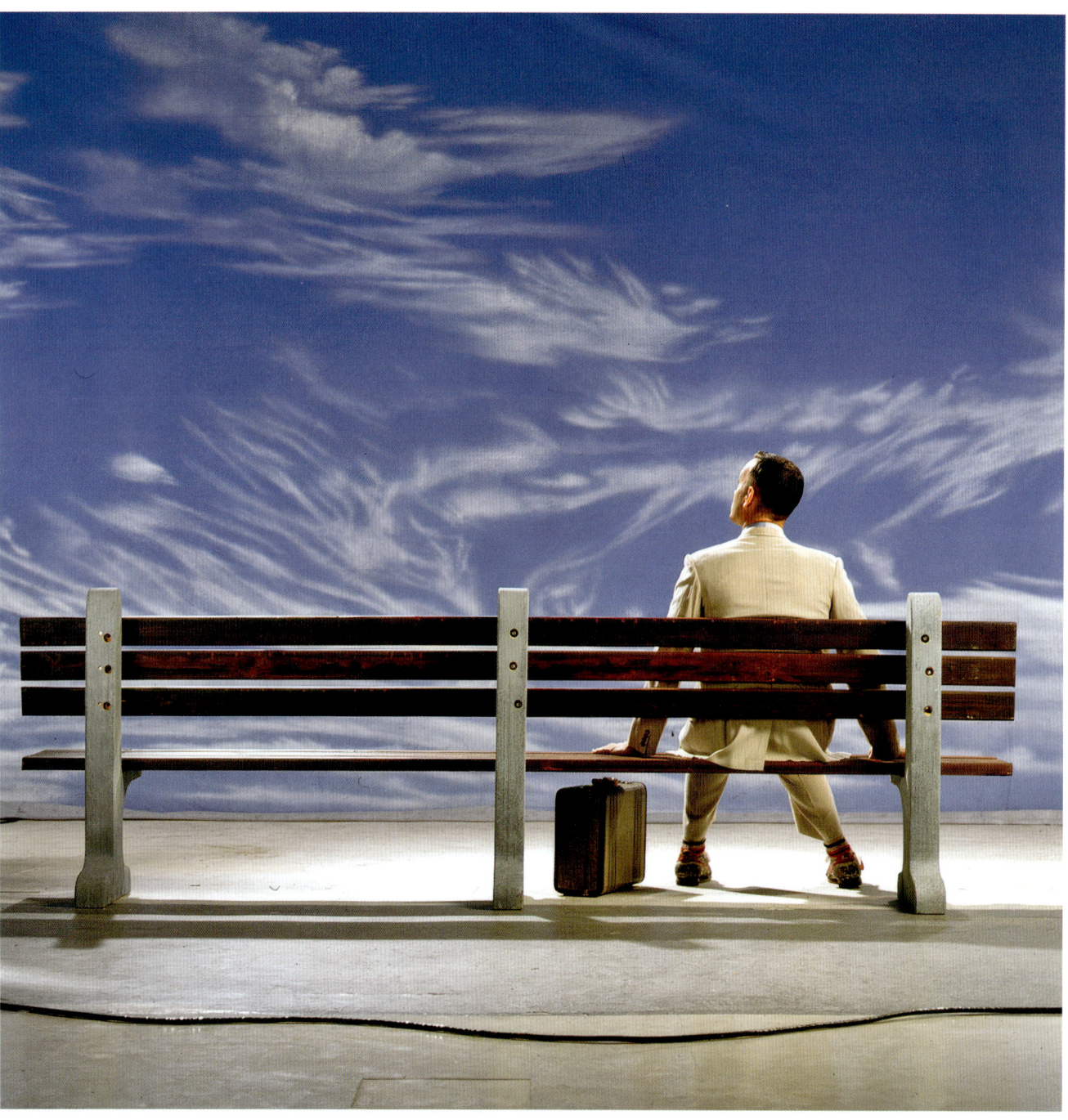

17 | I Got No Complaints

WHEN *FORREST GUMP* WAS released on July 6, 1994, the studio was still skeptical about the film and unsure of its prospects. The executives who had praised the film and had witnessed the preview apparently did not trust their own emotions. Box-office receipts would tell the tale. As the weeks went by, the excitement grew. Word on the street was good. Critical response was good. And the audience kept growing.

When the film hit the theaters, I was kayaking on Orcas Island. I called Bob from a phone booth for a box-office report and was astounded by what he told me. Folks were piling into the theaters. I thought we had made a great film, but you never know what will happen when you send it into the marketplace. I thought the film would resonate with my friends and those of my generation. But it appeared to play on a completely different level for a much wider audience. I discovered the film's reach when I got a letter from my brother-in-law's mother in Little Rock, Arkansas. She loved the movie. She loved it so much she was going to see it again with all her friends. All the risks were paying off, especially for Bob and Tom. They had bet on themselves and their film, and they won big time. No one was more deserving.

The ice at the studio was finally melting. When I returned from my kayaking trip, I received a call from Michelle Manning. The studio was going to reimburse me for my living expenses in post-production. Success begets forgiveness, I guess.

Next stop was the Venice Film Festival for the film's international premiere and European launch. When I got to the Cipriani Hotel, Tom Hanks stood up from the waterside bar and gave me a Gump-like wave, just like Forrest gave Lieutenant Dan when he recognized him at the dock. I only hoped that Tom wouldn't jump into the lagoon!

The entire festival was a celebration of the film and the filmmakers. That was a first for me. I had never been treated like royalty before: Liv and I had a nice suite at the Cipriani overlooking the pool. We lunched at grand villas. Sherry Lansing even hosted a dinner where she toasted all the filmmakers and cast individually. My toast seemed to go on forever as she showered me with lavish praise. Liv whispered, "She speaks so highly of you." Quietly, I said, "Don't take her too seriously. She's a good speaker and a great actress."

Then it was on to the premiere on the Lido. I remember less about the standing ovation after the movie than the boat ride back to the hotel. Jack Nicholson made the trip with us. I think he wanted to tell us personally how much he enjoyed the film. He went on and on. Was this the cynical Jack we all knew from his films? No, this was Jack the lover of movies, complimenting us from the bottom of his heart.

Later that fall I got a call from Sherry Lansing's office. She asked if I might be available for a meeting. I had not been in her office since we started work on the film. She had seemed pleasant enough in Venice, and with the success of the film, the bad feelings between us were beginning to fade. Still, I had no idea what the meeting could possibly be about. Arriving back on the studio lot filled me with the willies. When I entered Sherry's office, I was surprised to find Jonathan Dolgen there with her. The first and only time I had met him was after the tense preview screening on the lot. After a few pleasantries, Sherry complimented my work on the film. She asked if I was happy with how it had been received. I told her that I was very happy. Then came the reason for the meeting.

She thanked me for my hard work and dedication and said the studio owed me a debt of gratitude. She continued that if she had been the film's producer, she would have fought as hard as I did to protect the film and get it made right. I shifted in my seat, accepting her compliments, still not knowing where this was going. She went on to say that she knew I wouldn't be sharing in the film's financial success as Bob and Tom would, so the company wanted to give me a gift as a small token of its appreciation. Then she handed me an envelope. Inside was a check for $150,000.

I was stunned. I looked up and said thank you. I also thanked them for having the courage to make the film. With that, the meeting ended. As I left the office, my mind was racing, trying to process what had just happened.

When the astonishing numbers kept rolling in from home and abroad, the executives were suddenly the geniuses behind the making of *Forrest Gump*, taking credit wherever they could. But no matter. We were on cloud nine and soaking it in. Award show after award show came our way: the Writers Guild, the Directors Guild, the Golden Globes—fourteen in all. And finally came the Academy Awards: thirteen nominations and six Oscars.

A few memories from the Academy Awards ceremony stand out. Sitting with Liv in the side section of the theater, I told her to enjoy herself because this would never happen again. When Bob received his Best Director award, he thanked me. That meant a lot. Winning for Best Picture was bittersweet. Of course I was elated, but I was sad that my contribution to the film was rewarded while some of those whose shoulders I had stood on throughout the making of the film were not.

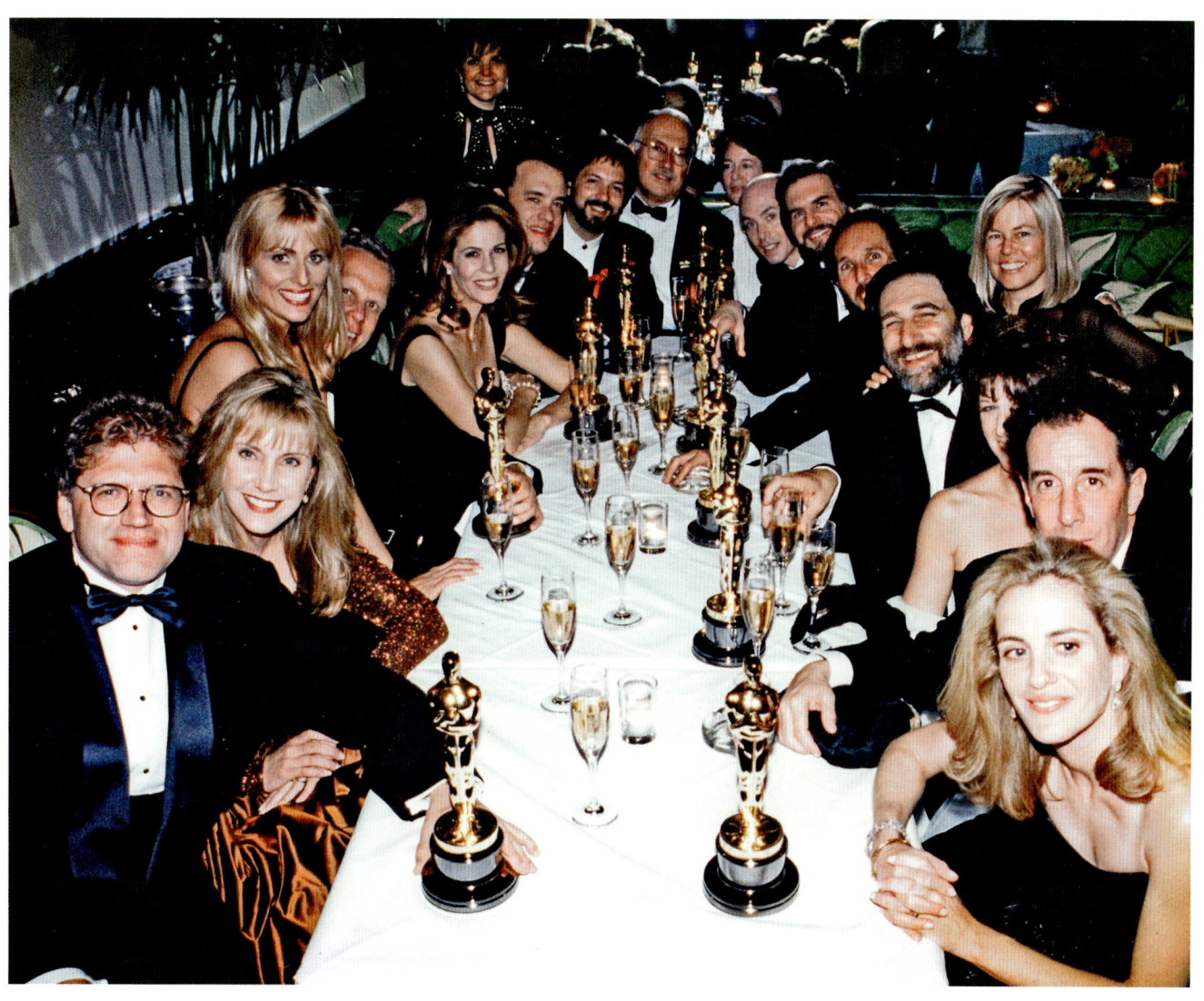

From left to right: Robert Zemeckis, Mary Ellen Trainor, Jamie Tisch, Steve Tisch, Rita Wilson, Tom Hanks, George Murphy, Artie Schmidt, Susan Schmidt, Steve Rosenbaum, Ken Ralston, Steve Starkey, Olivia Erschen, Eric Roth, Debra Greenfield, Mark Canton, Wendy Finerman

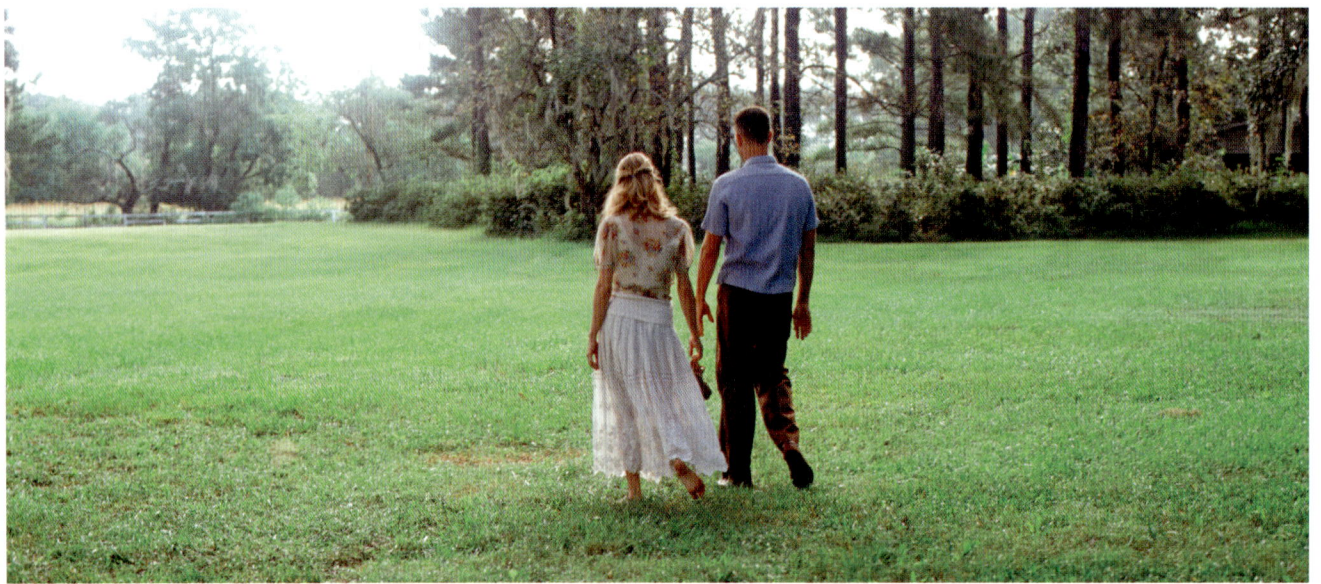

It felt awkward. I had to remind myself that the award honored everyone involved with the movie.

When I walked onstage, I shook hands with Robert De Niro and Al Pacino, who handed me my statue. I told them it was an honor to meet them. (I revered *The Godfather.*) When I spoke my few words of thanks, I looked down at the celebrities in the front row. That was a mistake, but I didn't falter from my short, prepared acceptance speech.

I couldn't eat at the Academy dinner, though I did manage to have a short conversation with Paul Newman, who was sitting at a table by himself. Why not? I had just won an Academy Award. Later Liv and I rode to the Paramount after-party with Alan Silvestri and his wife, Sandra. I was disappointed that Alan's score for the film had not won an award. I thought it was unsurpassed. The after-party itself was great fun. Liv and I sat at a long table with Goldie Hawn, Kurt Russell, Bob Zemeckis and his wife, Mary Ellen, and later commemorated the evening with an Oscar photo. And then it was over.

The next morning a replica of the bench from the film showed up at our home in Pacific Palisades. I stood at the door, exhausted and still sleepy, and wondered what I was going to do with it. I told the delivery guys to put it back on the truck and take it to our offices on the Universal lot and place it next to the mirror ball.

That ended my run on the movie. Just like Forrest said, "That's all I got to say about that."

Epilogue

THIRTY YEARS HAVE PASSED since the release of *Forrest Gump.* It has been embraced not only by those who saw the film decades ago but also by a new generation of filmgoers. Audiences are still taken by the charming and likable character portrayed by Tom Hanks. They are drawn to Forrest because they see something of themselves in him. They feel what Forrest feels. They worry, as he does, that they won't find their place in the world. And they pay attention when Forrest's mama tells him that life is like a box of chocolates—you never know what you're gonna get. She is Forrest's moral and ethical compass, and with her advice and guidance, he has the confidence to pursue his dreams.

Forrest's lessons have become ours. His mama teaches him that he is unlike anyone else and should embrace his differences. As she says, if we were meant to be the same, God would have given us all braces on our legs. How much more secure we would all be if we didn't feel the need to be like everyone around us and simply used our God-given strengths. In Forrest's case, that was his ability to run. By running, he was able to escape his boyhood tormentors. He excelled at football, allowing him to graduate from college and become an all-American. In Vietnam, he ran to save his life and the lives of the soldiers around him. Finally, he ran to overcome his grief over losing his mama and his love, Jenny. In running, Forrest found solace and discovered his destiny, as we each have to discover our own. His guileless approach to running attracted followers hoping to find answers to life's questions. When he suddenly stopped and headed home, they were left to find the answers for themselves.

When I started work on *Forrest Gump,* I was an innocent. I had worked with two of the titans in the industry, George Lucas and Steven Spielberg. I revered their movies and attempted to do the best work I could. Then, as luck would have it, I started a longtime collaboration with Robert Zemeckis. *Forrest Gump* was only my second project as a producer. I was very naïve, and my work was selfless. I was serving the vision of the director, and all my efforts were for the good of the film. Like a firefighter facing a burning building, I spent my days putting out fires when they arose on the set. Just as Forrest saved his fellow soldiers in Vietnam,

I fiercely protected my crew from the punishing studio. I was unaware of the consequences of my actions, but I was willing to take responsibility for them; stupid is as stupid does, after all. It seemed like the right thing to do.

Although he called himself a simple man, Forrest's rich moral fiber gave him strength and an uncanny ability to do the right thing. Those qualities allowed him to rise above calamity and learn important life lessons. In the face of adversity, often caused by circumstances beyond his control, Forrest overcame his difficulties, whether it was fighting in Vietnam or surviving in the shrimping business. Not even a hurricane could stop him. Forrest never hesitated to act on simple truths. When he spoke at the antiwar rally in Washington, he said, "Sometimes when people go to Vietnam they go home to their Mamas without any legs. Sometimes they don't go home at all and that's a bad thing. That's all I have to say about that." Are we meant to laugh or cry? It doesn't matter. Whether Forrest is neutral, bewildered, or confused, he still shines a light on the Vietnam War, while leaving the interpretation of history to us.

Forrest's unknowing impact on the cultural and political touchstones of the 1950s, 1960s, and 1970s are filled with irony and humor. We smile with appreciation as he demonstrates his hip shake to Elvis Presley and later inspires John Lennon's lyrics to "Imagine." He helps the first Black student gain entrance to the University of Alabama even as George Wallace takes a stand at the schoolhouse door. While receiving his Medal of Honor from President Johnson for his courage in Vietnam, Forrest bends over and shows the president the wound on his buttocks. He's only doing as he's told, just as his mama taught him. Then he unknowingly kicks off the Watergate scandal and Nixon's downfall by reporting to hotel security that he sees flashlights in a nearby room. He is even responsible for the happy face T-shirt and the "Shit Happens" slogan! No wonder we still smile when we watch Forrest after all these years.

As I started to work on this book, the memories came flooding in. How could I possibly remember those days with such vivid accuracy? Perhaps they're not as clear as I think they are, but my memory is my history. As I think of the difficulty and turmoil that surrounded the making of the film, I can only remain grateful for the experience.

People often ask if we knew beforehand that we had a good movie on our hands. I did not. There is no way to tell. We were too busy working on the film, quickly moving from one scene to the next. It was impossible to know anything about the film's ultimate outcome. You can only hope that what you've read in the script and watched during the production will add up to a good film. Now, having said that, when we filmed the scene at Jenny's grave, it was a very emotional moment. And when Forrest tells President Kennedy he has to pee, it definitely made me laugh.

Still, as we laughed and cried on the set, we had to wonder what the audience was going to think about a man in dirty tennis shoes sitting on a bench, waiting for a bus and telling his story to complete strangers. Would moviegoers be interested? Would they buy it? It was really a roll of the dice that required faith by everyone involved with the film. When I first watched the ending—when Forrest sits on the wall at the end of Oak Alley and watches the school bus carry his son to school, then stares off into space as a feather floats into the sky—I never knew how satisfied I would be decades later about a story so well told.

Acknowledgments

I AM SO THANKFUL for the opportunity to work on *Forrest Gump.* I must thank Robert Zemeckis for inviting me to the party. This was only my second film with Bob as a producing partner, and when I accepted the challenge, I had no idea what I was in for. It proved to be the most demanding and rewarding work I have ever done on a film. I am and will remain forever grateful for the experience.

I must thank Wendy Finerman, who discovered the novel by Winston Groom and hired Eric Roth to write his miraculous screenplay. Without the two of them, the picture never would have been made. All moviegoers and lovers of the film should thank them!

How do I thank Tom Hanks? Who can imagine the character of Forrest Gump played by anyone but Tom? I cannot. Without Tom Hanks there is no *Forrest Gump.* Much the same can be said for the cast surrounding him: Robin Wright as Jenny, Gary Sinise as Lieutenant Dan, Mykelti Williamson as Bubba, Sally Field as Mama Gump, Michael Conner Humphreys as Young Forrest, Hanna Hall as Young Jenny, and the list goes on. There were no small parts. Thanks to Ellen Lewis, every actor was carefully chosen, and they all stepped up to the challenge.

Bob told me that what made *Forrest Gump* a great picture to make was that everyone on the cast and crew was on the same page making the same movie. What he meant by that was that each person—whether a day player, the production designer, cinematographer, editor, costume designer, makeup and hair artists, special-effects and visual-effects teams, location and transportation teams, sound department, and music supervisor and composer—had an intimate understanding of the script and knew what the film called for. When this happens, one can only be grateful and in awe of the level of creativity and energy that each and every person brings to their part of the film. It is revealed every day in their work. I wish to thank all the talented individuals on the crew who I had the honor and pleasure of working with.

And, of course, where would I have been without my coproducer Charles Newirth and his staff in the production office; the assistant directing department led by Bruce Moriarty; and Cherylanne Martin, who not only organized my second unit but also took charge of the advance work of the first unit? Thanks to Rick Porras and Steve Boyd, who started by finding the archival footage we needed and ended up doing everything that was falling through the cracks. And finally, thanks to my assistant, Hayley Miller, who took care of every detail on the show for me. I could not have done my work without her.

Really, the list could go on and on.

Finally, ultimately, I must thank Paramount Pictures led by Sherry Lansing, John Goldwyn, and Michelle Manning. Although we had our differences and they had their doubts, they ultimately backed us and allowed us to make the picture of our dreams. We were also given wonderful support by Paul Haggar in post-production.

When I set out to scribble my memories of my experiences on *Forrest Gump,* the production department at Paramount leaped at the chance to help me. I must thank Lee Rosenthal and Momoko Fleming for providing me with production reports that helped me reconstruct the shooting days. I was also very fortunate to get permission to use the iconic photographs taken by the extraordinarily talented unit photographer Phil Caruso in the telling of my tale. I was given tireless support from the Paramount stills department, led by Larry McCallister and Alexandra Giffen. I thank them for spearheading my voyage of discovery.

I assembled the same trusted allies while finishing this book as I did on my first book. Joan Tapper guided me through editing, pushing me to make the writing better. John Balkwill was a designer and printer whose aesthetics I can only aspire to. I was graced to have his unique touches throughout my book and was saddened by his loss before we finished our work together. And thanks to Lindsay Rust, without whose guidance and artistry this book would never have been completed. Once again, my colleague and friend Doug Chiang provided inspiration and guidance to Ric Lim in the creation of the artwork that placed me on the bench for the title page of chapter 4.

Finally, I must thank my trusted ally and life partner, Olivia Erschen. Whenever I have moments of doubt, she encourages me and convinces me to trust my instincts. She means everything to me.

About the Author

ACADEMY AWARD–WINNING PRODUCER Steve Starkey is a longtime collaborator with legendary filmmaker Robert Zemeckis. After producing *Death Becomes Her,* his first film with Zemeckis, Starkey went on to produce and win the Academy Award for Best Picture on the film *Forrest Gump.* Following the film *Contact,* Zemeckis and Starkey formed the company ImageMovers with agent Jack Rapke.

The first of their distinctive films with the new company included *What Lies Beneath* and *Cast Away.* After producing *The Polar Express, Beowulf,* and *Monster House,* the first feature-length films using motion-capture technology, Zemeckis, Rapke, and Starkey launched a company at Disney, ImageMovers Digital, to make feature films using that technology. *A Christmas Carol* and *Mars Needs Moms* were made under their new banner.

During this time, Starkey produced films for a number of other directors, including *Matchstick Men* with Ridley Scott and *The Prize Winner of Defiance, Ohio* with Jane Anderson. Returning to live-action filmmaking, Zemeckis and Starkey continued their collaboration on *Flight, The Walk, Allied,* and *Welcome to Marwen.*

Starkey is also the author of *Breaking & Entering: The Education of a Film Producer.*

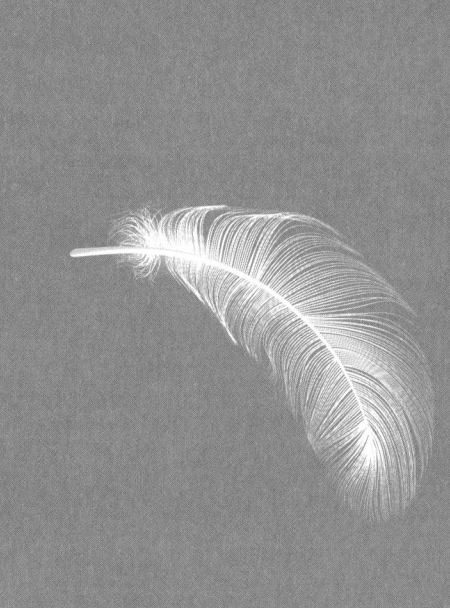